HOUSTON
PUBLIC LIBRARY

CITY HOUSTON TEXAS

An Empire for Slavery

An Empire for Slavery

. . . .

THE PECULIAR INSTITUTION IN TEXAS, 1821–1865

. . . .

Randolph B. Campbell

LOUISIANA STATE UNIVERSITY PRESS

BATON ROUGE AND LONDON

Manufactured in the United States of America
Designer: Barbara Werden
Typeface: Linotron Palatino
Typesetter: G&S Typesetters, Inc.
Printer: Thomson-Shore, Inc.
Binder: John H. Dekker & Sons, Inc.

First Printing
98 97 96 95 94 93 92 91 90 89   5 4 3 2 1

The paper in this book meets the guidelines for permanence and durability of
the Committee on Production Guidelines for Book Longevity of the Council on
Library Resources.♾

Library of Congress Cataloging-in-Publication Data

Campbell, Randolph, 1940–
    An empire for slavery : the peculiar institution in Texas,
  1821–1865 / Randolph B. Campbell.
      p.   cm.
    Bibliography: p.
    Includes index.
    ISBN 0-8071-1505-3 (alk. paper)
    1. Slavery—Texas—History—19th century. 2. Afro-Americans—
  Texas—History—19th century. 3. Texas—History—To 1846.
  4. Texas—History—1846–1950. 5. Texas—Race relations. I. Title.
  E445.T47C35   1989
  306'.362'09764—dc19   88-31357
                                                               CIP

To Diana

Contents

Illustrations

MAPS

Preface

American Negro slavery is a subject fraught with moral judgment and racial implications. No history of the Peculiar Institution, as antebellum southerners called it, regardless of perspective or method, has avoided questions of morality and race. Accordingly, this study of slavery in Texas begins with a statement of its underlying assumptions concerning those issues.

First, there is no intention to defend or attack the Peculiar Institution. Slavery was wrong, and special emphasis on the horrors of the institution is not necessary to prove its immorality. Even at its most benign, slavery could not have been "right" in the mid-nineteenth-century South. It was a moral anachronism by that time, an evil by definition in that most nations of the Western world had found it unacceptable for one man to own another.

Second, this study assumes that the enslaved blacks were simply human, nothing less and nothing more. Like other humans, they employed their intelligence and their moral and spiritual resources to survive in and attempt to influence the world in which they found themselves. Enslaved blacks were not an inherently inferior part of the human race, and slavery, regardless of the claims made by some of its defenders, was no school for civilization.

During my years of research and writing on slavery in Texas, I have incurred so many debts of gratitude that it is difficult to know where to begin the acknowledgments. The Faculty Research Committee at North Texas State University (now the University of North Texas) provided essential financial support, and the Department of History gave the time free from other responsibilities. My colleagues in the department's local history study group, especially Donald E. Chipman and Richard G. Lowe, read and critiqued portions of the manuscript and offered consistent encouragement. The county-outline maps of Texas are the work of Terry G. Jordan of the University of Texas Department of Geography.

The entire manuscript benefited immensely from careful readings by Alwyn Barr, Thomas W. Cutrer, Paul D. Lack, Carl H. Moneyhon, Robert G. Sherer, and Ron Tyler. Richard L. Himmel, David R. Lindsey, and Martin Sarvis of the North Texas libraries were unfailingly helpful, regardless of the demands on their time. Randal B. Gilbert of Tyler, Texas, provided much excellent material on Smith County and made me wish for such a "research assistant" in every county seat across the state. Two North Texas graduate students, Mark H. Atkins and David Minor, must be thanked for comments that, while not necessarily respectful, provided helpful perspective. Cecil Harper, Jr., my first doctoral student at North Texas, deserves a special note of acknowledgment for his invaluable assistance. I am afraid that Cecil gave so much time to helping with my research, listening to rehearsals of my ideas, and reading early drafts of the manuscript that he slowed progress on his own dissertation. The staff of the Louisiana State University Press, especially Senior Editor Margaret Fisher Dalrymple, who edited the manuscript, and Managing Editor Catherine F. Barton, have provided generous encouragement as well as expert advice.

Those who have read this manuscript in part or in its entirety have aided in locating sources, correcting factual errors, and refining interpretations. Weaknesses that remain are, of course, my own responsibility.

An Empire for Slavery

Introduction

There is a widespread popular misconception, particularly in Texas, that somehow the institution of Negro slavery was not very important in the Lone Star state. This is not really surprising in that many historians, writers, and creators of popular culture have preferred to see Texas as essentially western rather than southern.[1] The state thus becomes part of the romantic West, the West of cattle ranches, cowboys, and gunfighters and seemingly less compelling moral issues such as destruction of the Indians. So long as Texas is not seen as a southern state, its people do not have to face the great moral evil of slavery and the bitter heritage of black-white relations that followed the defeat of the Confederacy in 1865. Texans are thus permitted to escape a major part of what C. Vann Woodward called the "burden of Southern History."[2]

It is true that slavery had a relatively brief history in Texas. As an Anglo-American institution, it lasted about fifty years in Texas, from 1816

1. Perhaps the best indication that historians have preferred to see Texas as western rather than southern is the absence of any book-length study of slavery in the Lone Star state. Texas is the only former slave state, except Delaware, without such a study (see note 9 below). Moreover, the most famous Texas historian, Walter Prescott Webb, built his reputation on works such as *The Great Plains* (1931) and *The Texas Rangers* (1935), studies emphasizing the western character of Texas. The role of movie-makers is described in Don Graham, *Cowboys and Cadillacs: How Hollywood Looks at Texas* (Austin, 1983), 4–5.

Documenting a "popular misconception" is difficult because it appears most often in informal settings such as classroom discussions. A good example of the popular view of slavery in Texas appeared, however, in a column by Sam Kinch, Jr., in the Dallas *Morning News*, December 5, 1986, Sec. A, p. 31. In commenting on Texans' dislike for centralized government, Kinch, editor of the *Texas Weekly* political newsletter in Austin, wrote "we didn't like the Yankees telling us we couldn't have slaves—though few of us did." The meaning of "few" is debatable, but the implication of Kinch's remark seems clear—not enough Texans owned slaves to make slavery really important in the state.

Frank E. Vandiver, *The Southwest: South or West?* (College Station, 1975), 48, although recognizing the southern heritage of Texas, concludes that its people are "uniquely Southwestern." This position, while obviously defensible, also tends to allow Texans to avoid identification with the Old South.

2. C. Vann Woodward, *The Burden of Southern History* (Baton Rouge, 1960).

2 / AN EMPIRE FOR SLAVERY

or so until 1865, whereas in an original southern state such as Virginia its history extended from the mid-seventeenth century to the close of the Civil War, a period of more than two hundred years. Texas had a small fraction of the total slave population of the United States, less than 5 percent at the census of 1860, while, by comparison, Virginia had 12 percent and Louisiana, Texas's closest neighbor to the east, had more than 8 percent.[3] Also, slavery spread over only the eastern two-fifths of the Lone Star state before it was ended in 1865. The Peculiar Institution simply did not hold Texas as long or to the same extent numerically and geographically as it held older areas of the antebellum South.

The limited nature of Texas's historical experience with slavery, however, belies the vast importance of the institution to the Lone Star state. The great majority of immigrants to antebellum Texas came from the older southern states (77 percent of household heads in Texas in 1860 were southern born), and many brought with them their slaves and all aspects of slavery as it had matured in their native states. More than one-quarter of Texas families owned slaves during the 1850s, and bondsmen constituted approximately 30 percent of the state's total population. Proportions of slaveholders and slaves in the populations of Texas and Virginia during the last antebellum decade were closely comparable.[4] In this sense, then, slavery was as strongly established in Texas, the newest slave state, as it was in the oldest slave state in the Union.

In 1850 and 1860, more than 93 percent of Texas's free population and 99 percent of its slaves lived east of a line extending from the Red River at approximately the 98th meridian southward to the mouth of the Nueces River on the Gulf of Mexico. The area of slaveholding, although covering only the eastern two-fifths of Texas, was as large as Alabama and Mississippi combined (see map 1).[5] Even without further expansion to the west, it constituted virtually an empire for slavery.

3. U.S. Bureau of the Census, *Population of the United States in 1860: Compiled from the Original Returns of the Eighth Census* (Washington, D.C., 1864), ix, 193, 483, 515.
4. Randolph B. Campbell and Richard G. Lowe, *Wealth and Power in Antebellum Texas* (College Station, 1977), 27–30. James D. B. DeBow (comp.), *Statistical View of the United States . . . Being a Compendium of the Seventh Census* (Washington, D.C., 1854), 86, shows that slaves were 27.3 percent of the population of Texas in 1850 and 33.2 percent of the population of Virginia. In 1860, the comparable statistics were 30.3 for Texas and 30.8 for Virginia; see U.S. Bureau of the Census, *Population of the United States in 1860*, 483, 515. Approximately one-quarter of all families in Texas and Virginia owned slaves. Kenneth M. Stampp, *The Peculiar Institution: Slavery in the Ante-Bellum South* (New York, 1956), 30.
5. Campbell and Lowe, *Wealth and Power*, 15–17.

Map 1

Antebellum Texas

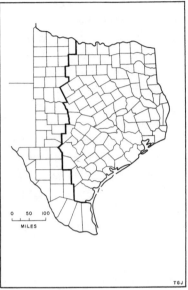

Antebellum Texans considered slavery vital to their future. The first settlers in Stephen F. Austin's colony brought slaves, and Austin himself, although not particularly devoted to slavery in the abstract, concluded by 1833 that "Texas *must be* a slave country. Circumstances and unavoidable necessity compels it. It is the wish of the people there, and it is my duty to do all I can, prudently, in favor of it. I will do so." As Texas moved from Mexican colony to independent republic to statehood, Austin's opinion was frequently repeated. "I hold," James S. Mayfield of Fayette County told his fellow delegates to the state constitutional convention of 1845, "that the true policy and prosperity of this country depend upon the maintenance and prosperity of that institution." "We want more slaves—we *need* them," wrote Charles DeMorse, Massachusetts-born editor of the Clarksville *Northern Standard*, in 1859. "We care nothing for . . . slavery as an abstraction—but we desire the practicality; the increase of our productions; the increase of the comforts and wealth of the population; and if slavery, or slave labor, or Negro Apprentice labor ministers to this, why that is what we want."[6]

6. Stephen F. Austin to Wiley Martin, May 30, 1833, in Eugene C. Barker (ed.), *The Papers of Stephen F. Austin* (3 vols.; Washington and Austin, 1924–28), II, 981 (hereinafter this collec-

Some observers recognized that slavery in Texas had importance transcending its role in shaping that state. As early as 1839, Frederic Gaillardet pointed out that Texas, with its rich soil and "location at the southern end of the American Union," was becoming a haven for slaveholding planters from the upper South: "In the enjoyment of this position lies the germ of Texas' future greatness. It will become in the more or less distant future, the land of refuge for the American slaveholders; it will be the ally, the reserve force upon which they will rest. . . . If . . . that great association, the American Union, should be one day torn apart, Texas unquestionably would be in the forefront of the new confederacy, which would be formed by the Southern states from the debris of the old Union." John Marshall, editor of the Austin *Texas State Gazette*, argued in 1858 that Texas was destined to become the "Empire State of the South," provided that the African slave trade could be reopened. Slavery was growing, but too slowly, Marshall wrote, "and until we reach somewhere in the vicinity of two millions of slaves, it is equally evident that such a thing as too many slaves in Texas is an absurdity." Texas was slavery's frontier during the late antebellum period; it held the promise of growth and vitality for years to come. Developments there were critical to the Peculiar Institution, not only in one state but to its future in the South as a whole.[7]

In spite of its obvious historical significance, slavery has received virtually no attention as a part of Texas' heritage. The second chapter of Alwyn Barr's *Black Texans* provides a useful general summary, and Ronnie C. Tyler and Lawrence R. Murphy's edited work, *The Slave Narratives of Texas*, contains a remarkably good introductory essay. However, there has never been a general study of slavery in Texas; the best state history text gives it less than three pages, and *The Handbook of Texas* has no entry on the subject.[8]

tion will be cited as Barker [ed.], *Austin Papers*); William F. Weeks (reporter), *Debates of the Texas Convention* (Houston, 1846), 532; Clarksville *Northern Standard*, February 19, 1859.

7. Frederic Gaillardet, *Sketches of Early Texas and Louisiana*, trans. and ed. James L. Shepherd, III (Austin, 1966), 68–69. George W. Featherstonhaugh, *Excursion Through the Slave States: From Washington on the Potomac to the Frontier of Mexico, with Sketches of Popular Manners and Geological Notices* (New York, 1844), 124–25, made similar predictions concerning the future of slavery in Texas. Austin *Texas State Gazette*, July 17, 1858.

8. Alwyn Barr, *Black Texans: A History of Negroes in Texas, 1528–1971* (Austin, 1973), 13–38; Ronnie C. Tyler and Lawrence R. Murphy (eds.), *The Slave Narratives of Texas* (Austin, 1974), xvii–xlviii; Rupert Norval Richardson, Ernest Wallace, and Adrian N. Anderson, *Texas: The Lone Star State* (4th ed.; Englewood Cliffs, N.J., 1981), 196–98; Walter Prescott Webb, H. Bailey Carroll, and Eldon S. Branda (eds.), *The Handbook of Texas* (3 vols.; Austin,

Historians have written extensively about slavery in southern states other than Texas. With the additional exception of tiny Delaware, the institution has received book-length attention in each of the fifteen states that permitted slavery in 1860. Most of these studies are relatively old, having been written before 1950. However, Julia Floyd Smith's *Slavery and Plantation Growth in Antebellum Florida, 1821–1860* (the first on that state) appeared in 1973, and Barbara Jeanne Fields's analysis of slavery and freedom in nineteenth-century Maryland was published in 1985. Important studies of slavery in particular states during more limited chronological periods also have appeared during the last two decades. Examples include Peter Wood's *Black Majority* dealing with South Carolina's slaves from 1670 through the Stono Rebellion (1739) and Clarence L. Mohr's examination of masters and bondsmen in Georgia during the Civil War. By and large, scholars have not revised the older studies of slavery in each state, but recent works indicate that interest in the institution as it existed in particular areas of the South remains strong. A general account of the Peculiar Institution in Texas is thus long overdue, and this study seeks to fill that need.[9]

1952, 1976). Elizabeth Silverthorne, *Plantation Life in Texas* (College Station, 1986), is a recent, semipopular account that deals with slavery on larger agricultural units.

A number of theses and dissertations examine slavery in Texas. Among the most general of these are Abigail Curlee, "A Study of Texas Slave Plantations, 1822–1865" (Ph.D. dissertation, University of Texas, 1932); Johanna Rosa Engelking, "Slavery in Texas" (M.A. thesis, Baylor University, 1933); Hallie M. McPherson, "Slavery in Texas" (M.A. thesis, University of Chicago, 1924); and Joleene Maddox, "Slavery in Texas, 1836–1860" (M.A. thesis, Southwest Texas State University, 1969).

9. James Curtis Ballagh, *A History of Slavery in Virginia* (Baltimore, 1902); John Spencer Bassett, *Slavery in the State of North Carolina* (Baltimore, 1899); Jeffrey R. Brackett, *The Negro in Maryland: A Study of the Institution of Slavery* (Baltimore, 1889); J. Winston Coleman, Jr., *Slavery Times in Kentucky* (Chapel Hill, 1940); Barbara Jeanne Fields, *Slavery and Freedom on the Middle Ground: Maryland During the Nineteenth Century* (New Haven, 1985); Ralph Betts Flanders, *Plantation Slavery in Georgia* (Chapel Hill, 1933); Frank Klingberg, *The Negro in Colonial South Carolina: A Study in Americanization* (Washington, D.C., 1941); Chase C. Mooney, *Slavery in Tennessee* (Bloomington, 1957); James Benson Sellers, *Slavery in Alabama* (University, Ala., 1950); Julia Floyd Smith, *Slavery and Plantation Growth in Antebellum Florida, 1821–1860* (Gainesville, 1973); Charles Sackett Sydnor, *Slavery in Mississippi* (New York, 1933); Joe Gray Taylor, *Negro Slavery in Louisiana* (Baton Rouge, 1963); Orville W. Taylor, *Negro Slavery in Arkansas* (Durham, 1958); Rosser Howard Taylor, *Slaveholding in North Carolina: An Economic View* (Chapel Hill, 1926); Harrison Anthony Trexler, *Slavery in Missouri, 1804–1865* (Baltimore, 1914). Recent studies of more limited scope include: Peter Wood, *Black Majority: Negroes in Colonial South Carolina from 1670 Through the Stono Rebellion* (New York, 1974); Clarence L. Mohr, *On the Threshold of Freedom: Masters and Slaves in Civil War Georgia* (Athens, Ga., 1986). See also Betty Wood, *Slavery in Colonial Georgia, 1730–1775* (Athens, Ga., 1984); Edmund S.

Scholars who have sought to describe and interpret American Negro slavery have produced a labyrinthine historiography with enough twists and turns to perplex even the most dedicated reader. There is no need for a detailed summary of these studies, especially since John B. Boles has recently published an outstanding synthesis of writings on slavery in *Black Southerners, 1619–1869* (1983).[10] However, the broad contours of their interpretations should be reviewed as background for a study of the Peculiar Institution in Texas.

Racist, proslavery views tended to dominate the writings of the first professional historians who dealt with slavery. This trend culminated with the work of Ulrich B. Phillips, who in 1918 portrayed slavery as an unprofitable, essentially benign institution providing social control and civilizing influences for an inferior race. State studies during the next thirty years generally echoed Phillips' conclusions. Ralph Betts Flanders' 1933 study of Georgia, for example, concluded: "As a means of social control slavery during the ante-bellum period was invaluable; . . . as a training school for the untutored savage it served to a large degree as a civilizing agency." The dominance of Phillips' interpretation began to disappear during the 1950s after Kenneth M. Stampp in *The Peculiar Institution* rejected the older work's racist assumptions and went on to describe slavery as profitable, brutal, and brutalizing. Some considered Stampp's assertion that Negroes are "only white men with black skins" insultingly patronizing, but, as the United States underwent a revolution in civil rights during the next two decades, blatant racism largely disappeared from the historiography of slavery. Stampp had provided an effective antidote to Phillips, although critics would find more subtle forms of racism in much of the work that followed.[11]

Since Stampp's work, no general histories of slavery have appeared. Instead, scholars have focused primarily on limited questions relating to key aspects of the slave experience. Stanley Elkins provoked a major controversy with the publication of a small volume entitled *Slavery* in 1959. Arguing that the time had come to agree on the immorality of slavery and

Morgan, *American Slavery, American Freedom: The Ordeal of Colonial Virginia* (New York, 1975); and C. Peter Ripley, *Slaves and Freedmen in Civil War Louisiana* (Baton Rouge, 1976).

10. John B. Boles, *Black Southerners, 1619–1869* (Lexington, Ky., 1983).

11. John David Smith, *An Old Creed for the New South: Proslavery Ideology and Historiography, 1865–1918* (Westport, Conn., 1985); Ulrich Bonnell Phillips, *American Negro Slavery: A Survey of the Supply, Employment, and Control of Negro Labor as Determined by the Plantation Regime* (New York, 1918); Flanders, *Slavery in Georgia*, 299–300; Stampp, *Peculiar Institution*, vii.

move ahead to seek a better understanding of its effect on bondsmen, Elkins concluded that the psychological impact of slavery was to reduce most male slaves to behavioral patterns associated with the childlike "Sambo" character. The Sambo personality, he insisted, was not a black characteristic; instead it was the reaction of most humans caught in a similar situation. His well-known comparison of slave plantations and Nazi concentration camps, where even Jewish intellectuals became Sambos in order to survive, argued this point by analogy. Elkins was criticized effectively for overstating his case, exaggerating the prevalence of Sambo-like behavior, and misinterpreting its meaning. Critics also denounced him, with much less justice, as a racist who had claimed that blacks were by nature weak-willed Sambos. When the novelist William Styron used the Sambo thesis as a key interpretive device in his "meditation on history," *The Confessions of Nat Turner* (1966), he was furiously condemned as a white racist.[12]

In *The Slave Community* (1972), John Blassingame argued that Sambo existed primarily in the minds of masters and that a careful examination of slave life revealed a culture shaped to a large extent by the bondsmen themselves. His was the first major study calling attention to the need to allow the slaves themselves to testify on what it was like to live in bondage. *The Slave Community* and George P. Rawick's *From Sundown to Sunup: The Making of the Black Community*, which made similar points and also appeared in 1972, marked another significant step forward in the historiography of slavery.[13]

Robert W. Fogel and Stanley L. Engerman also disagreed with Elkins, but their book, *Time on the Cross*, provoked even more controversy than his. Employing quantitative evidence and focusing on the economics of slavery, they argued that slaves, rather than being inefficient Sambos created by a brutal, closed system, were efficient workers who seized upon available opportunities to create an enviable record of black achievement under adverse circumstances. Significant numbers even attained special status as craftsmen and managers. *Time on the Cross* also con-

12. Stanley M. Elkins, *Slavery: A Problem in American Institutional and Intellectual Life* (Chicago, 1959); Ann J. Lane (ed.), *The Debate over Slavery: Stanley Elkins and His Critics* (Urbana, Ill., 1971); William Styron, *The Confessions of Nat Turner* (New York, 1966); John H. Clarke (ed.), *William Styron's Nat Turner: Ten Black Writers Respond* (Boston, 1968).

13. John W. Blassingame, *The Slave Community: Plantation Life in the Antebellum South* (New York, 1972); George P. Rawick, *From Sundown to Sunup: The Making of a Black Community* (Westport, Conn., 1972).

tended that most slaves escaped severe punishment and lived with material conditions not a great deal worse than those common for the working poor elsewhere. Critics quickly attacked Fogel and Engerman for having understated the brutality of slavery while painting an overly positive picture of material conditions. Much of the criticism was justified, but *Time on the Cross* made a contribution in its emphasis on how slaves occupied positions of responsibility.[14]

Eugene D. Genovese's *Roll, Jordan, Roll,* also published in 1974, is more of a general account of slavery than any study since Stampp's *The Peculiar Institution.* Employing Marxist theory to inform his study, Genovese argued that in the pre-capitalist antebellum South the planters' paternalistic ethos allowed the slaves room to control in some degree all aspects of their lives and build a culture of their own. His study does an excellent job of describing the subtleties of the master-slave relationship, but even it has not escaped entirely from charges of racial bias. Genovese's account of the influences that shaped the slaves' world, it has been said, gives too much credit to planter paternalism and not enough to the bondsmen's own efforts.[15]

Since the mid-1970s, historians interested in slavery have tended to focus on even more particular facets of the institution, especially the everyday lives and culture of bondsmen. The results have been important studies of slave family life, religion, music, education, and folklore. Scholars have also produced pioneering studies of slave women, who labored under the double burden of race and sex, and of particular groups such as the black drivers. The result is an ever-increasing awareness of the variety and complexity of the institution.[16]

14. Robert William Fogel and Stanley L. Engerman, *Time on the Cross: The Economics of American Negro Slavery* (2 vols.; Boston, 1974); Herbert G. Gutman, *Slavery and the Numbers Game: A Critique of "Time on the Cross"* (Urbana, Ill., 1975); Paul A. David *et al., Reckoning with Slavery: Critical Essays in the Quantitative History of American Negro Slavery* (New York, 1976).

15. Eugene D. Genovese, *Roll, Jordan, Roll: The World the Slaves Made* (New York, 1974); James D. Anderson, "Aunt Jemima in Dialectics: Genovese on Slave Culture," *Journal of Negro History,* XLI (1976), 99–114.

16. See, for example, Herbert G. Gutman, *The Black Family in Slavery and Freedom, 1750–1925* (New York, 1976); Albert J. Raboteau, *Slave Religion: The "Invisible Institution" in the Antebellum South* (New York, 1978); Thomas L. Webber, *Deep Like the Rivers: Education in the Slave Quarter Community, 1831–1865* (New York, 1978); Lawrence W. Levine, *Black Culture and Black Consciousness: Afro-American Thought from Slavery to Freedom* (New York, 1977); Leslie Howard Owens, *This Species of Property: Slave Life and Culture in the Old South* (New York, 1976); Deborah Gray White, *Ar'n't I A Woman? Female Slaves in the Plantation South* (New York, 1985); Jacqueline Jones, *Labor of Love, Labor of Sorrow: Black Women, Work, and the Family from*

As should be expected, the historiography of slavery, especially recent work on slave families, religion, and behavior and the role of bondsmen in shaping their own lives and culture, heavily influences this study. Some of the state-level historiography is influential, too, in that the extent to which slavery in Texas differed from the institution elsewhere in the South is considered. Throughout, however, there is no intention to test any one idea or interpretation and, at the same time, no determination to say anything novel for its own sake. A study of slavery in Texas is "new" by definition.

Finally, while recognizing the importance of theory in much recent historical scholarship, this work is based on the assumption that slave-holding society in the antebellum South was unique, "Sui Generis" as historian Bertram Wyatt-Brown has put it, and seeks to describe and interpret the Peculiar Institution in Texas without the aid of any particular theoretical model.[17] Instead of structuring a model and fitting the story to a theory, it proceeds simply by asking large questions and seeking answers in available sources. Every effort has been made to go only where the evidence leads in attempting to answer the essential questions posed by Texas' experience with the Peculiar Institution. These are: What factors explain the establishment and growth of slavery in Texas? How did slavery function as an economic and a legal institution in the Lone Star state? What were the physical and psychological conditions of servitude for Texas slaves? What was the impact of slavery on slaveholders and on slaveholding society in general? How did the Civil War affect slavery in Texas before the institution was destroyed in June, 1865?

Slavery to the Present (New York, 1985); William L. Van Deburg, *The Slave Drivers: Black Agricultural Labor Supervisors in the Antebellum South* (Westport, Conn., 1979).

17. Bertram Wyatt-Brown, Review of James Oakes's *The Ruling Race: A History of American Slaveholders*, in *Journal of Southern History*, XLVIII (1982), 561.

ONE

. . . .

The Colonial Period, 1821–1835

''TEXAS *MUST BE* A SLAVE COUNTRY''

Slavery as an institution of significance in Texas came with Anglo-American settlers during the 1820s, but the first slave arrived there nearly three hundred years earlier. Among the survivors of the Pánfilo de Narváez expedition shipwrecked on the coast of Texas in November, 1528, was a black man called Estevanico, the personal servant of Andrés Dorantes de Carranza. Estevanico survived nearly six years of servitude to the Indians before escaping with Dorantes, Alvar Núñez Cabeza de Vaca (the most famous member of this expedition), and Alonso Castillo Maldonado and wandering hundreds of miles through Texas and northern Mexico to the outpost of Culiacán near the Gulf of California. After reaching Culiacán in April, 1536, and then journeying to Mexico City, he was sold (or perhaps loaned) by Dorantes to the viceroy of New Spain, Antonio de Mendoza. Estevanico never returned to Texas, but he remained an adventurer. In 1539, he served as a guide for Fray Marcos de Niza, a trailblazer for the Coronado expedition. Exploring ahead of the main party and acting against instructions from de Niza, he entered Háwikuh, an Indian village in western New Mexico, and was killed by the natives.[1]

Negro slavery was permitted and protected from the early sixteenth century onward in New Spain, but the institution was relatively unim-

---

1. Webb, Carroll, and Branda (eds.), *Handbook of Texas*, I, 261–63, 574, II, 281; Richardson, Wallace, and Anderson, *Texas: The Lone Star State*, 15–16. Estevanico was from Azamor on the Atlantic coast of Morocco. One Spaniard who saw him in 1536 described him as being "brown." Cyclone Covey (trans. and ed.), *Cabeza de Vaca's Adventures in the Unknown Interior of America* (Albuquerque, N.M., 1983), 140–41.

portant outside Veracruz and the limited areas suitable for plantation agriculture. Certainly it had little opportunity to gain a foothold in Texas, for the Spanish themselves barely settled and controlled the northernmost reaches of their American empire. By the last quarter of the eighteenth century, in spite of continuing efforts to establish missions and presidios across the region, Spanish Texas had only three settlements large enough to be called towns—San Antonio, Nacogdoches, and La Bahía (now Goliad). The first reliable census of the province, taken in 1777, reported a sparse population of 3,103, including inhabitants of the missions. Of these settlers, only 20, less than 1 percent, were classified as Negroes and probably were slaves. Another census in 1785 enumerated 2,919 persons, 43 of whom were identified specifically as slaves (24 in San Antonio, 16 in Nacogdoches, and 3 in La Bahía). Five years later, officials reported that the province had 37 slaves in a total population of 2,417. During the next thirty years, as the Spanish period drew to a close, Texas' slave population remained small. Nacogdoches in east Texas reported 33 bondsmen in an 1809 census while slaves virtually disappeared from San Antonio and La Bahía, which together had only 9 persons of "African origin" in 1819. Obviously, then, although Negro slavery existed, the number of bondsmen in Spanish Texas was always far too small to give the institution a significant hold on the province.[2]

After 1800, as Spain's grasp on her American colonies weakened rapidly, the mother country's attention to Texas, always limited at best, diminished even further. This circumstance provided an opportunity for revolutionaries and pirates (it was often difficult to tell the difference) to carry on a slave trade from Texas into the United States. In 1816, Manuel Herrera, would-be representative to the United States of a revolutionary Mexican republic, created a government at Galveston with a Frenchman, Louis d'Aury, as governor and commander of the fleet. D'Aury began busily capturing Spanish vessels, including slave ships. No market for the captured slaves existed in Mexico or Texas, so they were smuggled into Louisiana in violation of United States law against the international slave

2. Alicia V. Tjarks, "Comparative Demographic Analysis of Texas, 1777–1793," *Southwestern Historical Quarterly*, LXXVII (1974), 295, 299, 324–25; Carmela Leal (comp. and trans.), "Translations of Statistical and Census Reports of Texas, 1782–1836, and Sources Documenting the Black in Texas, 1603–1803" (Microfilm Publication by the Institute of Texan Cultures, San Antonio, 1979); Lester E. Bugbee, "Slavery in Early Texas," *Political Science Quarterly*, XIII (1898), 389–90; Linda M. Purcell, "Slavery in the Republic of Texas" (M.S. thesis, North Texas State University, 1982), 1–2; Engelking, "Slavery in Texas," 7–8.

trade. In August, 1817, the customs collector at New Orleans complained to the secretary of state that he could not stop "the most shameful violation of the slave act, . . . by a motley mixture of freebooters and smugglers, at Galveston, under the Mexican flag."[3]

D'Aury left Galveston in August, 1817, to pursue the revolution against Spain, but he was quickly replaced by the notorious Jean Laffite who continued to capture Spanish slavers. Laffite's slaves reached buyers in the United States through agents who arranged purchases and deliveries. The most famous of these agents were the Bowie brothers, Jim, John J., and Rezin P. The Bowies bought slaves at Galveston for one dollar a pound (the average cost was $140) and then took them to the nearest customs house in Louisiana where they turned in their property for being smuggled into the United States. Louisiana law, which applied since Congress had never acted on the matter, provided for sale of confiscated property and payment of half the price to those who were informers in the case. The Bowies promptly bought back their slaves, received half of the purchase price as an informers' fee, and were off to sell their now legally held property to planters in Louisiana and Mississippi, at times for as much as $1,000 per bondsman. It is said that the brothers made $65,000 in the three years before Laffite was forced by the United States to leave Galveston.[4]

Even as Laffite was being put out of the slave trading business, Texas stood on the threshold of settlement by Anglo-Americans, many of whom would have been good customers for the pirate's slaves. In fact, slaveholders had begun to settle at Pecan Point on the south side of the Red River as early as 1816. A census of Miller County, Arkansas—a territory of vaguely defined boundaries extending from Arkansas into present-day Oklahoma and Texas—showed a population of 999 people, including 82 slaves, in 1820. Most of these bondsmen lived north of the Red River, but some resided south of the river in Texas. Between 1810 and 1820, other settlers from the United States began drifting across the border into the area of east Texas between Nacogdoches and Louisiana. Undoubtedly, a few of these settlers brought bondsmen with them. Jane Long, the wife of the filibuster James Long who planned to conquer

3. Eugene C. Barker, "The African Slave Trade in Texas," *Quarterly of the Texas State Historical Association*, VI (1902), 145–46.
4. *Ibid.*, 146–49; Amelia Williams, "A Critical Study of the Siege of the Alamo and of the Personnel of Its Defenders," *Southwestern Historical Quarterly*, XXXVII (1933), 92–93.

Texas after the Adams-Onís Treaty in 1819 proposed to "give away" the territory west of the Sabine River, spent the winter of 1821–22 at Bolivar Point opposite Galveston accompanied only by two children and a young slave woman named Kiamatia.[5]

These early settlers had no legal right to be in Texas and certainly no assurances that they could hold slaves there. But they represented the first trickle of a flood that Spanish and Mexican authorities would be unable to stem. Americans would soon pour into Texas legally, and no rule or regulation would deny them their slaves.

Moses Austin opened the way for legal settlement by Anglo-Americans in Texas when he traveled to San Antonio de Béxar in 1820 and received permission from Spanish authorities (on January 17, 1821) to settle a colony on the Brazos and Colorado rivers. He was accompanied, fittingly enough, by a slave named Richmond, the property of his son, Stephen F. Austin. As Negro slavery was legal in Spain's American empire, the subject did not arise in either Moses Austin's petition or the Spanish grant. Richmond became ill on the trip home and was left with Douglas Forsythe at the Sabine River. He soon recovered and worked for Forsythe to pay his doctor's bills and board. Moses Austin was less fortunate. After going home to Missouri, he died on June 10, 1821. His colonizing enterprise in Texas then fell to his twenty-eight-year-old son, Stephen F. Austin.[6]

During the summer of 1821, Stephen F. Austin retraced his father's steps to San Antonio, where he was confirmed as heir to the grant. Austin claimed and sold the slave, Richmond, as he entered Texas, but he was by no means unconcerned with the role of slavery in his colonizing efforts. His first proposal for the distribution of land in Texas provided generous grants for household heads, their wives, and children, and then called for the granting of fifty acres per slave. After gaining approval of

5. Rex Wallace Strickland, "Anglo-American Activities in Northeastern Texas, 1803–1845" (Ph. D. dissertation, University of Texas, 1937), 72–73, 97; Webb, Carroll, and Branda (eds.), *Handbook of Texas*, I, 954, II, 76, 523–24, 547–48; Anne A. Brindley, "Jane Long," *Southwestern Historical Quarterly*, LVI (1952), 211–38.

6. Bugbee, "Slavery in Early Texas," 390; Eugene C. Barker, "The Influence of Slavery in the Colonization of Texas," *Southwestern Historical Quarterly*, XXVIII (1924), 3–4; Sue Clark Wortham, "The Role of the Negro on the Texas Frontier, 1821–1836" (M.A. thesis, Southwest Texas State University, 1970), 12; Zoie Odom Newsome, "Antislavery Sentiment in Texas, 1821–1861" (M.A. thesis, Texas Tech University, 1968), 9–10; Receipt from Douglas Forsythe to Moses Austin, January 22, 1821, in Barker (ed.), *Austin Papers*, I, 375–76.

the colonizing contract and returning to the United States to recruit settlers, Austin persuaded authorities in San Antonio to increase the grant
per slave to eighty acres.[7]

Stephen F. Austin thus had no difficulty in proving himself heir to
Moses Austin's grant and in the process established terms that accepted
and actually encouraged the migration of slaveholders to Texas. However, just as he reached San Antonio in August, 1821, word came that the
revolution against Spain was finally successful. Mexican independence
raised questions about slavery because Mexican revolutionaries had always voiced strong opposition to the institution. Father Miguel Hidalgo,
the first leader of the revolt against Spain, issued several decrees in late
1810 demanding immediate manumission of all slaves on pain of death.
And José María Morelos' "Sentimientos de la Nación" of September 14,
1813, proclaimed that "slavery is forbidden forever." Given the relative
unimportance of Negro slavery in New Spain, these revolutionary sentiments were more theoretical than practical. But antislavery idealism continued after 1821 and soon cast a shadow over the future of slavery in
Texas, where the institution was far more than just a theoretical matter.[8]

Settlers from the United States began to move into Austin's colony
during late 1821 and early 1822, and they brought slaves. Josiah H. Bell,
for example, received a grant from Austin for himself, his wife, two sons,
and three slaves. Jared E. Groce, who arrived in January, 1822, from
Georgia, brought ninety bondsmen and established a plantation called
"Bernardo" on the Brazos River near the present-day site of Hempstead.
Groce could not occupy all the land to which he was entitled (7,200 acres
for his slaves alone). "Bernardo" consisted of "only" one league of land
(4,428 acres) on which his slave craftsmen built a plantation home and
cabins for themselves. Groce immediately demonstrated the promise of
Texas lands and slave labor by producing cotton crops that were sold to
neighbors and even in the interior of Mexico. It is said that he used his
slaves to transport the cotton by mule train.[9]

7. Austin to Antonio Martínez, August 18, 1821, and October 12, 1821, in Barker (ed.),
Austin Papers, I, 407, 417; Eugene C. Barker, *The Life of Stephen F. Austin: Founder of Texas,
1793–1836* (Nashville, 1925), 33–39.

8. Newsome, "Antislavery Sentiment in Texas," 90–91; Rosalie Schwartz, *Across the Rio
to Freedom: United States Negroes in Mexico* (El Paso, 1975), 6–7.

9. Barker, *Stephen F. Austin,* 40; Wortham, "Role of the Negro on the Texas Frontier,"
37–41; Rosa Groce Berleth, "Jared Ellison Groce," *Quarterly of the Texas State Historical Association,* XX (1917), 358–59; Jacquelyn Wooley Bornholst, "Plantation Settlement in the Brazos
River Valley, 1820–1860" (M.A. thesis, Texas A & M University, 1971), 29.

Shortly after these first settlers began to arrive, Austin and his colonists, especially the slaveholders, ran into difficulties with Mexican authorities. The provisional government at Monterrey refused to approve the contract awarded Austin at San Antonio in 1821 and indicated that his colonists could occupy land only provisionally. At the same time, the new national government in Mexico City was formulating a general colonization policy that would be critical to Texas. Austin, convinced that under these circumstances he needed to protect his interests in person, went to Mexico City, arriving on April 29, 1822, just as Agustín de Iturbide became constitutional emperor of Mexico. Austin remained in the capital city for more than a year, learning a great deal about Mexico and building for himself a reputation that would eventually greatly benefit Texas and the interests, including slavery, of its settlers.[10]

Austin found that the wheels of Mexican government turned slowly, especially, it seemed, in the passage of a colonization law. He sent memorial after memorial to the constituent congress and, in spite of the fact that slavery was obviously controversial, made it clear that his colonists expected to bring their bondsmen to Texas and receive land for them. Austin himself, he told congress on May 13, had slaves in his own "familia."[11]

The Mexican leaders found it extremely difficult to choose between the revolutionary ideal of liberty and the practical need to protect property interests and encourage settlement of their nation. Therefore, on August 20 the majority of the committee charged with formulating a bill reported a compromise proposal allowing settlers to bring in their slaves but ordering that the children born to those bondsmen in Mexico be freed at age fourteen. José Antonio Gutiérrez de Lara, the spokesman for this bill, deplored slavery and the slave trade but spoke also of the rights of property and the need for progress. A minority bill, reported at the same time, provided for immediate abolition and permanent prohibition of slavery. Following debate, both bills were recommitted. The minority bill was reported again a month later, but it was sent back to committee for further revision. Before any other action could be taken, Iturbide disbanded congress and created a forty-five man legislative junta to govern with him. This junta passed the original colonization bill in November, 1822, and

10. Barker, *Stephen F. Austin*, 45–49; Bugbee, "Slavery in Early Texas," 391–92; Purcell, "Slavery in the Republic of Texas," 3–4.

11. Austin to Mexican Constituent Congress, May 13, 1822, in Barker (ed.), *Austin Papers*, I, 512, 514.

Iturbide signed it into law on January 4, 1823. Article 30 of this so-called Imperial Colonization Law read as follows: "There shall not be permitted, after the promulgation of this law, either purchase or sale of slaves that may be introduced into the empire. The children of such slaves, who are born within the empire, shall be free at fourteen years of age."[12]

Austin, as he anxiously watched the progress of this colonization law during 1822, feared that congress would not pass any bill permitting slavery. Therefore he probably was relieved when Iturbide disbanded the legislative body in October. Even then, the emperor's junta proposed at first to free all slaves after ten years residence in Texas, and Austin had to talk to each member of the legislative body and convince them collectively to adopt the terms stated in Article 30. It was more than he had expected. Austin would later express doubts concerning slavery in Texas, yet he, more than any other individual, was responsible for gaining the approval of Mexican authorities for introducing the institution there.[13]

Emperor Iturbide was overthrown in February, 1823, and the Imperial Colonization Law was then annulled. Austin delayed his departure for Texas long enough to appeal successfully to the new constituent congress to approve his grant under the terms of the old law. His was the only colony in Texas settled according to the law of January 4, 1823. Upon his return to Texas, Austin found that his long absence and rumors concerning the attitude of Mexican authorities had greatly slowed immigration. He was able, however, to publicize the Imperial Colonization Law and reassure colonists so successfully that by the end of 1824 nearly all of his allotted three hundred families settled in Texas.[14]

Austin and his original settlers thus weathered the first Mexican threat to slavery, but this was by no means the end of the issue. A new constituent congress met in Mexico City in November, 1823, and on July 13, 1824, expressed its attitude toward slavery in a decree prohibiting the slave trade. Unfortunately, while the attitude of congress was clear, the meaning of this decree was not. "Commerce and traffic in slaves," it read, "proceeding from any country and under any flag whatsoever, is forever

12. Bugbee, "Slavery in Early Texas," 393–95 (Article 30 is quoted on 394); Newsome, "Antislavery Sentiment in Texas," 11–13; Barker, "Influence of Slavery in Colonization of Texas," 4–5.
13. Barker, "Influence of Slavery in Colonization of Texas," 5–6; Newsome, "Antislavery Sentiment in Texas," 12–13; Bugbee, "Slavery in Early Texas," 394–95.
14. Barker, "Influence of Slavery in Colonization of Texas," 6; Bugbee, "Slavery in Early Texas," 395, 396–97; Newsome, "Antislavery Sentiment in Texas," 13–14; George Nixon to Austin, November 14, 1823, in Barker (ed.), *Austin Papers*, I, 707.

prohibited in the territory of the United Mexican States." Slaves brought into Mexico in violation of this decree were to be freed. Did congress, however, mean to prohibit even the introduction of slaves by their owners, or did it mean only to stop the importation of bondsmen as merchandise? Mexican officials themselves did not know. Lucas Alamán, one of the most important leaders in the shaping of Mexico's policy toward Texas during the 1820s and 1830s, insisted later that the July 13, 1824, decree had outlawed any introduction of slaves. But the Congress of Coahuila and Texas, which wrote a state constitution for that portion of the Mexican federation in 1827, stated specifically that slaves could be brought in for six months after adoption of the state's fundamental law. Obviously, if the 1824 decree had prohibited all importations, the state congress was in violation of a national law. American settlers were greatly troubled, both for the slaves they had in Texas and for the future of the institution, but they were able to take advantage of the law's lack of clarity and continue to develop slavery in Texas.[15]

The constituent congress proceeded to adopt a new national colonization law on August 18, 1824, and a federal constitution on October 4, 1824. Neither mentioned slavery, so the institution appeared to have survived revolutionary Mexico's liberal sentiments.[16] Slaves could not be imported as merchandise, but no other constitutional or statutory prohibitions restricted bringing bondsmen into the province. Settlers in Austin's Colony were subject to the restrictions in Iturbide's Imperial Colonization Law that children born to their bondsmen be freed at age fourteen; other colonists would not face even that limitation.

Developments in 1822–24 were typical of Texas' experience with slavery during the entire period of Mexican rule. Mexican leaders showed disapproval of slavery but did nothing effective to abolish it. Anglo-Americans in Texas frequently expressed anxiety about the future of their institution, and the issue hindered the settlement of Texas because potential immigrants from the United States feared for the safety of their slave property once they came under the jurisdiction of Mexico. Austin received letter after letter expressing these fears. James A. E. Phelps, for example, wrote from Mississippi to voice concern about the meaning of the July 13, 1824, decree against the slave trade. "Nothing appears at

15. Barker, "Influence of Slavery in Colonization of Texas," 8–10, concludes that the law was intended to stop all importation of slaves. Bugbee, "Slavery in Early Texas," 397–401, is less certain. Bugbee quotes the entire text of the law.

16. Bugbee, "Slavery in Early Texas," 399.

present," he wrote, "to prevent a portion of our wealthy planters from emigrating immediately to the province of Texas but the uncertainty now prevailing with regard to the subject of slavery." Charles Douglas from Alabama expressed the same feelings to Austin. "Our most valuable inhabitants here own negroes," he wrote, and they are not willing to move without assurances that slaves will be "secured to them by the laws of your Govt." Austin responded to such letters with renewed appeals to Mexican authorities. In a letter of April 4, 1825, to Rafael Gonzales, governor of Coahuila and Texas, for example, he explained that the protection of slavery was "a matter of greatest importance." Without slavery, he wrote, Texas could not attract the people to make it a land of sugar and cotton plantations and would instead be populated by shepherds and the poor.[17]

During the years from 1822 to 1825, in spite of uncertainty about the future of slavery, many of Austin's colonists brought bondsmen with them and began to establish the institution just as it existed in the United States. Most basic was the definition of slaves as private property and their treatment as such. Stephen F. Austin demonstrated this in October, 1823, when he hired three slaves from Jared E. Groce for a year beginning on November 1. "The said negros are to be well treated by me," the contract read, "and the said Groce is to clothe them—should they run away or die the loss is to be Groces—sickness to be my loss—."[18]

Slavery, wherever it existed, needed protective laws, and Austin instituted such legal support in Texas. In January, 1824, he promulgated a set of Civil and Criminal Regulations for his colony and instructed the *alcaldes*—the most important local political and judicial authorities under Mexican law—to enforce them. Articles 10 through 14 of the Criminal Regulations constituted Texas' first "slave code." To steal or entice away a slave or harbor a runaway bondsman was a crime punishable by fines as high as $1,000 plus payment of damages to the owner. Anyone buying articles or produce from a slave without his master's approval could be fined as much as $100 and three times the value of the property bought. Slaves who stole could be given ten to one hundred lashes, unless their owners chose to spare them the whipping by paying an amount equal to

17. James A. E. Phelps to Austin, January 16, 1825, Charles Douglas to Austin, February 15, 1825, Austin to Governor Rafael Gonzales, April 4, 1825, all in Barker (ed.), *Austin Papers*, I, 1020–21, 1047, 1067.

18. Agreement of Austin and Jared E. Groce, October [1823], in Barker (ed.), *Austin Papers*, I, 701.

three times the value of the property stolen. Finally, any white person who found a slave away from home without a pass was to give him ten lashes and see to it that the bondsman returned home or was placed in the hands of an alcalde.[19]

By the fall of 1825, sixty-nine of the families in Austin's colony owned slaves, and the 443 bondsmen there were nearly 25 percent of the total population of 1,800. The next year, a census of the Atascosito District, an area to the east of Austin's Colony, showed 76 slaves (19 percent) in a population of 407. Although no enumerations are available for the mid-1820s, slaves were also present at the settlements in the Nacogdoches area and on the Red River.[20]

Slavery thus gained a foothold in Texas by 1825, but immigrants had not seen the last of Mexican opposition to their institution. A new threat came in 1825 from the constituent congress for the recently created state of Coahuila and Texas. Meeting in Saltillo, the state capital, in August, 1824, this congress remained in session until June, 1827. Its first step, the passage of a state colonization law on March 24, 1825, should have been reassuring to Anglo-Americans because it paid scant attention to slavery. The article on the subject read: "In respect to the introduction of slaves, the new settlers shall subject themselves to the laws that are now, and shall hereafter be established on the subject." This was, as Juan Antonio Padilla, the secretary of state at Saltillo, told Austin, too indefinite to mean anything. The slave trade decree of July, 1824—the only existing law affecting new settlers—could be interpreted as applying only to the slave trade, so, Padilla concluded, settlers could bring in slaves as they wished. Emigrants, he wrote, should apply a proverb favored by Mexican lawyers: "What is not prohibited is to be understood as permitted."[21]

As the constituent congress slowly worked toward a state constitution, however, the news from Saltillo became alarming for the slaveholding interest in Texas. Austin learned in July, 1826, that one article in the

19. Austin's Criminal Regulations are reprinted in Dudley G. Wooten (ed.), *A Comprehensive History of Texas, 1865 to 1897* (2 vols.; Dallas, 1898), I, 488–90. They are discussed in some detail in Joseph W. McKnight, "Stephen F. Austin's Legalistic Concerns," *Southwestern Historical Quarterly*, LXXXIX (1986), 256–57.

20. Barker, *Stephen F. Austin*, 98; Curlee, "Texas Slave Plantations," 24–25; Mary M. Osburn (ed.), "The Atascosito Census of 1826," *Texana*, I (1963), 299–321. Curlee points out that eleven of the sixty-nine slaveholders in Austin's Colony owned more than ten bondsmen. They held a total of 271 slaves—61 percent of the total.

21. Barker, *Stephen F. Austin*, 232–33; Juan Antonio Padilla to Austin, June 18, 1825, in Barker (ed.), *Austin Papers*, I, 1135–37.

proposed constitution would abolish slavery immediately and provide for indemnifying owners by a law to be passed later. He reacted by once more taking up his pen to argue that slavery had to be protected if Texas were to grow as he and Mexican authorities wished. To free slaves already in Texas, even with an indemnity, he told the congress in Saltillo, would be an act of bad faith. And, he asked, how would Mexico indemnify owners for property valued typically at $600 to $1,500 and up to $3,000? The *ayuntamiento* (town council) of San Antonio agreed with Austin's petition and sent a similar one to Saltillo. Austin, however, was pessimistic. "I think it probable," he wrote to his sister, Emily M. Perry, in August, 1826, "that slavery will not be allowed . . . tho the constitution will decide it." As rumors concerning the constitutional provisions spread, some settlers began to plan to act on the pessimism expressed by Austin. Jesse Thompson, for example, bemoaning the ruin of his "moast flattering prospects" in Texas, wrote: "I feel as though I shall make every arrangement so soon as is practicable to be in the United States with my property." In early September Austin informed José Antonio Saucedo, the political chief at San Antonio, that his settlers could not be counted on to defend against an expected Indian attack. "More than one half of these people," he wrote, "are awaiting the decision of Congress in regard to their slaves, as they intend to leave the Country if their emancipation is decreed."[22]

As the situation became critical, Austin employed yet another weapon in the struggle to protect slavery in Texas. His brother, James E. B. Austin, went to Saltillo on a personal mission to the congress. Brown Austin, as he was called, was optimistic as he prepared to leave. "I will go and see," he wrote his worried brother, "Try and keep the Slave holders from going until they hear the result of the Slave question—Tell them they are safe yet—and there is but little doubt but part of the laws will be favourable—that is—what—relates to the Slaves already in the Country—." One day in Saltillo, however, was enough to convince Brown Austin that the situation was indeed critical. He found Texas' representative in the

22. Barker, "Influence of Slavery in Colonization of Texas," 11–12; Barker, *Stephen F. Austin*, 234–36; Austin to State Congress, August 11, 1826, Austin to Ayuntamiento of Bexar, August 14, 1826, Austin to Emily M. Perry, August 21, 1826, Jesse Thompson and J. C. Payton to Sprowl, August 11, 1826, Austin to José Antonio Saucedo, September 11, 1826, all in Barker (ed.), *Austin Papers*, I, 1406–1409, 1422–23, 1427, 1405, 1452. Noah Smithwick, *The Evolution of a State, or Recollection of Old Texas Days*, comp. Nanna Smithwick Donaldson, (Austin, 1900), 37, confirms Thompson's intention to leave Texas and says that Thompson had neglected planting in favor of stock raising because he feared for the future of slavery.

congress, Felipe Enrique Neri, baron de Bastrop, hopelessly outnumbered by antislavery Mexicans led by Carlos Antonio Carrillo. Congress, he informed his brother, is "composed of members so inimical to the interests of Texas, that the *most* that can be obtained is permission for the 300 families to hold their Slaves—."[23]

Within a few weeks of Brown Austin's arrival, the petitions concerning slavery from his brother and the ayuntamiento of San Antonio came before congress. "The representation you made on the subject appeared so just and well founded that the Author of the *Article* himself (Carrillo) asked permission to withdraw it," Brown Austin reported. In November, Austin's friend Juan Antonio Padilla expressed the view that immediate, total abolition would destroy at one blow the population, property, and agriculture of an important part of the state. When the Constitution of the State of Coahuila and Texas was finally completed on March 11, 1827, the practical sentiments of Stephen F. Austin and Padilla and the persistent political efforts of Bastrop and Brown Austin bore fruit in an article that was not so lenient as the settlers had wanted nor as harsh as that originally proposed by Carrillo. Article 13 read as follows: "From and after the promulgation of the Constitution in the capital of each district, no one shall be born a slave in the state, and after six months the introduction of slaves under any pretext shall not be permitted."[24]

Six months later, on September 15, 1827, the congress issued a decree to put article 13 into effect. There was to be a census of all slaves within each municipality. Ayuntamientos were to keep a register of all births and deaths among slaves and report those statistics to the state government every three months. There were also several provisions concerning the condition of slaves and the treatment of those who were emancipated. One-tenth of the slaves belonging to any estate passed on by inheritance were to be freed at the change of ownership. Ayuntamientos were charged with providing an education for children emancipated by constitutional provision. Two months later the congress made one concession to the slaveholders by providing that slaves could be sold from one owner to another.[25]

23. James E. B. Austin to Austin, September 3, 1826, and September 23, 1826, both in Barker (ed.), *Austin Papers*, I, 1445–46, 1461–62.

24. J. E. B. Austin to Austin, October 10, 1826, Juan Antonio Padilla to Austin, November 30, 1826, both in *ibid.*, I, 1474, 1525; H. P. N. Gammel (comp.), *The Laws of Texas, 1822–1897* (10 vols.; Austin, 1898–1902), I, 424.

25. Gammel (comp.), *Laws of Texas*, I, 188–89, 202; Bugbee, "Slavery in Early Texas," 407–408; Barker, "Influence of Slavery in Colonization of Texas," 15.

Reactions to the state constitution's restrictions on slavery varied notably among Anglo-Americans. Brown Austin thought that immigrants should rush into Texas with their slaves during the six months allowed after promulgation of the constitution. "If there are any persons in your part of the country having *Slaves*, that wish to remove here—," he wrote his sister Emily Perry, "*hurry* them on before the expiration of the time—." Stephen F. Austin hinted at the same approach, reminding James F. Perry in May, 1827, that slaves in Texas would sell and hire very high once no more could be introduced.[26]

Austin knew, however, that the restrictions on slavery would almost certainly slow the migration of southerners to Texas. Reminders of that fact reached him regularly in 1827 and 1828 from correspondents across the Old South. Realizing that the development of Texas was at stake and that rushing in slaves before the constitution went into effect was a stopgap measure at best, Austin traveled to Saltillo in November, 1827, and appealed to the state legislature for a repeal of the restrictions.[27]

Failing in that quest, he began to look for sources of nonslaveholding settlers. In November, 1827, he wrote to Joel Roberts Poinsett in the United States, endorsing a project by David G. Burnet for colonizing farmers from Ohio in east Texas. Inhabitants of Ohio, he wrote, are known to be "principled" against slavery, and if the government of Mexico wishes to convert Texas from a useless wilderness to a civilized state, "sound policy, and expediency I should presume would approve of a decided encouragement of Ohio and other northern migration." On February 2, 1828, Austin explained his purposes quite candidly to Thomas F. Leaming of Philadelphia: "Slavery is prohibited by the Constitution of this Govt. which has checked the emigration from the Southern States, and I have had an idea of endeavouring to procure emigrants from Pennsylvania and other non slave holding States." Austin had not turned against slavery, but if the choice was between the Peculiar Institution and Texas, he would choose Texas.[28]

26. J. E. B. Austin to Mrs. E. M. Perry, May 24, 1827, Stephen F. Austin to James F. Perry, May 26, 1827, both in Barker (ed.), *Austin Papers*, I, 1644–45, 1645–46.

27. Examples of correspondents from the Old South expressing concern over the future of slavery include Ben R. Milam to Austin, March 30, 1827, and Richard Ellis to Austin, January 3, 1828, both in *ibid.*, I, 1021–22, II, 2–4. Austin's appeal to the state legislature at Saltillo is in *ibid.*, I, 1716–20.

28. Austin to Poinsett, November 3, 1827, in *ibid.*, I, 1703–1704; Austin to Thomas F. Leaming, February 1, 1828, in Andreas Reichstein (ed.), "The Austin-Leaming Correspondence, 1828–1836," *Southwestern Historical Quarterly*, LXXXVIII (1985), 254–55. Austin's own

Austin did not have to choose, however, for during the early months of 1828 settlers in Texas found a way around the constitutional restrictions on slavery. Negroes would be brought into Texas and held as indentured servants who were working to pay their former masters for freedom. In other words, Mexico's own system of debt peonage would be used to further slavery in Texas. Ellis H. Bean suggested this idea as early as July, 1826, and the ayuntamiento of San Felipe de Austin made a formal request for its legal adoption on March 31, 1828. "Considering the paralized state of immigration to this Jurisdiction from the U.S. arising from the difficulties encountered by Imigrants in bringing hirelings and servants with them, this Body conceive it their duty to propose to the Legislature of this state . . . a Law whereby emigrants and inhabitants of this state may be secured in the Contracts made by them with servants or hirelings in foreign countries." Austin endorsed this proposal to the authorities in San Antonio and Texas' representatives at Saltillo. On May 5, 1828, the congress, noting the "deficiency" of agricultural workers in the state, passed a decree that read: "All contracts, not in opposition to the laws of the state, that have been entered into in foreign countries, between emigrants who came to settle in this state, or between inhabitants thereof, and the servants and day laborers or workingmen whom they introduce, are hereby guaranteed to be valid in said state." The state congress, distracted by other matters and perhaps satisfied that debt peonage did not violate its antislavery principles, thus undid virtually everything that the Constitution of 1827 had done to rid Texas of slavery.[29]

The procedure for taking advantage of the May 5, 1828, decree was relatively simple. Before leaving the United States, slaveholders took their slaves before a notary public or other governmental official and drew up a contract showing that each bondsman wished to accompany his master to Texas. The slave would be free in Texas, but he owed his value plus the cost of moving specified in the contract to his master. This debt was to be paid by annual wages, set at very low rates, less the cost of clothes and other necessities. Slave children, once they reached the

---

view of slavery may be indicated by the fact that on February 6, 1828, he purchased a forty-year-old female from John Gibson for $350. Barker (ed.), *Austin Papers*, II, 13.

29. Ellis H. Bean to Austin, July 5, 1826, in Barker (ed.), *Austin Papers*, I, 1368–69; Eugene C. Barker (ed.), "Minutes of the Ayuntamiento of San Felipe de Austin, 1828–1832," *Southwestern Historical Quarterly*, XXI (1918), 311; Gammel (comp.), *Laws of Texas*, I, 213; Bugbee, "Slavery in Early Texas," 408–410; Barker, *Stephen F. Austin*, 240–41.

age of eighteen, were to serve on the same terms, and those born after removal to Texas were to serve the master without pay until they were twenty-five and then on the same terms as their fathers. Such a contract kept Negroes as firmly in servitude as if they had never left the United States.[30]

Within a few years slaveholders began employing less elaborate but equally effective indenture contracts to bring in bondsmen. James Morgan, for example, had the county court of Leon County, Florida, bind his slaves for ninety-nine years; the men and boys were to learn "the art and mystery of farming and planting" and the women "the art and mystery" of cooking and housekeeping. Marmaduke D. Sandifer signed a contract with Clarissa, "a girl of color," before the alcalde at San Felipe de Austin on Christmas Day, 1833, whereby she agreed to "conduct & demean herself as an honest & faithful servant, hereby renouncing and disclaiming all her right and claim to personal liberty for & during a term of ninety-nine years." In return, Sandifer promised to furnish her food, lodging, and medical care and, should she be disabled, to support her in a "decent and comfortable manner."[31]

Slaveholders were delighted with the subterfuge permitted by Mexican law. Frost Thorn informed Austin from Nacogdoches in July, 1828, that it was of "great service to this country." The decree was already creating positive feelings, Thorn wrote, and he intended to publicize it in New Orleans and across the South. Austin relaxed to the extent that his correspondence concerning northern immigrants ceased, but he was not really satisfied. Perhaps he recognized, as did General Manuel Mier y Terán who made an inspection tour of Texas for the Mexican federal government in 1828, that subterfuge is rarely a permanent way of dealing with the law. Terán saw that labor contracts permitted the introduction of slaves, but he also reported that American settlement was "restrained by the laws prohibiting slavery." "If these laws were repealed—," he wrote President Guadalupe Victoria on June 30, "which God forbid—in a few years Texas would be a powerful state which could compete in production and wealth with Louisiana." The first half of 1829 found Stephen F. Austin making inquiries at Saltillo and San Antonio about the

30. Bugbee, "Slavery in Early Texas," 411–12.
31. Indenture Agreement, April 20, 1831, in James Morgan Papers, Rosenberg Library, Galveston; Indenture Agreement, December 25, 1833, in Dr. W. E. Howard Collection, Dallas Historical Society Archives, Dallas.

possibility of repealing the constitutional provision against slavery or suspending it for ten years.[32]

A new threat to slavery in Texas appeared, as one historian put it, like "a bolt from the blue" in the fall of 1829. President Vicente Guerrero, influenced by José María Tornel who had been attempting for two years to have the Mexican congress abolish slavery, issued a decree on September 15, 1829, declaring immediate emancipation everywhere in the republic. (It was customary to free a number of slaves in the area of Mexico City on Independence Day, and Tornel persuaded Guerrero to extend this tradition to all slaves in the nation.) Guerrero's decree first reached Texas on October 16 in a letter from Governor J. M. Viesca at Saltillo to Ramón Músquiz, the political chief at San Antonio. Músquiz reacted in exactly the way Austin and his colonists would have wished. He withheld publication of the decree and appealed to the governor to have Texas excepted from its operation. Settlers in Texas, Músquiz said, had been guaranteed their property rights by federal and state colonization laws. And they could not develop Texas "without the aid of the robust and almost indefatigable arms of that race of the human species which is called negroes, and who, to their misfortune, suffer slavery." Furthermore, to free the thousand or more slaves in Texas would constitute a serious disturbance to public order. Governor Viesca agreed with Músquiz and, on November 14, 1829, appealed to President Guerrero for an exemption for Texas. He would have made the request, he said, even without prompting from Músquiz because the advancement of Coahuila and Texas depended on it. Viesca also added one other consideration—the possibility of violent reactions by the settlers in Texas. The colonists were not insubordinate, he said, but strong feelings result when men are "in danger of being ruined, as would happen to many of them whose fortune consists entirely of slaves."[33]

The slaveholding interest thus received prompt support from Mexican officials who appear to have been nearly as dedicated as Austin to the rapid settlement and development of Texas. Músquiz informed Austin of the decree and of his actions concerning it. He urged secrecy until a result

---

32. Frost Thorn to Austin, July 22, 1828, in Barker (ed.), *Austin Papers*, II, 74; Barker, "Influence of Slavery in the Colonization of Texas," 18; Alleine Howren, "Causes and Origins of the Decree of April 6, 1830," *Southwestern Historical Quarterly*, XVI (1913), 393, 396 (quotation from General Mier y Terán).

33. Barker, "Influence of Slavery in Colonization of Texas," 18–21.

was known, but unfortunately a copy of the decree somehow found its way to the alcalde at Nacogdoches and, although it was not published, caused near panic. "In the name of God what shall we do," John Durst, a prominent citizen wrote Austin on November 10, "for God's Sake advise me on the subject by the return of Mail[.] We are ruined for ever should the Measure be adopted." Austin, reassured to some extent by Músquiz's stand, obviously objected to the tone of Durst's letter. "There ought to be no vocifrous and visionary excitement or noise about this matter—," he replied. If the decree were published in Texas, he said, the people should use the ayuntamientos to appeal for their constitutional rights. "The constitution must be both our shield, and our arms, under *it*, and with *it* we must constitutionally defend ourselves and our property." The course he advised was "a very plain one—calm, deliberate dispassionate, inflexible *firmness*."[34]

Austin's intention to stand firm was not put to the test because President Guerrero issued another decree on December 2, 1829, exempting Texas from the general emancipation ordered on September 15. Possibly, the president acted in response to a letter from General Terán, now the military chief for Texas, and decided in mid-November to make the exemption before the petitions from Texas arrived at Mexico City. If this were the case, he acted only from general concern about the growth of Texas and the possibility of opposition there and not under any threat of resistance to his decree. In any event, Guerrero's order of December 2 was generally circulated in Texas by the end of that month; slavery had survived another threat, and colonists there were delighted.[35]

Stephen F. Austin used the status of slavery as a clinching argument in an optimistic letter of December 31, 1829, urging his brother-in-law, James F. Perry, to move to Texas. "All the difficulties as to Slaves . . . are removed," he wrote, "by a new law excepting Texas from the Genl. emancipation law of 15 Sepr." Although slaves could be brought in only under labor contracts at that time, Austin was convinced that in a few years Texas would be a "Slave State" and then quickly grow into "the best State in the Mexican Union." Three months later Austin wrote Perry that his hopes were being realized. Immigrants are pouring in, he told

34. John Durst to Austin, November 10, 1829, Austin to Durst, November 17, 1829, both in Barker (ed.), *Austin Papers*, II, 285, 288–89. Word of Guerrero's decree reached New Orleans and produced excitment there, too. Ira Ingram to Austin, January 11, 1830, in Samuel May Williams Papers, Rosenberg Library, Galveston.

35. Barker, "Influence of Slavery in Colonization of Texas," 23–24.

Perry. "We are getting the best men, the best kind of settlers. Pay no attention to rumors and silly reports but push on as fast as possible." In the meantime, the San Felipe de Austin *Texas Gazette* reminded Americans in Texas that Mexican authorities had granted them "all we could wish for, as colonists—the SECURITY of our PERSONS and PROPERTY."[36]

Once again, however, the issue of slavery was not long at rest. The federal government, concerned with the influx of settlers who evaded colonization laws in a variety of ways and appeared likely to draw Texas away from loyalty to Mexico, decided to end immigration from the United States. President Anastacio Bustamante issued a decree on April 6, 1830, which prohibited further immigration from Mexico's neighbor to the north. Lucas Alamán, Bustamante's secretary of relations who shaped this law, contended that the slave trade decree of July 13, 1824, had prohibited slavery in Texas. But he recognized that emancipation would draw strong resistance and conceded that slaves already in Texas would remain in bondage. The law of April 6, however, called for strict enforcement of rules against the further introduction of slaves.[37]

The law of April 6, 1830, obviously threatened to destroy all Stephen F. Austin's hopes for Texas. How could he persuade Mexican officials to permit renewed immigration from the United States? He decided that the main object of the decree had been "to keep out turbulent and bad men vagabonds and slaves"; therefore the way to reopen Texas was to acquiesce in Mexican views on slavery. He expressed his new position with complete candor in a letter of June 16, 1830, to Richard Ellis and other potential emigrants from Alabama. Austin explained how he had previously supported slavery in Texas on practical grounds but argued that the reasons "for a partial toleration of this evil, have now ceased." Moreover, Mexico meant to enforce its rules, "and I am of the opinion that Texas will never become a Slave state or country." He recognized that if immigration were reopened slaves could still be brought in as indentured servants but doubted that this arrangement offered enough security to slaveholders. "No one," he wrote, "will be willing to risk a large capital in negroes under contracts with them." All of this, Austin insisted, was for the best. Who could look to the future of a Texas overrun by slaves and

36. Austin to James F. Perry, December 31, 1829, and March 28, 1830, both in Barker (ed.), *Austin Papers*, II, 309, 352; San Felipe de Austin *Texas Gazette*, January 30, 1830. The *Gazette* echoed this idea again on April 3, 1830.
37. Howren, "Causes and Origins of the Decree of April 6, 1830," 395–98, 415–17; Bugbee, "Slavery in Early Texas," 660–61.

free negroes and "seriously wish that slavery should be entailed upon this country—"? Austin expressed similar sentiments during the summer of 1830 to other correspondents who could explain his position publicly, most notably Thomas F. Leaming and S. Rhoads Fisher in Pennsylvania. Once more, if the choice in Stephen F. Austin's eyes had to be between Texas and slavery, he would choose Texas.[38]

Austin's stand was not popular with the slave interest. He told Leaming in July that his opinions had drawn "the sarcasms of slaveholders." Perhaps more to his dismay, he was questioned even by nonslaveholders about the probable impact of closing Texas to slavery. "Do you believe," asked S. Rhoads Fisher from Pennsylvania in August, 1830, "that cane and cotton can be grown to advantage by a sparce white population? . . . We must either abandon the finest portion of Texas to its original uselessness or submit to the acknowledged, but lesser evil of Slavery—."[39]

Influenced no doubt by arguments so similar to those he had often made himself, Austin soon resumed efforts to have the Mexican government ease its restrictions on slavery in Texas. In September, 1830, he explained to Alamán that the main impediment to progress was the lack of labor. Most immigrants, he noted, were accustomed to the employment of slaves. Early in 1831 he wrote to Alamán again and also raised the subject with General Terán. Alamán was noncommittal, and Terán, while admitting that slavery would promote the growth of Texas, advised patience.[40]

Austin thus had no success with his appeals. In reaction, as on previous occasions when slavery had come under serious attack, he became critical of the institution and what it would mean to Texas. This time, however, he also indicated a growing conviction that for better or for worse slavery was in the province to stay. He told his business partner Samuel May Williams in April, 1831: "I sometimes shudder at the consequences and think that a large part [of] America will be Santa Domingonized in 100 or 200 years. The wishes of my colonists have hurried me into

38. Austin to Thomas F. Leaming, June 14, 1830, Austin to Richard Ellis et al., June 16, 1830, both in Barker (ed.), Austin Papers, II, 417–19, 421–23. See also Austin to Henry Austin, June 1, 1830, and Austin to S. Rhoads Fisher, June 17, 1830, both in ibid., II, 404–405, 425–29.

39. Austin to Thomas F. Leaming, July 14, 1830, in Reichstein (ed.), "Austin-Leaming Correspondence," 269; S. Rhoads Fisher to Austin, August 23, 1830, in Barker (ed.), Austin Papers, II, 469–70.

40. Austin to Lucas Alamán, September 20, 1830, Terán to Austin, March, 1831, both in Barker (ed.), Austin Papers, II, 491, 635; Barker, "Influence of Slavery in Colonization of Texas," 27–28.

this theory—but I am now in for the cuestion and there is no retreat." "The question of slavery," he told his cousin Mary Austin Holley in July, 1831, "is a difficult one to get on with." Either, he said, there will be slavery in Texas or a carefully regulated black "laboring class." "Which is best?" he concluded, "Quién Sabe? It is a difficult and *dark* question."[41]

While Austin concerned himself with repeal of the Law of April 6, 1830, and its prohibition of immigration, free and slave, from the United States, Americans continued to filter into Texas. Some brought slaves with them, thus violating the law twice by their entry. The Mexican government gradually strengthened enforcement, however, and on April 28, 1832, the government of Coahuila and Texas issued a new colonization law, containing an additional threat to the future of slavery in Texas. Article 36 of this decree read as follows: "Servants and day laborers, hereafter introduced by foreign colonists, cannot be obligated by any contract to continue in the service of the latter longer than ten years."[42] At this point, then, the introduction of slaves into Texas was prohibited by the state constitution (1827) and federal decree (Law of April 6, 1830) and, should immigration of free citizens of the United States be permitted again, the indentured servant loophole had been tightened notably. Slavery appeared thoroughly hemmed in by restrictions that, if enforced, could have prevented its development as an institution of much significance in Texas after 1832.

Before the year ended, however, developments in southeastern Texas presaged a revolution that would dramatically alter slavery's future course. There was a flare-up of insurrection aimed at the military commander at Anahuac on Galveston Bay, the unfair administration of tariff laws, and Mexican federal authority in general. American settlers held conventions in October, 1832, and April, 1833, at which they asked for reforms, including repeal of the Law of April 6, 1830, and the creation of a separate state government for Texas. Austin went to Mexico City to present these requests. A letter written when he stopped en route at Matamoros on May 30, 1833, revealed a significant commitment in his

41. Austin to Samuel May Williams, April 16, 1831, Austin to Mary Austin Holley, July 19, 1831, both in Barker (ed.), *Austin Papers*, II, 645, 676.

42. Andrew Phelps McCormick, *Scotch-Irish in Ireland and America as Shown in Sketches of . . . Pioneer Scotch-Irish Families . . . in North Carolina, Kentucky, Missouri, and Texas* (New Orleans, 1897), 132–37, describes how some colonists respected Mexican restrictions and did not bring in slaves, while others went ahead and brought in their bondsmen during the early 1830s. Gammel (comp.), *Laws of Texas*, I, 303.

attitude toward slavery as the conflict between Texas and the Mexican national government began: "I have been adverse to the principle of slavery in Texas. I have now, and for the last six months, changed my views of that matter; though my ideas are the same as to the abstract principle. Texas *must be* a slave country. Circumstances and unavoidable necessity compels it. It is the wish of the people there, and it is my duty to do all I can, prudently, in favor of it. I will do so." In actuality, while Austin had wavered according to changing circumstances, he had never been consistently adverse to slavery in Texas, and a willingness to do what was necessary for his colony had always outweighed any sort of opposition to slavery on principle. He had only made up his mind, not changed his basic course.[43]

Austin did not specify what he intended to do, "prudently," for slavery, but the separation of Texas from Coahuila certainly could have resulted in a new state colonization law allowing labor contracts without restrictions concerning duration. However, the national government, under the control of President Antonio López de Santa Anna, would not allow a separate state government for Texas, although Santa Anna agreed to a number of other reforms, including repeal of the restriction on immigration from the United States, which became effective in mid-1834. Austin was not in Texas to enjoy even this limited success. Instead, he was imprisoned in Mexico City from January until Christmas Day of 1834 for writing a letter "in a moment of irritation," suggesting that the ayuntamiento of San Antonio organize a state government without waiting for approval from the Mexican government.[44]

During Austin's absence in 1833–34, public affairs in Texas were relatively quiet. Settlers continued to hold Negroes as slaves (those brought in before restrictions in the state constitution of 1827 became effective) and as servants bound by labor contracts. When legal immigration from the United States resumed in 1834, more bondsmen were brought in under indentures. Moreover, a blurring of the distinction between bona fide slaves and labor contract servants apparently occurred. Travelers and Mexican officials tended to claim that all the blacks were held by subterfuge. One anonymous writer claimed in 1834 that Negroes were held as

43. Barker, *Stephen F. Austin*, 374–420; Ben Procter and Archie P. McDonald (eds.), *The Texas Heritage* (St. Louis, 1980), 42–44; Austin to Wiley Martin, May 30, 1833, in Barker (ed.), *Austin Papers*, II, 981.

44. Barker, *Stephen F. Austin*, 430–50; Procter and McDonald (eds.), *Texas Heritage*, 44–45.

slaves in "many" Texas homes, "although the laws of Mexico forbid it." A slaveholder can do this, he wrote, by getting his negroes to sign a bond promising to serve him for ninety nine years." Similar views were published by Amos A. Parker in 1835: "By the laws, slavery is not allowed in the province; but this law is evaded by binding the negroes by indenture for a term of years. You will, therefore, find negro servants, more or less, all over the country; but more on the lowlands, towards the bays and seacoasts. Large cotton plantations in this section of the country, are cultivated by negroes." When Juan N. Almonte inspected Texas for Vice-President Valentín Gómez Farías during the spring of 1834, he reported 2,000 Negroes (none in the Department of Béxar, 1,000 in the Department of Brazos, and 1,000 in the Department of Nacogdoches) in a total population, excluding Indians, of 21,000. These Negroes, he said, were introduced "under certain conditions granted by the state government."[45]

Settlers in Texas differed from Mexican observers by blurring the distinction between slaves and indentured servants in the direction of seeing all blacks in Texas as property pure and simple. Regardless of constitutional and statutory regulations, Negroes were bought and sold, hired out, inventoried as assets of estates, and bequeathed in wills. Early sales in Austin's Colony, such as one on November 16, 1824, involving a woman and her child, took the form of seventy-year hire contracts, "should the said negroes live that time," in order to evade the restrictions of the Imperial Colonization Law on selling and purchasing bondsmen. As the colony grew and the status of blacks in various areas became more ambiguous, however, transactions took a more direct form. Stephen F. Austin, for example, simply bought a slave woman named Mary at San Felipe de Austin in February, 1828, and William Barret Travis sold a five year-old-boy for $225 to Jesse Burnam on Christmas Day, 1834, warranting that he (Travis) had a clear "right and title" to the boy. Austin also set

45. For indications that slaves were brought in as indentured servants during the early 1830s, see Asa Hoxey to R. M. Williamson, December 2, 1832, in "Notes and Fragments," *Quarterly of the Texas State Historical Association*, IX (1906), 285–86, which discusses buying slaves in Virginia before moving to Texas, and W. G. L. Foleys to Austin [?], October 28, 1834, in Williams Papers, which asks for information on the proper method of introducing slaves to Texas. Travelers' observations include [Anonymous], *A Visit to Texas: Being the Journal of a Traveller Through Those Parts Most Interesting to American Settlers* (New York, 1834; rpr., Austin, 1952), 210, and Amos Andrew Parker, *Trip to the West and Texas . . . in the Autumn and Winter of 1834–5* (Concord, N.H., 1835), 162. For information on Almonte's inspection tour, see Helen Willits Harris, "Almonte's Inspection of Texas in 1834," *Southwestern Historical Quarterly*, XLI (1938), 195–211, and Juan N. Almonte, "Statistical Report on Texas, 1835," trans. Carlos E. Castañeda, *Southwestern Historical Quarterly*, XXVIII (1925), 177–222.

an example in the hiring of slaves from the onset of colonization, and the practice continued into the 1830s. Austin's will, written in 1833 before his last trip to Mexico City, specified that his slave woman Mary was to go to the wife of his business partner, Samuel May Williams. When individuals who were among Austin's "Old Three Hundred" settlers died, inventories of their estates often included slaves, some of whom were young children. This was the case with Alexander Jackson (1828), Jonathan C. Peyton (1834), and Thomas Westall (1834). These transactions and property arrangements could hardly have been legal under Mexican law. How, for example, could Travis sell a five-year-old in 1834? The boy could not have been legally born a slave in Texas or brought in as such, and no provision existed for selling indentured servants or their children. How could estates claim title to young children in 1834? Older slaves may have been in Texas legally before promulgation of the state constitution in 1827, but the children were born later. In sum, the status of Negroes in Mexican Texas during the early 1830s was often indeterminate, but the tendency among American settlers was to treat all blacks as de facto slaves and to get away with it.[46]

Slavery thus came to Texas with the first Anglo-American settlers and gained a foothold during the colonial period. Reasons for this development are not difficult to determine. First, most of the settlers were from slave states where the institution was commonplace. They generally considered blacks inherently inferior and thought bondage an essential form of social control. Virginia-born Stephen F. Austin, for example, spoke at times as a critic of slavery and protested that he objected to the institution in principle, but he personally held slaves and did more than any other individual to establish slavery in Mexican Texas. He expressed serious qualms about slavery only on the several occasions when he believed that he had to choose between it and Texas. The second, and probably more

46. Bill of Sale for Slaves, November, 1824, Austin to Jared E. Groce [hire agreement], October, 1823, both in Barker (ed.), *Austin Papers*, I, 969–70, 701; Bill of Sale, December 25, 1834, in William Barret Travis Collection, Sul Ross State University Library, Alpine, Texas; Estate of Stephen F. Austin, Brazoria County Probate Records (Wills, etc., Book A); Estate of Thomas and Sarah Westall, Brazoria County Probate Records (Wills, etc., Book A); Estate of Jonathan C. Payton, Austin County Probate Records (Succession Record, Book A); Estate of Alexander Jackson, Austin County Probate Records (Succession Record, Book B). Appendix 3 lists all counties from which local record information such as the estate records cited here was drawn. It also gives the office in which the records are located and the location of the courthouse within the county.

important, explanation of slavery's foothold in Texas is the belief that it was a practical necessity. The argument from necessity—that Texas could be settled and developed rapidly and profitably only with the employment of slave labor—was used compellingly by Austin and sympathetic Mexican officials. Many leaders of the Mexican governments, both federal and state, appear to have had genuine liberal convictions against slavery, but they regularly allowed themselves to be convinced that the institution was necessary to the growth of Texas.[47] Economic necessity overcame moral or theoretical considerations.

Even the limited and vacillating opposition presented by Mexican authorities obviously retarded the development of slavery in Texas. This contention is supported by the many letters Austin received from prospective immigrants expressing concern over the future of slavery, by the observations of General Terán in 1828, and by the low percentage of slaves in Texas during the early 1830s. Almonte, who was sympathetic to the settlers at that point, may have understated the number of slaves when he placed it at two thousand (9.5 percent of the total) in 1834. But had there been twice as many Negroes as he reported, they still would have constituted only about 20 percent of the population, a smaller proportion than would be expected under more favorable circumstances.

The impact of Mexico's limited opposition to the introduction of slaves tempts the asking of a "what if" question. Could Texas have been settled successfully without slavery? The answer has several parts and depends finally, of course, on the definition of "successfully." In the first place, firmness on the part of Mexican authorities, in spite of the difficulties involved in governing such an outlying province, could likely have blocked the introduction of slavery into Texas. Anglo-Americans certainly seemed to think that Mexico could prohibit slavery in Texas if she so wished. And this probably would not have meant a cessation of immigration from the United States. Stephen F. Austin's reaction when the Mexican government appeared ready to take a firm stand certainly suggests that it may have been possible to attract Anglo-Americans to Texas without permitting slavery. It appears equally certain, however, that Texas would not have attracted settlers or developed cotton production as rap-

47. General Mier y Terán indicated an even more cynical calculation in a letter to Lucas Alamán concerning the Law of April 6, 1830, in which he suggested that a Texas filled with slaveholding colonists would be hesitant to rebel against Mexico because of the fear of servile insurrection. See Ohland Morton, *Terán and Texas: A Chapter in Texas-American Relations* (Austin, 1948), 118–19.

idly without slavery. The estimated production in the area of Austin's original colony increased from 600 bales in 1827 to 2,000 bales by 1833, and the Nacogdoches District exported an estimated 2,000 bales in 1834. Slave labor was the key to this cotton culture. Texas could have been settled without slavery but not in the most immediately profitable way.[48]

Of course, the future of slavery in Texas was by no means determined in 1834–35. Instead, the institution was still threatened by constitutional and statutory restrictions. Children born to bondsmen belonging to Austin's original colonists (those who came under the Imperial Colonization Law of January, 1823) were to be free at age fourteen, although those masters affected had probably lost sight of this requirement in the passage of time.[49] More important, the 1827 Constitution of Coahuila and Texas prohibited the introduction of slaves and declared all slave children free at birth. The state law of 1832 limited the duration of labor contracts to ten years. Enforcement of these rules was hardly certain; nevertheless, slavery's foothold in Texas was far from secure as the revolution against Mexico developed in 1835.

48. The problems of governing so distant a province were mentioned by several observers; see, for example, [Anonymous], *A Visit to Texas*, 210. Tom V. Watson, "A Study of Agriculture in Colonial Texas, 1821–1836" (M.A. thesis, Texas Tech University, 1935), 30–37; Curlee, "Texas Slave Plantations," 12–13; Berleth, "Groce," 361.

49. The Texas Supreme Court ruled in 1847 in *Nathaniel Robbins' Administrator* v. *Hannah Walters*, 2 Tex. 130, that a slave born in Texas before the promulgation of the Constitution of Texas and Coahuila (March 11, 1827) could be held indefinitely in slavery.

TWO

. . . .

Slavery in the Texas Revolution, 1835–1836

"A DULL, ORGANIC ACHE"

To Benjamin Lundy, the noted abolitionist who traveled extensively in Texas between 1830 and 1835, the cause of Texas' revolt against Mexico in 1835–36 was obvious. "It is susceptible of the clearest demonstration," he wrote in 1837, "that the immediate cause and leading object of the contest originated in a settled design, among the slaveholders of this country, (with land speculators and slave traders,) to wrest the large and valuable territory of Texas from the Mexican Republic, in order to re-establish the SYSTEM OF SLAVERY; to open a vast and profitable SLAVE-MARKET therein; and, ultimately, to annex it to the United States." The British abolitionist John Scoble repeated Lundy's charges in more colorful language a few years later while arguing that Great Britain should not grant diplomatic recognition to the Texas Republic. That "robber state," he wrote, was settled by "hordes of characterless villains, whose sole object has been to re-establish slavery and the slave trade." José María Tornel offered a similar view from the Mexican perspective in 1837: "The land speculators of Texas have tried to convert it into a mart of human flesh where the slaves of the south might be sold and others from Africa might be introduced, since it is not possible to do it directly through the United States."[1]

1. Benjamin Lundy, *The War in Texas: A Review of Facts and Circumstances Showing that This Contest Is a Crusade . . . to Reestablish, Extend, and Perpetuate the System of Slavery and the Slave*

Logic supported the interpretation of the Texas Revolution presented by Lundy, Scoble, and Tornel. Settlers from the United States had always been concerned about establishing and maintaining slavery in Texas, and Mexican opposition, while vacillating, had bothered many immigrants and retarded development of the institution. Moreover, once the Texans gained their independence, they were quick to give slavery all the guarantees that it had never been afforded by Mexican governments. Under these circumstances, the claim that desire to protect slavery was at least a major cause of the insurrection appears plausible. If, however, this interpretation is valid, direct evidence of slavery's involvement should also be present. Did a Mexican threat to slavery prompt the revolt? Did the revolutionaries ever indicate that the protection of slavery was a primary cause of their actions? Answers to these questions depend on tracing revolutionary developments during the early 1830s to examine when and how slavery appeared as an issue.

If any single action could be said to have set in motion the train of events leading to revolution, it was the Law of April 6, 1830, which prohibited further immigration from the United States and called for the collection of customs duties and garrisoning of troops in Texas. Tariff collections under this law caused problems in 1831 when George Fisher, Mexico's new customs collector for ports east of the Colorado River, located his customhouse at Anahuac at the head of Galveston Bay and demanded that all ships departing Texas from his jurisdiction clear customs at Anahuac. This requirement meant that ships leaving from Brazoria on the Brazos River had to travel several hundred extra miles along the coast and up Galveston Bay before leaving Texas waters. After a bitter dispute in late 1831, a deputy collector was appointed at Brazoria. The issue still rankled Texans, however, especially since Colonel John D. Bradburn, a Kentucky-born officer who commanded Mexico's new military post at Anahuac, antagonized them in other ways at the same time. In January, 1831, Francisco Madero, a newly appointed general land commissioner of Texas, arrived on the Trinity River just north of Anahuac, established the town of Liberty, and began issuing land titles to American settlers in

Trade (Philadelphia, 1837), 3; John Scoble, Texas: Its Claims to be Recognized as an Independent Power by Great Britain; Examined in a Series of Letters (London, 1839), 3, 9; José María Tornel, Relations Between Texas, the United States of America, and the Mexican Republic (Mexico City, 1837), in The Mexican Side of the Texas Revolution by the Chief Mexican Participants, trans. Carlos E. Castañeda (Dallas, 1928), 328.

the area. Bradburn, believing that Madero was acting in violation of the Law of April 6, 1830, soon arrested him and annulled the ayuntamiento of Liberty. Bradburn further upset Anglo-Texans by using slave labor without compensating owners in erecting military buildings, by informing slaves that the intent of Mexican law was to make them free, and by refusing to turn over two runaway slaves from Louisiana to their owner. He arrested William B. Travis and Patrick H. Jack, apparently because they antagonized him with messages about an armed force coming from Louisiana to recover the runaways. In June, 1832, colonists demanded the release of Travis and Jack. When Bradburn refused and strengthened his post, the Texans sent to Brazoria for cannon and planned an assault. Serious insurrection appeared imminent.[2]

In the meantime, however, developments in Mexico worked to the advantage of the Americans in Texas. Antonio López de Santa Anna began a revolt against President Anastacio Bustamante with the intention of reinstating the liberal Constitution of 1824. Bradburn was a Bustamante appointee, so the Texans at Anahuac, while they waited for cannon to attack a Mexican fort, adopted the Turtle Bayou Resolutions, which asserted their loyalty to the apparently liberal-minded Santa Anna and the Constitution of 1824. Adoption of these resolutions proved wise when Colonel José de las Piedras, commander of Mexico's garrison at Nacogdoches, hearing of the troubles at Anahuac, arrived there with troops before the cannon came from Brazoria. Convinced that Bradburn's arbitrary rule was the problem, Piedras ordered the release of Travis and Jack. Bradburn resigned, and his garrison declared for Santa Anna and returned to Mexico. Meanwhile, resistance flared in other parts of Texas, only to be faced in August, 1832, with a large Mexican army commanded by Colonel José Antonio Mexía. Fortunately for the Texans, however, Mexía was a Santanista, so they could claim to be his allies in the war against Bustamante. Stephen F. Austin, on his way home from the state legislature in Saltillo, traveled with Mexía and made the same argument. Following a warm welcome at Brazoria, replete with a dinner and ball

2. David J. Weber, *The Mexican Frontier, 1821–1846: The American Southwest Under Mexico* (Albuquerque, 1982), 167–71; Margaret Swett Henson, *Juan Davis Bradburn: A Reappraisal of the Mexican Commander at Anahuac* (College Station, 1982), 72–75, 81–84, 58–67, 77–78, 89–98. Bradburn apparently thought that the indentured servant "loophole" in Mexican laws against the importation of slaves applied only to Austin's Colony. Miriam Partlow, *Liberty, Liberty County, and the Atascosito District* (Austin, 1974), 86–88, 94–96. Barker, *Stephen F. Austin*, 386–87.

and many toasts to Santa Anna, Mexía returned to Mexico. A near insurrection had turned into a demonstration of Texan loyalty to the next president of Mexico.[3]

Hoping that their support for Santa Anna would earn a favorable hearing for reform proposals, the Anglo settlers in Texas held two conventions at San Felipe de Austin: one in October, 1832, and a second in April, 1833. These conventions urged repeal of the Law of April 6, 1830, and asked that Texas be separated from Coahuila and made a state in Mexico's federal union. Such reforms, the delegates hoped, would prevent a recurrence of the problems that had led to the disturbances at Anahuac. The second convention went so far as to propose a constitution, drafted by a committee chaired by Sam Houston, for the new state of Texas.[4]

Slavery received no special mention at either of these conventions, but it likely was one among the many interests that Texans expected separate statehood to protect. Houston's proposed constitution did not mention slavery. Stephen F. Austin's statement of the second convention's purpose did not either, although he did complain that the existing political system "tends to check the growth of the country, and to produce confusion and insecurity, rather than to extend protection to lives and property." Austin, while preparing to take the second convention's petitions to Mexico City, also informed his cousin Henry Austin: "The sum and substance of the whole matter is that Texas must have a state Government. Nothing else will quiet this country or give any security to persons or property." He did not specify, but "property" certainly implied slaves. Within a month he was writing, "Texas *must be* a slave country." Benjamin Lundy claimed that during his visit to Texas in the summer of 1833 settlers told him that a desire to control their own laws on slavery was one reason for requesting separation from Coahuila. Lundy also wrote that, according to a Mr. Egerton from New York, Austin, when he presented the proposed constitution of Texas to the Mexican Congress, asked that settlers be allowed to hold slaves.[5]

3. Henson, *Bradburn*, 100–111; Barker, *Stephen F. Austin*, 387–403; Ernest Wallace and David M. Vigness (eds.), *Documents of Texas History* (Austin, 1963), 73.

4. Barker, *Stephen F. Austin*, 404–29; Weber, *Mexican Frontier*, 246; Wallace and Vigness (eds.), *Documents of Texas History*, 74–85.

5. Austin to Henry Austin, April 9, 1833, Austin to Wiley Martin, May 30, 1833, both in Barker (ed.), *Austin Papers*, II, 953, 981; Benjamin Lundy, *The Life, Travels, and Opinions of Benjamin Lundy, Including His Journeys to Texas and Mexico*, comp. Thomas Earle (1847; rpr. New York, 1971), 85–86; Eugene C. Barker, *Mexico and Texas, 1821–1835* (Dallas, 1928), 84.

One aspect of slavery, the African trade, did receive specific mention at the 1833 convention. David G. Burnet, who was destined to become the first president of the Texas republic, introduced a resolution stating that the convention held the African trade in "utter abhorrence" and calling on all "the good people of Texas" to avoid involvement in that "abominable traffic" and to work "to prevent the evil from polluting our shores." This resolution, prompted by the arrival of a foreign slaver from Cuba at Galveston, was published in Texas, New Orleans, and Mexico. Some Texans, particularly newcomers James W. Fannin, Jr., and Ben Fort Smith, ignored these sentiments and engaged in the African trade during 1833 and 1834. But leading Texans continued to oppose the practice with as much indignation as could have been expected of any Mexican official. John A. Wharton, brother of the chairman of the 1833 convention, William H. Wharton, complained to Burnet in July, 1834, that the trade was "disgraceful to ourselves, and ruinous to our country." It is, he wrote, an "outrage upon humanity" and a "defiance of the laws of almost all christendom" that should not go unpunished. Clearly, then, while Anglo-Texans meant to continue slavery, the only aspect of the institution receiving specific attention in the conventions of 1832 and 1833 and their immediate aftermath was the African slave trade. And it was not an issue likely to cause trouble between Mexico and most Texans, since both opposed it.[6]

For most of 1833 and 1834, developments in Mexico favored Texas. Vice-President Gómez Farías, a liberal reformer, governed during much of this period, and numerous changes were made. Texas was divided into three political departments, English was accepted for official purposes, the court system was revised, and religious toleration was granted. Texas, however, was not separated from Coahuila, and indeed this became an increasingly remote possibility after April, 1834, when President Santa Anna took over from Gómez Farías, repudiated liberalism, and moved to make Mexico a centralized dictatorship. In October, 1835, the Mexican Congress conceded to his wishes and replaced the Constitution

6. Resolution by David G. Burnet on African Slave Trade, April, 1833, in Barker (ed.), *Austin Papers*, II, 941–42; Mary Whatley Clarke, *David G. Burnet* (Austin, 1969), 45–46; Webb, Carroll, and Branda (eds.), *Handbook of Texas*, I, 582, II, 621; Edward Hanrick to Samuel May Williams, August 28, 1833, in Williams Papers; Dilue Harris, "Reminiscences of Mrs. Dilue Harris," *Quarterly of the Texas State Historical Association*, IV (1900), 97–99; John A. Wharton to David G. Burnet, July 8, 1834, in David G. Burnet Papers, Barker Texas History Center, University of Texas, Austin.

of 1824 with laws converting the states into mere departments of a centralized nation. Many Anglo-Texans were slow to see the direction of Santa Anna's policy because the state government of Coahuila and Texas had discredited itself with a dispute over location of the state capital and with dishonest land sales. By the summer of 1835, however, Santa Anna began to show Texas the real meaning of centralization. The result was revolution.[7]

The disturbance that led to insurrection came at Anahuac, and, as in 1832, the issue was customs collection. President Santa Anna sent soldiers to the Galveston Bay post in January, 1835, to support the collection of duties. Texans in the area opposed the operations of Mexican authority; violence and arrests followed. General Martín Perfecto de Cos, commander of the Eastern Interior Provinces, decided to reinforce the garrison at Anahuac, and a small group of militant Texans, learning of this intention, acted first and forced the surrender of Mexican troops there. A majority of Texans disapproved of this action and attempted to convince Cos of their loyalty. The general, however, insisted that leading opponents of Santa Anna's regime be arrested and that all colonists in Texas obey the central government. He made plans to bring reinforcements and take command personally at San Antonio. Conciliation appeared so hopeless by late summer, 1835, that a consultation of all Texans was called for October 15 at Washington on the Brazos. In September, the Central Committee of Safety of San Felipe reinforced the call for the consultation. "War is our only resource," wrote Stephen F. Austin, the committee's chairman. "There is no other remedy but to defend our rights, ourselves, and our country by force of arms." Fighting began at Gonzales on October 2, 1835.[8]

As the revolution developed in 1835, Texans saw the situation as a threat to slavery and, ironically, as an attempt to reduce them to the status of slaves. Ben Milam put these fears succinctly in a letter of July 5 warning Frank W. Johnson that a Mexican attack was imminent: "Their intention is to gain the friendship of the different tribes of Indians; and if possible to get the slaves to revolt. . . . If the Federal system is lost in Texas, what will be our situation? Worse than that of the most degraded

7. Barker, *Stephen F. Austin*, 434–35, 442, 461, 470–73; Weber, *Mexican Frontier*, 247–48; Oakah L. Jones, Jr., *Santa Anna* (New York, 1968), 56–58, 60–61.

8. Barker, *Stephen F. Austin*, 474–84 (quotation on 481); Weber, *Mexican Frontier*, 248–50.

slaves." In a Fourth of July address, R. M. Williamson told listeners at Bexar that Mexicans were coming to Texas in part "to compel you to liberate your slaves." Horatio Allsbery, who visited Monterrey during the summer, wrote a public letter informing Texans that Mexico intended to "put their slaves free and then loose upon their families." General Cos did nothing to dispel these fears when he issued a warning from Matamoros in July telling the colonists that the consequences of insurrection would "bear heavily upon them and their property." Texans thus feared for the security of their slaves, but at the same time they saw nothing incongruous in adopting resolutions explaining that their struggle was for "liberty" against impending slavery. As the Liberty Committee of Public Safety put it, "the contest is for liberty or slavery, for life or death."[9]

In the early fall of 1835, the fears of Anglo-Texans focused on the Brazos River area where slaves were the most numerous. The Committee of Safety for Matagorda resolved on September 30 that as "danger is apprehended from the slave population on the Brazos" citizens should adopt "prompt measures to prevent in our section both alarm and danger." A few days later Thomas J. Pilgrim, reacting to a rumor about Mexican troops landing at the mouth of the Brazos, asked Stephen F. Austin: "Would there not be a great danger from the Negroes should a large Mexican force come so near?" Then, apparently the Texans' worst fears nearly came true. "I have some unpleasant news to communicate," B. J. White wrote Austin from Goliad on October 17. "The negroes on Brazos made an attempt to rise. Major Sutherland came on here for a few men to take back, he told me—John Davis returned from Brazoria bringing the news that near 100 had been taken up many whipd nearly to death some hung, etc. R. H. Williams had nearly kild one of his." A postscript by White added that the plotters had planned to divide the cotton farms, make the whites work for them, and ship cotton to New Orleans.[10]

9. Ben Milam to Frank W. Johnson, July 5, 1835, Horatio Allsbury to Public, August 28, 1835, both in Barker (ed.), *Austin Papers*, III, 82–83, 107–108; Address of R. M. Williamson, June 22, 1835, General Martín Perfecto de Cos to Public, July 5, 1835, both in John Holmes Jenkins (ed.), *The Papers of the Texas Revolution, 1835–1836* (10 vols.; Austin, 1973), I, 199, 203; Partlow, *Liberty, Liberty County, and the Atascosito District*, 100–101. For similar sentiments, see San Felipe de Austin *Telegraph and Texas Register*, October 17, 1835, and Brazoria *Texas Republican*, September 26, 1835.

10. Resolutions of the Committee of Safety for Matagorda, September 30, 1835, Thomas J. Pilgrim to Austin, October 6, 1835, B. J. White to Austin, October 17, 1835, all in Barker (ed.), *Austin Papers*, III, 143–44, 162, 190.

Texans, even if distracted by the developing war with Mexico, were prepared and able to suppress any internal slave revolt in 1835–36, and they were ever vigilant concerning new threats. The rumor, for example, of a project for settling free blacks from the United States in Texas drew a heated protest from the Beaumont Committee of Safety in December, 1835. Free blacks, the committee wrote, would threaten the "peace and tranquility" of slave property.[11]

Texans could not, however, have protected slavery had they lost their war with Mexico. Defeat almost certainly would have meant the end of the institution. Santa Anna made his inclinations clear as he prepared to invade Texas in February, 1836. "There is a considerable number of slaves in Texas . . . ," he wrote his minister of war and marine, "who have been introduced by their masters under cover of certain questionable contracts, but who according to our laws should be free. Shall we permit those wretches to moan in chains any longer in a country whose kind laws protect the liberty of man without distinction of cast [sic] or color?" William H. Wharton, writing as "Curtius" in 1836, indicated that Texas leaders understood the implications of their contest with Mexico in the same way. The Mexicans, he wrote, are threatening us with a "sickly philanthropy worthy of the abolitionists of these United States." Stephen F. Austin went so far as to claim in one of his appeals for aid from the United States in 1836 that Santa Anna meant to exterminate the American population of Texas and fill "that country with Indians and negroes."[12]

By March, 1836, the revolution had progressed to the point that a convention, meeting at Washington on the Brazos, adopted a Declaration of Independence and wrote a constitution for the Republic of Texas. As these brave steps were being taken, however, it appeared that Mexican forces would render them meaningless. Santa Anna's army took the Alamo in San Antonio on March 6, offering no quarter to its defenders. Among the noncombatant survivors was a slave named Joe, the property

11. Beaumont Committee [of Safety] to Henry Millard, December 2, 1835, in William C. Binkley (ed.), *Official Correspondence of the Texas Revolution, 1835–1836* (2 vols.; New York, 1936), I, 161.

12. General Santa Anna to Minister of War and Marine, February 16, 1836, in *Mexican Side of the Texas Revolution*, 65; "Curtius" [William H. Wharton], February, 1836, in Jenkins (ed.), *Papers of the Texas Revolution*, IX, 240; Austin to Senator L. F. Linn, May 4, 1836, in Barker (ed.), *Austin Papers*, III, 345–46.

of William B. Travis. Two weeks later General José Urrea forced the surrender of a Texan army under James W. Fannin at Goliad and then, acting under orders from Santa Anna, murdered about 350 prisoners. The remaining Texas forces, now under the command of Sam Houston, retreated eastward across the Colorado and Brazos rivers, and Anglo-Texan settlers began a panic-stricken rush ahead of their army. The "Runaway Scrape," as it became known, saw families and their slaves fleeing into east Texas and across the Sabine River into Louisiana during March and early April. Then, on the afternoon of April 21, 1836, Houston's forces surprised Santa Anna's army at San Jacinto and in eighteen minutes won a crushing victory. Mexico would be a long time in accepting the fact, but this battle ended its ownership of Texas. The panic of the Runaway Scrape subsided after San Jacinto, and Texans soon began to capitalize on their newly won independence.[13]

Slavery and slaves played an important role in the events of early 1836. Houston's retreat and the Runaway Scrape may have been prompted in part by a concern for the reaction of bondsmen to the invading Mexican

13. O. Jones, *Santa Anna*, 66–69; James W. Pohl and Stephen L. Hardin, "The Military History of the Texas Revolution: An Overview," *Southwestern Historical Quarterly*, LXXXIX (1986), 289–99, 303–306; Procter and McDonald (eds.), *Texas Heritage*, 47–48; José Enrique de la Peña, *With Santa Anna in Texas: A Personal Narrative of the Revolution*, trans. and ed. Carmen Perry (College Station, 1975), 44. For an interesting account of the "Runaway Scrape," see Harris, "Reminiscences," 163–67.

The Battle of San Jacinto gave rise to the legend of the Yellow Rose of Texas. The story is that a slave woman named Emily Morgan, the property of James Morgan, "dallied" with General Santa Anna at his camp before the battle, giving Texas forces time to prepare their attack. In some versions, Emily is also credited with advising Sam Houston on how best to defeat the Mexicans. Professional historians do not believe that there is any truth to the legend, but even if Emily was involved with Santa Anna, she was not a slave. No Emily was among the slaves Morgan brought to Texas in 1831, and there is no evidence that he ever owned such a slave. An Emily D. West came to Texas from New York in 1835 with Emily West de Zavala, the second wife of Lorenzo de Zavala. In April, 1836, Emily, the servant, was captured at James Morgan's home where the De Zavala family had taken refuge. After escaping during the Battle of San Jacinto, she rejoined the de Zavalas and in 1837 returned to New York with Mrs. de Zavala. In short, there probably is no basis for the legend, and if there is, the story bears no relationship to slavery in Texas because Emily West was always a free woman. Margaret S. Henson, "She's the Real Thing," *Texas Highways*, XXXIII (April, 1986), 60–61. A good summary of the views of scholars is found in the Dallas *Morning News*, November 17, 1985, Sec. A, pp. 45, 50. For a more popular view, see Martha Anne Turner, *The Yellow Rose of Texas: Her Saga and Her Song* (Austin, 1976). For the continuing legend, see Stephen Harrigan, "The Yellow Rose of Texas," *Texas Monthly* XII (April, 1984), 152. San Antonio even has an Emily Morgan Hotel that advertises her as a "beautiful slave girl."

army. William Parker claimed that one of Houston's purposes was "to prevent the negroes from joining the enemy in small parties," and many Texans fled eastward with the conviction that Santa Anna meant to create a servile insurrection.[14] Some slaves did seek freedom with Mexican forces. General José Urrea recorded in his diary for April 3 the comment: "Fourteen Negro slaves with their families came to me on this day and I sent them free to Victoria." Ann Raney Coleman described how during the Runaway Scrape four of her husband's slaves ran away to the Mexican army, leaving him "inconsoleble at his loss." In contrast, however, Mrs. Dilue Harris remembered bondsmen loyally performing essential services in helping their owners' families move eastward along roads turned into quagmires and across rivers swollen by heavy rains. At least two slaves, Peter who belonged to the revolutionary leader Wiley Martin and Cary who belonged to Thomas F. McKinney, voluntarily aided the Texan cause to the point that their actions were cited as part of the justification for manumission requests in 1839. Other slaves supported the Texan cause, albeit involuntarily, when they were "pressed" with the intention of building fortifications on Galveston Island.[15]

The Treaties of Velasco, which Santa Anna agreed to in order to secure his release after San Jacinto, called for the return of "negro slaves, or indentured persons" who had been captured by or taken refuge with the Mexican army. General Vicente Filisola attempted to comply with this agreement, but General Urrea bitterly attacked his fellow officer for surrendering slaves who were illegally held in that status in the first place. "All the slaves within my jurisdiction," Urrea claimed, "continued to enjoy their liberty." He sent them to Victoria in Tamaulipas, Mexico. In sum, the fighting of the Texas Revolution afforded a few Negroes the opportunity to gain freedom with Mexican forces, but with the victory at San Jacinto, the great majority, who could not or had not sought to escape

14. William Parker to the Natchez *Free Trader*, April 29, 1836, in Jenkins (ed.), *Papers of the Texas Revolution*, VI, 123. For examples of Texans' fears of servile insurrection, see Resolutions of a Meeting at Brazoria, March 17, 1836, in *ibid.*, V, 98–99, and Henry Austin to James F. Perry, March 5, 1836, in Barker (ed.), *Austin Papers*, III, 318–19.

15. Diary of General José Urrea, in *Mexican Side of the Texas Revolution*, 238; Reminiscences of Ann Raney Thomas Coleman, in Ann Raney Thomas Coleman Papers, Barker Texas History Center, University of Texas, Austin; Harris, "Reminiscences," 163–67; James Morgan to Thomas Jefferson Rusk, April 8, 1836, in Binkley (ed.), *Official Correspondence*, II, 611; Thomas Jefferson Rusk to James Morgan, April 16, 1836, in Jenkins (ed.), *Papers of the Texas Revolution*, V, 493. Slaves who aided the revolution are discussed briefly in Barr, *Black Texans*, 6–7. The cases of Peter and Cary will be discussed and are documented below.

bondage, were more firmly than ever secured in their status as slaves.[16]

Official action to secure slavery during the Texas Revolution began even before the Declaration of Independence. The Consultation, which met at San Felipe in November, 1835, set up a provisional government for Texas consisting of a governor, lieutenant governor, and general council. On January 5, 1836, this council adopted an ordinance making it unlawful "for any free negro or mulatto to come within the limits of Texas." Violators were to be sold at auction. The council explained in very direct language that the measure was intended to protect the interests of slaveholders. "The infusion of dissatisfaction and disobedience into the brain of the honest and contented slave, by vagabond free negroes . . . cannot be too promptly and strongly guarded against." This ordinance did not go into effect because it was caught in the conflict between the council and Governor Henry Smith. Nevertheless, it indicated the attitude of Texas' leaders as the revolution developed.[17]

On March 1, 1836, a convention called by the general council to deal with the emergency and consider a lasting form of government met at Washington on the Brazos. In less than three weeks, this convention adopted a Declaration of Independence and wrote a constitution for the Republic of Texas. The declaration did not mention slavery as an issue in the revolution, but the constitution dealt with the institution in detail. The section on slavery, as it was originally written, provided that "all persons of color who were slaves for life, previous to their emigration to Texas, and who are now held as bonded servants or otherwise, shall remain in the like state of servitude in which they would have been held in the country from which they came." Congress could not prohibit the bringing of slaves to Texas by immigrants from the United States. It could not emancipate slaves; nor could slaveholders, unless provisions were made for removing the freedmen from the republic or congress agreed in advance that a particular slave's good conduct earned him the right to remain in Texas. Congress' permission was also required for any free Negro to emigrate to the republic. The original draft authorized congress to

16. Treaty of Velasco, May 14, 1836, in Jenkins (ed.), *Papers of the Texas Revolution*, VI, 274; Diary of General Urrea, in *Mexican Side of the Texas Revolution*, 269–70. De la Peña, *With Santa Anna in Texas*, 179, describes how he (de la Peña) helped a slave who had served Filisola as a coachman avoid being returned to slavery.

17. Barker, *Stephen F. Austin*, 490–91. The ordinance is in Jenkins (ed.), *Papers of the Texas Revolution*, IX, 490–91, and the General Council's reasoning is in Gammel (comp.), *Laws of Texas*, I, 720–22.

pass laws compelling the owners of slaves to treat them "with humanity" and provide sufficient food and clothing. When slaves were accused of crimes, no grand jury was necesssary, but they were to receive a jury trial. Congress could prevent the introduction of slaves "as merchandise" or from any country other than the United States. When discussion of the slavery article began, George C. Childress proposed an additional section outlawing the African slave trade. The Committee on Naval Affairs made the same recommendation. All civilized nations oppose the African trade, the committee said, so Texas, a "nation just ushered into existence," should take the same stand.[18]

Concern for the African trade was not new among Texans. The convention of 1833 condemned the practice. However, unsettled conditions in 1835–36 opened the way for adventurers to continue bringing Negroes from Cuba. James W. Fannin, Jr., for example, wrote a Major Belton on August 27, 1835: "My last voyage from the Island of Cuba (with 152) succeeded admirably." An English schooner reportedly landed blacks from Grenada at Galveston in January, 1836. In March of that year, William S. Fisher reported from Brazoria that the schooner *Shenandoah* had landed 170 Negroes belonging to Monroe Edwards and that Sterling McNeel had brought a cargo of Africans to the coast. The "traffic in Negroes," Fisher said, "is increasing daily."[19]

The convention adopted a final version of the constitution at midnight on March 16. Section 9 of its General Provisions read as follows:

> Sec. 9. All persons of color who were slaves for life previous to their emigration to Texas, and who are now held in bondage, shall remain in the like state of servitude: *provided*, the said slave shall be the bona fide property of the person so holding said slave as aforesaid. Congress shall pass no laws to prohibit emigrants from bringing their slaves into the republic with them, and holding them by the same tenure by which such slaves were held in the United States; nor shall

18. The Texas Declaration of Independence was published in the San Felipe de Austin *Telegraph and Texas Register*, March 12, 1836. Original draft of the constitution and discussion are in Jenkins (ed.), *Papers of the Texas Revolution*, IX, 338, 340, 362; Recommendation of Committee on Naval Affairs in Gammel (comp.), *Laws of Texas*, I, 896.

19. James W. Fannin, Jr., to Major Belton, August 27, 1835, William P. Harris to "Friend Hanks," January 19, 1836, both in Jenkins (ed.), *Papers of the Texas Revolution*, I, 373, IV, 72; William S. Fisher to Henry Smith, March 2, 1836, in Binkley (ed.), *Official Correspondence*, I, 477. For further discussion of the African trade at this time, see Fred H. Robbins, "The Origins and Development of the African Slave Trade into Texas, 1816–1860" (M.A. thesis, University of Houston, 1972), 73, 100–107.

congress have power to emancipate slaves; nor shall any slave holder be allowed to emancipate his or her slave or slaves without the consent of congress, unless he or she shall send his or her slave or slaves without the limits of the republic. No free person of African descent, either in whole or in part, shall be permitted to reside permanently in the republic, without the consent of congress; and the importation or admission of Africans or negroes into this republic, excepting from the United States of America, is forever prohibited, and declared to be piracy.

The original draft's specific inclusion of "bonded servants" had been altered to a more ambiguous reference to those held in "bondage," probably with the intention of being more inclusive, and the provisions concerning the treatment of slaves had been removed. The African slave trade was called "piracy," but there was no restriction on bringing slaves from the United States into Texas as merchandise. In short, the Constitution of 1836 in its final form was even more careful of the interests of slaveholders and less concerned with the situation of slaves than was the original draft.[20]

Fifteen years after the adoption of this constitution the Supreme Court of Texas gave a compelling statement of the "Founding Fathers' " primary purpose where slavery was concerned. "It was manifestly the intention of the convention in framing this provision," Justice Abner S. Lipscomb wrote, "to remove all doubt and uneasiness among the citizens of Texas in regard to the tenure by which they held dominion over their slaves." Mexico's "fluctuating and unsettled" legislation on slavery had created insecurity as to legal titles, said Lipscomb. He cited examples of Mexican actions creating this uncertainty before concluding that "the true object and meaning of the provision . . . was to fix and establish the title of the master, whatever may have been the legal effect of Mexican legislation to impair that right and to nullify all Mexican legislation on the subject, there is no doubt."[21]

20. Wallace and Vigness (eds.), *Documents of Texas History*, 104. Joseph E. Field, *Three Years in Texas: Including a View of the Texas Revolution and an Account of the Principal Battles, Together with Descriptions of the Soil, Commercial and Agricultural Advantages* (1836; rpr. Austin, 1935), 8, suggested that the term "bondage" was intended to include all blacks regardless of how they were held. David G. Burnet, serving as ad interim president of the republic, issued a proclamation on April 3, 1836, ordering all authorities of Texas to stop the African slave trade. See Binkley (ed.), *Official Correspondence*, II, 583–84.

21. *Guess* v. *Lubbock*, 5 Tex. 535 (1851).

What, then, was the role of slavery in the Texas Revolution? Circumstantial evidence supports the abolitionists' contention that slavery was the primary cause of conflict. Anglo-American settlers wanted their Peculiar Institution, and Mexico opposed it, at least in principle. Once they were independent, Texans made no pretense of hiding their determination to guarantee slavery in their new republic. They outlawed the African trade, but that was primarily a response to world opinion rather than an action against slavery.[22] The introduction of slaves from the United States was guaranteed. Given these results, slavery appears to have been a major cause of the revolution.

The difficulty with this interpretation, however, is the lack of direct supporting evidence. Slavery did not play a major role in developments from the passage of the anti-immigration Law of April 6, 1830, until the outbreak of fighting in the fall of 1835. The institution was not a primary issue in the disturbances of 1832 or the events of late 1835, and Mexico took no action threatening it directly or immediately during these years. Instead, the immediate cause of conflict was the political instability of Mexico and the implications of Santa Anna's centralist regime for Texas. Mexico forced the issue in 1835, not over slavery, but over customs duties and the generally defiant attitude of Anglo-Americans in Texas.

This, of course, is not to say that slavery was unimportant in the Texas Revolution. In the broadest sense, the conflict resulted from a clash of cultural traditions. Anglo-Americans were simply too different from Hispanic-Americans to accept Mexican government indefinitely. One of those differences was slavery. The institution was always there, never too far in the background, as what the noted Texas historian Eugene C. Barker called a "dull, organic ache." It was, therefore, an underlying cause of the struggle that began in 1835. Once the revolution came, slavery was an immediate concern. Texans worried constantly about the servile insurrection they accused the Mexicans of trying to foment, and Mexican leaders indicated that slavery would be one of the casualties in their conquest of the rebels. The war did disturb slavery and give some bondsmen the opportunity to escape. After San Jacinto, however, the institution became more secure than it had ever been in Texas. Protecting slavery was

22. J. Pinckney Henderson as minister to Great Britain and France from the Republic of Texas pointed to the outlawing of the African trade as proof that Texas had "abolished the most offensive features of slavery." George P. Garrison (ed.), *Diplomatic Correspondence of the Republic of Texas* (3 vols.; Washington, 1908–11), I, 827–28.

not the primary cause of the Texas Revolution, but it certainly was a major result.[23]

23. Samuel Harmon Lowrie, *Culture Conflict in Texas, 1821–1835* (New York, 1932), 59–60, 179–81; Barker, *Mexico and Texas*, 86. On Texans' fears concerning slavery, see Eugene C. Barker, "Public Opinion in Texas Preceding the Revolution," in *Annual Report of the American Historical Association for the Year 1911* (Washington, D.C., 1913), 219. Mexico did indeed end slavery in 1837. See Josefina Zoraida Vázquez, "The Texas Question in Mexican Politics, 1836–1845," *Southwestern Historical Quarterly*, LXXXIX (1986), 317. Paul D. Lack, "Slavery and the Texas Revolution," *Southwestern Historical Quarterly*, LXXXIX (1985), 181–202, is the most recent review of the subject of this chapter. Lack places somewhat greater emphasis on slavery as a cause of the revolution and on the efforts of slaves to use the crisis to obtain freedom, but there is no fundamental difference between his article and the views presented here.

THREE

· · · · · · · · · ·

Growth and Expansion, 1836–1861

''THE EMPIRE STATE OF THE SOUTH''

Independence opened an era of rapid growth for slavery in Texas that did not end until the institution was destroyed in the Civil War. Stephen F. Austin symbolized the optimism underlying this expansion when, in November, 1836, he paid $1,200 for a twenty-seven-year-old male slave for whom he had no immediate use. Austin sent his very expensive purchase to his brother-in-law James F. Perry, saying that he expected not to reclaim the bondsman until the fall of 1837. Protections for slavery in the Constitution of 1836 undoubtedly encouraged Austin and other Texans to make such investments in human property. Andrew P. McCormick, for example, remembered how his nonslaveholding father sent money to the United States in 1837, once slavery was "recognized and established by law in Texas," to buy a man and a woman.[1]

Older Texans were not alone in expanding slavery; the institution proved attractive to new arrivals and nonsoutherners too. Ashbel Smith, the Connecticut-born doctor and future political leader who moved to Texas in 1837, paid $2,200 for two preteenaged boys and a teenaged girl at New Orleans in April, 1838. He immediately shipped his purchases to Galveston. "I intend to sell some land the first good opportunity," A. M. Clopper informed his brother in Cincinnati in June, 1837, "so as to enable me to purchase a couple of negro fellows and a house Girl." Otis M. Wheeler, a native of Massachusetts, wrote his brother in New York in January, 1844, that he had succeeded beyond his own expectations since

---

1. Austin to James F. Perry, November 11, 1836, December 2, 1836, both in Barker (ed.), *Austin Papers*, III, 453, 462, 464; McCormick, *Scotch-Irish in Ireland and America*, 145.

settling near Sabinetown in east Texas. Wheeler planned to plant one hundred acres in cotton and fifty in corn that year and half-jokingly questioned the effect it would have on "your abolition principals when I tell you that I own the negros to do the work."[2]

The rapid expansion of slavery that began after the revolution and continued through the 1850s meant that thousands of new bondsmen came to Texas each year. Almost certainly, although the quantitative evidence necessary for conclusive proof does not exist, the majority migrated with their owners. Immigrants to Texas were overwhelmingly southern-born, and they brought their slave property with them.[3] A study of the age and sex distribution of the slave population in Texas suggests that this was how most bondsmen came to the Lone Star state. If Texas were importing most of its slaves from older states in the Upper South, then there should have been a high proportion of males and prime-age slaves in its slave population—the assumption being that bondsmen of this sort would be more desirable as a labor force without children and old people. The fact was, however, that Texas' slave population was highly similar in age and sex characteristics to those of Upper South states such as Virginia. In other words, a demographic analysis of Texas' slaves suggests that most came to the state with their owners. A sample of 181 narratives given by Texas freedmen to WPA interviewers in the 1930s supports this conclusion. These former bondsmen were, of course, generally young at the time of freedom, so most (62.4 percent) were born in Texas. But 28.2 percent of the 181 recalled coming to Texas with their owners while only 5.5 percent were sold there through the domestic slave trade.[4]

2. Bill of Sale, April 14, 1838, Shipping Manifest, April 16, 1838, both in Ashbel Smith Papers, Barker Texas History Center, University of Texas, Austin; A. M. Clopper to Nicholas Clopper, June 27, 1837, in "The Clopper Correspondence, 1834–1838," *Quarterly of the Texas State Historical Association*, XIII (1909), 143; Otis Marshall Wheeler to "Dear Brother," January 25, 1844, in Avery Turner Papers, Department of Manuscripts and University Archives, Cornell University Libraries, Ithaca, N.Y.

3. Campbell and Lowe, *Wealth and Power*, 29. A good example of the movement of slaves from the Old South to Texas is found in an agreement between Churchill Jones and Aylett Dean on October 22, 1849, wherein Dean agreed to move Jones's slaves from a plantation on the Conecuh River in Alabama to Texas. Churchill Jones Papers, Barker Texas History Center, University of Texas, Austin.

4. Richard G. Lowe and Randolph B. Campbell, "The Slave-Breeding Hypothesis: A Demographic Comment on the 'Buying' and 'Selling' States," *Journal of Southern History*, XLII (1976), 401–12. Interviews with ex-slaves conducted by the WPA during the late 1930s, commonly called the slave narratives, constitute one of the major sources on slavery in Texas and

The activities of slave traders in Texas indicate that many bondsmen, although not a majority, came to the state as merchandise. Dealers from out-of-state commercial centers regularly advertised in the newspapers of towns that were remote from Texas' few cities. For example, the Marshall *Texas Republican*, which began publication in Harrison County in 1849, carried cards at various times from H. M. Farrior & Co. and George J. Pitts of Shreveport, Louisiana, and Joseph Bruin of New Orleans. Pitts's advertisement of January 21, 1860, was typical. "I have," he said, a "choice lot of Virginia, Carolina and Georgia Negroes, consisting of field hands, cooks, house servants, washers, ironers, and seamstresses; and will be receiving fresh supplies during the season, which I offer for sale low for cash or approved paper." Galveston and Houston, the only towns in antebellum Texas other than San Antonio and Austin that could aspire to the title of "city," had resident slave dealers. Within a few years of annexation, the Houston *Telegraph and Texas Register* carried the cards of H. S. and L. G. Bachelder, Samson & Co., and F. Scranton. In August, 1850, for example, the latter, calling himself "the old Texian," offered four men, six women, four girls, and three children "to sell for cash." At the close of the 1850s, Edward Riordan, "Negro and Real Estate Broker" located on Congress Street in Houston, advertised in Galveston, Columbus, and even in Dallas, nearly 250 miles to the north. In Galveston, McMurry and Winstead informed would-be customers that "we have made arrangements for fresh supplies during the season and will always have on hand a good assortment of field hands, house servants and mechanics." These partners faced strong competition, however, because Galveston was the home of John S. Sydnor, reputed to be the single larg-

---

are virtually the only evidence on slavery from the bondsmen's point of view. These interviews are published in George P. Rawick (ed.), *The American Slave: A Composite Autobiography*, Series 1 (7 vols.; Westport, Conn., 1972); Series 2 (12 vols.; Westport, Conn., 1972); *Supplement*, Series 1, (12 vols.; Westport, Conn., 1977); and *Supplement*, Series 2, (10 vols.; Westport, Conn., 1979) (hereinafter cited as *Am. Slave*).

Volumes 4 and 5 of Series 1 contain 181 narratives by slaves who, unlike many of those interviewed in Texas during the 1930s, actually experienced slavery in Texas. I examined those 181 interviews in detail and made a quantitative summary of all important information. Nine additional volumes of Texas narratives appeared later, in 1979, as part of *Supplement*, Series 2. Some of those narratives were new, and some were more detailed versions of ones that had appeared in Series 1. The narratives published in the supplementary series provided much useful descriptive information, but quantitative analysis throughout this study was limited to the 181 interviews in the first series. The reliability of the slave narratives as a historical source is discussed in detail in Appendix 1.

est slave dealer in Texas. Sydnor, one-time mayor of his city and, ironically, a friend of the abolitionist Stephen Pearl Andrews, personally auctioned off slaves at his market throughout the last antebellum decade.[5] Thus a majority of the bondsmen in Texas before 1861 came with their owners, but, had this type of migration ended, there would have been no shortage of slaves available through the domestic trade.

Finally, the African trade, although outlawed by the constitution of the republic, supplied a few of the slaves who arrived between 1836 and 1861. There is little or no documentary evidence of this criminal activity occurring after independence. However, documented cases of importations from Africa during 1833–35 immediately before the revolution do exist, and rumors of such activity persisted for years after 1836. For example, Joseph Crawford, the British vice-consul at New Orleans, reported in 1837 that slavers from Cuba had landed Africans in Texas. Francis Sheridan, Britain's colonial secretary, visited Galveston in 1840 and complained that Texas was doing too little to enforce its laws against the African trade and urged that British cruisers be ordered to extend their antislaver activities to the Gulf Coast. During the same year, a visiting English lawyer, Nicholas Doran P. Maillard, claimed that American ships were carrying one hundred slaves from Cuba to Texas twice a month. Such charges persisted well into the statehood period. Oral tradition has it that the United States War Department's experiment with camels as pack animals on the southwestern "deserts" served as a cover for the importation of a shipload of Africans at Indianola, Texas, in 1856. Arthur T. Lynn, the British consul at Galveston, reported in 1858 that a new state law permitting free blacks voluntarily to enslave themselves was in fact a scheme to cover the importation of Africans. Some of these rumors, especially those in the early years of the republic, must have had some basis in fact, but the most careful studies estimate that no more than two thousand slaves came to Texas in this way between 1836 and 1860.[6]

5. Marshall *Texas Republican*, June 15, 1849, May 16, 1850, March 11, 1859, January 21, 1860; Houston *Telegraph and Texas Register*, March 23, 1848, February 18, October 25, 1849, August 7, 1850; Galveston *Weekly News*, January 4, 1859, March 6, 1860; Dallas *Herald*, November 30, 1859; Columbus *Times*, April 14, 1860, quoted in Lillie E. Atkinson, "Slavery in the Economy of Colorado County, 1822–1863" (M.A. thesis, Prairie View A & M, 1954), 19; Tyler and Murphy (eds.), *Slave Narratives of Texas*, xxv–xxvi.

6. Robbins, "Origins and Development of the African Slave Trade into Texas," 111, 119–20, 139–40; Willis W. Pratt (ed.), *Galveston Island, or, a Few Months Off the Coast of Texas: The Journal of Francis C. Sheridan, 1839–1840* (Austin, 1954), 89–90; Barker, "African Slave

In short, only a tiny fraction of the state's bondsmen were brought in by the illegal African trade.

Precise statistics on the slave population of Texas at the time of the revolution are unavailable, but several sources, particularly tax rolls, provide reasonable approximations and indicate how rapidly the number of bondsmen increased during the following years. In August, 1836, Henry M. Morfit, President Andrew Jackson's envoy to investigate conditions in Texas following the revolution, reported that the new republic had a population of 30,000 Anglos, 5,000 Negroes, 3,470 Mexicans, and 14,500 Indians. If the Indians are excluded, slaves were 13 percent of the total population. Morfit's estimate was significantly higher than the 2,000 Negroes reported by Almonte in 1834, but, as noted above, the latter had reasons to understate the number of bondsmen in Texas.[7] The rough accuracy of Morfit's estimate is also supported by evidence from the republic's first tax rolls compiled in 1837.

Taxation of personal property required an enumeration of slaves, thereby creating annually a near "census" of bondsmen years before there was any effort to count the entire population of Texas systematically. It appears that tax assessors undercounted slaves by 10 to 20 percent, no doubt because infants and aged individuals had little value and because slaveowners were allowed to "forget" a few bondsmen as a means of lowering their assessments. Nevertheless, the undercounting was generally consistent from year-to-year and county-to-county, so that totals from the tax rolls give an acceptable idea of increases in the slave population over periods of time.[8]

Tax-roll information is available for fifteen of Texas' twenty-five counties in 1837. These data show 4,212 slaves in the republic. Of the ten

Trade in Texas," 156–57; Laura A. White, "The South in the 1850s as Seen by British Consuls," *Journal of Southern History*, I (1935), 38.

7. Henry M. Morfit to John Forsyth, August 27, 1836, in Wooten (ed.), *Comprehensive History of Texas*, I, 759.

8. Tax records for nineteenth-century Texas are available on microfilm on a county-by-county basis as Records of the Comptroller of Public Accounts, Ad Valorem Tax Division, County Real and Personal Property Tax Rolls, 1837–1900, Archives Division, Texas State Library, Austin. Hereinafter these records will be cited as County Tax Rolls with the appropriate year or years. The suggestion that tax assessors undercounted by 10 to 20 percent is based on a comparison of the numbers of slaves they taxed in 1850 and 1860 with the numbers of slaves enumerated by United States census takers in those years.

counties for which no rolls exist, three—Matagorda, Montgomery, and Red River—undoubtedly contained sizable numbers of bondsmen. Thus, Morfit's estimate of 5,000 slaves in Texas when it became a republic probably represented a reasonably accurate approximation.[9]

By 1840, Texas had thirty-two counties. Tax rolls are available for twenty-six of them, and of those likely to have had significant numbers of slaves, only Matagorda and Harrison are missing. These rolls enumerated 12,570 slaves in Texas, an increase of at least 150 percent from the total in 1836. In 1845, as the republic period came to a close, the tax rolls for thirty-two of Texas' thirty-six counties reported a total of 27,555 slaves. This amounted to an increase of more than 100 percent since 1840 and more than 450 percent during the years of the republic. No general census is available, but it is clear that the white population did not grow as rapidly as the slave. As noted above, Morfit's estimate placed slaves at 13 percent of the total in 1836. In 1847, two years after annexation ended the republic, a state census enumerated 102,961 whites, 295 free blacks, and 38,753 slaves. This census, although less than perfect in several ways, showed slaves at 27 percent of the total. Even with allowances for errors in Morfit's estimate and the state census, these statistics indicate that the slave population increased at a tremendous rate once the institution was reasonably secure in Texas.[10]

Rapid growth continued throughout the early statehood years. Whereas the state census of 1847 had reported 38,753 slaves in a total population of 142,009, the first United States census three years later, enumerated 212,592 people in Texas, including 58,161 slaves. Ten years later, there were 182,566 bondsmen and 412,649 whites and free blacks, comprising a total population of 604,215. The number of slaves increased 50 percent in roughly three years from 1847 to 1850 and 214 percent over the next ten years. The free population also increased 50 percent during the late 1840s, but its rate of gain from 1850 to 1860 was 173 percent. With

9. County Tax Rolls, 1837; Curlee, "Texas Slave Plantations," 15–16. The tax rolls for Austin and Liberty counties for 1837 are not available on microfilm, but Curlee, using original tax rolls still preserved in the comptroller's office during the early 1930s, provided data on the numbers of slaves taxed in those two counties.

10. County Tax Rolls, 1840 and 1845. "Report of the Secretary of the Treasury," *Appendix to the Journals of the Senate of the First Legislature of the State of Texas* (Clarksville, Tex., 1848), 68–69, contained a convenient summary of 1845 county totals. In a few cases, the number of slaves was not printed; then, the original rolls were consulted. William R. Hogan (comp.), "The State Census of 1847," *Southwestern Historical Quarterly*, L (1946), 117–18.

Table 1. Slave Population of Texas, 1846–1861 (from Tax Rolls)

Year	Population	Year	Population
1846	30,505	1854	90,003
1847	39,056	1855	105,186
1848	40,308	1856	113,139
1849	42,759	1857	124,782
1850	48,145[1]	1858	133,737
1851	58,740	1859	146,370
1852	68,584	1860	160,467[2]
1853	78,306	1861	169,166

[1] This number is 20.8 percent less than the U.S. Census count of 58,161.
[2] This number is 13.8 percent less than the U.S. Census count of 182,566.

slaves increasing more rapidly than whites, they were by 1860 a larger percentage of the total (30.2 percent) than they had been in 1847 (27.3 percent) and 1850 (27.4 percent).[11]

Tax-roll data permit a somewhat different perspective on the growth of slave population because, as noted above, they are available on an annual basis. Table 1, compiled from comptrollers' reports and the annual county tax rolls, shows an increase from 30,505 slaves in 1846 to 169,166 by 1861. This represents a gain of 455 percent over a period of fifteen years. When these data are divided at five-year intervals, the rates of growth are as follows: 93 percent from 1846 through 1850, 93 percent from 1851 through 1855, and 50 percent from 1856 through 1860.[12] Perhaps the rate of increase virtually had to decline as the number of slaves in Texas grew larger and larger. Where, for example, an increase of 28,235 bondsmen from 1846 through 1850 amounted to a 93-percent gain in the total, the addition of almost twice as many (56,027) from 1856 through 1860 constituted only 50-percent increase. Nevertheless, the rate of increase did slow after 1855.

Texas' slave population did not expand at the same rate into all areas of the state. In the early years, slaves were concentrated geographically in three areas (see maps 2 and 3). The oldest area of major slaveholding

11. DeBow (comp.), *Statistical View of the United States*, 40, 86; U.S. Bureau of the Census, *Population of the United States in 1860*, 486.

12. Table 1 was compiled from data in the County Tax Rolls, 1846–61, and from Biennial Reports of the Comptroller of the State of Texas. For the sake of convenience, the Comptroller's Reports were used as far as possible, and missing data were then filled in from the original rolls. (Appendix 2 presents statistics on the growth of slavery in each Texas county during selected years from 1837 to 1864.)

Map 2

Slave Population of Texas in 1840

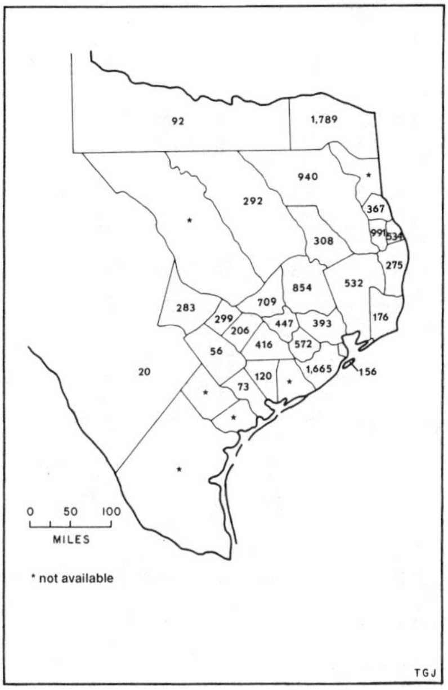

Map 3

Slave Population of Texas in 1845

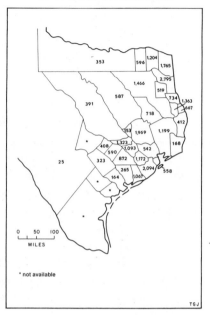

was that part of Austin's Colony extending from the Gulf Coast inland along the Brazos and Colorado rivers. This included Brazoria and Matagorda counties on the coast and the inland counties of Fort Bend, Colorado, Austin, and Washington. Taken together, these six counties had approximately one-third of Texas' slaves in 1840. Owners in Brazoria alone paid taxes on 1,665 bondsmen that year. In 1845, after five years of rapid growth, these counties still reported more than one-quarter (7,621) of all the slaves listed on the state's tax rolls. A second area of concentration was in east Texas centering on San Augustine County. The 1840 tax rolls show San Augustine third in the state behind only Brazoria and Red River counties in the number of slaves reported. In the northeastern corner of Texas, the third area of concentration, the institution grew so rapidly during the early 1840s that Harrison, Bowie, and Red River counties together had 5,764 slaves (21 percent of the total) by 1845. Other settled areas reported bondsmen, too, but they did not—especially in deep east Texas (Jasper and Jefferson counties) and the region along and southwest of the San Antonio River (where the tax rolls for many counties have been lost)—show any signs of matching the areas of concentration in the extent of their slave population.

The United States Census of 1850, the first such enumeration in Texas, showed nineteen of the state's counties with one thousand or more slaves (see map 4). They were located along the Brazos and Colorado rivers in the area of Austin's Colony and from the east Texas region around Nacogdoches and San Augustine northward through Harrison and Cass counties to the Red River border where Bowie, Red River, and Lamar counties all had large numbers of bondsmen. Thus sizable slave populations remained concentrated in the regions of the earliest settlements in Texas and in areas with at least some access by water to outside markets. Texas rivers could never be called reliable sources of transportation, but in a state of such great distances and no railroads or canals, any major watercourse was an inducement to settlement. By 1860 (see map 5), settlement had expanded along the rivers (including the Trinity in the east and the San Antonio in the west as well as the Brazos and the Colorado) and then into the areas between so that 64 of the 105 counties in antebellum Texas had one thousand bondsmen or more. Only the westernmost counties and several small enclaves in the southeast and north had not reached that level of slave population.

Sheer numbers demonstrate the spread of slavery across Texas by 1860, but the percentage of slaves in each county's total population provides a better indicator of where the institution was especially significant. In 1850 only six counties, Brazoria, Fort Bend, Matagorda, and Wharton on the lower Brazos and Colorado rivers, and Harrison and Bowie in northeast Texas had a black majority (see map 6). Twenty-nine other counties in the far eastern and south-central regions had slave populations constituting one-quarter to one-half of the total. Ten years later, as the institution grew with special rapidity along the middle Trinity from Polk and Walker to Limestone counties, thirteen counties had 50 percent or more slaves. Bondsmen were at least one-quarter of the population in most east and south-central Texas counties, but in those southwest of the San Antonio River and in the more remote north-central portion of the state, bondsmen still constituted less than 25 percent of the total population (see map 7).

Did slavery in 1861, after twenty-five years of rapid expansion, face any significant limitations on its future growth in Texas? Indians appeared to constitute a formidable barrier on the northwestern frontier, but that threat could have been overcome in a reasonably short time, probably with help from many of the slaves themselves. Texas' Indians and slaves were rarely friends or allies. More often they were enemies.

Map 4

Texas Counties with 1,000 or More Slaves, 1850

Map 5

Texas Counties with 1,000 or More Slaves, 1860

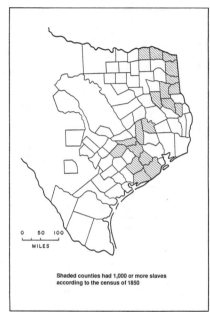

Shaded counties had 1,000 or more slaves
according to the census of 1850

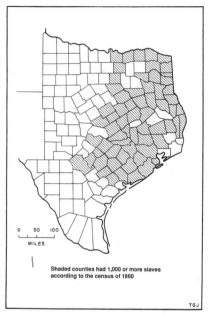

Shaded counties had 1,000 or more slaves
according to the census of 1860

Culturally, the Indians of Texas were divided into two large groups. Most of those living in eastern, northeastern, and east-central Texas were sedentary, agricultural Indians such as the Caddo and Wichita groups, who were original inhabitants of the region, and tribes such as the Cherokee, Alabama, and Creeks, who were migrants from east of the Mississippi. During the late 1830s and early 1840s, intermittent warfare between Anglo-Americans and these east Texas Indians resulted in the Indians' expulsion from the area. Some slaves looked to the Indians, particularly the Cherokees, as a way to escape to a milder form of bondage, and a few actually joined in the fight against the Texans. Other bondsmen, however, especially those on the Red River frontier, were loyal to their masters and joined in the fight against the Indians. In short, relations with the sedentary, agricultural tribes of Texas, many of whom were already familiar with the Peculiar Institution and were willing to hold slaves themselves, did little to slow the growth of slavery.[13]

The other main group of Texas Indians was the "uncivilized," non-

13. Kenneth Wiggins Porter, *The Negro on the American Frontier* (New York, 1971), 371–73, 375–92.

Map 6
Percentages of Slaves in Populations
of Texas Counties, 1850

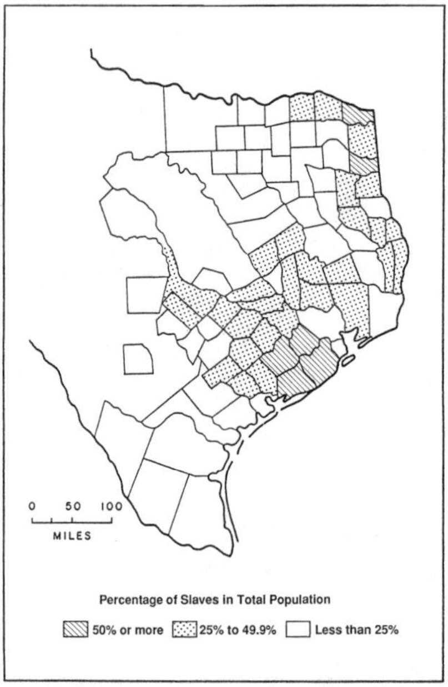

Map 7
Percentages of Slaves in Populations
of Texas Counties, 1860

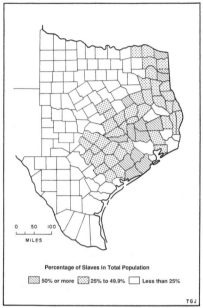

Percentage of Slaves in Total Population

▨ 50% or more ░ 25% to 49.9% ☐ Less than 25%

Percentage of Slaves in Total Population

▨ 50% or more ░ 25% to 49.9% ☐ Less than 25%

TGJ

agricultural tribes such as the Karankawa of the Matagorda Bay area, the Tonkawa of the area in the interior between the Brazos and San Antonio rivers, and the fearsome Comanche and Kiowa who roamed the plains just beyond white settlements. To these Indians, Negroes were essentially the same as their masters; they dressed in the same fashion, spoke the same language, and did the same work. Therefore, depredations were committed against white and black alike. The Comanches in particular treated frontier settlers without racial discrimination. They killed white and black men and killed or captured white and black women and children. In general Negroes had no choice but to reciprocate the murderous hostility of the "wild" Indians. As early as 1824, when Stephen F. Austin led an expedition against the Karankawa, thirty armed, mounted slaves who belonged to Jared Groce joined his force. On the Texas frontier during the forties and fifties, the appearance of the Comanches meant that Negroes had to fight for their lives alongside their masters. Historian Kenneth Porter's words summarize the situation well: "Relations between Negroes and Indians on the Texas frontiers reveal a general pattern of mutual hostility similar to that which existed between Indians

and white frontiersmen; they certainly give no encouragement to the belief in a mystical bond of unity between members of the darker races." In
1860–61, Comanche raids on the settlements edging into the plains of
northwest Texas constituted a serious threat to that part of the frontier.
But even warriors so fierce as the Comanche were only a temporary impediment to white expansion. Within twenty years, the Civil War not-
withstanding, the Indians would be overcome and driven out.[14]

Indians did not constitute a significant limit on slavery's growth, either
by stopping white expansion or by offering hospitality to runaways, but
there may have been other obstacles of a more permanent nature. Did the
decline in the overall rate of numerical expansion after 1855 and the presence of relatively few slaves on the southwestern and northern frontiers
in 1860 indicate that the institution had reached natural boundaries to its
further growth in Texas? As early as 1841, William Kennedy, an Irish-
born journalist who visited Texas, expressed the opinion that the area
was "not geographically adaptable to the great extension of slavery." Cotton production, he wrote, could not extend into west Texas, and slaves
were not good herdsmen. In the 1920s, the idea that slavery had natural
limits in Texas was developed by Charles W. Ramsdell into a major interpretive point supporting the thesis that the Civil War was "needless"
because slavery would soon have died from its own limitations. Ramsdell
argued that the cotton plantation economy faced at least two serious
problems—transportation and fencing—once it reached the blackland
prairies of central Texas. These, he admitted, were only "a temporary
barrier to the westward movement of the slave plantation" because railroads would move cotton and supplies and imported rails or barbed wire
would enclose the fields. But then, Ramsdell contended, settlers would
reach the Cross Timbers and the semi-arid plains that lay beyond. "The
history of the agricultural development of the Texas plains region since
1880," he wrote, "affords abundant evidence that it would never have
become suitable for plantation slave labor." By the time cotton farmers
developed the windmill, dry-farming techniques, and drought-resistant
feed crops, slavery would have declined toward extinction. Slavery in the
southwestern frontier area faced a double-barrelled problem in that the

14. *Ibid.*, 373–75, 392–401, 420–21; J. H. Kuykendall (ed.), "Recollections of Early Texans," *Quarterly of the Texas State Historical Association*, VII (1903), 35; Rupert Norval Richardson, *The Comanche Barrier to South Plains Settlement: A Century and a Half of Savage Resistance to
the Advancing White Frontier* (Glendale, Cal., 1933), 267–397.

soil was not promising for cotton production and proximity to Mexico increased the problem of runaways.[15]

Ramsdell's natural limits interpretation cannot be accepted or rejected conclusively because it is in the nature of "what if" history. First, he was correct in pointing out that prior to 1861 the expansion of slavery in Texas correlated very closely with the increase in cotton production. In 1850, of nineteen counties with 1,000 or more slaves, fifteen produced 1,000 or more bales of cotton. Only five counties with fewer than 1,000 slaves grew at least 1,000 bales of cotton. Ten years later, sixty-four counties had 1,000 or more slaves, and all except eight produced 1,000 or more bales. Only six with fewer than 1,000 bondsmen managed to grow as much cotton. Second, Ramsdell was also correct in recognizing that the transportation and fencing problems in north-central Texas were only temporary barriers. By 1880, even without slavery, the blackland prairie counties in the area centered just to the east of Dallas were producing cotton crops almost beyond anything that might have been imagined during the antebellum period. Third, Ramsdell's view of the problems for slavery's future in the area southwest of the San Antonio River was also correct. That area did not have great potential for cotton production and never would have matched the north-central region in growing the fleecy staple. In 1880, for example, the ten counties of antebellum Texas southwest of the San Antonio produced 3,076 bales, whereas in the north-central area Dallas and Collin counties alone grew 43,614 bales. Slavery also was less secure on the southwestern frontier because of its proximity to Mexico, a matter that deserves some elaboration.[16]

From 1836 onward, Texas slaveholders complained about their property escaping to freedom in Mexico. The congress of the republic passed

15. William Kennedy, *Texas: The Rise, Progress, and Prospects of the Republic of Texas* (London, 1841), 758; Charles W. Ramsdell, "The Natural Limits of Slavery Expansion," *Mississippi Valley Historical Review*, XVI (1929), 155–58.

Kennedy may have erred in one respect. Slaves were good herdsmen. As will be discussed in chapter 6, they proved their capabilities as cowboys on the Gulf Coastal Plains during the antebellum years. Herding never would have required large numbers of bondsmen like the plantation agriculture Ramsdell wrote of, but it was an economic activity that could have employed slaves across west Texas.

16. DeBow (comp.), *Statistical View of the United States*, 308–19; U.S. Bureau of the Census, *Population of the United States in 1860*, 484–86; United States Bureau of the Census, *Agriculture of the United States in 1860; Compiled from the Original Returns of the Eighth Census* (Washington, D.C., 1864), 140–51; United States Bureau of the Census, *Report on the Productions of Agriculture as Returned at the Tenth Census, 1880* (Washington, D.C., 1883), 242–44.

a special law to promote the capture of runaways west of the San Antonio River, but enough Negroes still escaped to upset slaveowners. Shortly after annexation, Texas called on the United States government to nego- tiate a treaty permitting extradition of slaves from Mexico. All efforts at reaching such an agreement failed, however, because the government of Mexico had several reasons for encouraging runaways to escape across the Rio Grande. Mexican leaders reasoned that runaways weakened slav- ery in Texas and thereby reduced the possibility of further territorial ag- gression by the United States. They also concluded in the late 1840s that military colonies composed of former slaves and friendly Indians would be useful in protecting the borders against invaders from the United States and "wild" Indians. In 1849, for example, the Seminole chief Wild Cat migrated across Texas from the Indian Territory to Coahuila and settled near present-day Zaragossa. Mexican authorities welcomed his colony of Seminoles, their slaves, and free Negroes, much to the disgust of Texas planters.[17]

By 1851 Texans estimated that three thousand fugitive slaves had crossed the Rio Grande, and in 1855 the famed Ranger, John Salmon "Rip" Ford, claimed that another thousand had fled in the previous four years. "Something should be done," the San Antonio *Herald* said in May, 1855, "to put a stop to the escape of Negroes into Mexico. If the General Government cannot protect us, we should protect ourselves." Not sur- prisingly, in light of the situation and public demands for action, bor- der incidents soon followed. In the fall of 1855, three companies of Texas Rangers under the command of James H. Callahan crossed the Rio Grande under the authority of orders to pursue marauding Lipan Apaches. Most historians believe, however, that Callahan's expedition, which was driven out of Mexico and burned the town of Piedras Negras to cover its retreat, was as much concerned with seeking runaways as with chasing Indians. During the same year, when Santiago Vidaurri led a rebellion in the northern Mexican states of Nuevo Leon and Coahuila, "Rip" Ford offered assistance in return for an opportunity to capture run- aways. In 1859 the San Antonio *Herald* suggested that Texans needed no excuse for crossing the Rio Grande in search of escaped slaves. "We have often wondered," the editor wrote, "why some bold and enterprizing

17. Ronnie C. Tyler, "Slave Owners and Runaway Slaves in Texas" (M.A. thesis, Texas Christian University, 1966), 4–5, 9–15; Ronnie C. Tyler, "Fugitive Slaves in Mexico," *Journal of Negro History*, LVII (1972), 2–5.

men in our state do not club together and go into Mexico and bring away the large number of fine likely runaways known to be not far over the line, forming a pretty respectable African colony."[18]

There were never enough runaways to Mexico to constitute a significant threat to slavery in Texas as a whole, but the situation in the region west of the San Antonio River, when coupled with the limited prospects for cotton production there, undoubtedly limited the expansion of slavery in the area. Frederick Law Olmsted, the noted antislavery critic who traveled to Texas in 1854, voiced the opinion while in San Marcos that proximity to Mexico "will go far to prevent this from becoming a great enslaved planting country." The editor of the *Texas Almanac for 1857* seemed inclined to agree. Closeness to Mexico, he wrote, is "making this kind of property [slaves] a very uncertain one."[19]

If Ramsdell were correct in these various specific parts of his interpretation, was he then accurate in general about the future of slavery in Texas? Again, this question cannot be answered conclusively, but it does not have to be in order to see one major problem with Ramsdell's argument. That is, he overlooked the size and potential of the area of antebellum Texas that even he conceded to slavery. The seventeen counties in the blackland prairie region extending from the Red River southward into central Texas just north of Austin comprised 16,220 very fertile square miles that would by 1880 produce 246,352 bales of cotton, an amount equal to 57 percent of the entire state's crop in 1860. Obviously, the cotton plantation had a bright future in this area, and yet in 1860 these seventeen counties had only 22,232 slaves, just 12 percent of the state's total. The Grand Prairie soil region, while not quite so promising for cotton, included ten counties with 10,434 square miles and 3,114 slaves in 1860. These counties produced 64,070 bales of cotton by 1880. These two prairie

18. Tyler, "Slave Owners and Runaway Slaves," 22, 36; San Antonio *Herald*, May 29, 1855; Ronnie C. Tyler, "The Callahan Expedition of 1855: Indians or Negroes?" *Southwestern Historical Quarterly*, LXX (1967), 574–85; J. Fred Rippy, "Border Troubles Along the Rio Grande," *Southwestern Historical Quarterly*, XXIII (1919), 100; Rosalie Schwartz, "Runaway Negroes: Mexico as an Alternative for United States Blacks, 1825–1860" (M.A. thesis, San Diego State University, 1974), 50–60; San Antonio *Herald*, February 8, 1859.

19. Frederick Law Olmsted, *A Journey Through Texas: Or, A Saddle-Trip on the Southwestern Frontier, With a Statistical Appendix* (New York, 1857), 68; *The Texas Almanac for 1857: With Statistics, Historical and Biographical Sketches, Etc., Relating to Texas* (Galveston, 1856), 70. The presence of relatively large numbers of Mexican Americans west of the San Antonio River was also a potential limit on the expansion of slavery into that area. As will be explained in Chapter 11, Texas planters generally felt that Mexican Americans were too willing to consort with slaves and aid runaways.

Map 8

The Blackland Prairie and Grand Prairie Counties of Texas

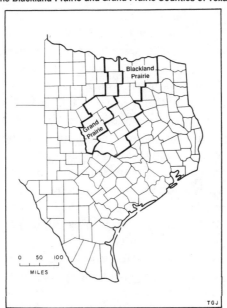

regions combined (see map 8) constituted a cotton frontier more than three-quarters as large as the state of South Carolina with only 6 percent as many slaves.[20]

Slavery may indeed have had natural limits in western Texas, especially in areas where geographical factors received support from proximity to Mexico in limiting the institution, but there was so much territory to develop, territory with great potential for cotton production and slaveholding, that Texas would have helped maintain the strength of slavery for many years after 1860. The institution was not threatened with an immediate or even short-term demise due to natural boundaries in Texas. Certainly contemporaries did not think so during the late 1850s. John Marshall of the Austin *Texas State Gazette*, in one of his numerous edito-

20. U.S. Bureau of the Census, *Agriculture of the United States in 1860*, 140–51, 240–42; U.S. Bureau of the Census, *Agriculture, 1880*, 242–44; U.S. Bureau of the Census, *Population of the United States in 1860*, 402, 406. The number of square miles in these Texas counties was taken from descriptions of each in Mike Kingston (ed.), *The 1986–1987 Texas Almanac and State Industrial Guide* (Dallas, 1985), 237–376. A few new counties were created from those in the Blackland and Grand Prairie areas in 1860. They were taken into consideration in calculating the total square miles in this region. South Carolina has an area of 31,055 square miles according to *The World Book Encyclopedia* (22 vols.; Chicago, 1977), XVIII, 513.

rials calling for re-opening the African slave trade, argued that "until we reach somewhere in the vicinity of two millions of slaves, it is evident that such a thing as too many slaves in Texas is an absurdity." Editorials in the Marshall *Texas Republican*, Clarksville *Northern Standard*, and Matagorda *Gazette*, none of which were located in the areas likely to grow the most rapidly, echoed similar opinions. "There are," wrote Charles DeMorse of the Clarksville paper, "in all the Southern States, not more Negroes than could be profitably employed in Texas." Robert W. Loughery of the *Texas Republican* contended the cotton lands of Louisiana, Arkansas, and Texas together would become home to between eight and sixteen million slaves. The Matagorda *Gazette* did not talk of opening the African trade or importing millions of bondsmen, but its point was the same: "We are no advocates for the repeal of the United States laws upon the slave-trade, but we confess that we would be pleased to hear of a few thousand accidently dropping along on this coast. We want to see some more of our rich lands under cultivation." [21]

Thus, during Texas' early statehood period from 1846 to 1861, slavery expanded numerically and geographically with tremendous rapidity. Natural limits to this expansion may have existed in western Texas, but their effect would have been minimal for years to come. The mood of Texans toward slavery, at least as it received public expression, was one of buoyant optimism. [22]

21. Austin *Texas State Gazette*, July 17, 1858; Marshall *Texas Republican*, December 10, 1858; Matagorda *Gazette*, April 11, 1860; Clarksville *Northern Standard*, February 19, 1859.

22. Optimism extended even into areas such as Clay County, which was west of the Grand Prairie region. "White labor *makes the truck*," wrote one resident in 1861, "but it is only because we are too poor to buy darkies at the present high prices—*we want them bad enough*." *The Texas Almanac for 1861: With Statistics, Historical and Biographical Sketches, Etc., Relating to Texas* (Galveston, 1860), 189.

Urban slavery did not hold the key to the future of the institution in Texas, but even in the towns slavery was not on the verge of extinction in 1860. Paul Dean Lack, "Urban Slavery in the Southwest" (Ph.D. dissertation, Texas Tech University, 1973), 339.

FOUR

. . . .

The Economics of Slavery in Texas

''WE WANT MORE SLAVES, WE NEED THEM''

Slavery came to Texas and flourished there primarily as an economic institution. Stephen F. Austin's colonists and the impresario himself believed that a province so land-rich and labor-poor could be settled and brought into large-scale, profitable production much more rapidly with slave than with free labor, and Texans generally remained unshaken in this view throughout the antebellum period. An anonymous traveler summarized their belief succinctly in 1840: "There are a considerable number of negro slaves in this country, and their labor is thought to be profitable. The principal reason for this opinion probably is that land is so cheap, and cropping so profitable, that very few even poor men consented to be hired, preferring to work their own lands. Owing to these circumstances no one could cultivate a large plantation by free labor." Even many of those who were inclined to oppose slavery in principle argued that economic need made it essential in Texas. James P. Newcomb of the San Antonio *Herald*, for example, wrote in 1855: "We look upon it as one of those evils that must be left to root itself out, which it will do, as soon as free labor becomes as cheap and reliable, and not until then." In 1859, Charles DeMorse of the Clarksville *Northern Standard* told his readers that only slave labor could develop the resources of Texas. "We want more slaves," he wrote, "we need them."[1]

---

1. [A. B. Lawrence], *Texas in 1840: or, The Emigrant's Guide to the New Republic, Being the Result of Observations, Inquiry, and Travel into that Beautiful Country* (New York, 1840), 233;

Throughout the antebellum years observers and publicists regularly reminded Texans and prospective immigrants of slavery's tremendous potential in cash-crop agriculture. Even George W. Featherstonhaugh, the antislavery Englishman who visited Texas in 1834–35, claimed that on Texas' blackland prairies every working slave produced six to eight bales of cotton a year. James D. Cocke, who came from Virginia to Texas in 1837, contended that the republic's prosperity would be unbounded if only there were a bank to loan money for the purchase of slaves. On the Brazos and Colorado rivers, he wrote, each hand could produce $1,000 in crops per year (eight bales of cotton worth $400 and four hundred bushels of corn worth $600). The Matagorda *Gazette* told its readers in 1858 that a successful planter could have field hands pay for themselves in three years. If he began with twenty slaves, the newspaper said, he could have forty in three years, "and in six years will be rich." "We had rather have a plantation on Old Caney than a gold mine at Pike's Peak," the editor enthused.[2]

Contemporaries, when they wrote of the need for slavery and of its promise in Texas, were obviously thinking of plantation agriculture. A sizable majority of Texans, however, were not slaveholders and certainly not plantation owners. In 1850, only 30.1 percent of the state's families owned slaves, and a miniscule 2.3 percent held twenty or more bondsmen and therefore qualified as planters. Ten years later, the proportion of slaveholding families had declined to 27.3 percent, and only 3.0 percent were planters. In absolute numbers, 466 individuals in the state in 1850 owned twenty or more slaves, and the planter class numbered only 2,163 in 1860.[3] Thus, in a sense, Texas was not a land of slaveholders and planters. Nevertheless, as chapter 11 will explain in detail, small slaveholders and nonslaveholders did not generally oppose slavery or planters in any way and definitely not on economic grounds. Those who owned a few slaves found them valuable in many ways and hoped to acquire

Ferdinand Roemer, *Texas: With Particular Reference to German Immigration and the Physical Appearance of the Country*, trans. Oswald Mueller (San Antonio, 1935), 89; Bornholst, "Plantation Settlement in the Brazos River Valley," 197; San Antonio *Herald*, May 22, 1855; Clarksville *Northern Standard*, February 19, 1859.

2. Featherstonhaugh, *Excursion Through the Slave States*, 124; [James D. Cocke (?)], *A Glance at the Currency and Resources Generally of the Republic of Texas, By A Citizen of the Country* (Houston, 1838), 11–14; Webb, Carroll, and Branda (eds.), *Handbook of Texas*, I, 368; Matagorda *Gazette*, December 4, 1858.

3. Campbell and Lowe, *Wealth and Power*, 43–45; DeBow (comp.), *Statistical View of the United States*, 95; U.S. Bureau of the Census, *Agriculture of the United States in 1860*, 242.

more. Most nonslaveholders apparently recognized that owning slaves was a measure of financial success and wanted to hold bondsmen themselves. In short, slavery as an economic institution rested primarily on the plantation system's need for labor, and that involved only a minority of Texans. Support of an essentially economic nature, however, was far more widespread than the numbers of planters would suggest.

The basic question to ask about slavery as an economic institution in Texas is, "did it pay?" A common sense answer is that it must have paid or at least that Texans certainly thought it did. Demand for bondsmen was so strong throughout the antebellum period that even with more than a 200-percent increase in the slave population from 1850 to 1860, prices, as will be seen, nearly doubled. Assuming that Texans were economically rational, the best logical explanation of this circumstance is that slave labor was profitable on cotton plantations and that slaves were a valuable capital investment. Some Texas newspaper editors certainly saw it that way. Robert W. Loughery of the Marshall *Texas Republican*, for example, in commenting on high prices paid in Harrison County in January, 1854, concluded: "The natural inference would be that a country must be very productive when people can afford to pay such prices for labor." Some contemporary observers, however, insisted that slavery was not profitable even in Texas, and some early twentieth-century historians apparently included the Lone Star state as they indicted the institution for unprofitability across the South. The argument of unprofitability and Ramsdell's "natural limits" thesis were combined by these historians to support the "Needless War" interpretation of the struggle from 1861 to 1865. This general interpretation has been largely discredited since the 1950s; nevertheless, just as it is important to see precisely the weaknesses in Ramsdell's thesis for Texas, it is necessary to see how and to what extent slavery was profitable in the Lone Star state.[4]

Appreciation in slave values was one potential source of profit in a rapidly growing area that had so much land and so little labor. During the years prior to the revolution, slaves did not increase notably in value, probably because actions by the Mexican government kept the institution's future in doubt. Data are scarce, but a bondsman, regardless of age,

4. Marshall *Texas Republican*, January 7, 1854. For similar views, see Galveston *Weekly News*, February 19, 1861, and Austin *Texas State Gazette*, October 20, 1860. Contemporary observers who questioned slavery's profitability included Roemer, *Texas*, 58–59, and Olmsted, *Journey Through Texas*, 182, 205–207, 459. Phillips, *American Negro Slavery*, contended that slavery was generally unprofitable across the South.

sex, or condition, averaged approximately $450 in value between the mid-1820s and 1836. Rapid expansion after independence pushed values up in 1837 and 1838, but then the Panic of 1837 led into the most serious economic collapse in the history of the United States to that date. For Texas, the panic's most important result was a decline in the price per pound of ginned cotton from 13.3 cents in 1837 to 8.9 cents in 1840 and 5.6 cents by 1845. Slave prices matched this downward plunge, falling from an average of approximately $575 per slave regardless of age, sex, or condition in 1837 to $450 in 1840 and $345 in 1845 (see table 2). The slave property belonging to the estate of Elisha Davis in Matagorda County provides an interesting case study in declining values over these years. Davis' slaves were appraised in April, 1837, and again in May, 1844, as indicated in table 3. Charles lost $200 in value despite the fact that he became a prime-age worker during these years, and Esther, although still in her twenties, declined in value, too. Overall , in the eyes of the appraisers, the average value of these six slaves fell from $587.50 to $425.00.[5]

The depression of the early forties did not stop the growth of slavery, but it was at least discouraging. In 1843, when the New York *Sun* charged that Africans were still being imported into Texas, the Houston *Morning Star* replied that in light of the scarcity of money and the cheapness of slaves, such a trade was economically impractical. An "unseasoned" African, the Houston editor said, would not sell for more than $100 in cash. Some Texans apparently became so discouraged with low values for cotton and slaves that they were willing to consider a future based on attracting independent farmers rather than planters. James Morgan suggested this in a letter of January 26, 1844: "I wish to be free and hope to see Texas free'd of slavery—because it will be to *my interest* as a land holder. My land will increase in value faster—yes be worth double in half the time by an emigration of a white population who come to till the soil—and densely populate the country—and there are thousands in this country who are of the same opinion."[6]

5. Curlee, "Texas Slave Plantations," 63–64; Estate of Elisha Davis, Matagorda County Probate Records (Inventory Record, Book A). Scattered estate inventories from Austin, Jackson, Matagorda, and Nacogdoches counties yielded appraisals of thirty-one slaves during the years from 1828 through 1836 (11 males, 13 females, and 7 children). The average value of these slaves was $449.74.

6. Margaret Swett Henson, "Development of Slave Codes in Texas, 1821–1845" (M.A. thesis, University of Houston, 1969), 71–72; James Morgan to Mrs. Jane M. Storms, January 26, 1844, in Morgan Papers.

Table 2. Mean Value of Slaves in the Republic of Texas, 1837–1845

Year	No. of Slaves[1]	Average Value	Cotton, Cents per Lb.
1837	117	$568	13.3
1838	84	$629	10.1
1839	71	$495	13.4
1840	260	$444	8.9
1841	81	$480	9.5
1842	53	$471	7.9
1843	132	$331	7.3
1844	153	$314	7.7
1845	174	$345	5.6

Sources: Table 2 is based on appraisals found in estate inventories located in the probate records of Austin, Brazoria, Colorado, Fayette, Fort Bend, Matagorda, Milam, Montgomery, Nacogdoches, Red River, Shelby, Travis, and Washington counties. A list of the estates involved is too long to include here, but the number of slave values found for each year is given in the table.
[1] Number of slaves in sample from which mean values were calculated.

Table 3. Appraised Value of Slaves of Elisha Davis Estate, 1837 and 1844

Slave	1837		1844	
	Age	Value	Age	Value
Charles	14	$750	21	$550
Phil	7	$400	14	$350
Frank	6	$350	14	$350
Mary Ann	45	$475	44[1]	$350
Edy	28	$800	35	$450
Esther	22	$750	25[1]	$500

[1] Although the ages are obviously incorrect, the two women, Mary Ann and Esther, were clearly the same individuals at both appraisals.

Economic recovery brought higher cotton prices in the mid-1840s, however, and slave values then followed an upward trend to an all-time high around 1860. A brisk business in both private and public sales flourished throughout the early statehood period. Newspapers regularly carried advertisements of bondsmen for sale, and the first Tuesday in each month was understood by all as the day for auctions in county-seat towns across the state. Slaves typically sold for cash or for twelve-month notes bearing 10 to 12 percent interest. These notes generally were secured by mortgages on the slave property involved in the transactions.[7]

7. Curlee, "Texas Slave Plantations," 58–62; Hal Robbins, "Slavery in the Economy of Matagorda County, Texas, 1839–1860" (M.A. thesis, Prairie View A & M College, 1952),

Accounts of tremendous prices being paid at public auctions doubtless encouraged the rise in slave values during the early statehood period. By 1854, the Marshall *Texas Republican* was reporting the sale of field hands for $1,500 to $1,800. Four years later, the Gilmer *Democrat* told its readers of a ten-year-old boy selling for $1,206 and a twelve-year-old girl for $1,255. In 1860, a slave carpenter reportedly sold for $2,755 in Marshall, and the next year a woman with seven small children brought $5,800 at auction in Brenham. Private records bear out these public reports. Hobart Key of Marshall paid $1,350 for a twenty-seven-year-old woman and her three small children in 1852, telling his wife that this "is as low as negros are selling." Two years later, Thomas W. Chambers paid $1,300 for a twenty-year-old male and $1,500 for another who was twenty-seven. In May, 1859, James W. Lawrance of Grimes County bought five slaves from a seller in Mississippi, paying $1,200 each for two twelve-year-old boys and $1,000 each for two girls aged twelve and thirteen. The following year, Reuben Hornsby, Jr., of Travis County paid $6,800 for a thirty-five-year-old woman and her seven children aged sixteen to three. Probate records also contain numerous examples of rapidly rising values. The Brazoria County estate of Thomas S. Baird, for example, had among its bondsmen a twenty-five-year-old slave (Bob) appraised in June, 1855, at $1,000, an eighteen-year-old (Squire) valued at $800, a forty-five-year-old woman (Esther) worth $600, and a fifteen-year-old girl (Irene) appraised at $800. Bob was sold less than two years later for $1,510; the others in 1860 for $2,000 (Squire), $730 (Esther), and $1,420 (Irene) respectively. Thus, four slaves valued at $3,200 in 1855 sold for $5,660 within five years.[8]

37–43. For evidence on the use of mortgages to secure the purchase of slaves on credit, see Marshall *Texas Republican*, December 3, 1859; Clarksville *Northern Standard*, January 11, 1851; Estate of William and Nancy Davis, Newton County Probate Records (Probate Minutes, Book B); and Faydell Lomma Barrett, "Slavery in the Economy of San Augustine County, Texas, 1837–1860" (M.A. thesis, Prairie View A & M College, 1963), 53.

8. Marshall *Texas Republican*, January 7, 1854, February 20, 1858, February 11, 1860; Galveston *Weekly News*, February 19, 1861; Matagorda *Gazette*, February 12, 1859; Hobart Key to Mary Key, October 24, 1852, quoted in Randolph B. Campbell, *A Southern Community in Crisis: Harrison County, Texas, 1850–1880* (Austin, 1983), 127; Bills of Sale, February 11 and December 4, 1854, in Thomas W. Chambers Papers, Bill of Sale, May 10, 1859, in James W. Lawrance Papers, Bill of Sale, August, 1860, in Reuben Hornsby Papers, all in Barker Texas History Center, University of Texas, Austin; Estate of Thomas S. Baird, Brazoria County Probate Records (Wills, etc., Books B and C). Another good example is found in the estate of James Gay. Its fourteen slaves, appraised at $12,750 in December, 1859, sold for $17,866 in May, 1860. Estate of James Gay, Fayette County Probate Records (Probate Records, Book E).

Table 4. Mean Value of Slaves in Texas, 1843–1862

Years	Number of Slaves[1]	Mean Value per Slave
1843–47	494	$345
1848–52	982	$440
1853–57	1,810	$625
1858–62	2,433	$765

Sources: Table 4 is based on data drawn from appraisals located in estate inventories in forty-four Texas counties during the years from 1843 to 1862. The lists of counties (see Appendix 3) and estates are too lengthy to include here, but the total number of slaves involved is provided in the table.

[1] Number of slaves in the sample from which mean values were calculated.

The increase in slave values during the statehood period as indicated in newspaper reports, private bills of sale, and probate records may be summarized systematically by utilizing information from the appraisals of thousands of slaves who belonged to estates undergoing probate. A summary reveals that the approximate average value of bondsmen in Texas regardless of age, sex, or condition increased from $345 in the mid-1840s to $440 around 1850, $625 in the mid-fifties, and $765 around 1860 (see table 4). This represented an increase of 122 percent in fifteen years. That, to return to the point of profitability, was an obvious source of financial gain for slaveowners. This upward trend, of course, might have stopped within a few years; values might even have fallen in the future. The fact remains, however, as economist Gavin Wright has put it, "that virtually every slaveholder who was careful enough to keep his slaves alive made at least a normal profit during the 1850s from capital gains alone." Thus, high prices indicated slavery's viability and were in themselves one way that the institution "paid" during the late 1840s and 1850s. Obviously, there could have been a repetition of the collapse following the Panic of 1837, but Texans, especially since the Panic of 1857 affected the North far more than the South, were not disposed to look back or be pessimistic.[9]

9. Gavin Wright, The Political Economy of the Cotton South: Households, Markets, and Wealth in the Nineteenth Century (New York, 1978), 141. The rise in slave prices during the 1850s was not part of a major inflationary trend in the Southwest at that time. The wholesale price index of commodities at New Orleans stood at 103 in 1850 (with the average from 1824–42 = 100), 103 in 1855, and 105 in 1860. The lowest point during the decade was an index of 85 in 1852; the highest, 136 in 1857. Statistical History of the United States from Colonial Times to the Present (Stamford, Conn., 1965), 122. James L. Huston, The Panic of 1857 and the Coming of the Civil War (Baton Rouge, 1987), 33–34, 60–65, discusses how the panic had less impact on the South than on the North.

Slaveowners, of course, did not justify slavery as an economic institution on the basis of capital gains. Instead, they emphasized its role in providing the labor for cotton farming, thus narrowing the broad question—did slavery pay?—to a more specific one: how productive and profitable was the application of slave labor to cotton production? Random pieces of information relative to this question, such as examples of production per acre or per slave, appear in contemporary newspapers, travelers' accounts, and the records of planters, but any attempt at a broad, systematic answer depends on data from the United States Censuses of 1850 and 1860. This is because only the manuscript census returns provide information on each farm operator, such as the number of slaves owned, the number of improved acres in the farm, cash value of the farm, value of farm implements and livestock, and the size of various crops such as cotton. These data thus permit an analysis of productivity and profitability limited to only those farmers who owned slaves and actually produced cotton.

Table 5 indicates that the application of slave labor to cotton production generally yielded satisfactory returns to farmers in antebellum Texas. With the exception of small slaveholders (1–9 slaves), all groups enjoyed rates of return (that is, profits as a percentage of investment) of approximately 6 percent or better in 1850 and 1860. By 1860, assuming 9-cent cotton, even these smallest slaveholders were over the 6-percent mark. Alfred H. Conrad and John R. Meyer pointed out in their 1958 path-breaking study of slavery's profitability that in "contemporary chronicles . . . southerners and northerners alike considered 6–8 per cent a reasonable rate of return and a reasonable asking price for loans." Furthermore, they noted that these rates were also consistent with returns from investments in commercial paper in the northeastern United States. Thus, when considered in the terms of either an accountant (percent of return) or an economist (return from an alternate use of capital), the rate of return per bondsman for slaveholding cotton farmers in Texas, especially for those with ten or more slaves, was at least reasonable and perhaps highly satisfactory during the last antebellum decade.[10]

10. Alfred H. Conrad and John R. Meyer, "The Economics of Slavery in the Ante Bellum South," *Journal of Political Economy*, LXVI (1958), 101–103; Frederick L. Meier, "A Study of Slavery in Microcosm: Lamar County, Texas, 1850–1860" (M.A. thesis, Fort Hays State University, 1971), 71–98; and Reba W. Palm, "Slavery in Microcosm: Matagorda County, Texas" (M.S. thesis, Texas A & I University, 1971), 131, reach similar conclusions, although their methods of investigation differ from those used here.

Table 5. Rate of Return per Slave for Slaveholding Cotton Farmers in Texas, 1850 and 1860[1]

Size of slaveholding	Average pounds pro- duced per slave	Rate of return: 8-cent cotton	Rate of return: 9-cent cotton
1850			
1–9	437[2]	4.45%[2]	5.04%[2]
10–19	612	6.23%	7.03%
20–49	536	5.75%	6.51%
50 & over	788	8.09%	9.12%
All holders	540[2]	5.64%[2]	6.37%[2]
1860			
1–9	774[2]	5.62%[2]	6.21%[2]
10–19	1,130	7.40%	8.22%
20–49	1,292	8.79%	9.79%
50 & over	1,512	11.05%	12.35%
All holders	1,134[2]	7.83%[2]	8.70%[2]

[1] The method of selecting two samples of slaveholding farmers (1,156 from the census of 1850, and 1,117 from the census of 1860) and the methodology utilized in calculating the productivity and profitability of those farmers' slaves in cotton production are explained in detail in Richard G. Lowe and Randolph B. Campbell, *Planters and Plain Folk: Agriculture in Antebellum Texas* (Dallas, 1987), 26–35, 159–70, 191–98.

[2] Denotes inclusion of free labor in the calculation for holders of fewer than ten slaves.

Did slaveholding farmers in antebellum Texas, in their quest for profit, concentrate on cotton to such an extent that they did not produce enough food for the human and animal populations on their farms? Certainly there was increasing emphasis on cotton production during the years from 1850 to 1860. Table 6 indicates that the ratio of corn to cotton grown by slaveholding farmers in Texas decreased dramatically from eighty-nine bushels for each bale of cotton in 1850 to thirty-two bushels to the bale in 1860. This pattern of increasing emphasis on cotton held true for all classes of slaveholders through the decade. It does not necessarily follow, however, that self-sufficiency was being sacrificed. Perhaps slaveholders were able to produce enough food even with greater emphasis on cotton.

Table 7 shows that even with increased emphasis on cotton production slaveholding farmers in Texas produced as much corn per person (free and slave) on their farms in 1860 as in 1850 (50.0 bushels each year). If, as the most systematic study of food self-sufficiency has suggested, humans consumed an average of thirteen bushels of corn per year, Texas' slaveholding farmers were meeting this requirement with a good deal to

Table 6. Ratio of Corn (Bushels) to Cotton (Bales) Produced, 1850 to 1860

Size of Slaveholding	1850	1860
1–9	155 bus./1 bls.	62 bus./1 bls.
10–19	71 bus./1 bls.	31 bus./1 bls.
20–49	59 bus./1 bls.	24 bus./1 bls.
50 & over	55 bus./1 bls.	18 bus./1 bls.
All slaveholding farmers[1]	89 bus./1 bls.	32 bus./1 bls.

[1]This category represents a recalculation of all the corn and all the cotton produced by slaveholding farmers.

spare for their livestock.[11] Table 7 also indicates that Texas' slaveholding farmers did not rely solely on corn for food. Other grains such as wheat, oats, and rye and food crops including peas, beans, and potatoes provided another ten to twenty bushels per person to the food supply in both 1850 and 1860. Finally, slaveholding farmers slaughtered $7 to $10 worth of livestock for home consumption in 1850 and increased the amount to between $10 and $15 by 1860. Hogs were valued at $2 to $5 each during this period, so it is possible that average Texas slaveholding farmers slaughtered at least two hogs for every person living on their farms in 1850 and 1860.

In sum, antebellum Texas plantations and farms employing slave labor were generally self-sufficient in food supply. Of course, not every agricultural unit conformed to the overall averages for the production of grain, other food crops, and livestock for slaughter. Some may indeed have concentrated on cotton to the point of having to purchase foodstuffs. As a whole, however, the state's slaveholding farmers were feeding themselves. Grains and meat could be, and were, exchanged locally rather than having to be imported from other states.[12]

Finally, the broad question—did slavery pay?—must be asked not only about individual farmers and planters who utilized slave labor but also for the state as a whole. In this case, the more specific question is: did slavery retard the economic development of antebellum Texas? The answer depends first on a definition of "economic development." If the term means expansion in the agricultural sector of the economy marked

11. Richard G. Lowe and Randolph B. Campbell, *Planters and Plain Folk: Agriculture in Antebellum Texas* (Dallas, 1987), 170–74, provides a general description of the debate over self-sufficiency. The number of free residents on slaveholding farms in 1850 was calculated by multiplying the number of farms by 5.44, the average size of a white family in Texas. For 1860, the average number of people per white family was 5.49.

12. Roemer, *Texas*, 58, described farmers selling corn.

Table 7. Volume of Food Crops Harvested per Resident on Slaveholding Farms, 1850 and 1860

Size of Slaveholding	1–9	10–19	20–49	50 +	Total, All Farms
1850					
Free residents	4,657	1,050	506	76	6,289
Slave residents	3,138	2,584	2,671	1,076	9,469
Total residents	7,795	3,634	3,177	1,152	15,758
Bushels of corn per resident	49.2	51.5	48.9	53.0	50.0
Bushels of food crops per resident[1]	63.7	69.0	63.0	77.3	65.8
Value of animals slaughtered per resident	$9.60	$7.35	$7.32	$9.79	$8.64
1860					
Free residents	4,145	1,180	670	137	6,132
Slave residents	2,950	2,978	3,653	2,019	11,600
Total residents	7,095	4,158	4,323	2,156	17,732
Bushels of corn per resident	48.7	48.8	53.0	51.2	50.0
Bushels of food crops per resident[1]	62.9	61.1	63.1	61.8	62.4
Value of animals slaughtered per resident	$14.66	$11.53	$10.19	$11.17	$12.41

[1]Food crops are a combination of the corn, the other grains such as wheat, and the potatoes and peas harvested on these farms.

by an increasing value of farm production per capita, there is little question that Texas, led by her slaveholding farmers, enjoyed notable development during the 1850s. Tables 8 and 9 demonstrate the approximate cash value of the major crops produced by Texas' slaveholding farmers in 1850 and 1860. When the values of cotton (the major cash crop), corn (the major noncash crop), other grains (wheat, oats, and rye), food crops (peas, beans, sweet potatoes, and Irish potatoes), and animals slaughtered for home consumption are combined and divided by the number of people (free and slave) on the farms that produced them, the dollar value per capita of farm output was $63.71 in 1850. Ten years later, value per capita had increased by approximately 60 percent to $102.20. All slaveholding farmers, regardless of the number of bondsmen they held, shared in this gain, although the larger the slaveholder, the higher the per capita value of his agricultural production.

Economic development, however, is not limited to the agricultural sector. If the term means commercialization, urbanization, and industrialization, then there is no question that Texas demonstrated very slow and limited development during the 1850s. Storekeepers made a living in small towns across the state and a few large merchants and factors thrived in Galveston and Houston, but commerce constituted a relatively minor sector of the economy. Less than 5 percent of all household heads in Texas reported commercial occupations in 1850 and 1860. The state had no urban place with as many as 10,000 people in 1860; San Antonio was the largest with a population of 8,200. Industry, other than some manufacturing of farm machinery such as cotton gins and processing of agricultural products, was largely unknown. Only 1 percent of Texas' household heads in 1850 and 1860 reported manufacturing occupations.[13]

The responsibility for this lack of commercial, urban, and industrial development in antebellum Texas did not rest on any single factor. First, part of the explanation was geographical—climate and soil gave Texas an advantage compared to most regions of the United States in plantation agriculture and thus helped create an overwhelmingly agricultural economy. Second, politics contributed, too, in that the Democrats who dominated Texas wrote the old Jacksonian bias against banks into a constitutional prohibition during the early statehood period. It is diffi-

---

13. Campbell and Lowe, *Wealth and Power*, 30, 90; Raymond E. White, "Cotton Ginning in Texas to 1861," *Southwestern Historical Quarterly*, LXI (1957), 255–69; Vera Lee Dugas, "Texas Industry, 1860–1880," *Southwestern Historical Quarterly*, LiX (1955), 151–85.

Table 8. Per Capita Value of Major Farm Crops Harvested: Slaveholding Farmers, 1850

Size of Slaveholding	1–9	10–19	20–49	50+	Total, All Farms
Total residents	7,795	3,634	3,177	1,152	15,758
Bales of cotton harvested	2,477	2,648	2,636	1,100	8,861
Value of cotton	$89,172	$95,328	$94,896	$39,600	$318,996
Value per capita	$11.44	$26.23	$29.87	$34.38	$20.24
Bushels of corn harvested	383,696	187,295	155,350	61,000	787,341
Value of corn	$191,848	$93,648	$77,675	$30,500	$393,671
Value per capita	$24.61	$25.77	$24.45	$26.48	$24.98
Bushels of other grain harvested	15,441	6,294	2,744	800	25,909
Value of other grain	$12,353	$5,035	$2,195	$640	$20,727
Value per capita	$1.58	$1.39	$.69	$.56	$1.32
Bushels of potatoes and peas harvested	97,727	57,209	41,987	27,220	224,143
Value of potatoes and peas	$58,636	$34,325	$25,192	$16,332	$134,486
Value per capita	$7.52	$9.45	$7.93	$14.18	$8.53
Value of animals slaughtered	$74,849	$26,728	$23,250	$11,275	$136,102
Value per capita	$9.60	$7.35	$7.32	$9.79	$8.64
Total value of all crops per capita	$54.75	$70.19	$70.26	$85.39	$63.71

Table 9. Per Capita Value of Major Farm Crops Harvested: Slaveholding Farmers, 1860

Size of Slaveholding	1–9	10–19	20–49	50+	Total, All Farms
Total residents	7,095	4,158	4,323	2,156	17,732
Bales of cotton harvested	5,614	6,493	9,584	6,067	27,758
Value of cotton	$202,104	$233,748	$345,024	$218,412	$999,288
Value per capita	$28.49	$56.21	$79.81	$101.30	$56.36
Bushels of corn harvested	345,268	202,705	229,000	110,300	887,273
Value of corn	$172,634	$101,353	$114,500	$55,150	$443,637
Value per capita	$24.33	$24.38	$26.49	$25.58	$25.02
Bushels of other grain harvested	53,642	20,364	9,745	4,975	88,726
Value of other grain	$42,914	$16,291	$7,796	$3,980	$70,981
Value per capita	$6.05	$3.92	$1.80	$1.85	$4.00
Bushels of potatoes and peas harvested	47,602	30,894	33,984	17,981	130,461
Value of potatoes and peas	$28,561	$18,536	$20,390	$10,789	$78,277
Value per capita	$4.03	$4.46	$4.72	$5.00	$4.41
Value of animals slaughtered	$104,013	$47,947	$44,030	$24,090	$220,080
Value per capita	$14.66	$11.53	$10.19	$11.17	$12.41
Total value per capita	$77.56	$100.50	$123.01	$144.90	$102.20

cult to imagine significant commercial and industrial development in an economy without banks. Finally, slavery also appears to have been a major factor retarding commercialization and industrialization. Slave labor made the plantation possible. Free laborers were not available in large numbers where inexpensive land was readily available, and if they had been, they would never have worked as long or as hard as slaves. Productivity on plantations was high in part precisely because the bondsmen were employed so intensively. No need existed for the invention and manufacture of farm machinery in order to produce cash and food crops that meant both profits and self-sufficiency. Thus the planters, who were after all among the richest and most enterprising men in Texas and those who would have had to lead any move to change its economic structure, reaped large enough profits from combining land and slave labor that they generally saw no need to risk investments in commerce or industry. This was especially true since they also generally approved of the social arrangements that accompanied farming and slavery. Planters concentrated on agricultural self-sufficiency and on increasing their slave forces—actions that reduced local demand for the goods and services of merchants and manufacturers—and on the cultivation of cotton, a crop that quickly passed out of Texas for processing elsewhere with a minimum involvement of local merchants along the way. Texas would probably have been more agricultural than commercial or industrial had slavery never entered the state; certainly it remained overwhelmingly agricultural for generations after the institution ended. But the slave plantation made the state's comparative advantage in farming even more pronounced and in that sense at least retarded the development of commerce and industry.[14]

A discussion of the economics of slavery in Texas does not end with consideration of rising values, productivity and profitability, agricultural self-sufficiency, and economic development because the institution's flexibility permitted slaveholders to benefit economically in numerous other

14. This discussion is of necessity largely theoretical. It draws on the following work: Robert E. Gallman, "Slavery and Southern Economic Growth," *Southern Economic Journal*, XLV (1979), 1007–1022; Heywood Fleisig, "Slavery, the Supply of Agricultural Labor, and the Industrialization of the South," *Journal of Economic History*, XXXVI (1976), 572–97; Robert V. Anderson and Robert E. Gallman, "Slaves as Fixed Capital: Slave Labor and Southern Economic Development," *Journal of American History*, LXIV (1977), 24–46; and Fred Bateman and Thomas Weiss, *A Deplorable Scarcity: The Failure of Industrialization in the Slave Economy* (Chapel Hill, 1981).

ways. As George R. Woolfolk has pointed out, the value of an economic institution may be judged by the functions it performs as well as by the profit-and-loss balance sheet.[15] Slavery's flexibility and functional utility was demonstrated in the slave-hire system, in the mortgaging of slaves to secure loans, in the management of estates, and in the assessing and collecting of taxes.

Slave hiring in Texas began almost as soon as slaveholders arrived in the region. On October 19, 1823, Stephen F. Austin contracted with Jared E. Groce, the largest slaveholder in his colony, to hire three Negroes for a year beginning on November 1. The following April, Austin, acting in effect as a probate judge, hired out a male slave, the property of Richard Barrett's heirs, for a period of three months. Settlers at times hired out their slaves to pay for land in Texas. For example, on August 1, 1824, Thomas Westall hired four slaves to Stephen F. Austin until January 1, 1826, and agreed that the hiring money would be credited against the costs of land in the latter's colony. The hiring system continued through the colonial period and then, like all aspects of slavery, flourished during the republic and early statehood years. Historians have long been aware of slave hiring in the Old South, but only those interested in urban and industrial slavery have paid close attention to the system. Texas, of course, was a rural, agricultural state, so a look at the hire system there reveals a little-examined function of slavery as an economic institution.[16]

Individual slaveowners hired out their bondsmen when, for example, they had surplus labor or were unable for some reason to provide supervision, but the most common source of bondsmen for hire was estates

15. George R. Woolfolk, "Cotton Capitalism and Slave Labor in Texas," *Southwestern Social Science Quarterly*, XXXVII (1956), 43–52.

16. Austin to Jared E. Groce, October 19 [1823?], Agreement for hire of a slave, April 12, 1824, Contract for hire of slaves, August 1, 1824, all in Barker (ed.), *Austin Papers*, I, 701, 763, 869–70. For information on slave hiring in general works, see Frederic Bancroft, *Slave-Trading in the Old South* (Baltimore, 1931), 145–64; and Stampp, *Peculiar Institution*, 67–72. Studies that describe hiring in industrial and urban settings include Robert S. Starobin, *Industrial Slavery in the Old South* (New York, 1970), 128–37; Richard C. Wade, *Slavery in the Cities: The South, 1820–1860* (New York, 1964), 38–47; and Claudia Dale Goldin, *Urban Slavery in the American South, 1820–1860: A Quantitative View* (Chicago, 1976), 35–42, 69–75.

Texas, of course, had fledgling towns, and slave hiring was common there, too, during the antebellum years. See Kenneth W. Wheeler, *To Wear a City's Crown: The Beginnings of Urban Growth in Texas, 1836–1865* (Cambridge, Mass., 1968), 106–10, 143–48; Lack, "Urban Slavery in the Southwest," 30–33, 58–59, 73–74; and Earl Wesley Fornell, *The Galveston Era: The Texas Crescent on the Eve of Secession* (Austin, 1961), 118–22. For examples of court cases arising from nonagricultural hires, see *Schrimpf* v. *McArdle*, 13 Tex. 368 (1855) and *Clark* v. *Southern Pacific Railroad*, 27 Tex. 100 (1863).

undergoing probate. Estate guardians and administrators, needing a cash income to support widows and minor children and unable to manage or provide management for the farm or plantation under their control, frequently hired out the estate's slaves. Hiring out thus made slavery economically useful in two ways: it helped support women and children who could not fully provide for themselves, and it provided additional labor on a temporary basis for those who probably could not afford it otherwise. The workings of the slave-hire system may be demonstrated by using the Westall family of Brazoria County as a case study.

Henson G. Westall died in January, 1853, leaving a wife and three minor children. A "verbal will" made on the day of his death provided that his four heirs were to receive equal shares of his estate and that his brother, Andrew E. Westall, was to rear his son, Andrew E. Westall, Jr. Westall had so many debts that his administrator, William C. Hill, kept the estate together, hiring out most of its sixteen slaves and selling off its cattle and part of its land, for three years before the creditors involved would agree to a partition of the slave property. The estate's slaves were divided into four lots on January, 1856, one for each heir, including the widow who had since remarried. Andrew E. Westall, Jr., inherited a man, a woman, and two children valued in total at $2,800; Eliza H. Westall, two men and a woman together worth $2,900; and Ann M. Westall, a woman and three teenaged slaves (two girls and a boy) valued at $3,400. Andrew, Jr., who was eleven at the time, and eight-year old Eliza became the wards of Andrew E. Westall. Ann M. Westall, who was only about three years of age, also had a guardian, A. T. Morris. For nearly ten years, these three children's main source of support was the hiring out of their slave property. In the case of Andrew Jr. and Eliza, their guardian, A. E. Westall, hired the slaves himself and credited their estate with the proceeds annually. By 1859, with income derived solely from the hires, Westall reported that each of his wards had a positive balance of more than $500 in their accounts with him. The children began attending school away from home in 1860 or 1861, and in 1863 Andrew Jr. was enrolled at Austin College in Huntsville while Eliza attended the Cummins School in Chapel Hill. Income from slave hiring paid the costs of their schooling and continued to provide a favorable balance with their guardian. In the meantime, A. T. Morris earned money to support Ann M. Westall by hiring her slaves out to various individuals in the area. During a period of eight years from 1857 through 1864, the four slaves under his control served a total of eighteen different masters for at least one year. Ann M. Westall, who had just reached her teens by 1864, was supported by income from hiring through this whole period. Obviously, slavery had, through the hiring system, been of great benefit economically to the Westall children and their guardians for more than a decade of the late antebellum years.[17]

The slave-hire system was important enough that it should be examined systematically as well as described through case studies. Again, probate records provide the necessary data. Estate managers hired out slaves everywhere slavery existed in Texas, but in areas with relatively few slaves there were not enough cases to justify a search of the probate records for hire data. Therefore, this study is limited to the portion of eastern and south-central antebellum Texas where slaves constituted at least one-quarter of the population by 1860 and slave hiring was common enough to generate a sizable number of estate-manager reports in the probate records of most counties. More precisely, the area of investigation was marked by a line running southwestward from Lamar County on the Red River to Matagorda County on the Gulf Coast (see map 9). In 1860, with the exceptions of Falls and McLennan, every Texas county having slaves as 25 percent or more of its total population was to the east of that line. Twenty counties were chosen according to geographical location to represent this region of extensive slave population. These sample counties contained 74,529 slaves in 1860, approximately 41 percent of all the slaves in Texas.[18]

A sample of 754 slave hires for the period from 1848 to 1862 was drawn from the probate records of these twenty sample counties. Some guardians and administrators reported hires for only one year; others managed the same estate year after year and reported annually. Thus the 754 observations of slave hirings did not necessarily involve 754 different slaves. Some individual hirers appeared more than once in the records, too. All the observations, however, were for separate hire agreements and were treated as such in analyzing the age-sex distribution of hired slaves and hire rates.[19]

17. Estate of Henson G. Westall, Brazoria County Probate Records (Wills, etc., Books B, C, and D).

18. U.S. Bureau of the Census, *Agriculture of the United States in 1860*, 240–42.

19. Analysis was limited to hires during the years from 1848 to 1862 because by 1848 slaves were numerous enough in most of these counties to create reasonably large numbers of hire cases and by the end of 1862 the currency system of Texas was being upset by the Civil War. Probate records from years prior to 1848 and from 1863 to 1865 were read, but information drawn from them was used only for purposes of general description.

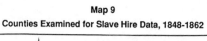

Map 9

Counties Examined for Slave Hire Data, 1848-1862

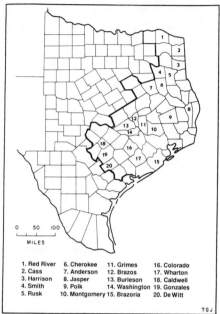

1. Red River	6. Cherokee	11. Grimes	16. Colorado
2. Cass	7. Anderson	12. Brazos	17. Wharton
3. Harrison	8. Jasper	13. Burleson	18. Caldwell
4. Smith	9. Polk	14. Washington	19. Gonzales
5. Rusk	10. Montgomery	15. Brazoria	20. De Witt

Although instances occurred when slaves were hired during every month of the year and for periods of time ranging from a day to a few days or a month to a few months, hiring usually took place in early January for the period of one year. More specifically, hiring usually took place on the first of January, and slaves generally returned to their owners on December 25. The form of payment typically was a twelve-month note to be paid when the hire period expired.[20] Most hiring was done at public

20. These statements are based largely on the reports of the hiring of more than six hundred slaves in Texas between 1848 and 1862. Estate managers hired out bondsmen whenever necessary and for varying periods of time. Newspaper advertisements indicate that the hire system operated year around. Slaves for hire were, for example, advertised in the Galveston *Weekly News*, February 24, 1844; Clarksville *Northern Standard*, November 12, 1845; Houston *Telegraph and Texas Register*, March 1, 1849; Marshall *Texas Republican*, June 3, 1859; and San Antonio *Herald*, October 28, 1859. A Harrison County slave brickmason named Richmond provided a good example of daily hires. His master, John B. Webster, regularly hired him out at three dollars per day. John B. Webster Plantation Journal, 1858–59, in East Texas Baptist University Library, Marshall.

Most hires reported in the probate papers, however, were arranged in early January, and newspaper comments indicate that the first of the year was the time for what the Marshall *Texas Republican*, January 7, 1854, called "annual sales and the hiring of property." Some hire contracts specified December 25 as the expiration date, but others simply provided for a year's service. In any case, Christmas seems to have been accepted as the end of the year and

outcry in front of the county courthouse, and state law required that all public hirings be advertised in three places, including the local courthouse door. It was possible, however, for slaves to be hired out directly from their owners' residences. In Texas, unlike some of the more developed slave states, the hire system did not commonly depend on agents who specialized in the business. Instead, at least where the many slaves managed by guardians and administrators were concerned, the only expenses were the costs of advertising and an auctioneer to handle the bidding. In some cases, even these expenses were avoided by petitioning the county judge to permit a private hiring arrangement in which the guardian or administrator simply worked out a contract with a prospective hirer.[21]

Guardians and administrators wishing to hire out slaves under their control rarely were unable to find a hirer. The examination of hundreds of estate records revealed only a handful of slaves who could not be hired. For example, one Washington County administrator in 1858 hired out twenty-six slaves but reported that John, his wife, and four children were "not hired no one wanting them." Other instances of failure to hire appear to have been due to exceptional circumstances. Louisa R. Bennett, administrator of the Elisha D. Little estate in Washington County, reported in 1857 that she had sold a teenaged girl named Kate who had become "so vicious and unmanageable that when hired out no person to whom she was hired would keep her."[22] Slaves like Kate were not numerous, however, and most hired out with little difficulty to the administrator.

The great majority of slave hires involved a single hirer, but there were cases in which two or more individuals combined to rent the services of

a special time for slaves. This is borne out by an 1846 law against slaves hiring their own time except for one day a week. The rule did not apply "in the Christmas holidays." Gammel (comp.), *Laws of Texas*, II, 1502.

21. Estate of Timothy Wortham, Red River County Probate Records (Probate Minutes, Book G); Estate of John Banks, Cherokee County Probate Records (Probate Minutes, Book E-F); Williamson S. Oldham and George W. White (comps.), *A Digest of the General Statute Laws of the State of Texas* (Austin, 1859), 175. Bancroft, *Slave-Trading in the Old South*, 149–52, discusses hiring agents. An example of a private hiring is found in Estate of N. H. Wiggins, Cherokee County Probate Records (Probate Minutes, Book E).

22. Estate of William Routt, Washington County Probate Records (Final Record, Book G). (One other example of the inability to hire out slaves was found in Estate of James Wasson, Cass County Probate Records [Final Record Probate Court, Book 3.]) Estate of Elisha D. Little, Washington County Probate Records (Final Record, Book G).

a bondsman. In Gonzales County, for example, a nine-year-old boy was hired to H. G. Zumwalt and Thomas Eldridge for $35 in 1860, and the services of a twenty-seven-year-old woman in the same estate went to four hirers for $150. It was even possible, as one district-court case from Cass County demonstrated, to subhire a slave. Noble A. Birge and Charles S. Hynson hired a bondsman to work in their livery stable but then sublet him to another who allowed the man to drown. The owner won damages from the original hirers, not because subhiring was unlawful but because they had not asked his permission to do so.[23]

Annual slave-hire contracts in Texas varied somewhat in detail on everything except food and housing, which were always the responsibility of the hirer. Even in the matter of clothing, which was almost always the responsibility of the hirer, some contracts mentioned only the "usual amount of clothing" while others specified the number of pants, shirts, dresses, blankets, pairs of shoes, and hats. Medical care was mentioned more often than clothing in hire contracts. The hirer was usually responsible for the costs of doctors and medicine, but there were cases in which the guardian or administrator was directed to pay all medical expenses. Apparently some county judges felt that maintenance of the health of an estate's slaves was too important to be left solely in the hands of hirers. Hired slaves' sicknesses or injuries generally meant a loss to the hirers, but there were cases in which time lost for medical reasons was deducted from the hire. In Cass County, for example, a cook woman who had a baby while hired out in 1857 had her hire rate reduced by $35—$12.50 for the time lost, $12.50 for the hire of another cook, and $10 for the doctor.[24]

The hire system also had provisions concerning slaves who died or ran away while hired out. Those who died generally were considered a

23. Estate of Thomas McGuffey, Gonzales County Probate Papers; Estate of C. B. Harris, Cass County Probate Records (Final Record Probate Court, Book 4); Minutes of the Cass County District Court (Book B).

24. Estate of Elisha D. Little, Washington County Probate Records (Final Record, Book G), has the "usual amount of clothing" statement. Clothing was specified in detail in hire contracts found in Estate of William Steen, De Witt County Probate Records (Final Record Deceased Persons, Book A); Estate of Gray Blackburn, Cass County Probate Records (Final Record Probate Court, Book 1); and Estate of Thomas Saunders, Washington County Probate Records (Final Record, Book B). The Texas Supreme Court ruled in 1849 that "the hirer of a slave, not the owner is responsible for medical attendance, where the attendance is not requested by the owner, and where there is no special agreement." *McGee* v. *Currie*, 4 Tex. 217 (1849). Estate of Fanny Rush, Cass County Probate Records (Final Record Probate Court, Book 5).

loss to their owners, and the hire rate was reduced in proportion to the time they had served. Even this general rule could have contractual exceptions, however. When William W. Hill hired two slaves in Washington County in 1843, it was agreed that he, not the owner, was accountable in the case of abduction or death by Indians. Runaways generally, although not invariably, meant a loss to the hirer (at least for the period of the hire). When Thomas Eborn of Travis County hired fourteen-year-old Jo for 1857, the contract stipulated that if the boy ran away the loss would be the owner's. Jo ran away in December, one week before the contract expired, and Eborn interpreted this to mean that he did not owe any part of the hire money. He lost his argument, however, in district court and on appeal in the state supreme court, which ruled that he was due only a one-week abatement in the cost of Jo's hire. Justice Oran M. Roberts commented that Eborn was in effect fortunate to receive any reduction in costs since the hirer commonly bore the loss in such cases.[25]

Contemporary observers of the slave-hire system in Texas were inclined to emphasize how much hirers paid for labor. Frederick Law Olmsted, for example, wrote of ordinary field hands in Gonzales bringing from $150 to $250 and a black mechanic in Austin who hired for $280. He had heard, he reported, of a cook who hired for $600. The Marshall *Texas Republican* described men hiring for $235 to $312 during 1854 in that town, while the same year at Greenville Alfred Howell wrote of women going for as much as $200. The Crockett *Printer* told of a blacksmith who brought $555 in 1859, and the Memphis *Weekly Avalanche* of January 31, 1860, reported that nearly half of a group of thirty-one slaves hired at Columbia, Texas, for more than $300 each.[26]

Most of these reports on hiring were no doubt accurate, but they represented the upward limits rather than typical rates. Table 10 presents a summary of what was more commonly paid to rent slave labor during the period from 1848 to 1862 in Texas. It is based on estate managers' reports

25. The general rule concerning slaves who died while hired out was stated by the supreme court in *McLemore* v. *McClellan*, 17 Tex. 122 (1856), and *Townsend* v. *Hill*, 18 Tex. 422 (1857). The exception is in Estate of Thomas Saunders, Washington County Probate Records (Final Record, Book B). The general rule concerning slaves who ran away while hired out is stated in *Eborn* v. *Chote*, 22 Tex. 32 (1858).

26. Olmsted, *Journey Through Texas*, 48, 53, 140; Marshall *Texas Republican*, January 7, 1854; Alfred Howell to his brother, January 1, 1854, in Alfred Howell Letters, Tennessee State Library, Nashville; Crockett *Printer*, quoted in the Marshall *Texas Republican*, January 14, 1859; Memphis *Weekly Avalanche*, January 31, 1860, cited in Bancroft, *Slave-Trading in the Old South*, 160–61.

Table 10. Texas Slave Hire Rates, 1848–1862

Years	Number of Slaves: Ten or Older	Number of Slaves: Under Ten	Value of Average Hire: All Slaves
1848–52	59	24	$ 70
1853–57	297	97	$103
1858–62	245	49	$119

concerning 771 slaves—292 males, 309 females, and 170 children under the age of ten. The average hire rate rose from $70 in 1848–52 to $103 in 1853–57 to $119 by 1858–62. The inclusion of young children, because they were an expense and a burden on their mothers' time, undoubtedly lowered these overall hire rates. However, most children under the age of ten were hired with one or both parents rather than alone, so it is only realistic to include them when discussing general hire rates in rural Texas.[27]

Table 11 gives a more precise indication of how age and sex affected individual slave hires from 1848 to 1862. Boys and girls aged ten to fourteen hired for approximately $60 during most of this late antebellum period. Males and females in their late teens cost more than $100 per year, and many hirers were willing to pay nearly $200 for the services of a prime-age male. Men continued to bring $150 or more per year until they were more than fifty years old. After the age of fifteen, females generally hired for somewhat lower rates than males, but the cost of a woman with children was nearly $100 per year from 1853 to 1862.[28]

These rates indicate that the hiring of a slave was relatively expensive in antebellum Texas. Land generally cost less than ten dollars an acre across the state during the 1850s; hirers paid more than ten times that amount for the labor of a single adult male slave for one year. By the same token, those who hired out bondsmen earned significant returns for the estates under their control. Table 12, based on the actual evaluations and hires of 122 individual slaves of all ages and both sexes reported by guardians and administrators, shows that the hiring out of bondsmen

27. The statement that most children under ten years of age were hired out with a parent is an impression based on reading the reports of hundreds of hire arrangements. Some children under ten were hired separately (see table 11).

28. It is impossible to make precise comparisons of these rates with those suggested in previous studies because the latter are not age-specific. Bancroft, *Slave-Trading in the Old South*, 157, says that in Texas men hired for $166, women for $109, and youths not under fourteen for $80 in 1860.

Table 11. Texas Slave Hire Rates According to Age and Sex, 1848–1862

	(Number of Observations in Parentheses)		
	1848–52	1853–57	1858–62
Males 0–9	n/a	$26 (8)	$29 (10)
Females 0–9	$36 (1)	$23 (9)	$38 (6)
Males 10–14	$56 (8)	$70 (34)	$74 (16)
Females 10–14	$49 (4)	$65 (38)	$77 (29)
Males 15–19	$94 (6)	$161 (29)	$141 (9)
Females 15–19	$112 (5)	$126 (21)	$125 (31)
Males 20–29	$158 (9)	$202 (56)	$197 (38)
Females 20–29	$121 (3)	$141 (20)	$134 (18)
Males 30–39	$174 (3)	$210 (14)	$213 (22)
Females 30–39	$103 (3)	$128 (5)	$146 (23)
Males 40–49	$200 (1)	$170 (12)	$177 (19)
Females 40–49	$60 (3)	$82 (4)	$128 (3)
Males 50 +	$60 (1)	$134 (11)	$91 (4)
Females 50 +	$66 (1)	$84 (11)	$103 (14)
Males 18–30	$158 (10)	$200 (65)	$195 (45)
Females 15–49 (with children)[1]	$72 (12 + 23)	$85 (42 + 80)	$102 (19 + 33)

[1]Not included in listing of females above.

Table 12. Texas Hire Rates as a Percentage of Slave Value, 1848–1862

	Number of Cases	Total Evaluation	Total Hire	Hire as % of Evaluation
1848–52	26	$15,625	$2,579.60	16.5%
1853–57	38	$34,650	$4,704.50	13.6%
1858–62	58	$60,930	$9,358.00	15.4%
TOTALS	122	$111,205	$16,642.10	15.0%

worth slightly more than $110,000 earned more than $16,500 for their estates. The hired slaves thus returned approximately 15 percent of their total value each year. Profitability in the sense of return on investment was generally not the chief interest of guardians and administrators. They simply wanted to keep the slaves busy and bring in money to pay debts and support those dependent on the estate. But if profitability were to be measured by estimating and factoring in all the costs such as taxes on the bondsmen, interest on the capital each slave represented, and the expenses of maintenance in the future, it is likely that hiring provided a reasonable rate of return for that period.[29]

29. An estimate of the cost of land per slave in Texas is found in Lowe and Campbell, *Planters and Plain Folk*, 166–68. This same work shows (p. 169) that rates of return of invest-

Some contemporary critics insisted that slave-hire rates were too high, especially in comparison to the costs of free labor elsewhere, and indicated a weakness in the system. Olmsted made this observation in the 1850s, as did Judith Trask, an immigrant from Massachusetts, in 1835. She had to pay $11 a month, she complained to her father, for a Negro girl who would not be worth fifty cents in the North. Complaints of this sort, however, overlooked the simple fact that hire rates were high primarily because Texans considered slave labor worth the cost. Even Trask admitted that hired servants were so expensive because people wanted them to produce cotton. And proslavery editors rarely missed an opportunity to make the same point. "The natural inference," wrote Robert W. Loughery of the Marshall *Texas Republican* in 1854, "would be that a country must be very productive when people can afford to pay such prices for labor." John Patterson Osterhout summarized the implications of the hire system very well in February, 1860, while trying to explain the attitude of Texas toward slavery and secession to his brother in Pennsylvania. When lands, he wrote, "sell for 30 to 40 dollars per acre and negro men hire out for from 200 to 500 dollars per year & have to be fed, clothed, and doctored in the bargain it would seem that men ought to know that slavery is popular & will be likely to continue for many years yet."[30] Hire rates indicated vitality, not weakness.

Critics such as Olmsted favored free labor, but that was not really a viable alternative in Texas. Free farm workers were not numerous, and in cotton culture, which required labor virtually year-round, they tended to be very expensive. Monthly wages for a farm hand with board were $19 per month in 1860 in the sample counties examined in this study. This rate would mean an annual cost of at least $228 for a worker who could not be expected to labor as long or as hard as a hired slave. Moreover, the slave's labor could be assured for a year while the free worker, especially in a state with plentiful, cheap land, might leave at any time. In these same counties, the wage for a female domestic worker with board was approximately $3.25 per week. Her services for fifty weeks of a year

---

ments in slave labor and cotton production in Texas did not exceed 10 percent, except for the very largest planters in 1850 and 1860. The rates of return from hiring in rural Texas match almost perfectly those given in Bancroft, *Slave-Hiring in the Old South*, 156.

30. Olmsted, *Journey Through Texas*, 53; Judith Trask to Israel Trask, July 5, 1835, in Trask Family Papers, Texas Collection, Baylor University, Waco, Tex.; Marshall *Texas Republican*, January 7, 1854; John P. Osterhout to Orlando Osterhout, February 1, 1860, in John Patterson Osterhout Papers, Fondren Library, Rice University, Houston, Tex.

would cost $162.50, significantly more than the hire rate for a female slave.[31]

In sum, slave hiring demonstrated and promoted the economic vitality of slavery in antebellum Texas. Hired slaves were expensive, but they cost less and were more dependable than free labor. It seems that hiring out slaves was so profitable and so easy to accomplish that there should have been individuals who made it a business, owning bondsmen solely for the purpose of hiring them out. There is, however, no evidence from newspapers or other contemporary sources that this practice existed. Slave hiring was important to the system in Texas but not a business in itself. Above all, it was a testimonial to the flexibility of slavery and the many functions it performed.

Critics sometimes charge that southern money was "tied up" in slaves, but in fact bondsmen functioned as a highly liquid form of capital. Texas slaveholders counted on being able to convert them to cash whenever necessary. For example, the 1842 will of Alexander F. Johnson of Fort Bend County directed that his debts be paid from the proceeds of selling his "Negro boy Austin." Ten years later, R. M. Roseborough, in explaining to Ashbel Smith his plans for moving to Texas, inquired about the price he could expect to get for his slave if cash were needed. George and Louisa Goff, a husband and wife from Alabama, demonstrated the use of slaves virtually as money when they moved to Texas during the 1850s. Before migrating, they bought two slave girls with money inherited from Louisa's father. Settling in Bosque County in 1854, they sold the girls to acquire land. Two years later, they moved to Grayson County, trading their land for two men before leaving. They purchased 495 acres in Grayson for $3,960, getting $2,200 for the two men and giving a note for the remaining $1,760. George Goff died that year, whereupon Louisa sold a slave woman and three children, also inherited from her father, for $2,200 and paid off the note. Estate administrators regularly sold slaves as a means of raising money to pay debts. The guardians of minors, if they could not obtain enough income from hiring, could sell bondsmen,

31. The relatively high costs of free labor in cotton production are explained in Carville Earle and Ronald Hoffman, "The Foundation of the Modern Economy: Agriculture and the Costs of Labor in the United States and England, 1800–1860," *American Historical Review*, LXXXV (1980), 1066. Wages for free farm hands and female domestics were calculated from data in the manuscript returns of the Eighth Census of the United States, 1860, Schedule 6 (Social Statistics), Archives Division, Texas State Library, Austin.

too. When, for example, John James, a minor in Rusk County, needed money to pay for schooling in 1859, his guardian sold a twenty-five-year-old female named Rachel for $1,000 in cash.[32] These Texans and their antebellum neighbors probably would have been surprised had they been told that, as individuals, their money was "tied up" in slaves.

Slaves did not necessarily have to be sold in order to raise money; they could also be used as security for cash loans and promissory notes given for goods or services. In December, 1858, for example, Harriet Simmons of Austin County gave Frank Lipscomb her note in payment for a $200 cash loan and $100 in legal services. The note was secured by a deed of trust conveying two female slaves to Leonard W. Groce as trustee. If Simmons defaulted on payment, Groce was to sell the slaves, pay Lipscomb, and return any additional money from the sale to her. When Ashbel Smith needed to borrow $700 in 1857, he was informed that the money was available at 12-percent interest, "secured by a mortgage on Sam." John Buchanan of Jackson County mortgaged a six-year-old boy in 1839 to secure a $363 account at Clark L. Owen's store. Thomas and Minerva Penrice of Austin County found an even more specialized use of slaves as financial security in 1860 after losing a civil suit brought against them and owing the plaintiff $364 and court costs. Wishing to appeal and needing a $700 appeal bond, the Penrices executed a deed of trust on three of their slaves to secure the costs of any execution against them.[33] Similar mortgage arrangements were made all over antebellum Texas, some involving dozens of slaves and thousands of dollars.

Slavery functioned effectively in myriad ways in estate settlements. Property in slaves generally was divisible among multiple heirs, and in a state with plentiful inexpensive land but little labor, Texans viewed slaves as the most valuable form of property that could be left to heirs. Probate records provide literally thousands of estate distributions involving slaves. The case of Henson G. Westall of Brazoria County, cited above, may be taken as typical in most respects. On January 1, 1856, the

32. Estate of Alexander F. Johnson, Fort Bend County Probate Records (Probate Record, Book A); R. M. Roseborough to Ashbel Smith, April 20, 1852, in Smith Papers; Grayson County District Court Minutes (Book A); Estate of George, William, and John James, Rusk County Probate Records (Probate Record, Book D).

33. Deed of Trust executed by Harriet Simmons, December 6, 1858, and Deed of Trust executed by Thomas and Minerva Penrice, November 20, 1860, Austin County, County Clerk's Miscellaneous Records (Records, 1849–65); Estate of John Buchanan, Jackson County Probate Records (Final Estates, Book A); H. F. Gillet to Ashbel Smith, October 25, 1857, in Smith Papers.

sixteen slaves of his estate were divided by court-appointed commissioners "into four lots according to families." His widow and each of his three
children received one "lot" of bondsmen. James Blair of De Witt County
directed a somewhat different handling of his slaves in a will written in
1846, leaving all to his wife during her "widowhood." The sole use of his
bondsmen, Blair wrote, was to be "that of promoting her happiness as it
relates to the comfort of life or the improving of the domicile or Plantation
in such manner as the aforesaid Catherine Blair shall choose to direct."
David White of Bell County demonstrated yet another variation of handling slave property. He left his one slave to his wife to hold for eight
years and then sell, with the proceeds being equally divided among his
heirs. William Wade of Austin County, apparently not wishing to trust
a will or the probate process, distributed slaves as gifts to his four sons,
six bondsmen to each boy, but reserved to himself "the use and enjoyment of a life estate in and to the same without accountability therefor."
Haden Edwards of Rusk County provided a final example of the importance of slaves in estate settlements. He left his wife "three sound young
negroes . . . of good character," two males and one female, who were to
be hired out or otherwise employed to support her. Edwards, however,
did not own these slaves. Instead, he directed that all but one thousand
acres of his headright was to be sold to provide purchase money.[34]

In a few cases, estate settlements even used slaves to create what
might be called endowments. Mary A. Hall of Brazoria County, for example, willed her two slaves to her husband, but at his death their value
was to be placed at the disposal of the Brazos Presbytery of the Old
School Presbyterian Church to pay the expenses of traveling ministers or
be used otherwise as the presbytery might direct. Joseph T. Hefford of
Matagorda County provided that at the deaths of all his heirs his two
slaves and their offspring would become the property of the Town of
Matagorda for use in supporting the public school fund.[35]

Slave property was a major source of tax revenue in antebellum Texas.
A revenue act of June, 1837, called for the enumeration of slaves along

34. Estate of Henson G. Westall, Brazoria County Probate Records (Wills, etc., Books B,
C, and D); Estate of James Blair, De Witt County Probate Papers (Final Record of Deceased
Persons, Book A); Estate of David White, Bell County Probate Records (Will Record); Estate
of William Wade, Austin County, County Clerk's Miscellaneous Records (Records, 1849–65);
Estate of Haden Edwards, Nacogdoches County Probate Records (Book of Wills).

35. Estate of Mary A. Hall, Brazoria County Probate Records (Wills, etc., Book B); Estate
of Joseph T. Hefford, Matagorda County Probate Records (Transcribed Will Record).

with other personal property to be taxed at the rate of one-half of one percent ad valorem. In 1840, the tax on slaves was made a per-capita tax, with those under fifteen years of age costing their owners one dollar; those fifteen to fifty, three dollars; and those over fifty, two dollars. These rates were changed in 1842 to twenty-five cents each on slaves under ten and seventy-five cents on all aged ten to sixty. After statehood, legislators returned to the original practice of taxing slaves on an ad-valorem basis. Although assessors probably allowed slaveholders to "forget" a few bondsmen at tax time, the value of slaves constituted more than one-third of the state's total tax assessment during the 1850s. In an agrarian society, the only other common objects of taxation were land and livestock. Taxes on slave property thus fell on those best able to pay. Tax rates were low, but that was due in part to yet another use of slavery. The upkeep of public roads, one of the few functions of government during the antebellum years and therefore something that might have required public funds, was largely handled by slave labor in many counties. The commissioners' court simply appointed a number of slaveholders and their "hands" to be responsible for particular sections of the road or roads in their neighborhoods.[36]

In conclusion, slavery was the key to an agricultural economy in antebellum Texas that was profitable, self-sufficient in food production, and growing. The institution may have helped retard commercialization, urbanization, and industrialization, but it was satisfactory to a great majority of the state's economic leaders. Moreover, it performed numerous functions that, while not appearing in the profit-or-loss column on a balance sheet, were of great benefit to many Texans. Perhaps slavery may have reached its natural limits on the plains of western Texas or its future may have been ruined by a collapse in world cotton markets, but those possibilities did not represent current or pressing problems during the 1850s. Slavery was not economically moribund in antebellum Texas; the institution was flourishing and had plenty of room to grow.

36. Gammel (comp.), *Laws of Texas*, I, 1319–20, II, 190, 779. Tax rates at the end of the antebellum period were set at 12.5 cents per $100 for the state and one-half that amount for the counties. There was also a 50-cent poll tax on all males aged twenty-one to fifty. *Ibid.*, IV, 1130–33. Assessments on slaves constituted 35 percent of the total in 1850 and 36 percent in 1860. *Biennial Report of the Comptroller, For the Years 1850 and 1851* (Austin, 1851), 218; *Biennial Report of the Comptroller of Texas . . . 1860–1861* (Austin, 1861), 60. Documentation of the role of slaves in maintaining the roads may be found in the Commissioners' Court Minutes of any Texas county that had a sizable black population during the antebellum years.

FIVE

· · · · · · · · · ·

The Law of Slavery in Texas

"NEGROES ARE, IN THIS COUNTRY, PRIMA FACIE SLAVES"

Texans always recognized that slavery could not exist without protection of the law. In January, 1824, only two years after settlement began in his colony, Stephen F. Austin issued his Criminal Regulations, containing five articles that constituted the province's first "slave code."[1] More extensive rules to protect the institution and govern slave conduct could not be promulgated while Texas remained part of Mexico. But once the Constitution of 1836 provided the necessary fundamental guarantees, the law of slavery developed rapidly. Then, following statehood and the adoption of a new constitution in 1845, Texas' legislators and judges brought to maturity an extensive system of statutory and case law dedicated to the maintenance and regulation of the Peculiar Institution.

The law of slavery in Texas was a complex and sometimes curious matter because it dealt with a unique form of property—humans whom

1. Texas never had a slave code in the sense of a systematic collection of all the constitutional provisions, statutes, and case law dealing with slaves and slavery. Codifications of civil and criminal law and criminal procedure, however, did contain sections summarizing rules and regulations pertaining to the Peculiar Institution. See, for example, Oldham and White (comps.), *Digest of the General Statute Laws*, 407–409, 539–43, 559–62, 670–73. In general, the laws of slavery in Texas were patterned on practices elsewhere in the South. Mark Tushnet, *The American Law of Slavery, 1810–1860: Considerations of Humanity and Interest* (Princeton, 1981), does not deal with Texas and does not make a state-by-state comparison, but it is clear that Texans generally copied the legislative practices of older slave states. Also, Texas judges regularly cited decisions made in other states when deciding cases involving slavery.

other humans owned as private possessions. If slaves had been simply items of personal property like horses or wagons, without human intelligence or will, laws could have operated only on their owners rather than on the bondsmen themselves and masters would rarely have allowed considerations other than economic interest enter into the handling of their bondsmen. Slaves, however, because of their human capabilities, could not be treated as property pure and simple. The state held bondsmen legally responsible for their own actions—a practice that threatened owners' property rights when slaves were punished or executed for particular criminal offenses.[2] Masters at times recognized their servants' humanity by granting them freedom—an action that was widely regarded as a threat to the entire institution. The law of slavery revealed how Texans wrestled with and resolved these and other conflicts arising from the paradoxical practice of holding humans as property.

Texas' slave code dealt with five related but distinct aspects of the institution. Each required particular constitutional provisions, laws, or legal rulings, so each must therefore be examined in turn. First, the code had to guarantee the right to own slaves and provide essential civil protections for property rights in bondsmen. Second, laws defining criminal acts against slave property, such as stealing a bondsman, had to be enacted. Third, the conduct of the slaves themselves had to be regulated. Fourth, the constant problem of runaways had to be addressed. And, finally, there was the matter of free blacks, whose presence alone was regarded by many as an intolerable threat to slavery.[3]

The first critical step toward development of a slave code for Texas came when the Constitution of 1836 swept away all questions created by Mexican authorities concerning the legality of slavery in the new republic. Negroes held in bondage at the time of the revolution were to remain in servitude, and immigrants could bring their bondsmen to Texas and hold them just as slaves were held in the United States. Congress could not deprive owners of their human property through emancipation. When the first state constitution was written in 1845, no need existed to clarify the status of blacks in bondage, but the assurances concerning

2. The Texas Supreme Court ruled in *Grinder* v. *The State*, 2 Tex. 338 (1847) that a master was not responsible for court costs in a case involving a capital offense by one of his slaves. "Public justice was satisfied," Justice Abner S. Lipscomb wrote, "in the person of the slave."

3. Texas' slave code also had provisions concerning the "rights" and protections due bondsmen. This aspect of the law of slavery is dealt with below in chapters 7 and 8.

slaveholding immigrants and the restrictions on forced emancipation were repeated.[4]

Such constitutional guarantees provided the most fundamental protection possible for the right to own slaves as property. Legislation was not necessary to permit or protect simple ownership. Some Texans, however, felt that property rights in slaves deserved special consideration. On January 27, 1841, two years after congress passed a law exempting homesteads in the republic from forced sale under execution to pay debts, slavery's advocates secured the adoption of a measure extending similar protection to Negro property. This law was instantly controversial, primarily because it arrayed one type of property interest against another. Creditors lamented the denial of forced sales for debt collection. Other Texans applauded the measure because it encouraged immigration, especially during the depression that extended into the 1840s after the Panic of 1837. One editor, D. H. Fitch of the Houston *Morning Star*, defended the law with the argument that the master-slave relationship was akin to family ties. "Is it not only right that this 'property' not be sold?" he asked. Fitch's resort to such an argument suggests the depth of feelings evoked by the law. Defense of property rights with concern for the property's humanity was ironic and probably hypocritical as well, since many slaveholders were willing to sell their bondsmen so long as the sale was not forced under execution for debt. In any case, the law was repealed within less than twelve months. The idea appeared again in 1856 with a senate bill proposing to exempt up to five of a master's slaves from "execution or forced sales." This bill was tabled, however, and never came to a vote.[5] Texans revered slave property, but the majority stopped short of placing it on a level with their homesteads.

The business of buying and selling slaves, which obviously involved property rights, was carried on according to such long-established practices that it required no statutory framework. Sellers typically gave warranties that the bondsmen involved in a transaction were slaves for life

4. The relevant portions of the constitutions of 1836 and 1845 are found in Gammel (comp.), *Laws of Texas*, I, 1079, II, 1296.

5. Webb, Carroll, and Branda (eds.), *Handbook of Texas*, I, 830; Gammel (comp.), *Laws of Texas*, II, 515, 697; Houston *Morning Star*, quoted in Henson, "Development of Slave Codes in Texas," 75; Archie P. McDonald (ed.), *Hurrah for Texas! The Diary of Adolphus Sterne, 1838–1851* (Waco, 1969), 27; *Journal of the Senate of the State of Texas* [6th Legislature], (Austin, 1856), 19.

and sound in body and mind. Buyers, once they accepted such a warranty, were obligated to pay for the property according to the agreed-upon terms. Numerous suits arose, however, from charges concerning the sale of unsound bondsmen, with the result that Texas courts established a great deal of case law protecting the rights of both parties in the sale of slaves. In cases where bondsmen were warranted sound by sellers but died shortly after the transaction from some proven long-standing defect, the courts ruled that the purchaser deserved compensation.[6]

In cases where considerations other than the physical and mental soundness of the slaves as property were involved in a transaction, however, the court tended to rule for the seller. For example, in 1846 a Bowie County slaveowner named McKinney, planning to move to Collin County and not wishing to separate one of his female slaves from her husband who belonged to a Dr. Fort, bought the man for 13,000 pounds of ginned cotton. The man, who was only twenty-two, died in 1847, and McKinney sued Fort for his value. He lost in district court and also on appeal to the Texas supreme court. Chief Justice John Hemphill commended McKinney for his benevolent sympathies but pointed out that Fort had not been asked for a warranty. McKinney, Hemphill said, determined to make the purchase from considerations other than the soundness of the property involved and therefore could not recover any damages. Even in cases where a warranty of soundness in mind and body had been given, the court was inclined to recognize evidence that considerations of the slave's humanity, rather than his status as property pure and simple, had been involved. The case of *James Nations* v. *John G. Jones* provides an interesting example of this point. Jones sold a slave to Nations with the verbal warning that the "boy" was a "chuckle-headed fool" to which the latter replied "this was the kind of Negro he wanted." Nations soon concluded that the slave was in fact an idiot and sued for a reduction in the purchase price. He lost in both the district court and, on appeal, the supreme court because, as Chief Justice Hemphill put it: "He desired to have a chuckle-headed fool, that had just sense enough to do what he was told." Nations complained, Hemphill wrote seemingly with tongue-in-cheek, "that the slave had a little more of the valuable quality

6. *Scranton* v. *Tilley*, 16 Tex. 183 (1856); *Wade* v. *DeWitt*, 20 Tex. 398 (1857); *Blythe* v. *Speake*, 23 Tex. 429 (1859); *Rogers* v. *Crain*, 30 Tex. 284 (1867). There had to be clear evidence that the defect existed prior to the sale. See *Murphy* v. *Crain*, 12 Tex. 297 (1854).

of mental weakness than he bargained for or intended to purchase," but the evidence was that he had gotten just what he wanted.[7]

Texas courts thus appear to have balanced the rights of sellers and buyers of slaves so that both parties to such transactions, especially if they gave primary attention to the actual condition of the property involved, were legally protected. The courts afforded even more certain protection to slaveholders who suffered property losses due to the actions of others. This was especially true in the many cases that arose from the slave-hire system. In one of the earliest decisions rendered by the state supreme court, Henry Mims won damages from Isaac N. Mitchell because the latter had hired his slave girl and mistreated her so badly that she died. Justice Royal T. Wheeler, in rendering what became a landmark decision, wrote: "The hirer of a slave is bound to observe towards the slave the same care which a discreet, humane and prudent master would observe in the treatment of his own slaves." This general concept was later extended to cases in which hired slaves were killed while performing duties not "normally" performed by bondsmen, cases in which an overseer or foreman rather than the actual hirer was responsible for the loss, and cases in which the hired slave died as a result of being moved to a less healthy climate. The court even ruled for the owner in a case that rose from a hirer mistreating a slave so badly that he ran away and was killed later while breaking into a house. Justice Wheeler concluded that the "wrongful" mistreatment led to the loss so the hirer was responsible. In short, owners who hired out their slaves could be certain that their property interests were protected.[8]

Property rights in slaves were even protected by law against losses resulting from action by the state. An act of January 24, 1852, permitted masters to collect indemnities for any slave convicted and executed for committing a capital offense, provided that the owner did not try to "evade or defeat the execution of the law." The jury that convicted the

---

7. *McKinney v. Fort*, 10 Tex. 220 (1853); *Nations v. Jones*, 20 Tex. 300 (1857). A general warranty of soundness did not cover defects that were plain and obvious to the purchaser. See *Williams v. Ingram*, 21 Tex. 300 (1858).

8. When a man named Philips captured a runaway belonging to O. M. Wheeler and then used the slave to clean out a well during which job the bondsman was accidentally killed, the owner successfully sued for damages (*Philips v. Wheeler*, 10 Tex. 536 [1853]). *Mims v. Mitchell*, 1 Tex. 443 (1846); *Clark v. Southern Pacific Railroad*, 27 Tex. 100 (1863); *Sims and Smith v. Chance*, 7 Tex. 561 (1852); *Mills v. Ashe*, 16 Tex. 295 (1856); *Echols v. Dodd*, 20 Tex. 191 (1857); *Pridgen v. Buchannon & Others*, 24 Tex. 655 (1859); *Robinson v. Varnell*, 16 Tex. 382 (1856).

slave assessed his value, not to exceed $1,000, and the state treasury paid one-half of it to the owner. The legislature appropriated $5,000 to support this act, and the fund was used. Apparently no one appreciated the irony of treating slaves as human enough to be responsible for their crimes and property enough to be paid for when destroyed by execution for capital offenses. In fact, there was an attempt in 1857 to extend compensation to the owners of bondsmen "executed by the people without the authority of law"—i.e., those who fell victim to mob action. The Texas senate rejected this idea, however, because, as a committee report put it, such a law "would encourage our citizens to take the law into their own hands, whenever inclination, passion or prejudice may prompt them." Owners who lost slaves to mob action were advised to turn to the courts for redress.[9]

In addition to guaranteeing the right to own slaves and protecting property rights in bondsmen, the law of slavery had to define and prohibit criminal interference with the institution. Stealing or enticing away slaves was one such offense that drew attention from the outset. In December, 1836, the first congress of the republic made it a felony punishable by death to steal a bondsman or entice him into leaving his master. This draconian penalty was reduced in 1840 to thirty-nine lashes and a prison sentence of one to five years. Further revisions of the penal code during the 1850s eliminated whipping as part of the punishment but broadened the offense to include attempts at stealing or enticing away slaves as well as the acts themselves. The penalty for this crime in 1860 was a prison sentence of five to fifteen years. In a similar vein, the law also provided that any boat captain who carried a slave away from his home county without his owner's permission could be sent to the penitentiary for ten to thirty years.[10]

Harboring a runaway bondsman also became a crime very early in the development of Texas' slave code. An act of January, 1839, provided punishments for this offense, ranging up to a $1,000 fine and a year in jail. Although these penalties were changed from time to time, the law remained in force and was broadened to include simply concealing fugitives and advising or aiding slaves to run away. In 1860 the offenses of

9. Gammel (comp.), *Laws of Texas*, III, 911–12, 1454; *Journal of the Senate of Texas; Seventh Biennial Session* (Austin, 1857), 255–57.

10. Gammel (comp.), *Laws of Texas*, I, 1247, II, 240, III, 1511; Oldham and White (comps.), *Digest of the General Statute Laws*, 540.

harboring or concealing runaways drew only a $100 to $500 fine, but re-
peat offenders could be sentenced to three to ten years in the penitentiary. The first conviction for aiding or advising bondsmen to run away
merited a similar sentence.[11]

Unauthorized trading with slaves was defined as a criminal offense in
February, 1840. Throughout the remainder of the antebellum period, any
person who bought valuable produce or articles from a slave without the
written consent of his or her owner was liable to a fine of as much as
$200. Liquor dealers who sold or gave their wares to bondsmen without
written approval from their masters were subject to the same penalty.[12]

Aiding or inciting a slave insurrection was not defined specifically as
a crime until surprisingly late in the development of Texas' slave code.
An act of December, 1837, provided the death penalty for free blacks
found guilty of "insurrection, or any attempt to excite it," but no law
encompassing whites as well as blacks and specifying aiding, planning,
or inciting a *slave* rebellion was passed until 1854. The crime was punishable by death until a revision of the state's penal code in 1858 reduced the
penalty to a prison sentence of ten years to life. "Insurrection of slaves"
was defined as an "assemblage of three or more, with arms, with intent
to obtain their liberty by force." After 1858 the law also provided a penalty of five to fifteen years in prison for any person who tried to render a
slave "discontented with his state of slavery."[13]

A good many Texans ran afoul of one or the other of these laws
against criminal interference with slaves. The Texas State Penitentiary in
1856–57, for example, had eighteen inmates serving sentences for "Negro Stealing" or "Enticing Away Negroes." State supreme court reports
indicate that others escaped prison only through technicalities. James
Cain, "yeoman" of Fayette County, had his conviction for slave stealing
reversed because the word "feloniously" was omitted from his indictment. Samuel Lovett of Upshur County was convicted of enticing away a
slave on the testimony of individuals who overheard him talking to the
bondsman in December, 1856, about the possibility of leaving the follow-

11. Gammel (comp.), *Laws of Texas*, II, 46–47, 650; Oldham and White (comps.), *Digest of the General Statute Laws*, 541.

12. Gammel (comp.), *Laws of Texas*, II, 345–46; Oldham and White (comps.), *Digest of the General Statute Laws*, 542.

13. Gammel (comp.), *Laws of Texas*, III, 1511; Oldham and White (comps.), *Digest of the General Statute Laws*, 539. Oliver C. Hartley (comp.), *A Digest of the Laws of Texas* (Philadel-phia, 1850), the most recent digest made before a general revision began in the mid-1850s, had no law specifying penalties for inciting slave insurrection.

ing spring. Justice Royal T. Wheeler reversed the district court on the grounds that such a discussion so far before the fact did not constitute an actual effort or an attempt by Lovett to commit the offense in question.[14]

Records of the various district courts across Texas also reveal case after case arising from violations of the laws against interfering with slaves, especially the offenses of selling liquor to bondsmen or buying from them without the consent of their owners. Thomas Kerchoff of Red River County, for example, was found guilty in 1860 on three counts of selling liquor to a slave and fined $20 on each charge. J. and N. Alexander of Smith County were each fined $25 for buying corn from one of D. R. Jeffries' slaves without his written consent. Convictions of this sort were also appealed at times to the supreme court, which showed the same concern for procedures that it demanded in cases involving more serious offenses. When S. M. Kingston of Gonzales County appealed a conviction for buying five chickens from a slave, Justice James H. Bell, noting that the eighteen-year-old son of the bondsman's owner was present at the transaction and that the indictment did not specify "written" permission, remanded the case to the lower court. John M. Allen won a similar reversal on a charge of selling liquor to a slave when Chief Justice Hemphill ruled that, since no money had changed hands, the whiskey was a gift, and gifts of liquor from whites to blacks were not illegal.[15]

Laws governing the conduct of bondsmen were also an essential part of Texas' slave code. An act of December, 1837, made insurrection, poisoning, rape of a white female, assault on a white with intent to kill, maiming a white person, arson, murder, and burglary into capital offenses if committed by a slave. All other crimes and misdemeanors "known to the common law of England" committed by slaves could be punished at the discretion of county courts "so as not to extend to life or limb." These lesser offenses did not require grand jury action, but a jury trial was mandatory. Any slave who used "insulting or abusive language" to a white person could be arrested by a justice of the peace and punished by twenty-five to one hundred lashes. In 1840 Congress provided that slaves could not carry a gun or deadly weapon without the written per-

14. *Report of the Directors, Superintendent and Agent of the Texas Penitentiary for the Years 1856 and 1857* (Austin, 1857), 44; *Cain v. The State,* 18 Tex. 387 (1857); *Lovett v. The State,* 19 Tex. 174 (1857).

15. Red River County District Court Minutes, Book F; Smith County District Court Papers, Case #706; *Kingston v. The State,* 25 Supp. Tex. 166 (1860); *Allen v. The State,* 14 Tex. 663 (1855).

mission of their owners. Any white person could take such weapons away from a bondsman who did not have the proper authorization.[16]

After 1845 the Texas legislature simply built upon the republic's laws defining criminal conduct by slaves and setting the penalties for those crimes. By 1860 the state's penal code provided only two punishments for bondsmen: death and whipping. Death by hanging was the punishment for those who committed murder, insurrection, or arson; rape or attempted rape of a white woman; and robbery, assault with the intent to commit murder or robbery, or assault with a deadly weapon on a white person. Lesser offenses such as petty larceny, public drunkenness, and insolence to a white person were punishable by whipping. All capital offenses were tried in district courts while lesser crimes went to justices of the peace. In any case involving an offense greater than the theft of property worth less than twenty dollars, slaves had the right to a jury trial. Slaves could not be held as accessories to crimes committed by their masters, and they were not responsible for offenses occurring while they were under their owner's supervision or control. Anytime, however, that bondsmen acted outside the immediate custody of their masters they were legally responsible for their acts.[17]

Undoubtedly many slaves were punished by their masters without regard to the law, especially in cases of minor violations, but it was not uncommon for bondsmen to be tried in court. Justice of the peace courts heard cases involving lesser offenses and at times handed out severe penalties. A Polk County slave, for example, accused in 1856 of stealing a bell and rope worth two dollars and injuring a mare, was found guilty of the first charge and innocent of the second. His punishment, set by the justice, was thirty lashes by the county sheriff. A Hunt County jury in January, 1856, directed that a slave found guilty of larceny be given "76 stripes well laid on." In one Smith County justice court, a slave named Charles received a jury trial because he was accused of stealing property valued at more than twenty dollars. He was found guilty and sentenced by the jury to be given "three hundred lashes on his bare back to be well laid on

16. Gammel (comp.), *Laws of Texas*, I, 1385–86, II, 346.

17. Oldham and White (comps.), *Digest of the General Statute Laws*, 482, 559, 562; *Guffey v. Moseley*, 21 Tex. 408 (1858); *Ingram & Wife v. Atkinson & Wife*, 4 Tex. 270 (1849). It must be remembered that laws concerning offenses by slaves gave masters a great deal of latitude in punishing their slaves without going to any other authority. This will be dealt with below in chapter 7.

with a leather strap in such manner as not to inflict great bodily injury." It is difficult to imagine just how the sheriff complied with this order. In a similar case in 1860, Governor Sam Houston intervened to abate the severity of punishment. E. V. Stanley's slave, Abe, found guilty of burglary, was sentenced to 750 lashes to be administered at stated intervals over a period of time, but Houston pardoned him before the full penalty was exacted.[18]

Bondsmen who committed more serious offenses against whites often were dealt with by lynch law. The Austin *Texas State Gazette* expressed approval of this form of "justice" in October, 1860. "A negro has been arrested for a rape on a respectable white lady," the editor wrote. "We expect he has been hung up a tree before this." Lynchings were common enough that Texas newspapers reported at least three in 1859 alone. At Smithfield, Tarrant County, in May, one of James Roper's slaves, angered because his master did not buy his wife in Alabama and bring her to Texas, killed Roper and burned his body. Local whites forced the slave to confess and then burned him on the same spot. A similar incident occurred in Polk County during May or June. In Hopkins County, after a slave was arrested for the attempted rape of a white woman, a mob broke into the jail and hanged him.[19]

Lynch law did not always prevail, however. Two slaves who murdered their owner, William Gaffeney, near Clarksville in April, 1853, were duly tried, sentenced, and executed according to the law. The two were valued at $1,879.16 by the jury that sentenced them to death. When three of Richard S. Bostick's slaves killed him in January, 1858, they met the same fate as Gaffeney's bondsmen. Following their execution in October, the administrator of Bostick's Jackson County estate subtracted $3,100, the appraised value of the three males aged forty-six, thirty-five, and twenty-five, from the property under his control. Peter, a sixteen-year-old boy from Red River County, also received a procedurally correct, albeit very swift, application of the law in early 1859. Accused of killing his mistress,

18. Polk County Justice of the Peace Records, JP Book, Precinct 4; Hunt County Commissioners' Court Minutes, Book A-1, pp. 96–97; Smith County Justice of the Peace Papers, Case #25; Amelia W. Williams and Eugene C. Barker (eds.), *The Writings of Sam Houston* (8 vols.; Austin, 1938–43), VIII, 3.

19. Austin *Texas State Gazette*, October 20, 1860; Enda Junkins, "Slave Plots, Insurrections, and Acts of Violence in the State of Texas, 1828–1865" (M.A. thesis, Baylor University, 1969), 50–51; Matagorda *Gazette*, July 23, 1859.

he was indicted on January 6, tried and found guilty on the twelfth, sentenced on the seventeenth, and hanged on the twenty-eighth. The jury that found Peter guilty fixed his value at $800.[20]

The case of Dave, a Smith County bondsman accused of assault with intent to commit murder, demonstrates a concern for procedures that was not uncommon when slaves committed serious offenses. A grand jury sitting at Tyler on June 4, 1861, indicted Dave for an April 15 assault on the son of his master, William C. Gober. Dave had stabbed Young Gober, who was "then and there a free white person," three times "with a certain knife then and there being held in the hands of him the said . . . slave." The attack with a deadly weapon had so injured its victim that "the life of him the said Gober was despaired of." Dave had a court-appointed attorney and entered a plea of not guilty. District Judge R. A. Reeves conducted his trial and at the conclusion charged the jury as follows:

> If the jury believe from the evidence that the defendant assaulted Young Gober with a knife as charged in the indictment and that it would have been murder if death had been the result, the assault is deemed in law to have been made with intent to commit that offense and the punishment is death. And if you find the defendant guilty as charged in the same indictment, return a verdict accordingly. If you find him not guilty so say by your verdict. If you have a reasonable doubt of his guilt, he is entitled to the benefit of such doubt and to an acquittal. If you find him guilty of the assault to murder you will also assess his value and state whether his owner has attempted to evade the law against the negro.

The jury found Dave guilty and set his value at $1,000. Dave's attorney appealed for a new trial, but Judge Reeves denied the motion and imposed the death sentence. Dave was hanged on July 11, 1861, on a gallows erected within the Smith County jail. In April, 1862, William C. Gober collected $500 from the state comptroller.[21]

20. Clarksville *Northern Standard*, April 9, June 4, 11, 1853, January 29, 1859; San Antonio *Herald*, October 20, 1858; Estate of Richard S. Bostick, Jackson County Probate Records (Final Estate Record); Red River County District Court Minutes, Book F.

21. Smith County District Court Papers, Case #754. The voucher for $500 paid to Gober is in the Papers of the Comptroller of Public Accounts, Texas State Library and Archives, Austin. Young Gober was twenty years old in 1860. He survived the attack and still lived in Smith County at the census of 1870. Eighth Census, 1860, Schedule 1 (Free Inhabitants);

Although a strong presumption of guilt was apparent, slaves charged with offenses against whites were not always found guilty and punished. The case of Elizabeth, who belonged to James Threatt of Robertson County, provides a good example. When her owner's young son disappeared in June, 1863, Elizabeth and another slave named Ned were beaten with a rope to extort information or confessions. Ned claimed that Elizabeth had put the child in a well, whereupon she said he was lying and took witnesses to the child's badly bruised body in a pond of water near the master's home. Ned and Elizabeth were indicted for murder. He, having met his death shortly thereafter (another lynching?), was not tried, but Elizabeth was convicted. Her court-appointed lawyer appealed to the Texas supreme court and won a new trial. Justice Moore ruled that the evidence obtained after coercion was admissible in court but concluded that it did not sustain a murder verdict. Elizabeth's cognizance of the child's murder and the body's hiding place "does not prove that she killed it," he wrote, "or was an accomplice in its being done." Once the case was remanded to Robertson County and then moved to Falls County on a change of venue, she was found not guilty. Pompey, a slave in Wharton County, won an acquittal on charges of attempting to poison his master after telling the jury how harshly he had been treated. A Burleson County bondsman received a full pardon from Sam Houston in 1860 after "sundry Citizens" petitioned the governor to explain that the assault which led to a death sentence had taken place "under peculiar and aggravated Circumstances" and left "no permanent injury."[22]

There were also cases in which slaves were prosecuted for capital offenses against their fellow bondsmen. When, for example, Jack was accused of killing his wife Nicey in Guadalupe County, a jury convicted him and imposed a death sentence. His case was appealed to the state supreme court in 1861 on several grounds, including the failure of the jury to set his value. Justice James H. Bell, however, denied the validity of the appeals and confirmed the district court's decision. Nels and Calvin were more fortunate than Jack. Nels, convicted of murder in Red River County in 1846, won a reversal because the jury in his trial had not been

Ninth Census of the United States, 1870, Schedule 1 (Inhabitants), National Archives, Washington, D.C.

22. *Elizabeth, A Slave* v. *The State*, 27 Tex. 329 (1863); Falls County District Court Minutes, Book B, Case #288; Annie Lee Williams, *A History of Wharton County, 1846–1961* (Austin, 1964), 106; Williams and Barker (eds.), *Writings of Houston*, VIII, 86–87.

sworn. Calvin, a Rusk County bondsman, was convicted in 1858 after his indictment was altered during the trial to clarify ownership of the victim and how she had died. Justice Bell found this procedure too improper to support a conviction. "The law of the case," he wrote, "is precisely the same as if the accused were a free white man, and we cannot strain the law 'in the estimation of a hair,' because the defendant is a slave." [23]

Many offenses by slaves against fellow blacks probably went without formal prosecution because owners feared the loss of valuable property to criminal punishment. This possibility is suggested in an interesting case that came to the supreme court in 1866, the year after emancipation in Texas. Mary and Maria, who belonged to B. D. Arnold of McLennan County, had quarreled in October, 1863, over the need to punish Maria's child, who supposedly had told a lie on Mary. According to witnesses, Mary smacked the child, whereupon Maria screamed: "You whip my child, God drast your eyes! I will kill you!" and stabbed her with a butcher knife. Mary lived for a month after the attack but died on November 29, 1863. Maria was not indicted for any crime for two years, probably, in the words of the statement of facts presented when the case finally came to the supreme court in 1866, because her master "was unwilling to incur the additional loss of punishing the murderer by law." A similar case apparently occurred in Washington County during 1857. The administrator of the Elisha D. Little Estate informed the probate court that a man named Anderson was unmanageable and had committed an offense "which if prosecuted would have forfeited his life." This report did not specify that Anderson's offense was against another black, but that was likely. [24]

Laws concerning runaways constituted a fourth aspect of Texas' slave code. An act of February, 1841, gave all Texans the lawful right and responsibility to apprehend runaway slaves and take them before a local justice of the peace. The runaway was then returned to his owner, if known, or jailed. If, after six months, during which time notices were to be placed in local newspapers, the slave had not been claimed, he was to

23. *Nels, A Slave* v. *The State*, 2 Tex. 280 (1847); *Calvin, A Slave* v. *The State*, 25 Tex. 789 (1860); *Jack, A Slave* v. *The State*, 26 Tex. 1 (1861).

24. *Maria, A Freedwoman* v. *The State*, 28 Tex. 698 (1866); Estate of Elisha D. Little, Washington County Probate Records (Final Record, Book G). The law providing compensation for owners who lost their property due to capital punishment by the state also indicated an awareness that masters might attempt to evade such punishment and losses. As noted above, compensation depended on the owner's having made no attempt to evade the law.

be sold at auction. However, if the original owner appeared and proved title to his property within the next three years, he was to receive the amount paid for the slave. By 1844, when the number of bondsmen escaping to Mexico had become troubling to slaveholders, the state congress made it legal for anyone capturing runaways west of the San Antonio River to demand a fifty-dollar reward for each plus two dollars for every thirty miles traveled to return them to the rightful owner.[25]

Laws established under the republic concerning the capture and disposal of runaways remained in effect through the statehood period, as did the system of special rewards for the capture of slaves west of the San Antonio River. In 1858 the state legislature, upset at the number of slaves escaping to Mexico and the Mexican government's refusal to respond to the situation, passed a measure entitled "An Act to Encourage the Reclamation of Slaves Escaping Beyond the Limits of the Slave Territories of the United States." This act entitled any person who captured a slave attempting such an escape and delivered his captive to the sheriff of Travis County at Austin to a payment from the state treasury amounting to one-third of the slave's value. The state would recover its costs either from the slave's master when the property was reclaimed or from the sale of the slave. The wording of this measure was such that it did not call for capturing slaves who had escaped to Mexico—only those who were "escaping." But this was a nicety that might easily have been overlooked by zealous slave catchers.[26]

In May, 1846, the Texas Legislature took an important step toward stronger enforcement of the various laws protecting slavery—those dealing with criminal interference by free persons and with runaways as well as those regulating slave conduct—by creating a formal slave patrol system. The law directed county courts to appoint a patrol consisting of a captain and as many as five privates for each "district or division" in the county. One-half of the members of a patrol were to be slaveholders. Their period of service was three months, and they were required to patrol their district at least once a month "and as much oftener as the tranquility thereof may require." Patrols were empowered to search suspected places for harbored or runaway slaves. If they captured a runaway, patrol members divided the fees that would have come to any in-

25. Gammel (comp.), *Laws of Texas*, II, 345–46, 950–51.

26. *Ibid.*, IV, 1074–75; Oldham and White (comps.), *Digest of the General Statute Laws*, 407–409.

dividual "for similar services." Any white person found associating with slaves without the permission of their owner was to be taken before a justice of the peace to be fined (five to fifty dollars) and imprisoned (up to thirty days). Slave patrols became a feared part of life for bondsmen. The role of "patterollers," as slaves called them, will be discussed further in chapter 9.[27]

One final protection for slavery involved the harsh constitutional and statutory restrictions on free Negroes in Texas.[28] The Constitution of 1836 provided that free blacks could not reside in the republic without permission of congress. In June, 1837, a congressional joint resolution permitted all free blacks who were in Texas at the time of the declaration of independence to remain "as long as they choose." The number was not large, probably no more than 150. However, another act on February 5, 1840, provided that after the passage of two years all "free persons of color" in Texas were to leave the republic. All who remained after that time, without the permission of congress, were to be sold as slaves. The law also prohibited immigration by free Negroes. Some free blacks received special exemption from the February, 1840, law, and in December, 1841, President Sam Houston granted a two-year extension of the "grace period" to all who requested the extra time. Nevertheless, the point was clear—free blacks were unwelcome in Texas. Those who were permitted to stay were often subjected to the same laws as slaves. For example, all the crimes such as insurrection, poisoning, or rape of a white female that were capital offenses if committed by slaves were to be punished in the same way if a free black was the offender. Free Negroes who stole or enticed away slaves or harbored runaways were to be fined an amount equal to the value of the slave or slaves in question. If the fine could not be paid, the offender would be sold as a slave for life.[29]

27. Gammel (comp.), *Laws of Texas*, II, 1497–1501.

28. For most of the antebellum period, any free person descended from Negroes, with one-fourth or more Negro blood, was considered a free black or "free person of color." Oldham and White (comps.), *Digest of the General Statute Laws*, 462. Early in 1858, however, the legislature amended the rule to define free persons of color as anyone with at least one-eighth African blood. Gammel (comp.), *Laws of Texas*, IV, 1115. No degree of diminution of Negro blood could result in freedom for a child born of a slave mother. *Gaines* v. *Ann*, 17 Tex. 211 (1856).

29. Gammel (comp.), *Laws of Texas*, I, 1292, 1385–86, II, 325–26, 468–69, 549–50, 789. The most thorough study of free blacks in Texas prior to 1845 is Harold Schoen, "The Free Negro in the Republic of Texas," *Southwestern Historical Quarterly*, XXXIX (1936), 292–308; XL

Discrimination against free Negroes would have been present, of course, on racist grounds alone; special regulations were common across the antebellum United States, North as well as South. But protection of slavery was the primary motive. Several members of the Texas senate made this quite clear during the debate in 1839 on a proposal to free Peter, a slave belonging to Wiley Martin, and allow him to remain in the republic. Peter had loyally aided the Texas revolution and accumulated a fortune of $16,000. Senator S. H. Everett, representing Jasper and Jefferson counties, opposed his manumission, calling it a bad precedent to allow a freed slave to stay in Texas. He would, he said, "take no hand in bringing destruction and bloodshed upon his country." Senator George W. Barnett agreed. Yes, he said, Peter should be rewarded for his help during the revolution "when this boy gratuitously furnished supplies," but not with freedom in Texas. With all his money, Barnett contended, Peter would cooperate with abolitionists, and "that would strike at the very root of our most useful domestic institutions, and at the peace and security of ourselves and our families." Peter eventually gained his freedom in 1842 and lived in the town of Richmond in Fort Bend County. He made a living as a peddler and cook, hired his wife from her master so that his family could be together, and lived a responsible life until his death in April, 1863. Of course, Peter Martin's example would hardly have reassured those who opposed his manumission. He had not cooperated with abolitionists or brought death and destruction to Texas, but he had demonstrated the validity of a slightly more subtle fear voiced by another of the senators who opposed his freedom. Manumission, he said, "sweeps from us our strongest ground, in refutation of the doctrine of the abolitionists, for we have always insisted that slaves and free negroes are incapable of self government."[30] Free blacks constituted a threat to one of

---

(1936), 26–34, 85–113; XL (1937), 169–99, 267–89; XLI (1937), 83–108. For the entire antebellum period, see Andrew Forest Muir, "The Free Negro in Jefferson and Orange Counties, Texas," *Journal of Negro History*, XXXV (1950), 183–206; and Andrew Forest Muir, "The Free Negro in Harris County, Texas," *Southwestern Historical Quarterly*, XLVI (1943), 214–38. For studies of one notable Texas free black, see Diane Elizabeth Prince, "William Goyens, Free Negro on the Texas Frontier" (M.A. thesis, Stephen F. Austin State College, 1967); and Victor H. Treat, "William Goyens," in Alwyn Barr and Robert A. Calvert (eds.), *Black Leaders: Texans for Their Times* (Austin, 1981), 19–47.

30. Harriet Smither (ed.), *Journals of the Fourth Congress of the Republic of Texas, 1839–1840* (3 vols.; Austin, 1929), I [Senate Journal], 63–64; Estate of Wiley Martin, Fort Bend County Probate Records (Probate Record, Book A); Seventh Census of the United States, 1850,

slavery's most basic assumptions, and the Republic of Texas generally treated them accordingly.

Statehood brought no significant changes in attitudes or practices concerning free blacks. The Constitution of 1845 created some confusion about their status by permitting manumission without specifying what was to become of the slaves thus gaining their freedom. But the supreme court ruled in 1854 that, in light of other restrictions in the constitution and in the laws of the republic, manumission could occur legally only when the slave in question was "sent without the limits of the state."[31] The court was notably careful of the rights of owners to manumit their slaves and of the rights of legally freed Negroes to maintain their freedom. The basic view of antebellum Texas justice toward blacks, however, was stated succinctly by Justice Oran M. Roberts in 1859: "Negroes are, in this country, *prima facie* slaves. While held as such, they are slaves *de facto*, whether *de jure* or not. If they are dissatisfied with their condition, and have a right to be free, our courts are open to them . . . to assert their right. As long as they fail to do so, they recognize this *status* as slaves." Any other doctrine, said Roberts, would confuse the "simplicity and certainty" necessary to both master and slave.[32]

The census of 1850 reported 394 free blacks (.19 percent of the whole population) in Texas, and that of 1860 enumerated only 355 (.06 percent of the total). An equal number of blacks, however, probably were not counted as free and perhaps not at all because they fell into a gray area between slavery and freedom. These were people such as a female slave who came to Texas with A. J. Hamilton in 1847, was set free by her master during the 1850s, then arrested for residing in the state as a free person without the legislature's permission, and finally allowed to choose Aaron Burleson as a "guardian" and remain in Travis County. The case of Jim Brigham provides another example. He bought freedom for himself, his

Schedule I (Free Inhabitants), National Archives, Washington, D.C.; Eighth Census, 1860, Schedule I (Free Inhabitants); *Becht* v. *Martin*, 37 Tex. 719 (1872–73).

31. *Purvis* v. *Sherrod*, 12 Tex. 140 (1854). This ruling was confirmed in *Armstrong* v. *Jowell*, 24 Tex. 58 (1859). Bequests of freedom were void, however, if they did not provide for the removal of the freed blacks from Texas. *Philleo* v. *Holliday*, 24 Tex. 38 (1859). In the years after statehood, the legislature did occasionally permit free blacks to remain in Texas. See Gammel (comp.), *Laws of Texas*, III, 1042, 1045, for the cases of Mary Madison and Thomas Cevallos.

32. *Boulware* v. *Hendricks*, 23 Tex. 667 (1859). For evidence of the court's respect for the rights of freed blacks, see *Moore* v. *Minerva*, 17 Tex. 20 (1856); and A. E. Keir Nash, "The Texas Supreme Court and the Trial Rights of Blacks, 1845–1860," *Journal of American History*, LVIII (1971), 622–42.

wife, and one of his children before the Civil War and lived as a free man in Hunt County. The commissioners' court of that county even appointed him as one of those responsible for upkeep of the Greenville-Paris road in 1859. Following the war, he helped found a town for freedmen called Neylandville. Jim Brigham does not appear in the census of 1860, and there is no indication that his residence in Texas had been approved by the state legislature, yet it is clear that he lived for years as a free black. There were also instances in which slaves were manumitted in their masters' wills but remained in Texas indefinitely after being emancipated. These former slaves could not own property and enjoy the other rights of free men so long as they lived in Texas, but they were not anyone's property either. The Rusk *Texas Enquirer* claimed in 1860 that Texas had 1,000 free Negroes, an estimate suggesting that this group, probably because of a failure to count those who were quasi-free, was more than twice as large as the census indicated.[33]

Free blacks, although constituting only a tiny fraction of Texas' total population even if all had been counted, still posed in the eyes of the Texas legislature a threat to slavery and to the belief that Negroes were fit only to be slaves. Accordingly, in January, 1858, the legislature passed a law permitting free persons of African descent to choose masters and voluntarily enslave themselves. Free Negroes over the age of fourteen could appear before a district court and, following an investigation by the district attorney to show that fraud or compulsion were not involved, become slaves for life. Children under the age of fourteen could become slaves with their mothers. Some free Negroes actually enslaved themselves under the terms of this act. Proslavery newspaper editors gleefully reported such cases as evidence that slavery was better than freedom for Negroes. District court records, however, give absolutely no hint as to the motivations of the blacks involved.[34] In any case, the legislature had

33. DeBow (comp.), *Statistical View of the United States*, 308–19; U.S. Bureau of the Census, *Population of the United States in 1860*, 486; *Am. Slave, Supp.*, Ser. 2, V, 1614–20 (James Grumbles); Cecil Harper, Jr., "Slavery Without Cotton: Hunt County, Texas, 1846–1864," *Southwestern Historical Quarterly*, LXXXVIII (1985), 399; Hunt County Commissioners' Court Minutes (Book A); Webb, Carroll, and Branda (eds.), *Handbook of Texas*, II, 278; *Webster* v. *Heard*, 32 Tex. 685 (1870); Rusk *Texas Enquirer*, quoted in Marshall *Texas Republican*, March 10, 1860. Ira Berlin, *Slaves Without Masters: The Free Negro in the Antebellum South* (New York, 1974), a very thorough recent study of the subject, does not mention free blacks in Texas, perhaps because so few were there.

34. Gammel (comp.), *Laws of Texas*, IV, 947–49. Free blacks could not voluntarily enslave themselves before this act in 1858. See *Westbrook* v. *Mitchell*, 24 Tex. 560 (1859). For examples of voluntary enslavement under the 1858 law, see Austin *Texas State Gazette*, December 11,

made its point of view clear: free Negroes constituted an unwelcome anomaly in Texas. Only a few would be allowed to remain in the state, and those would be encouraged to return to their "natural condition" as slaves.

Constitutional conventions, legislatures, and courts thus developed the body of law necessary to protect and regulate slavery in antebellum Texas. This slave code, written and interpreted largely by Anglo-Americans, drew its inspiration and precedents from practices in the southern United States, not from Hispanic America. The law of slavery was complex and sometimes curious primarily because bondsmen, as humans, could not be dealt with purely as private possessions. Slaves received some recognition of their humanity, but masters were assured even greater protection for their property.[35]

1858, June 4, 1859; Dallas *Herald*, February 2, October 26, 1859; La Grange *True Issue*, October 29, 1859; Smith County District Court Civil Minutes, Book D; Hunt County District Court Minutes, Book A; Barbara A. Ledbetter, "Black and Mexican Slaves in Young County, Texas, 1856–1865," *West Texas Historical Association Yearbook*, LVI (1980), 102. Berlin, *Slaves Without Masters*, 370–79, points out that there was an enslavement movement across the South during the late 1850s aimed at forcing free blacks either to accept bondage or leave the state.

35. Henson, "Development of Slave Codes in Texas," 91. Tushnet, *The American Law of Slavery*, analyzes the law of slavery from a Marxist perspective with the intent of determining if it was "slave" (precapitalist) or "bourgeois" (capitalist). He concludes that it does not fit perfectly into either category.

SIX

· · · · · · · · · ·

Work and Responsibility

"FROM CAN SEE TO CAN'T SEE"

Wesley Burrell, an aged former slave from Washington County, told a WPA interviewer in the late 1930s: "A White lady was here the other night wanted to know about slavery time and when I started to tell her she said she didn't want to hear that stuff. I told her the half hadn't been told if she didn't want to hear that, it wasn't nothing to tell." Obviously the old man was not talking about how slavery was established in Texas or about its expansion before 1861 or about its economic importance to the state. He was talking instead, from experience inside the institution, about what it was like to be a slave.[1] That was the vitally human aspect of the Peculiar Institution, and it had two dimensions—the physical and the psychological. The first is the subject of the next two chapters.

In one sense, of course, the physical conditions of servitude are insignificant. Slaves in Texas could have been worked lightly, afforded more than adequate food, clothing, and shelter, and rarely punished; and slavery would have been equally wrong. Jeff Hamilton, a slave who belonged to Sam Houston, made this point succinctly in his memoirs: "Human slavery was an awful thing, and it's a good thing it's been outlawed by civilized nations. Twas the feeling about it you had that you couldn't do what you wanted to and not so much the work, as my own work didn't amount to much, and the master and missus were sure good to me."[2] No set of physical circumstances could make slavery right; nevertheless,

1. *Am. Slave, Supp.*, Ser. 2, III, 537 (Wesley Burrell).
2. Jeff Hamilton, *My Master: The Inside Story of Sam Houston and His Times*, ed. Lenoir Hunt (Dallas, 1940), 22–23.

work loads, material conditions, and punishments determined the day-to-day existence of a slave.

Contemporary observers generally were eager to describe the physical conditions of slaves in Texas, but they presented strongly conflicting views. During the republic era, for example, William Kennedy and William Bollaert, both natives of the British Isles, emphasized the mild treatment accorded Texas slaves. "I can bear witness," Bollaert wrote, "that they are not over-worked, or ill used." In sharp contrast, the Englishman Nicholas Doran P. Maillard presented case after case of "heartless conduct" by slaveowners. And Carl, Prince of Solms-Braunfels, concluded that "in Texas as a whole I have noticed the treatment of the negro to be brutal and savage." Similarly conflicting views were typical after statehood, too. Frederick Law Olmsted found slavery unrelievedly brutal, whereas Jane McManus Cazneau (writing as "Cora Montgomery") sarcastically described the anger of a fellow traveler from Pennsylvania when he saw only "laughing, well-clad blacks" after being prepared to be "agonized by the shrieks and sufferings of the slaves."[3]

The problem with these contemporary views is that they were usually influenced by considerations other than simple observation. Bollaert, for example, held Texas bonds and was deeply interested in the republic's success whereas Maillard held Mexican securities and therefore could see horrors of servitude that not even Benjamin Lundy or Olmsted perceived. Some travelers became so disgusted from their experiences with inefficient and careless slave laborers that they began to "see" how the institution provided good treatment for an inferior race. In short, travelers' accounts often told at least as much about the observer as about the actual conditions of servitude.[4]

Fortunately, there is no need to rely solely on contemporary observers because better informed witnesses on the physical circumstances of slaves—the bondsmen themselves—left their testimony. Their stories might be expected to create a uniform indictment of the institution for day-to-day harshness, but they do not. Instead, the slaves themselves

3. Kennedy, *Texas*, 763; William R. Hogan, *The Texas Republic: A Social and Economic History* (Norman, Okla., 1946), 22; Nicholas Doran P. Maillard, *The History of the Republic of Texas: From the Discovery of the Country to the Present Time and the Causes of Her Separation from the Republic of Mexico* (London, 1842), 263–65; Prince Carl of Solms-Braunfels, *Texas, 1844–1845* (Houston, 1936), 53; Olmsted, *Journey Through Texas, passim*; Jane McManus Cazneau [Cora Montgomery], *Eagle Pass: or Life on the Border* (New York, 1852), 17.
4. Marilyn McAdams Sibley, *Travelers in Texas, 1761–1860* (Austin, 1967), 132–39.

provided striking evidence of widely varying experiences. Ben Simpson of Travis County, for example, called his master a "killer." On the way from Georgia to Texas, when Simpson's mother tired out from walking, the master shot her and left her body on the road. Later, he sexually abused Simpson's sister. After reaching their new home, Simpson and the other slaves were worked naked and kept chained to a tree at night. Their master married a young Mexican woman whom he whipped for feeding the slaves more than he wanted to give them. Simpson gained his freedom only after his owner was hanged as a horse thief. By contrast, Laura Cornish of Liberty County belonged to a man who would not permit his bondsmen to call him "master." Isaiah Day's slaves called him "papa." He never whipped his bondsmen and even bought those who ran away from other owners because of mistreatment. There was no work on his plantation on Saturday or Sunday or even on especially hot days. Cornish and the other slaves were told that they had white souls and were just "sunburnt" on the outside. When freedom came, none of Day's bondsmen left for at least two years. When Cornish's family finally moved, it was to land acquired from "Papa Day."[5]

The experiences of Ben Simpson and Laura Cornish probably represent extremes of the physical conditions of servitude in Texas. They also demonstrate the difficulties inherent in any attempt to generalize on this subject. A bondsman's physical circumstances varied according to the number of other slaves with whom he lived, the jobs he had to perform, and above all, the personality and character of his owner. As Prince Carl of Solms-Braunfels put it, "their welfare . . . depends on the whim and humor of their master." Jacob Branch, an ex-slave from Chambers County, was even more succinct. "The history of slavery . . . was pretty rough," he said. "Every plantation have to answer for itself." Nevertheless, with this caveat in mind, there must be an effort to balance all the individual cases in support of a reasonable generalization on the physical conditions of servitude in Texas. That can be done only through an examination of the work demanded of slaves, the material conditions of their daily lives, and the extent to which they suffered punishment and harsh treatment.[6]

The vast majority of Texas slaves lived in rural areas and did farm

5. *Am. Slave, Supp.*, Ser. 2, IX, 3549–55 (Ben Simpson), III, 937–43 (Laura Cornish). Isaiah Day paid taxes on fifty-two slaves in 1860. Liberty County Tax Rolls, 1860.

6. Solms-Braunfels, *Texas*, 51; *Am. Slave, Supp.*, Ser. 2, II, 410 (Jacob Branch).

labor. In both 1850 and 1860, approximately 94 percent of the state's bondsmen belonged to masters who reported agricultural occupations in the census. Only 6 percent were the property of non-farmers, and only a part of that small minority actually lived in towns. Most urban slaves, as would be expected, lived in small holdings of fewer than ten bondsmen. A majority in rural areas, however, belonged to individuals holding at least ten slaves. The percentage owned by small farmers having fewer than ten bondsmen declined from 38 to 29 percent of the total between 1850 and 1860, while approximately one-quarter (26 percent) belonged to small planters owning ten to nineteen slaves in both census years. The proportions held by medium (20 to 49 slaves) and large planters (50 or more) rose from 25 to 30 percent and 10 to 16 percent respectively during the decade.[7] In short, Texas slaves typically lived on at least a small plantation, and, therefore, their work patterns may be discussed primarily in terms of plantation labor.

Jacob Branch in recalling his youth as a slave on a farm near Double Bayou said, "Us ain't never idle." Given the annual agricultural cycle of plowing, planting, cultivating, and harvesting, he was guilty of very little exaggeration. Plowing usually began in January, and fields were bedded and ready for the planting of corn and cotton in February and March. Cultivation of both crops began shortly after the plants emerged from the soil. Cultivator plows broke the surface and took out grass and weeds between the rows, while hoes were used to work the earth around the plants and thin them to a "stand." Plowing and hoeing, especially of the cotton crop, went on into June. Corn matured during June and July, and slaves then pulled the ears and leaves off the stalks. Cotton picking began by early August and generally continued at least into December. By the time the last ginned and baled cotton went to market, it was time to begin plowing for another year.[8]

The cycle of labor associated with growing cotton and corn was only the beginning of the work required of agricultural slaves. First, lesser crops had to be cultivated. Farmers and planters generally grew black-

7. Campbell and Lowe, *Wealth and Power*, 43–45, 97, 99.

8. *Am. Slave, Supp.*, Ser. 2, II, 408 (Jacob Branch). The annual cycle of labor associated with growing cotton and corn is found in Lowe and Campbell, *Planters and Plain Folk*, 14–17, 21–22; Curlee, "Texas Slave Plantations," 154–74, 197–205; John B. Webster Plantation Journal; Thomas E. Blackshear Diary and Memorandum Books, Vol. 3 (Diary for 1859), in Thomas E. Blackshear Papers; Daily Journal for Sunset Plantation, 1860, in James B. and Virginia C. Billingsley Papers; John B. Walker Plantation Books, 1861–64, in Green C. Duncan Papers, all in Barker Texas History Center, University of Texas, Austin.

eyed peas, sweet potatoes, and garden vegetables. Some planted small grains, such as wheat, rye, and oats, too. Second, the livestock required attention. Work horses and mules were kept penned and had to be fed. Cattle and hogs were branded or marked, and hog killing was a major task every winter. Third, planters generally cleared new ground during the winter, and that involved cutting trees, splitting logs, grubbing undergrowth, and burning brush. Finally, myriad odd jobs and chores had to be done on every farm, such as cutting and splitting firewood, shelling corn, mending fences, digging drainage ditches, and maintaining wells.[9]

Most slaves, male and female alike, worked at both the cultivation of crops and everyday chores. Men handled the heaviest work, such as plowing, felling trees, and ditching, but women sowed corn and cotton seed, drove horses pulling harrows to cover the seed, and worked as hoe hands. Virtually all served as cotton pickers during the height of the season. Children worked from an early age, beginning with jobs like carrying water, gathering firewood, and knocking down old cotton stalks, and then, as they got a little older, had the responsibility for tending livestock. Most began to do some field work by the time they reached their teens. Jacob Branch remembered that "by the time us good sprouts us picking cotton" and contemporaries considered it remarkable that John Rugeley of Matagorda County did not send his children to the fields until they were fifteen.[10]

Slaves who did field work on farms and plantations generally remembered laboring from "sun to sun" or, as one put it, from "can see to can't see." The model plantation rules drawn up by Charles William Tait, a large Colorado County planter, indicate that the bondsmen were exaggerating very little. Tait called for his slaves to be prepared to work at sunrise during the months from April to October. This meant that in mid-July, for example, they were to be up and ready to go to the field by approximately 5:30 A.M. Tait did not specify a quitting time, but the sun does not set in Texas in mid-July until after 7:30 P.M. The day was broken by a "dinner" period of one to two and one-half hours, depending on the

9. Curlee, "Texas Slave Plantations," 205–11. All the plantation journals cited in note 8 also contain evidence on cultivating lesser crops, managing livestock, and chores.

10. The John B. Webster Plantation Journal is especially good in showing the variety of work done by men, women, and children. *Am. Slave, Supp.*, Ser. 2, II, 408 (Jacob Branch); Palm, "Slavery in Microcosm: Matagorda County," 60. On the work done by women and children, see Ann Patton Malone, *Women on the Texas Frontier: A Cross-Cultural Perspective* (El Paso, 1983), 34–38.

weather. Thus in mid-July, Tait's slaves worked about twelve hours a day in the fields. From October until April, the rules required slaves to begin work at daylight and take one hour off at midday. In Texas, sunrise in mid-January is around 7:30 A.M., and daylight comes approximately thirty minutes before that. Sunset is at 5:30 P.M. or so and reasonably good light lasts for another half hour. In mid-January then, the work day for Tait's slaves was about ten hours long.[11]

Tait's rules were only models, of course, and there was considerable variation among plantations and according to the season. For example, some slaves had time for breakfast after they began work. Others remembered being worked far harder than Tait's rules recommended. Martin Ruffin of Harrison County said that those who fed the livestock got up at 3 a.m. and the others at 4. They worked until "good dark." Wes Brady, also of Harrison County, remembered that "the overseer was straddle his horse at three o'clock in the morning, rousting the hands off to the field." He gave them fifteen minutes for "dinner" and whipped anyone who tried to take more time. Long hours were especially common during cotton-picking season. Slaves worked so late into the night that cotton had to be weighed in by candlelight. At other times, of course, the workday was reduced by inclement weather or less pressing seasonal demands for labor. In short, although agriculture has rarely offered the modern ideal of an eight-hour day to anyone, slave workers could expect to labor a good deal longer day after day throughout the year.[12]

Slaves did not generally do field work on Sunday. "The Sabbath is required to be respected as a day of rest," wrote one advisor on plantation management, and virtually all slaveowners agreed. Even those slaves who described unremittingly harsh conditions indicated that they usually had Sundays off. There were exceptions, however, to the general rule of rest on the sabbath during the busiest weeks of cultivating and picking cotton or grinding sugar cane. Lee Pierce, for example, remembered that when he worked for Henry Fowler of Hopkins County "us never stopped work no day, lessen Sunday, and not then if grass in the

11. For typical comments from slaves on their hours of labor, see *Am. Slave, Supp.*, Ser. 2, II, 12 (Will Adams), II, 96 (Lizzie Atkins), VII, 2640 (Susan Merritt), VIII, 3040 (Ellen Payne), VIII, 3377–78 (Martin Ruffin). Charles William Tait Papers, Barker Texas History Center, University of Texas, Austin. The times of sunrise and sunset are from Kingston (ed.), *1986–1987 Texas Almanac*, 86–87. Ashbel Smith's slaves "claimed" two hours at midday. John Bauer to Ashbel Smith, June 13, 1841, in Smith Papers.
12. Berleth, "Groce," 361–62; *Am. Slave*, Ser. 1, IV, Pt. 1, pp. 133–36 (Wes Brady), V, Pt. 3, pp. 265–76 (Martin Ruffin).

field or crops suffering." Working slaves on Sunday apparently became common enough that the state legislature, as part of a general "blue law" passed in December, 1863, made it illegal. Legislative piety did have limits, however, in that the law did not apply to sugar plantations during the cane-processing season or to "any work that may be necessary to save a crop."[13]

Some planters regularly allowed their bondsmen to stop field work at noon on Saturday, and others did so occasionally. Ashbel Smith's slaves "claimed," as one overseer put it, half the day for themselves, but by contrast Thomas E. Blackshear did not necessarily permit so much free time. He recorded on Saturday, June 11, 1859: "Finished hoeing 'grave yard' field and gave my negroes a part of the day." The entry of Saturday, July 11, however, read: "Put up fodder all day." H. R. Hardy, overseer on the Walker Plantation in Wharton County during 1864, handled the slaves under his direction in similar fashion. The entry for Saturday, April 30, in his "Daily Record" read: "Stayed work at 12 o'clock." Hardy's slaves also left the fields by noon on May 7 and May 21, but on June 4 he recorded: "Chopped cotton with all hands all day." A few slaves remembered Saturday as a day wholly free of farm labor for their master. Betty Bormer, who belonged to M. T. Johnson in Tarrant County, often went to Fort Worth on Saturday, and in Harrison County Dave Caven's bondsmen used the time to work their own small parcels of land. Hardy's entry concerning the Walker Plantation slaves for Saturday, June 25, 1864, read: "The Negroes working their own patches today."[14] Two-day weekends were far from typical, however.

In addition to Sundays, holidays provided a break in slaves' work routines. Gill Ruffin, who lived in Houston County, said he "didn't know any more about a holiday than climbing up a tree backward," but most slaves were more fortunate. Bondsmen traditionally did not work during the week from Christmas to New Year's Day. This was recognized even in hire contracts, which generally specified that individuals who were

13. Matagorda *Gazette*, April 16, 1859, quoted in Palm, "Slavery in Microcosm: Matagorda County," 144. For examples of slaves who faced harsh conditions but had Sunday off, see, *Am. Slave, Supp.*, Ser. 2, II, 6 (S. B. Adams), II, 397–401 (Wes Brady), VIII, 3093 (Lee Pierce). Gammel (comp.), *Laws of Texas*, V, 690.

14. Crystal Sasse Ragsdale (ed.), *The Golden Free Land: The Reminiscences and Letters of Women on an American Frontier* (Austin, 1976), 126–27; John Bauer to Ashbel Smith, June 13, 1841, in Smith Papers; Blackshear Diary and Memorandum Books, in Blackshear Papers; Walker Plantation Books, in Duncan Papers; *Am. Slave, Supp.*, Ser. 2, II, 342 (Betty Bormer), II, 12 (Will Adams), III, 939 (Laura Cornish).

hired out returned to their owners on December 25. There was time for slaves to rest, to have parties, to visit, and to go to nearby towns. Charles DeMorse of the Clarksville *Northern Standard* commented rather sourly in December, 1861, that Negroes enjoyed a longer vacation at Christmastime than whites had all year. He urged owners not to let their slaves go en masse to town during the week. The slaves' other major holiday, albeit only a single day, was July 4. Otis M. Wheeler of Coldspring described one such day off in a letter to his mother in 1860: "I am celebrating the 4th July today by sitting in the shade writing & listening to the shouts yells wild laughter of 40 negroes playing marbls & cutting all sorts of anticks in the yard & quarter." In 1858, when the fourth fell on a Sunday, John B. Webster's plantation journal for July 3 read: "Gave all hands a holiday." Some owners gave holidays when the cotton crop was "laid by" or when ginning and baling were completed for a year, but this was strictly an individual matter.[15]

A minority of the slaves who lived on farms and plantations were not field workers, at least not primarily. Instead, they spent most of their time at other jobs, many of which required special training and skills. Men worked as blacksmiths, carpenters, brickmasons, coopers, cobblers, tanners, and in the general repair of farm implements and machinery. The proportion of such workers among Texas' agricultural slaves cannot be determined with any precision, but it appears that most owners of ten or more bondsmen had at least a few engaged largely in nonfield labor. Abner Jackson's Lake Jackson Plantation, for example, had a blacksmith, two coopers, a carpenter, a brickmason, and an "engineer" among its eighty-eight slaves in 1862. In the same county, the inheritance of William Black in 1859 included only ten slaves, but one of them was a blacksmith valued at $3,000. The slave force on John B. Webster's Harrison County plantation included a brickmason and another man who spent most of his days working in the "shop." Matthew D. Ector, as administrator of the estate of Hugh W. Ector in Rusk County, placed three of his eight slaves "with the best carpenters the county could afford and this materi-

15. *Am. Slave, Supp.*, Ser. 2, VIII, 3377 (Gill Ruffin); Curlee, "Texas Slave Plantations," 275–77; John B. Webster Plantation Journal; H. McLeod to Stephen Perry, December 17, 1854, in James F. and Stephen S. Perry Papers, Barker Texas History Center, University of Texas, Austin; Lucadia N. Pease to Maria N. Moor, January 14, 1856, December 31, 1856, both in Pease-Graham-Niles Family Papers, Austin Public Library, Austin, Tex.; Clarksville *Northern Standard*, December 21, 1861; Otis Marshall Wheeler to "Dear Mother," July 4, 1860, in Turner Papers.

ally enhanced their value and skill as workmen." Several of these bonds-men later helped build a Presbyterian church in Henderson.[16]

Slave women worked as cooks, laundresses and ironers, seamstresses, and spinners and weavers. As in the case of skilled male workers, the proportions of females who did such work is impossible to determine. Most slaveholders, however, used slave cooks, and some larger planta-tions employed one for the owner's family, one for the overseer, and one or more for the slaves. Many of the women who worked at spinning and weaving did so at night after laboring in the fields during the day, al-though some practiced textile skills full time. Laura Cornish, for example, remembered that her mother "was the seamstress and don't do nothing but weave cloth . . . and make clothes."[17]

There were also nonfield workers who, without practicing any par-ticular skill, simply served in and around their owner's household. These included house servants, usually females, who waited on tables and did general chores. Men served as gardeners, hostlers, and carriage drivers. On the largest plantations, there were likely to be butlers and body ser-vants to the owner and his family. Although unskilled in the sense of having a trade, household slaves were specialized enough in their knowl-edge and services that they were not freely interchangeable with field workers. When, for example, Zachariah Abney of Harrison County died and his family moved off their plantation, the estate's administrator peti-tioned to sell one female house servant in part because she did not know

16. It is unfair, of course, to imply that field workers were totally unskilled. Working horses and oxen, for example, required training and some skill. S. M. Swenson indicated this in a letter of December 6, 1845, to John Adriance in which he commented disgustedly that one slave "has not sense enough to be fit for anything but a howhand[*sic*]." John Adriance Papers, Barker Texas History Center, University of Texas, Austin. Estate of Abner Jackson, Brazoria County Probate Records (Wills, etc., Book C); Estate of William Black, *ibid.*; John B. Webster Plantation Journal; Estate of Hugh W. Ector, Rusk County Probate Records (Probate Records, Book D). For examples of slave testimony concerning black craftsmen, see *Am. Slave, Supp.*, Ser. 2, III, 938 (Laura Cornish, whose father was a carpenter), IV, 1364 (Sarah Ford, whose father was a tanner and her uncle a shoemaker).

17. For examples of slave women who were cooks, see Clarksville *Northern Standard*, February 3, 1855, March 1, 1856, August 17, 1861. For female slave spinners and weavers, see John Michael Vlach, "Afro-American Folk Crafts in Nineteenth Century Texas," *Western Folklore*, XL (1981), 151–55; and *Am. Slave, Supp.*, Ser. 2, VII, 2516 (C. B. McRay), III, 937 (Laura Cornish); Walker Plantation Books, in Duncan Papers (which show a female weaver at work for the entire month of May, 1864). For general statements on work by females and their role as house servants, see Malone, *Women on the Texas Frontier*, 36–38, and White, *Ar'n't I A Woman?* 49–50.

how to work in the fields and was not needed in the home. By the same token, field hands could not step in effectively as gardeners or hostlers and carriage drivers.[18]

A few slaves, especially in southeastern Texas, spent most of their time as early-day cowboys. For example, Governor Francis R. Lubbock owned several bondsmen who were very good with the horses and cattle on his ranch near Houston. One, a man named Willis, had, as Lubbock put it, "a great desire to be free, so he could manage his stock to suit himself." Lubbock obliged by allowing the man to buy his freedom. James Taylor White, Texas' first "cattle baron," also used black drovers and handlers for the thousands of head of cattle he owned in the Atascosito District. Slave herders worked along the Gulf Coastal Plain as far to the southwest as Jackson County. In 1854 Amanda Wildy, as administrator of her husband's estate, explained to the court that she did not wish to sell any slaves or horses to pay debts because "it will require the service of the principal part of the horses and negroes to take care of and manage the stock of cattle." The estate had thirteen slaves, forty horses, and 2,800 head of cattle. There were few slave cowboys west of the Nueces River, partly because Mexican herders were numerous and partly because freedom in Mexico was too tempting to men with horses.[19]

Slaves who worked primarily at skilled occupations or as house servants had, in one sense at least, an easier daily routine than did the field workers. They did not work outdoors all day under the summer sun and in the winter cold, and their jobs generally were less burdensome physically. Leander H. McNeel of Brazoria County made this clear in his will, which directed that two of his bondsmen, probably elderly servants, were not to work in the fields but were to do only such "light jobs" as he had recently required of them. The hours of labor for nonfield workers, however, were equally long and in some cases probably longer than those

18. Lucadia N. Pease to Augusta N. Ladd, March 18, 1851, in Pease-Graham-Niles Family Papers, describes slaves who worked as cooks, waiters, and gardeners at her home in Brazoria. Estate of Zachariah Abney, Harrison County Probate Papers.

19. Terry G. Jordan, *Trails to Texas: Southern Roots of Western Cattle Ranching* (Lincoln, Neb., 1981), argues that Texas cattle ranching began in the southeastern part of the state. Philip Durham and Everett L. Jones, *The Negro Cowboys* (New York, 1965), 14–17; C. W. Raines (ed.), *Six Decades in Texas, or Memoirs of Francis Richard Lubbock, Civil War Governor* (Austin, 1900), 136–37; Partlow, *Liberty, Liberty County, and the Atascosito District*, 125, 127; Estate of Samuel Wildy, Jackson County Probate Records (Final Estate Records, Books C and D). Monroe Brackins of Medina County remembered working as a "horse breaker." *Am. Slave, Supp.*, Ser. 2, II, 378.

required of field hands. Craftsmen, livestock herders, and house servants worked at least from sun to sun, and it seems doubtful that the latter received much free time on Sundays and holidays either. Slaveowners and their families were not likely to cook, clean their houses, or drive carriages for themselves on the sabbath or during Christmas week when they were accustomed to being served by slaves the rest of the year.[20]

A small minority of the slaves in Texas, part of the 6 percent who did not belong to farmers or planters, lived in the state's towns and four fledgling cities. Most of the women were domestic servants. Men worked at a considerable variety of jobs. Some were laborers on the docks at Galveston and Houston, while others worked in brickyards and at cotton presses and warehouses. Bondsmen assisted masters who were craftsmen such as tailors and saddlemakers. Also, a good many apparently had personal service or skilled occupations. Henry Millard's will, for example, directed that his slave Philip, who was a barber in Galveston, continue in that occupation. The money he earned was to be used to pay Millard's debts. Slave men with skills in the use and repair of tools and machines were numerous enough that white mechanics in several towns lodged public protests. A Marshall Mechanics Association was formed in 1853 with the main purpose of preventing "as far as possible, mechanical labor by slaves, from coming in competition with that of white men." Five years later, the Houston Mechanics Association adopted a resolution "that we heartily deprecate the practice adhered to by some of *making contracts* with the negro mechanics to carry on work, *as a contractor*."[21]

Town slaves, much like their nonfield worker counterparts on farms and plantations, generally had somewhat better conditions of work day-to-day than did field hands. They had time off on Sundays, at least during the afternoon, and on holidays, and the urban setting afforded them an opportunity to get out and visit each other. Writing from Brazoria in 1851, Lucadia N. Pease noted that "Sunday is quite a holiday with the negroes who are all dressed in their Sunday best and walking the streets." Lieutenant Colonel Arthur J. L. Fremantle of Her Majesty's Coldstream Guards, describing a Sunday in Houston in May, 1863, wrote of "innumerable Negroes and Negresses parading about the streets in

20. Estate of Leander H. McNeel, Brazoria County Probate Records (Wills, etc., Book B).

21. Lack, "Urban Slavery in the Southwest," 30–33; Susan Jackson, "Slavery in Houston: The 1850s," *Houston Review*, II (1980), 79–82 (quotation from Houston Mechanics Association is on p. 81); Estate of Henry Millard, Williamson County Probate Records (Probate Minutes, Book 2); Marshall *Texas Republican*, June 18, 1853.

the most outrageously grand costumes." In Galveston's traditional May Day parade, slaves drove their owners' carriages and rode their horses. Bondsmen in towns were still slaves, but where occupations and work routines were concerned, few would have willingly changed places with their counterparts in the country.[22]

All Texas slaves, regardless of where they lived or what kind of labor they had to perform, worked under the ultimate supervisory authority of whites, either owners, hirers, or overseers. Some, however, held positions requiring them to take a great deal of responsibility for their own daily routines and even for the work of others. These bondsmen, although not typical, had a significant degree of influence on the physical conditions of servitude for themselves and others. As Rose Williams of Navarro County said of one such slave, "he was a little more important than the rest of us."[23]

A few slaves, in the absence of their masters, managed farms and plantations. Ashbel Smith's slave Peter, for example, took care of the plantation called "Headquarters" for a time in the early 1840s while Smith represented the Republic of Texas in Europe. Smith's cousin, Henry F. Gillette, wrote on July 4, 1844: "Old Peter is on the Bay [Galveston] and . . . has the finest crop ever raised on the place for this season of the year." B. L. Holcomb of Harrison County lived in Marshall during the early 1850s and left slave overseers in control of his two outlying plantations. The giving of such responsible positions to slaves apparently became common enough that some proponents of the Peculiar Institution found it disturbing. State Senator Henry E. McCulloch introduced a bill in 1858 "to prohibit the owners of slaves from placing them in charge of farm or stock ranches, detached from the home or residence of the owner or employer." This law eventually passed, but it did not necessarily stop masters from making their bondsmen into estate managers. Andrew Goodman of Smith County, for example, remembered being left in charge when his owner joined the Confederate army, and Mollie Kirkland's master appointed his "head slave," Henry Majors, overseer when he left. Majors ran the plantation just like the master, she said. Peter Marsh of

22. Lucadia N. Pease to Maria N. Moor, March 30, 1851, in Pease-Graham-Niles Family Papers; Walter Lord (ed.), *The Fremantle Diary, Being the Journal of Lieutenant Colonel Arthur James Lyon Fremantle, Coldstream Guards, on His Three Months in the Southern States* (Boston, 1954), 58; Fornell, *Galveston Era*, 116–17.

23. *Am. Slave, Supp.*, Ser. 2, X, 4126 (Rose Williams).

Smith County apparently also violated this law during the war. He was indicted for the offense, a jury sworn, and testimony given, but the district attorney then dismissed the case. How numerous slave overseers and managers were cannot be proven, but their use continued, it seems, even after the practice became illegal.[24]

Black "drivers"—that is, assistant overseers or foremen—were far more common than slave farm managers in antebellum Texas. James F. Perry, Thomas E. Blackshear, and J. W. Devereux, large planters whose extensive records have been preserved, all used slaves in positions of managerial responsibility. Devereux's man Scott worked directly under his master because the plantation had no overseer. In 1851 Lucadia N. Pease described Tom, one of her husband's thirteen bondsmen, as "the director of the other negroes at their work." Joseph McCormick of Brazoria County gave a slave named Mary authority over a work gang of other women and said that she had "intelligence and the bossing-faculty equal to her brother Joe, and was more trustworthy." Slaves themselves also testified to the frequent use of drivers. Charley Bowen, for example, said that his master used one driver for the hoe hands and one for the plow hands, and Bert Strong from Harrison County remembered how his master (Dave Caven) had fired a white overseer for "cutting and slashing" the slaves and made his uncle "overlooker." In another instance involving a black driver, the Matagorda *Gazette* informed its readers about a white man who spent the night at a plantation when no other whites were present. When he left he stole a pair of boots belonging to the black foreman who had permitted him to stay the night. The driver followed the thief to town and, with aid of a "young gentleman," recovered his boots. The editor probably told this story with the intention of showing fair treatment of the slave and apparently found it entirely unexceptional that a plantation would be left under his control in the first place.[25]

24. Henry F. Gillette to Ashbel Smith, July 4, 1844, in Smith Papers; Elizabeth Silverthorne, *Ashbel Smith of Texas: Pioneer, Patriot, Statesman, 1805–1886* (College Station, 1982), 66, 94; Joan M. Kahn, "Slave Labor on an Ante-Bellum Texas Plantation as Revealed in the Ashbel Smith Papers" (M.A. thesis, Columbia University, 1951), 25; Curlee, "Texas Slave Plantations," 111; *Journal of the Senate of Texas; Seventh Biennial Session* (1857), 380–81; *Am. Slave, Supp.*, Ser. 2, V, 1526 (Andrew Goodman), VI, 2240 (Mollie Kirkland), Smith County District Court Papers, Case #815.

25. Curlee, "Texas Slave Plantations," 113; Diary of J. W. Devereux, in Julien Sidney Devereux Papers, Barker Texas History Center, University of Texas, Austin; Lucadia N. Pease to Augusta N. Ladd, March 18, 1851, in Pease-Graham-Niles Family Papers; Brazoria County Tax Rolls, 1851; McCormick, *Scotch-Irish in Ireland and in America*, 151; *Am. Slave, Supp.*, Ser. 2, II, 347 (Charley Bowen), IX, 3756 (Bert Strong); Matagorda *Gazette*, May 21, 1859. B. E.

A good many slaves who were neither managers nor drivers also had special responsibilities placed on them from time to time. It was common, for example, for bondsmen to drive wagons and oxcarts to deliver cotton to shipping points and pick up plantation supplies. Stephen F. Austin's body servant, Simon, served the James F. Perry plantation in this capacity for years after his master's death in 1836. John B. Webster of Harrison County had several of his slaves haul cotton to the Southern Pacific Railroad in 1859 as the first step in reaching markets in New Orleans. Slaves from the Walker Plantation in Wharton County went to Eagle Lake in November, 1864, to sell hay and potatoes. During the spring of 1853, Felix W. Robertson trusted his slave John to drive a wagonload of cotton pulled by five yoke of oxen from Washington to Houston. John ran into trouble with another planter's overseer for taking down a fence in an effort to get his wagon out of a bog in the road and disappeared, either having run away or been killed. Robertson sued for damages and won in both the district court and, on appeal by the defendants, the Texas supreme court. Justice Royal T. Wheeler's opinion made it clear that the delegation of such responsibility to slaves was common enough to be legally acceptable. John, he said, had committed no trespass but had acted "necessarily, in the performance of his master's service, in the pursuance and execution of the authority and duty confided" to him.[26]

Otis M. Wheeler had one of his men stay at a place on the banks of the Trinity River two miles from the main plantation to tend livestock and keep fishing hooks and lines. "If we want fish or turtle," Wheeler wrote his mother, "it is only to send a little Negro at night & he returns in the morning with a horse packed." John B. Webster's brickmason, Richmond, was hired out on a daily basis throughout northeastern Harrison County. He went and came on his own. When J. B. Edwards of Marshall joined the army in 1862, he informed readers of the *Texas Republican* that his saddle shop would be run by "the boy HART" who will do work for "CASH, as he is unable to keep books."[27]

For some slaves, especially individuals with skills who lived in or near

Roper to Ashbel Smith, February 18, 1857, in Smith Papers, reported to Smith that the overseer at his Evergreen Plantation was not present when he (Roper) last visited. All was well, however.

26. Maddox, "Slavery in Texas," 42; John B. Webster Plantation Journal; Walker Plantation Books, in Duncan Papers; *Hedgepeth* v. *Robertson*, 18 Tex. 858 (1857).

27. Otis M. Wheeler to "Dear Mother," May 5, 1856, in Turner Papers; John B. Webster Plantation Journal; Marshall *Texas Republican*, March 15, 1862.

towns, it was only a short step from accepting responsibility for their work to taking the initiative in seeking employment and keeping some of their earnings. These bondsmen hired their own time; that is, they reached agreements with their owners whereby they paid a set amount per day or month and then found work for themselves at a higher rate. This practice had the double advantage of giving the slave greater control over the conditions of his employment and enabling him to keep some part of the proceeds. Owners permitted it because they received a cash income and were spared all the inconveniences of management. Many slaveholders, however, argued that allowing bondsmen to control their own time was permitting far too much freedom for individuals who were supposed to be slaves. There are no statistics to indicate just how many slaves actually hired themselves, but the practice had become enough of an issue by 1846 that the first legislature to meet after statehood passed an act to outlaw it. Slaves could not be permitted to hire their own time for more than one day a week except during the Christmas holidays. Owners who violated this law faced a $100 fine for every offense. It was to be enforced by arresting the offending slave and holding him until the owner paid the fine and all costs. If the owner did not appear within a set period, the slave was to be sold to the benefit of the county.[28]

This law was violated widely from the time of its passage. A German traveler commented in 1849 that slaves "often" carried on their own businesses by paying their masters a monthly sum. The Austin *Texas State Gazette* complained in July, 1851, that "nearly half the negroes in town hire their own time." Later that year, when the chief justice of Bexar County warned that he intended to enforce the law there, the *State Gazette*'s editor applauded and complained that "daily violations" continued in Austin. In 1856, the city council of Galveston passed an ordinance limiting the period that slaves could hire their own time to one week. This contradicted the state law's rule of one day per week, yet it was presented as a move to tighten restrictions on bondsmen in the city. The Clarksville *Northern Standard* also contained editorial warnings against the practice in 1856.[29]

28. Gammel (comp.), *Laws of Texas*, II, 1501–1504. Ashbel Smith permitted his bondsmen to hire their own time. See J. D. Groesbeck to Smith, March 12, 1841, Henry Gillette to Smith, July 10, 1843, both in Smith Papers. Gillette informed Smith that a female named "Easter" was doing well "on the Island." Sometimes she found it "difficult to pay her wages and house rent but some way always opens for her to get along."
29. Austin *Texas State Gazette*, July 19, September 13, 1851; Galveston *Weekly News*, October 7, December 9, 1856; Clarksville *Northern Standard*, December 20, 1856.

Slaves were able to continue hiring their own time because owners who found the practice advantageous generally escaped prosecution for violating the 1846 law. When efforts to use the statute occurred, the Texas supreme court found it virtually unenforceable. When the Travis County district court convicted Elijah Rawles of allowing a slave to hire his own time in 1855, he appealed. Justice Abner S. Lipscomb ruled that the law in question was "exceedingly awkward" in that it worked almost entirely upon the slave rather than the master. He found it unacceptable to take property without trial and then force an owner to pay to get it back. "It is very unfortunate that," he wrote, "on a subject of so much interest and importance, in regulating and keeping under proper discipline our slaves, there should be such imperfect legislation." Rawles's conviction was reversed, and the case dismissed. Two years later, J. M. Anderson of Guadalupe County won a similar dismissal. Citing *Rawles* v. *The State*, Justice Oran Roberts said that the offense was not indictable. Not surprisingly, owners continued to let some bondsmen hire themselves so long as slavery lasted in Texas. In 1863, for example, W. D. Williams of Liberty County, in appointing Pryor Bryan his agent, explained that two of his men were hiring their own time. John lived in Houston and paid $25 per month, while Dirk was "employed on the cars between Houston and Orange" and also paid $25 monthly. "They have never observed strict regularity in paying their monthly wages," Williams wrote, "and in case they should be behind time with you I would not urge payment if it was likely they needed money to defray their necessary expenses."[30]

Thousands of ordinary bondsmen, although not in positions of responsibility and unable to hire their own time, nevertheless had opportunities to work for themselves and be paid for their labor. This circumstance arose primarily from the widespread practice of giving slaves a plot of land, in some cases as much as an acre per family, to cultivate for themselves. Bondsmen generally worked their crops during their time off from regular labor. Ashbel Smith specified that his slaves were to have one-half of every other Saturday for this purpose, and the Matagorda *Bulletin* told about a bondsman who produced five hundred bushels of sweet potatoes and two hundred bushels of corn by working "after his usual task." Some bondsmen, either because their hours were so long or

30. *Rawles* v. *The State*, 15 Tex. 581 (1855); *Anderson* v. *The State*, 20 Tex. 5 (1857); Appointment of Pryor Bryan as agent for W. D. Williams, January 2, 1863, in Watson A. Neyland Collection, Sam Houston Regional Library and Research Center, Liberty, Tex.

they were so eager to produce, were highly inventive in making time to work their plots. Ben Chambers of Jasper County described how his fellow slaves erected five-foot high scaffolds and built fires on them to provide light to work by at night.[31]

Slaves generally used their patches to grow cotton, which they sold to their master or had him sell for them. Some earned significant sums. Bondsmen on Julien S. Devereux's Monte Verdi plantation in Rusk County received $737.05 for their crops in 1850. After Devereux died in 1856, his widow continued the practice. Her slaves sold 20,158 pounds of seed cotton worth $403.16 in 1857. The administrator of Charles K. Reese's Matagorda County estate reported in January, 1860, that he had "paid the Negroes on the Plantation for their cotton [5 bales]." Smaller earnings were common. The bondsmen on James W. W. Cook's estate in Rusk County earned $16.90 for cotton in 1854, and those belonging to Robert Ligon in Smith County received $32.50 in 1856. John R. Hill kept a ledger entitled "Negro Accounts" showing the amounts earned by each of his slaves. For example, Edmund earned $68.96 between December, 1861, and early 1864, while Dick Little received $81.93 during the same period.[32]

Slaves also earned small sums from a wide variety of other activities. Some kept hogs and chickens and sold meat and eggs. There were masters who paid for extra work at the height of the sugar or cotton harvest. Benjamin Decherd of McLennan County paid one of his slave women ten dollars to take care of two very young children who were orphaned when their mother died. The administrator of Charles K. Reese's estate reported

31. Abigail Curlee, "The History of a Texas Slave Plantation, 1831–1863" *Southwestern Historical Quarterly*, XXVI (1922), 109; Evergreen Plantation Purchase Ledger, in Smith Papers; Christopher C. Goodman to Brother, June 8, 1855, in Frances Jane Leathers (ed.), "Christopher Columbus Goodman: Soldier, Indian Fighter, Farmer, 1818–1861," *Southwestern Historical Quarterly*, LXIX (1966), 359; Matagorda *Bulletin*, October 18, 1838; *Am. Slave, Supp.*, Ser. 2, III, 672 (Ben Chambers). J. S. Wilson, M.D., advised readers of the Matagorda *Gazette*, June 20, 1860, to give their slaves time to work their "patches." For an example of an overseer who followed this advice, see Walker Plantation Books, in Duncan Papers.

32. Dorman H. Winfrey, *Julien Sidney Devereux and His Monte Verdi Plantation* (Waco, 1962), 75; L. D. Sanders v. Sarah A. Devereux, 25 Supp. Tex. 1 (1860). For examples of slaves who grew cotton on their patches, see *Am. Slave, Supp.*, Ser. 2, III, 672 (Ben Chambers), VII, 2603–2604 (Louisa Matthews), II, 284 (Charlotte Beverly), VI, 2300 (Lu Lee); Estate of Charles K. Reese, Matagorda County Probate Records (Inventory Record, Book A-2); Estate of James W. W. Cook, Rusk County Probate Records (Probate Record, Book D); Estate of Robert Ligon, Smith County Probate Papers; Ledger Book, in John R. Hill Papers, Barker Texas History Center, University of Texas, Austin.

in 1860 that he had "paid Alex Ewing's Negro woman for attending two Negro women in childbirth . . . $10." His accounting for 1863 carried the entry: "To cash pd. Negro boy Joe for catching Horace when run-away—$10." William J. Herndon paid a man $2.50 for finding a lost horse belonging to an estate in Matagorda County.[33]

Texas slaves had no legal right to the crops produced on their patches or to the money earned from the sale of those crops or other goods and services. State law required bondsmen to have written permission from their masters in order to sell any goods or produce. Chief Justice Royal T. Wheeler of the state supreme court emphatically explained how they had no title to earnings in *Sanders* v. *Devereux*: "The right to private property belongs, in this country, exclusively to freemen. The slave is denied the right as completely as he is the right of personal liberty. His person and his time being entirely the property of his master, whatever he may accumulate by his own labor, or may otherwise acquire, becomes immediately the property of his master." Fortunately for the slaves, most owners did not push their property rights to the legal limits; bondsmen who earned money generally kept and spent it.[34]

In summary, the majority of Texas slaves worked on farms and plantations. Men, women, and children shared, as their physical capabilities permitted, in clearing and improving land, cultivating field crops and gardens, tending livestock, and performing necessary chores. Inclement weather and slack seasons undoubtedly gave some relief from labor, as did the common practice of allowing bondsmen to have Saturday afternoons and Sundays as free time; nevertheless, long hours of hard and monotonous work were the rule. A sizable minority of slaves, perhaps 10 to 20 percent of the total, served as skilled hands or house servants or lived in towns. They enjoyed an advantage over field hands in that their work generally was less physically burdensome, but in many cases they

33. Lucadia N. Pease to Maria N. Moor, March 30, 1851, in Pease-Graham-Niles Family Papers (descripton of buying eggs and poultry from a slave); Ashbel Smith notebook, November 10, December 25, 1853, in Smith Papers; Estate of Eudocia C. Holder, McLennan County Probate Records (Probate Records, Book C); Estate of Rowland Rugeley, Matagorda County Probate Records (Inventory Record, Book A-2); Estate of Charles K. Reese, Matagorda County Probate Records (Inventory Record, Book A-2); Estate of H. J. Powell, Matagorda County Probate Records (Inventory Record, Book A-2).

34. Oldham and White (eds.), *Digest of the General Statute Laws*, 542; *L. D. Sanders v. Sarah A. Devereux*, 25 Supp. Tex. 1. For examples of slaves being allowed to keep money they earned, see *Am. Slave, Supp.*, Ser. 2, II, 12 (Will Adams), II, 284 (Charlotte Beverly), VI, 2300 (Lu Lee). The uses that Texas slaves made of their money will be discussed below in chapter 7.

probably worked longer hours under closer supervision by whites. Some Texas bondsmen held positions of responsibility, and a few were even able to take the initiative in determining the work that they did. Many had the opportunity to earn at least a little money of their own. Unremitting labor and the acceptance of responsiblity, however, did not necessarily earn satisfactory material conditions and decent physical treatment for all Texas slaves.

SEVEN

· · · · · · · · · ·

Material Conditions and Physical Treatment

"A TIGHT FIGHT"

The Republic of Texas had no constitutional or statutory provisions concerning the material conditions of slaves' lives. This circumstance changed, however, with the Constitution of 1845, which empowered the state legislature to pass laws requiring the masters of bondsmen "to provide for their necessary food and clothing." On the basis of this provision, the legislature defined the failure to supply a slave "with comfortable clothing, or a sufficient quality of wholesome food" as "cruel treatment," a criminal offense punishable by a fine of $100 to $2,000.[1] Definitions of "comfortable," "sufficient," and "wholesome" were highly debatable, however, so material conditions did not depend primarily on enforcement of these legal protections. Instead, except in the most extreme cases, the quality of food, shelter, clothing, and medical care was left to the discretion of individual slaveowners.

Common sense and direct evidence both suggest that the majority of slaves in Texas had at least an adequate supply of food. In the first place, bondsmen represented the single largest investment most slaveholders had. Questions of humanity aside, it was simply a matter of economic

1. The first draft of the constitution for the Republic of Texas had provisions concerning the treatment of slaves, but those protections were removed in the final draft (see chapter 2). The provisions on the material conditions of slaves in the first state constitution are in Gammel (comp.), *Laws of Texas*, II, 1296. Statutory provisions at the close of the antebellum period are in Oldham and White (comps.), *Digest of the General Statute Laws*, 542.

self-interest to heed the advice printed in the Matagorda *Gazette* that "an abundance of good and wholesome food should always be on hand to supply the wants of each and every slave." Second, Texas' farms and plantations grew large quantities of food crops, which, since the state did not export such produce, must have been available to feed the bondsmen. Finally, the slaves themselves did not commonly complain of being poorly fed. In a sample of 181 former slaves interviewed during the 1930s, 58 percent remembered having good or adequate food, while less than 5 percent said that they had not had enough to eat.[2]

Corn and pork were the main components of slave diets. C. William Tait's "Plantation Rules," for example, called for giving every working hand two and one-half to three and one-half pounds of bacon a week and a peck of meal. If other foods were available, these rules provided for less pork and corn to be given, but bacon and meal were the essentials. Most former slaves who commented on their food remembered eating, as Wes Brady of Harrison County put it, "fat pork and cornbread." Tesban Young said that her master had "hogs on top of hogs . . . for to make the meat." She had no illusions as to his motive: "The master says, 'the nigger must have plenty of food . . . for to work good.' "[3]

Pork and corn were thus central to the Texas slave's diet, but great variety existed beyond these two staples. In addition to hog meat, bondsmen at times also had fresh or dried beef, poultry, and wild game, including venison, turkey, rabbit, squirrel, and opossum. Slaves themselves provided some of the poultry and much of the wild game as well as fish from the state's rivers and streams. Owners generally put in gardens for their slaves and also encouraged them to grow vegetables on part of the small plots allotted to them. Sweet potatoes, black-eyed peas (cowpeas), watermelons, and turnips were grown almost like field crops on larger plantations. Molasses generally provided sugar in the slave diet. Milk was the most common drink, although coffee was not uncommon. Some-

2. Matagorda *Gazette*, April 16, 1859, quoted in Palm, "Slavery in Microcosm: Matagorda County," 144. Production of food crops in Texas is discussed above in chapter 4. The sample of 181 Texas slave narratives is described above in chapter 3, note 4. The other 37 percent of the narratives either did not mention food or gave no opinion concerning it. The economic condition of many elderly blacks during the Great Depression when the interviews were conducted may have contributed to their positive memories of the food available during slavery times. Nevertheless, their testimony cannot be totally discounted.

3. "Plantation Rules," in Tait Papers; *Am. Slave*, Ser. 1, IV, Pt. 1, pp. 133–36 (Wes Brady), V, Pt. 4, pp. 235–36 (Tesban Young).

times masters provided coffee, and sometimes slaves had to provide it for themselves. Wheat flour, regarded as a great delicacy, was one food item that bondsmen almost never had, unless they bought it with their own money.[4]

The manner of distributing and preparing food varied from one owner to another. Most common, it seems, was the method suggested in Tait's "Plantation Rules." A week's supply was distributed according to the needs of each slave, and the bondsmen then did their own preparation. This created problems at times because, as Betty Powers put it, a week's rations "am not enough for heavy eaters and we has to be real careful or we goes hungry." Moreover, the distribution of food by the week required that female slaves, after a day's work, spend additional time cooking a meal. To avoid these problems, some planters had all food prepared at one central kitchen and apportioned among the bondsmen. This was the practice at Jared Groce's Bernardo plantation and James F. Perry's Peach Point even during the 1830s and apparently became more common by the 1850s. Lewis Jones remembered that on the Fred Tate place in Fayette County all the slaves ate together in a hall with long tables.[5]

Some slaves suffered from not having enough food to provide the energy to work. Betty Powers, who described the problems "heavy eaters" had making their food ration last all week, said that "them short rations causes plenty trouble, because the niggers has to steal food and it am the whipping if they gets catched. They am in a fix if they can't work for being hungry, because it am the whipping then, sure, so they has to steal, and most of them did and takes the whipping, they has the full stomach anyhow." Annie Row said that she had been so hungry as a child that she took food away from a dog and was whipped for it. Most slaves, however, remembered having at least an adequate amount of food, and many described it as good. Bert Strong, after describing the variety of things to

4. Curlee, "Texas Slave Plantations," 243–50; Berleth, "Groce," 361–63; John B. Webster Plantation Journal; Lucadia N. Pease to Maria N. Moor, March 30, 1851, in Pease-Graham-Niles Family Papers. For examples of slave comments on food variety, see *Am. Slave, Supp.*, Ser. 2, VIII, 3377 (Gill Ruffin), VIII, 3041 (Ellen Payne), IX, 3756 (Bert Strong), VIII, 3093–94 (Lee Pierce), III, 897–98 (Andrew Columbus), III, 670 (Ben Chambers). Slaves on the Charles K. Reese plantation earned $200 for their cotton in 1859 and spent $44 of it for a sack of coffee and two barrels of flour. Estate of Charles K. Reese, Matagorda County Probate Records (Inventory Record, Book A-2).

5. "Plantation Rules," in Tait Papers; Curlee, "Texas Slave Plantations," 250–53; *Am. Slave*, Ser. 1, V, Pt. 3, pp. 190–91 (Betty Powers); *ibid., Supp.*, Ser. 2, VI, 2108–14 (Lewis Jones).

eat on Dave Caven's plantation, concluded: "That am good food, too. I ain't never hope to see no better food than that."[6]

The quality of a diet, of course, does not depend solely on the amount of food or its energy-producing content. The matter of nutrition must also be considered. A diet too dependent on pork and corn can provide enough calories for workers and yet be seriously deficient in necessary vitamins and minerals. Undoubtedly weaknesses of this sort existed in the diets of Texas slaves and, for that matter, of whites as well, since all ate essentially the same foods prepared in the same way. The magnitude of nutritional deficiency in the slave diet does not appear, however, to have been great in Texas. Extensive evidence, much of it provided by the bondsmen themselves, indicates that their diets were notably varied. This was, to some extent, a seasonal matter since many vegetables and fruits could not be preserved for the winter, but sweet potatoes, a highly nutritional food, and black-eyed peas could be, and winter is a relatively short season in much of Texas. The growing season in a coastal county like Matagorda is 296 days, and even in Bowie County in northeastern Texas plants can be cultivated 235 days of the year.[7]

In sum, Texas slaves generally had a diet that was adequate to provide the energy to work and the nutrition necessary for health. This was recognized even by some who disdained slavery and knew that no amount of food could make the institution right. As the German traveler W. Steinert put it in 1849: "I admit that the lot of many Negroes with regard to eating and drinking is much better than that of many factory workmen in Germany, but man does not live by bread alone."[8]

Slaves' housing was generally far less satisfactory than their food supply. William Fairfax Gray was appalled at conditions on an Oyster Creek plantation when a norther blew through in April, 1837. "The log huts of the poor negroes are more open than the log stable in Virginia," he wrote, "and some of them have no chimneys." Frederick Law Olmsted

6. *Am. Slave*, Ser. 1, V, Pt. 3, pp. 190–91 (Betty Powers), V, Pt. 4, pp. 70–72 (Bert Strong); *ibid.*, *Supp.*, Ser. 2, VIII, 3368–79 (Annie Row).

7. For an interesting discussion of the slave diet, see Richard Sutch, "The Care and Feeding of Slaves," in David *et al.*, *Reckoning with Slavery*, 231–301. This essay was written to refute the claims made by Fogel and Engerman in *Time on the Cross* concerning the quality of the slave diet. For a more balanced discussion of this subject, see Boles, *Black Southerners*, 88–96. Kingston (ed.), *1986–1987 Texas Almanac*, 247, 328, provides information on growing seasons.

8. Gilbert J. Jordan (ed. and trans.), "W. Steinert's View of Texas in 1849," *Southwestern Historical Quarterly*, LXXXI (1977), 65.

described how Sabine County slaves lived in ten-foot square log cabins with no windows and the cracks barely chinked. Most slaves had little good to say about their housing. For example, Wash Anderson of Orange County said: "The slaves just had little log huts. There weren't no floors to them, nothing but the ground. Them little huts just had one room in them." John Barker compared his home to a "chicken house." Exceptions, such as Anthony Christopher who belonged to Charles Patton of West Columbia, remembered having brick quarters with wood floors. But only one-quarter of a sample of 181 slave narratives described good or adequate housing, whereas one-quarter were noncommittal or remembered it as poor and one-half did not comment.[9]

Slave quarters ranged in size from one or two cabins on some farms to virtual small villages on the large plantations. Jared Groce's bondsmen lived in a row of houses facing a lake three-quarters of a mile from the plantation home, and William T. Scott quartered his more than one hundred slaves in cabins built around a hollow square. Each slave family generally had a separate cabin measuring approximately twenty by twenty feet square. Some families were very large, however, and there were cases in which more than one family was put under the same roof. The only standard pieces of furniture in slave cabins were beds, generally attached to the walls. Any tables or benches were provided by the bondsmen themselves. Most had a fireplace for heat and for cooking. Windows had shutters and no glass. In short, slave housing was likely to be crowded, ill-furnished, and very cold or hot depending on the season.[10]

Texas planters were warned that the "white-wash brush should be seldom idle or cease its work of purification." Some followed this advice, at least in a general way, if not with whitewash specifically. Tait's "Plantation Rules" called for inspection of cabins every Sunday. Thomas E. Blackshear's diary entry for May 28, 1859—a Saturday—read: "Gave my negroes half of to-day to scald their houses." Since cleanliness was only

9. Allen Charles Gray (ed.), *From Virginia to Texas, 1835: Diary of Col. Wm. F. Gray Giving Details of His Journey to Texas and Return in 1835–1836 and Second Journey to Texas in 1837* (Houston, 1909), 228; Olmsted, *Journey Through Texas*, 18–19. Emma M. Altgelt, a German pioneer woman, described slave housing on a farm near San Antonio in 1855 as "huts," in Ragsdale (ed.), *Golden Free Land*, 140. *Am. Slave, Supp.*, Ser. 2, II, 167 (John Barker), III, 719 (A. Christopher).

10. Curlee, "Texas Slave Plantations," 237–38; H. G. Smith to Ashbel Smith, January 7, 1850, in Smith Papers; *Am. Slave, Supp.*, Ser. 2, X, 4317 (Tesban Young), VIII, 3136 (Betty Powers).

a matter of common sense, it seems likely that most made some provisions in this respect. Evidence is very limited, however.[11]

The housing in which most Texas slaves lived was at best uncomfortable. In extreme weather, especially during winter northers, it was probably inadequate. The rest of the time, it was barely adequate as a shelter from the elements, and slaves apparently felt that there was little they could do to effect improvements.

Slave clothing did not compensate for barely adequate housing. Texas bondsmen typically received new clothes twice a year. Men usually received two pairs of pants, two shirts, a hat, and a pair of shoes in the spring. Women were given two dresses, two chemises, and a pair of shoes. Children wore only long shirts or frocks and had no shoes until they worked in the field. Clothing for the winter was the same, with the addition of coats or jackets for men and women who worked in the fields. Men received hats, but apparently women did not. Some owners provided handkerchiefs, but there is virtually no evidence of slaves having underwear or socks.[12]

Cloth for slave clothing had to be cheap and durable. A great deal of homespun was used, much of it made by the slaves themselves, but manufactured fabrics were common, too. Slaveholders brought lowell, a light cotton material, for summer clothing, and linsey, a heavier combination of wool and cotton, for winter outfits. Kersey, a woolen fabric, was used for winter pants and coats. Osnaburg, a heavy cotton product later used for upholstery and drapes, was also imported in large quantities by some slaveholders. Of these fabrics, linsey and osnaburg are both described as "coarse," and only the light cotton lowell was likely to have been at all comfortable. "Negro shoes," as they were called, were commonly called brogans or russet shoes from the color of the leather. They were notoriously rough and stiff, and apparently no effort was made

11. Matagorda *Gazette*, April 16, 1859, quoted in Palm, "Slavery in Microcosm: Matagorda County," 144; "Plantation Rules," in Tait Papers; Diary for 1859, in Blackshear Papers.

12. Curlee, "Texas Slave Plantations," 255–56; Estate of Wiley W. Pridgen, De Witt County Probate Records (Final Record, Book B); Estate of William Steen, De Witt County Probate Records (Final Record, Book A). All show slaves receiving two outfits twice a year. Some received only one outfit at a time. See Estate of Thomas Saunders, Washington County Probate Records (Final Record of Estates, Book B); Walker Plantation Books, in Duncan Papers. Many slaves commented on the quantity of their clothing. See *Am. Slave, Supp.*, Ser. 2, II, 175–76 (Joe Barnes), IX, 3756 (Bert Strong), X, 4216 (Rube Witt). For evidence on handkerchiefs and underwear, see Daily Journal for Sunset Plantation, in Billingsley Papers; *Reavis v. Blackshear*, 30 Tex. 753 (1868).

to determine the sizes needed by different individuals. Shoes generally were imported from manufacturers, but most owners, even if they bought cloth, had their slaves' clothes made on the farm or plantation where seamstresses were concerned with function rather than style. It was virtually impossible, too, to keep clothes clean. With only two outfits and no time except Saturday afternoon or Sunday to do washing, most slaves probably wore clothing that was not only coarse and without any style but dirty, too.[13]

In some particular cases, of course, slaves were extremely well dressed. The German traveler, Steinert, rode on a stagecoach from New Braunfels to Austin with a slave woman who wore a blue dress with white floral designs and white lace trim and a white silk hat with a black veil. She also wore gloves and carried a white parasol. It was his opinion that she dressed so well because her master wanted to make a "show." Bondsmen in Galveston often dressed in their owners' old finery for Sunday afternoons and other special occasions. Lucadia N. Pease described how the bride of one of her husband's slaves wore a dress of white muslin with red ribbons. In contrast, some slaves had little or almost nothing to wear. The administrator of Catherine A. Paulk's estate in Brazoria County reported in 1862 that her slaves "were almost destitute of clothes when they came into his possession." He hired them out to raise money to buy clothing. Criminal charges were brought against James Steen of Smith County in 1848 for mistreating three of his slaves in several ways, including working them in the fields virtually naked. None of these circumstances could be considered typical, however.[14]

Bondsmen were decidedly unhappy with their clothing. Slightly fewer than one-quarter of a sample of 181 remembered it as good or adequate,

13. Curlee, "Texas Slave Plantations," 260, 257. Materials to make slave clothing are mentioned in the following estate records: Estate of Rowland Rugeley, Matagorda County Probate Records (Inventory Records, Book A-2); Estate of Alfred H. Devereux, Grimes County Probate Records (Probate Minutes, Book N); Estate of George W. Cannon, Cherokee County Probate Records (Probate Minutes, Book F); Estate of George W. Hadnot, Jasper County Probate Records (Probate Minutes, Book C). For information on an attempt to manufacture material for slave clothing in Texas, see Campbell, *Southern Community in Crisis*, 76–77. Maddox, "Slavery in Texas," 64–65; Clarksville *Northern Standard*, September 18, 1852; "Plantation Rules," in Tait Papers; Diary for 1859, in Blackshear Papers; *Am. Slave, Supp.*, Ser. 2, IX, 3756 (Bert Strong).

14. Jordan (ed. and trans.), "Steinert's View of Texas in 1849," 408–10; Fornell, *Galveston Era*, 116–17; Lucadia N. Pease to Maria N. Moor, March 30, 1851, in Pease-Graham-Niles Family Papers; Estate of Catherine A. Paulk, Brazoria County Probate Records (Wills, etc., Book C); Smith County District Court Papers, Case #43.

while others were more negative, had no opinion, or simply did not mention the subject. Many slaves used money earned from their own small crops and other extra work to purchase additional clothing and shoes. Their clothing, like their housing, was barely adequate, but they were able to do more about what they wore than where they lived.[15]

Texas slaves suffered from a great variety of illnesses and injuries. They were beset by, to give a partial list of sicknesses, chills and fevers, colds and pneumonia, intestinal disorders, rheumatism, and several dreaded contagions including cholera and yellow fever. Childbirth was dangerous to slave women, and children suffered from whooping cough and other childhood diseases. Accidental injuries also were common among field workers. There were cuts, burns, broken bones, hernias, and snake bites. John B. Webster's journal for his plantation worked by about sixty slaves reported that at least a few were sick or "laying up" virtually every day in 1858 and 1859. All illnesses and injuries caused suffering and sometimes death; diseases like cholera could decimate an entire plantation. For example, an outbreak in the area of Columbus in Colorado County during 1850 reportedly killed thirty-three bondsmen on one plantation, sixteen on another, and nine on a third. Another outbreak in 1852 claimed the lives of thirteen slaves on John Hume's place near Huntsville and eight on Bolton's plantation in Wharton County. Hume's seven-year-old son and Bolton's overseer and his son died, too. The administrator of Mary A. Ewing's plantation in Matagorda County reported that the "bloody flux" (probably cholera) had killed eleven bondsmen in the spring of 1864 and that "no human precaution could have avoided it."[16]

Slaves had many health problems, but they did not generally suffer from a lack of medical attention. Masters and mistresses did much "doctoring" themselves, and a few overseers may have believed that holding down medical costs was part of their job. However, the evidence is over-

15. Curlee, "Texas Slave Plantations," 109–10; Winfrey, *Julien Sidney Devereux*, 75.

16. Curlee, "Texas Slave Plantations," 263–64, 266–68; John B. Webster Plantation Journal. For examples of concern over chills and fever along the coast, see Estate of Lewis M. Mayes, Colorado County Probate Records (Probate Records, Book D); Estate of Wiley W. Pridgen, De Witt County Probate Records (Final Record, Book B). For examples of accidents, see Estate of J. R. Davis, Grimes County Probate Records (Probate Minutes, Book N) (slave killed by runaway horse); Estate of E. M. Hill, Brazoria County Probate Records (Wills, etc., Book C) (slave ruptured); James Perry to Stephen Perry, February 29, 1844, in Perry Papers (slave killed at press). P. A. Davenport to John Adriance, August 6, 1850, in Adriance Papers; Estate of Mary A. Ewing, Matagorda County Probate Records (Inventory Record, Book A-2); *Young* v. *Lewis*, 9 Tex. 73 (1852).

whelming from plantation journals, probate records, and slave narratives
that serious illnesses and injuries were treated by doctors. Julien S.
Devereux regularly paid physicians for treating slaves, as did James F.
Perry. The latter sent one favorite house servant to a clinic in Houston
when she developed breast cancer. From there, she was transferred to a
hospital in New Orleans and surgery performed. All the attention was in
vain, however, as the woman died several years later. Estate administrators and guardians made annual reports showing large sums spent on
doctors and medicines. The estate of Sarah Droddy in Milam County paid
doctors $48 for treating a thirty-year-old woman in 1845 and $55 for the
woman and her child in 1846. The administrator of John G. Rives's estate
in Cass County, which had forty slaves, paid $140.65 in doctors' bills for
the first ten months of 1846. William J. Blocker's family owed a Harrison
County doctor $335 in 1864, nearly all as a result of attention to their
slaves. Estate after estate reported paying doctors and midwives to assist
in the delivery of slaves' babies. Bondsmen themselves remembered being visited by doctors. They had no illusions as to the role of self-interest
as well as humanity in their treatment. Armstead Barrett of Walker
County said: "Old Massa have doctor for us when us sick. We's too valuable." William Byrd was more succinct: "We too valuable to die." [17]

Slaves did not lack for medical attention; the problem was the state of
medical science in antebellum Texas. Physicians, regardless of their educational backgrounds, simply did not know very much. Some still used
treatments such as bleeding, cupping, and blistering, and most were
powerless against many of the diseases and internal injuries that afflicted
slaves. Inadequate medical science obviously took its toll on whites as

17. Curlee, "Texas Slave Plantations," 271–73; Maddox, "Slavery in Texas," 67–69.
Lucadia Pease told her sister in 1851: "I practice physic without having received a diploma."
Pease to Augusta N. Ladd, March 18, 1851, in Pease-Graham-Niles Family Papers. Winfrey,
Julien Sidney Devereux, 75; Estate of Sarah Droddy, Burleson County Probate Records (Probate
Minutes, Book 1); Estate of John G. Rives, Cass County Probate Records (Final Record Pro-
bate Court, Book 1); Estate of William J. Blocker, Harrison County Probate Papers. Examples
of estates reporting doctors and midwives assisting in the delivery of babies include: Estate
of Joseph Stevens, De Witt County Probate Records (Final Record, Book C); Estate of C. N.
Breen, Williamson County Probate Records (Probate Minutes, Book 3R); Estate of Charles H.
Whitaker, McLennan County Probate Records (Probate Records, Book B); Estate of G. W.
Hadnot, Jasper County Probate Records (Probate Minutes, Book C); *Am. Slave, Supp.*, Ser. 2,
II, 197 (Armstead Barrett), III, 578 (William Byrd), II, 146 (Henry Baker), V, 1910–14 (Nancy
Jackson). It was possible to obtain life insurance on slaves. James Morgan insured a sixteen-
year-old boy for $800 with the British Commercial Life Insurance Company in 1853. The
policy, which cost $33.25, is in Morgan Papers.

Table 13. Distribution of White and Slave Populations According to Age, 1850 and 1860

Ages	Slaves		Whites	
	Number	Percent	Number	Percent
1850				
0–9	19,061	32.8	50,158	32.6
10–14	8,243	14.1	19,802	12.9
15–49	28,093	48.3	75,449	50.0
50–65	2,080	3.6	6,610	4.3
65+	684	1.2	2,015	1.3
1860[1]				
0–9	59,474	32.7	136,880	33.0
10–14	24,782	13.6	52,913	12.8
15–49	88,614	48.8	199,606	48.1
50–65	6,459	3.6	19,412	4.7
65+	2,289	1.3	5,727	1.4

[1]In 1860 the total population figures included 948 slaves and 6,353 whites who were the result of estimates by census takers. No ages were available for these individuals.

well as blacks, but slaves generally had less adequate material conditions, did heavier work, and therefore suffered from more diseases and injuries. Still, their life expectancy, as it can be measured roughly from census reports, was only slightly lower than that of whites. In both 1850 and 1860, the proportions of the slave and white populations that fell into five age categories ranging from childhood (0 to 9 years) to old age (65 and over) were very comparable (see table 13). Whites who lived to be fifty or older were less than 2 percent more of the whole white population (5.6 percent in 1850 and 6.1 percent in 1860) than were similarly aged blacks as a part of its slave population (4.8 percent in 1850 and 4.9 percent in 1860).[18]

Every bondsman in Texas knew that the material conditions of servitude were vitally important; for many, punishment and cruel treatment held nearly equal significance. The constitution of the republic had no provi-

18. For examples of treating slaves with bleeding, blistering, etc., see Estate of Sarah Droddy, Burleson County Probate Records (Probate Minutes, Book 1). Age distributions are in DeBow (comp.), *Statistical View of the United States*, 52–53, 89–90; U.S. Bureau of the Census, *Population of the United States in 1860*, 482–83.

sions concerning physical abuse, but in February, 1840, congress provided that anyone who "shall unreasonably or cruelly treat, or otherwise
abuse any slave" could be punished, upon conviction, with a fine of $250
to $2,000. Any person who murdered a slave or caused death through
cruel treatment was to be tried for a felony, as in any case of murder.
District judges were to enforce these provisions, but they were undoubtedly hampered by a law of December, 1836, that provided that blacks
and mulattoes could not be witnesses "in any case whatsoever, except for
and against each other." This was taken to mean that slaves could not
testify against whites, so cases involving the mistreatment of slaves depended solely on the willingness of whites to protect slaves against other
whites.[19]

The Constitution of 1845 permitted the legislature to pass laws requiring slaveowners "to treat them [slaves] with humanity" and to pass laws
requiring slaveowners "to abstain from all injuries to them extending to
life or limb." It also contained a section providing that "any person who
shall maliciously dismember, or deprive a slave of life, shall suffer such
punishment as would be inflicted, in case the like offense had been committed upon a free white person, and on the like proof—except in case
of insurrection of such slave." On the basis/of these constitutional provisions and the 1840 law protecting slaves from physical cruelty and murder, the Texas legislature developed a code defining the power of masters
to punish their bondsmen and the points at which punishment became
cruel treatment.[20]

At the close of the antebellum period, Texas slaves could be punished
by their masters (or anyone such as an administrator or hirer having lawful control of them) according to the following general principles:

> 1ST. The right of the master to the obedience and submission of his
> slave, in all lawful things, is perfect, and the power belongs to the
> master to inflict any punishment upon the slave, not affecting life or
> limb, and not coming within the definition of cruel treatment, or un-
> reasonable abuse, which he may consider necessary for the purpose
> of keeping him in such submission, and enforcing such submission to

19. Gammel (comp.), *Laws of Texas*, I, 1265–66, II, 346. The willingness of whites to
protect slaves against other whites will be discussed in detail below.

20. *Ibid.*, II, 1296, III, 29. In 1848, the fine for cruel treatment or unreasonable abuse was
lowered from $250–$2,000 to $20–$500. During the 1850s, however, the penalty would be
increased to $100–$2,000.

his commands; and if, in the exercise of this right, with or without cause, the slave resists and slay his master, it is murder.

2ND. The master has not the right to kill his slave, or to maim or dismember him, except in cases mentioned in Article 564 [cases of insurrection or forcible resistance to a white] of this Code.

3RD. A master, in the exercise of his right to perfect obedience on the part of the slave, may correct in moderation, and is the exclusive judge of the necessity for such correction; and resistance by the slave, under such circumstances, if it results in homicide, renders him guilty of murder.

In addition to these powers of punishment legally accorded masters, any white man, when faced with "insolence" on the part of a slave, could inflict "moderate chastisement, with an ordinary instrument of correction." Also, any free white person could give a bondsman a "moderate whipping" for any one of seven different offenses, such as using "insulting language or gestures" toward a white or being drunk and making a disturbance in public.[21]

The penal code also attempted to define the points at which punishment became unreasonable abuse or cruel treatment and provided fines of $100 to $2,000 for offenders. "Unreasonable abuse" was the inflicting of punishment "greatly disproportionate to the nature of the offense" or beating with "unusual implements." "Cruel treatment" was "to torture or to cause unusual pain and suffering" or to punish severely enough to injure a slave's health or "depreciate his value." If a slave was maimed or disfigured, the person responsible could be charged with unreasonable abuse and cruel treatment. If mistreatment resulted in the death of a slave, the offence was murder. Finally, the code provided fines of as much as $100 for any person who, "without sufficient provocation," whipped or struck a slave that was not his property or under his lawful control.[22]

Slaveholders, in exercising their right to "obedience and submission" from their bondsmen, inflicted a variety of punishments. Whipping was most common, and the instruments used varied from switches to sticks to leather whips. Some owners also used jails, chains, clogs (leg weights),

21. Oldham and White (comps.), *Digest of the General Statute Laws*, 560–61.
22. *Ibid.*, 542–43.

and other special devices. Gus Johnson, for example, remembered that his mistress jailed her slaves in a hole dug in the ground with a weighted "drop door" to close it. The driver on the Kit Patton place forced workers to drag a chain as they worked in the field, and J. S. Devereux bought a fifteen-pound clog "to put on negro man Ben" in 1850.[23]

Slaves were whipped for many reasons, including running away, stealing, fighting, insolence, and failure to complete their work on time and to their masters' satisfaction. Jacob Branch's mother was whipped for letting flies speck the clothes she washed; Fannie Brown, for her slowness in learning how to spin. Others were whipped for poor cooking, for not keeping their row up with the other slaves' rows, and for letting livestock escape. Efforts to determine the proportion of all slaves who suffered whippings and how frequently they were punished are futile. Some masters never whipped or permitted it on their places. Others were like the master in Limestone County, who, in the words of one of his slaves, "had to beat somebody every day." Clearly, many slaves were whipped, and the practice was common enough that all were aware that they could be so punished. Every slave did not have to receive a whipping in order to be impressed with the frightening possibility that it could happen to him. One woman who ran away and was later caught expressed what was likely the typical bondsman's view on this form of punishment. When asked by her owner if she had not been afraid of wild animals, she replied: "I'm more scared of you than the animals, they don't whip."[24]

Slaveowners tended to view whippings as a necessary disciplinary measure, not as cruel treatment. For example, John Bauer, Ashbel Smith's overseer, in his annual report for 1842, wrote: "I am from principle disinclined to ill treat a beast far less a human being." He also reported that when Albert tried to run away he had been caught and given a "sound whipping." Regardless, however, of what masters and overseers such as Bauer thought, nearly any whipping was painful enough to border on

23. Curlee, "Texas Slave Plantations," 126–27; Winfrey, *Julien Sidney Devereux*, 73; *Am. Slave, Supp.*, Ser. 2, II, 226 (Harrison Becket), VI, 1992 (Gus Johnson), III, 629 (Richard Carruthers).

24. *Am. Slave, Supp.*, Ser. 2, II, 146 (Henry Branch), II, 410 (Jacob Branch), II, 462 (Fanny Brown), VII, 2767–68 (William Moore), VII, 2641 (Susan Merritt). *Ibid.*, II, 352 (Harrison Boyd), III, 475 (James Brown), are examples of the many slaves who said they were never whipped. William Moore (*ibid.*, VII, 2767), said his owner had to whip someone every day; Walter Rimm (*ibid.*, VIII, 3314), told about the woman who was more afraid of her owner than of wild animals. Roemer, *Texas*, 163–64, told of a slave blacksmith who had never been whipped.

cruel treatment. Moreover, severe beatings were not uncommon. The LaGrange *True Issue* in July, 1860, described how a master in Coryell County whipped a girl from sunrise until noon. One observer said the slave, who was accused of stealing, was the most inhumanely whipped creature he had ever seen, including horses and oxen. Mollie Dawson of Navarro County remembered her horror at the first whipping she ever saw. She was visiting her father who lived on a neighboring plantation when she saw a man with his feet and hands tied stripped naked and lying on the ground.

> This white man was whipping him and the blood was all over this nigger and he was saying "o, master, o, master, I pray you not to hit me any more. Oh, Lordy, oh, Lordy, has mercy on me. Master, please has mercy on me, please has mercy." But this man wouldn't stop a minute and spits tobacco juice and cuss him and then starts in whipping him again. This nigger was jumping around on the ground all tied up, just like a chicken when you chops his head off when this man was whipping him and when the white folks would stop awhile this nigger would lay there and roll from side to side and beg for mercy.
>
> I runs off a good piece when this white folks started whipping him and stopped and looks back at him, I was so scared that I just stood there and watched him till he quit. Then he tells some of the slaves to wash him off and put salt in the cut places and he stood there to watch them to see that they did. He was chewing his tobacco, spitting and cussing that nigger and when they gets him washed off and puts salt in the raw places he sure did scream and groan.
>
> But when he groaned they just keeping putting the salt in to the wounds on his poor old beat up body.
>
> The first thing that I know my father was patting me on the back and said, "Honey, you better run along home now," and I sure did and I didn't go back over there any more. That was the only slave I ever saw get a whipping.

Another bondsman, Andy Anderson, never forgot or forgave the first whipping he received. For accidentally breaking part of a wagon while gathering firewood, he was tied to a stake and given ten lashes every half hour for four hours. "I have that in my heart until this day," he told his WPA interviewer during the 1930s. Jacob Branch said that when his mistress beat his mother with a cowhide whip, it "look like she cut my mama in two."[25]

Some whippings were fatal. In 1861, for example, William R. Wilson of Harris County killed a slave named Ned by inflicting six hundred lashes with a "gutta percha strap." The manager of Andrew M. Echols' sawmill in Burleson County whipped a hired slave to death in 1856. The *Texas State Gazette* of October 7, 1854, carried an account of an overseer's administering a fatal beating to a slave woman.[26]

Cases of unreasonable punishment and cruel treatment, sometimes to the point of death, that did not involve whipping also were reported. When, for example, Eda Rains fell asleep while fanning a baby of the family to whom she was hired, her mistress struck her with the turkey wing fan and scarred her forehead for life. David Chandler of Travis County killed a slave belonging to David Conner because the bondsman, for some unspecified reason, "raised his hand" against Chandler. J. D. Nix of Harris County assaulted a slave woman and cut her with a knife. John Farrett was indicted in Red River County for assault with intent to murder after he wounded a slave girl named Catherine. James H. Callihan of Guadalupe County attempted to take a pistol away from a hired slave and then, when he ran away, shot and killed him. Thomas Presley, in the words of an Anderson County indictment, "did . . . without just provocation, inflict unusual pain . . . upon . . . a negro slave . . . the property of Millings, . . . murdering him." Charles U. Brady, an overseer in San Augustine County, shot and permanently disabled a slave as the result of an altercation stemming from the latter's having said something "impudent." The overseer on William T. Scott's Harrison County plantation killed a slave who physically resisted discipline. Another planter in the same county informed his son in 1859: "Dr. Stewart shot his man John for insubordination but it is thought he will not die." In April, 1852, Benjamin E. Roper, Ashbel Smith's overseer, cut a slave named Lewis with a knife. Roper informed Smith that the slave would remain with a doctor "until he is able to bear punishment when I shall bring him home

25. John Bauer to Ashbel Smith, December 26, 1842, in Smith Papers; La Grange *True Issue*, July 5, 1860; *Am. Slave, Supp.*, Ser. 2, IV, 1120–21 (Mollie Dawson), II, 52 (Andy Anderson), II, 410 (Jacob Branch). Advertisements for runaways sometimes testified to permanent scars left by whippings. See, for example, San Augustine *Red-Lander*, September 9, 1841; Marshall *Texas Republican*, March 10, 1865.

26. *Wilson* v. *The State*, 29 Tex. 240 (1867); *Echols* v. *Dodd*, 20 Tex. 191 (1857); Austin *Texas State Gazette*, October 7, 1854.

and give him a *very severe whipping.*" If "*any* negro . . . should ever give me the like provocation," Roper wrote, "I will deliberately take his life."[27]

At some point then, punishment and the exercise of whites' power over slaves went beyond discipline and became abuse, cruel treatment, and even murder. Slaves were supposed to have the protection of the law in such cases, but relatively few actions were brought against masters for cruel treatment or murder of their own slaves. Perhaps this was because only a small minority of owners subjected their own valuable property to extreme mistreatment. On the other hand, few white witnesses probably were available or willing to bring charges and testify against a master for what he did to his own bondsmen on his own farm or plantation, and blacks could not testify in court for each other or against whites.[28] Under these circumstances, legal actions against masters for mistreatment of their own slaves appear to have been brought only in especially aggravated cases.

One such case involved the Steen family of Smith County. Thomas Steen was indicted in 1847 for cruel treatment of three young slaves by denying them adequate food or clothing, exposing them to inclement weather, and whipping them with unreasonable severity. He was acquitted, but the next year his son James Steen was indicted on identical charges. At the trial in 1850, witnesses testified that they had seen two of the slaves, an eleven-year-old boy and a thirteen-year-old girl, working naked in the fields and had seen them, in the words of one witness, "whipped and whipped pretty badly." Thomas Steen, testifying in his son's behalf, claimed that the children had "always been part of his family," were well cared for, and worked very little. They had been whipped some, he said, "but not as much as they deserved." District Judge Lemuel D. Evans, in his charge to the jury, explained the law on food and clothing and provided some interpretation of his own on cruel treatment. "Whipping," he said, "or infliction of punishment not required in order to enforce obedience to the master's commands or to keep

27. *Am. Slave, Supp.,* Ser. 2, VIII, 3222 (Eda Rains); *Chandler* v. *The State,* 2 Tex. 305 (1847); *Nix* v. *The State,* 13 Tex. 575 (1855); *State of Texas* v. *John Farrett,* Red River County District Court Minutes, Book E; *Callihan* v. *Johnson,* 22 Tex. 597 (1858); *Presley* v. *The State,* 30 Tex. 160 (1867); *Brady* v. *Price,* 19 Tex. 285 (1857); Houston *Telegraph and Texas Register,* December 5, 1851; Levin Perry to Theophilus Perry, June 20, 1859, in Person Family Papers, Perkins Library, Duke University, Durham, N.C.; Benjamin E. Roper to Ashbel Smith, May 3, 1852, in Smith Papers.

28. In the case of *Doty* v. *Moore,* 16 Tex. 591 (1856), a district court decision was reversed because a slave was allowed to testify, in effect, against a white.

the slave in proper subjection to the master is cruel treatment." Steen was found guilty and fined $118. His lawyer filed a list of exceptions, appealed, and had the conviction reversed and remanded for further action. A second trial in Smith County resulted in another conviction and a much larger fine of $262.49.[29]

Legal actions for abuse and cruel treatment were much more common in cases involving slaves that did not belong to the person indicted. James Bumpus of Upshur County, for example, was tried in 1856 for laying "violent hands on a negro slave" belonging to Jacob Fisher and proceeding to "unmercifully whip and abuse said boy." Erwin Chancey of Smith County was accused of unreasonable abuse and cruel treatment and whipping another master's slave without due provocation because he beat William Kelley's man George with a stick. In 1855, John Stephenson was indicted in Washington County for assault and battery after he whipped Malissa who belonged to Linsay P. Rucker. In the other cases of abuse, cruelty, and murder mentioned above, Wilson, Chandler, Nix, Farrett, and Presley all faced legal action. All had in some way mistreated or attacked someone else's slave.[30]

The decisions in these cases suggest that juries were willing to give slaves protection of the laws against unreasonable abuse and cruel treatment, at least to the point of assessing fines against violators. But in general they were unwilling to convict whites of more serious offenses against bondsmen. William R. Wilson, for example, charged with murder and with cruel and unusual punishment for whipping a slave to death, was acquitted on the first charge but found guilty on the second and fined $2,000. Thomas Presley's case had exactly the same result, although his fine was only $240. Eventually both convictions were overturned by the Texas supreme court on the grounds that, according to the law, cruel treatment resulting in death had to be considered murder. Wilson and Presley could not be found guilty of the lesser offense when it had obviously led to a more serious one. Bumpus was found guilty of assault and battery and fined $40. In Chancey's case, the jury found him not guilty of

29. Smith County District Court Papers, Case #3 (Thomas Steen); Case #43 (James Steen). The James Steen case papers include the indictment, testimony, and Judge Evans' charge to the jury, plus all the information on the aftermath of the case.

30. *Bumpus* v. *Fisher*, 21 Tex. 561 (1858); Smith County District Court Papers, Case #705 (Erwin Chancey); *State* v. *Stephenson*, 20 Tex. 151 (1857). The Wilson, Chandler, Nix, Farret, and Presley cases are cited above in notes 26 and 27.

cruel treatment, an offense with a minimum fine of $250 at the time, but convicted him of whipping William Kelley's slave without due provocation and fined him $25.[31] Chandler was found guilty of manslaughter, a felony carrying a minimum penalty of one year in prison. Nix was convicted of assault and battery, for which he was fined $25 and sentenced to ten days in jail. Stephenson won an acquittal on assault and battery charges. Chandler and Nix appealed to the supreme court primarily on the grounds that they had not been charged with violating any specific provisions of the laws protecting slaves against abuse, cruelty, or murder. Chandler's lawyers argued, for example, that there was no law concerning manslaughter of a slave. The supreme court ruled, however, that, since slaves had always been treated as "persons" in the application of criminal law, the common law extended to offenses against blacks as well as whites when no special rules existed for bondsmen. As Justice Royal T. Wheeler wrote in the Chandler case: "It seems especially to have been the intention of our legislation . . . to throw around the *life* of the slave the same protection which is guaranteed to a free man." The convictions of Chandler and Nix were affirmed. Stephenson's acquittal was appealed by the state, whereupon the supreme court reversed the district court and remanded his case for further action. A slave is not, said Justice Oran M. Roberts in his decision, "property only, as a horse or any other domestic animal." Instead, bondsmen have personal rights, and every white person does not have the right to whip any slave.[32]

Laws against abuse, cruelty, and murder and the supreme court's willingness to extend the common law to bondsmen thus provided Texas slaves with some protection from extreme physical mistreatment, especially if offenses against them were committed by someone other than their own masters. Constitutional and legislative protections represented general public disapproval of cruelty, and the possibility of legal action may have restrained some whites. Nevertheless, courts were unwilling to convict masters or other free men of murdering slaves and extremely reluctant to interfere with what Justice James H. Bell of the supreme court called "the delicate and responsible relation of master and slave." Legiti-

31. All these cases are cited above in either notes 26, 27, or 30.
32. The penalty for manslaughter at the time of Chandler's conviction is in James Wilmer Dallam (comp.), *A Digest of the Laws of Texas* (Baltimore, 1845), 167. The Chandler, Nix, and Stephenson cases are cited above in notes 27 and 30.

mate punishment was so common and the line between it and cruel treat-ment so imprecise that legal protections for slaves were minimal at best. "Much," according to Justice Bell, "is left to the master's judgment, dis-cretion, and humanity."[33] Those qualities varied, as every slave well knew, from master to master.

33. *Callihan* v. *Johnson*, 22 Tex. 597 (1858).

EIGHT

. . . .

Family, Religion, and Music

''THE STRENGTH TO ENDURE''

His wife having been sold, and facing punishment himself, a slave who belonged to Irving Jones in Anderson County committed suicide. He "stood it as long as he could," said the bondsman who told the story. Slave suicides were not at all common, however.[1] Bondsmen, although most faced a lifetime of manual labor with at best adequate material conditions while subject to punishment largely at the whim of their masters, very seldom took their own lives. Their instinctive will to live was threatened by the harshness and hopelessness of bondage, but at the same time it was encouraged by several institutions that mitigated the psychological conditions of servitude. What aspects of Texas slaves' lives contributed to the mental and emotional strength to endure, and what behavioral adjustments did bondsmen make in order to survive? These questions serve as a focus for the next two chapters.

Sizes of slaveholdings affected the psychological as well as physical conditions of servitude. Approximately one-third of Texas bondsmen belonged to small holders, whereas the great majority were on farms and plantations having at least ten slaves. Those who lived in smaller holdings, especially the few who resided in towns, benefited mentally and emotionally from having greater control over their own working and living conditions than did their plantation counterparts. Some may have had an advantage also in that closer daily contact with their masters led to greater recognition of their humanity. At the same time, these bonds-

1. *Am. Slave, Supp.*, Ser. 2, VI, 2140 (Steve Jones), VII, 2578 (Adeline Marshall, who told of an old man who was whipped until he committed suicide).

men, particularly those on small farms, were likely to spend most of their time under the close supervision of their owners with only a few other people who shared their situation. The presence of as many or more whites than blacks probably served as an oppressive reminder of their inferior status as slaves while reducing their opportunity to share the support that bondsmen could give each other. These slaves endured, but only the plantation majority had an opportunity to demonstrate the truth of an old adage about strength in numbers. They were in a better position to create families, worship according to their own religious ideas, and have their own music.[2]

Slave families had no legal existence in Texas. A treatise on the state's laws affecting married women, written in 1901, concluded that "since there can be no valid marriage between persons who are incapable of assenting to any contract, it follows that slaves could not marry, even with the consent of their master, so as to constitute them husband and wife. . . . Contubernism was their matrimony; a permitted cohabitation not partaking of the nature of lawful marriage, which they could not contract." Since slave marriages had no standing under the law, it followed that fathers and mothers had no legally protected relationship with their children. The state supreme court demonstrated this in 1849 when it ruled that a district court jury had erred in assessing the value of a woman and her child together in determining the damages due for the theft of the two bondsmen. The two had to be assessed separately, the court said, since they were distinct pieces of property. Obviously, slaveowners had no legal compulsion to create or respect family ties of any sort.[3]

A few masters went to the extremes possible under these circumstances and forced their slaves to reproduce without regard to any family relationships. Women were put with men, Annie Row remembered, like "the cows and the bull" and bred for "bigger niggers." Other former

2. Campbell and Lowe, *Wealth and Power*, 44. The distribution of slaves among slaveowners is discussed in greater detail in chapter 6 above. For an extreme example of a case in which being part of a small slaveholding apparently meant closeness between master and slave, see the narrative of Mandy Hadnot in *Am. Slave, Supp.*, Ser. 2, V, 1626–29. Hadnot's owner gave her a pony and decorated a Christmas tree for her. The importance of large slaveholdings in providing an opportunity for slaves to develop their own culture has been emphasized in many recent studies. The first major work to make this point was Blassingame, *The Slave Community*.

3. Ocie Speer, *A Treatise on the Law of Married Women in Texas* (Rochester, N.Y., 1901), ch. 1, sec. 5, p. 5; *Blakely's Administrator* v. *Duncan*, 4 Tex. 184 (1849).

slaves spoke of "breeding," "traveling," or "stud" Negroes who in some cases went from one plantation to another to sire slave children. Fannie Brown said that although she had children before 1865, "I never did have no special husband before the war. I marries after the war." Children who were simply "bred" as animal-like property could be treated as such as they grew older. "We mostly were like cattle and hogs are today," said Jane Cotten.[4]

Some owners, unwilling to "breed" their slaves but determined to insure reproduction, forced "marriages" between their men and women. Seventeen-year-old Rose Williams, for example, did not understand what was expected when her master told her to move from her parents' cabin and live with one of his male bondsmen. She fought back at first and drove the man from her bed and the cabin. Finally, however, after remonstrances and threats from her owner, she gave in. The circumstances of this "marriage" marked her for life. When asked by a WPA interviewer if she had married after slavery, she replied: "Married? Never! No sir! One experience enough for this nigger. After what I'se do for the master, I never want any truck with any man." Other former slaves indicated that Williams' "marriage" was not an isolated case. Betty Powers, for example, fairly snorted when her WPA interviewer inquired about slave marriages. "Did we'uns have weddings?" she said. "White man, you know better than that. Them times colored folks am just put together. The master say, 'Jim and Nancy you go live together,' and when that order give it better be done."[5]

Most masters, however, did not interfere in the sexual lives of their slaves to the point of "breeding" or forcing "marriages." Instead, they permitted the formation of families and the bearing and rearing of children within a family setting. In some cases, a woman and her children were referred to as a "family." In 1860, for example, when Reuben Hornsby, Jr., of Austin bought a woman and her seven children, the bill of sale described his purchase as "a family of eight Negroes." A Johnson

4. *Am. Slave, Supp.*, Ser. 2, VIII, 3369 (Annie Row), II, 462 (Fannie Brown), III, 944 (Jane Cotten). Other slaves who commented on "breeding" include Lewis Jones (*ibid.*, VI, 2109); S. J. Washington (*ibid.*, X, 3985); S. Robertson (*ibid.*, VIII, 3332); George Austin (*ibid.*, II, 105); Jeptha Choice (*ibid.*, III, 709).

5. *Ibid.*, X, 4121–23 (Rose Williams), VIII, 3139 (Betty Powers). Other examples of forced marriages are found in *ibid.*, V, 1580 (James Green), II, 406 (Jacob Branch), and IX, 3473 (Hannah Scott). This type of interference in the courtship patterns of slaves and other methods of encouraging reproduction are discussed in Malone, *Women on the Texas Frontier*, 38–42.

County bill of sale referred to "a certain family of Negroes, Viz Emily aged about twenty-six years and her four children." Such records suggest that the female-headed black family at least existed during slavery. Generally, however, the word *family*, as it was used by slaveholders and slaves alike, meant the nuclear social unit—a man, his wife, and their children.[6]

Texas bondsmen themselves provided extensive evidence concerning the existence of nuclear families. In a sample of 181 slave narratives, 60 percent remembered living with both parents on the same home place and another 9 percent recalled that their fathers lived nearby on a neighboring farm or plantation. Inventories from probate records also provide numerous examples of nuclear families existing among bondsmen. Jared E. Groce's Austin County estate, for example, had sixty slaves when it was inventoried in February, 1840. Kinship ties were specified for forty-four bondsmen, while sixteen were not identified with a particular family. Most of the families consisted of a man, his wife, and their children, and others, while not "complete" in this way, gave evidence of long-term kinship ties. One, for example, was made up of an "old woman" (age fifty-eight), two of her sons aged twenty-eight and eighteen, and a six-year-old granddaughter. Another was headed by a fifty-two-year-old blacksmith who had five children aged sixteen to three but no wife. The Joseph Mims estate in Brazoria County had seventy-two slaves in January, 1845. Fifty-nine of these lived in twelve family units, only one of which was headed by a female. John Millican of Brazos County owned sixty-seven slaves at the time of his death in 1859. Ten were not identified with particular families, but the others lived in twelve families, eight headed by husbands with wives, three by women, and one by a man with no wife. William Ward of Brazoria County had eighty-two slaves in 1864, and only two did not belong to one of the nineteen families on his plantation. Eighteen of these families were headed by men. Abram Sheppard of Matagorda County owned only ten slaves in 1856, but eight of them belonged to one family headed by a fifty-year-old man. In Cass County in 1849, eight of W. M. Freeman's thirteen bondsmen belonged to one family. Two of the other five slaves were a sixty-year-old woman and her sixteen-year-old son, but they were not desig-

6. Bill of Sale for Slaves, 1860, in Hornsby Papers; Bill of Sale for Slaves, 1857, in Preston R. Rose Papers, Barker Texas History Center, University of Texas, Austin; Estate of Edith J. Johnson, Red River County Probate Records (Will Record, Book B).

nated a "family" in the inventory. In short, the evidence from slaves and slaveholders alike strongly suggests that the majority of bondsmen in Texas lived at least part of their lives within a traditional family setting.[7]

Masters had good reasons for permitting and even encouraging their slaves to live in families. Treating bondsmen with humanity and having them reproduce within a secure family setting, regardless of what the law allowed, was more socially acceptable than "breeding" or forced "marriages." Moreover, owners recognized how determined slaves were to have families and how important family ties were to the mental and emotional state of their bondsmen. Masters could see that the family led both to children and to ties and obligations that made their bondsmen more controllable in servitude. Considerations of humanity aside, few would deliberately deny an institution that served their own purposes so well. Masters were advised that "marital rights and conjugal ties ought to be scrupulously respected." Nevertheless, there was noticeable variation in what they were willing to do to permit and preserve slave families.[8]

When a man and woman on the same place wished to marry, they had to get their owner's permission. This was generally no problem, but the wedding ceremonies that followed varied markedly from one master to another. Some couples, once they had permission, simply moved into a cabin together, whereas others had elaborate wedding ceremonies with ministers presiding. The most common celebration was a "broomstick wedding" in which the bride and groom literally jumped over a broomstick together. According to one legend, the first one over would "rule" the family. In any case, such weddings essentially amounted to, as one former slave said in disgust, "no ceremony, no license, no nothing, just marrying."[9]

7. Estate of Jared E. Groce, Austin County Probate Records (Succession Record, Book B); Estate of Joseph Mims, Brazoria County Probate Records (Wills, etc., Book A); Estate of John Millican, Brazos County Probate Records (Probate Minutes, Book E); Estate of William Ward, Brazoria County Probate Records (Wills, etc., Book D); Estate of Abram Sheppard, Matagorda County Probate Records (Inventory Record, Book C); Estate of Williamson M. Freeman, Cass County Probate Records (Final Record Probate Court, Book 2). The probate records of Brazoria County alone contain at least four additional estates that inventoried slaves by family.

8. Edward Smith, *Account of a Journey Through Northeastern Texas Undertaken in 1849 for the Purposes of Emigration* (London, 1849), 83–84; Matagorda *Gazette*, April 16, 1859, quoted in Palm, "Slavery in Microcosm: Matagorda County," 144.

9. *Am. Slave, Supp.*, Ser. 2, II, 174 (Joe Barnes), III, 709 (Jeptha Choice), IV, 1132 (Mollie Dawson), VI, 2298 (Lu Lee), VIII, 3249 (Joe Rawls, who said that broomstick weddings were "just marrying"). Mandy Hadnot (*ibid.*, V, 1629–30) remembered being married by a white

A good many families began when men and women from neighboring farms made matches and asked their respective masters for permission to marry. For example, J. W. Devereux's diary for January 25, 1846, noted a marriage between one of his females and Sam Loftus "by consent of all parties. Sam brought a consent and good recommendation from his master." Henry Lewis who lived in Jefferson County described such a match from the slave's point of view: "My first wife named Rachel and she lived on Double Bayou. She belong to the Mayes place. First time I see her I was riding the range seeing about cattle. I was living on Master Bob's place in Jefferson County and I have to get a pass to go to see her. I tell Master Bob I want to get married and he say, 'all right.' Then I have to go and ask Mr. Mayes and he say, 'all right.' Us had a big wedding." When slaves on different farms and plantations married, they generally had to remain apart during the week and be together only on weekends and special holidays such as Christmas week. Such arrangements were far from ideal for the bondsmen, and they were not good business for the owner of the husband either, in that children born to such unions generally belonged to the owner of the mother. It was not uncommon, however, for one slave or the other, usually the man, to be bought or traded so that the couple could live together. For example, Hattie Cole, George Sells, Martha Spence Bruton, and Gill Ruffin all remembered their fathers being bought from other masters in order to unite them with their wives and children. At times, women were sold for similar reasons. When, for example, George Scott prepared to buy a slave named Liddy from Thomas B. Huling in 1860, the latter wrote his mother, "I have no objections to sell her as she has her husband belonging to Scott." [10]

Slave families tended to be large, since, after all, children were valu-

---

minister in her master's home, and Josephine Ryles from Galveston (*ibid.*, IX, 3405–3406) insisted that broomstick weddings were not typical. Malone, *Women on the Texas Frontier*, 46–47, also discusses slave weddings.

An example of consent for a marriage being refused is found in a letter to Samuel Maas from his daughter on May 16, 1864. The slave Mary should not be allowed to marry the man of her choice, the daughter said, because he had once urged another slave to set fire to their house. Samuel Maas Family Papers, Garrett Collection, University of Texas at Arlington Library.

10. Diary of J. W. Devereux, January 25, 1846, in Devereux Papers; Thomas B. Huling to his mother, January 21, 1860, in Thomas Byers Huling Papers, Barker Texas History Center, University of Texas, Austin; *Am. Slave, Supp.*, Ser. 2, III, 776 (Hattie Cole), IX, 3493–94 (George Sells), III, 521 (Martha S. Bruton), VIII, 3376 (Gill Ruffin), II, 156–57 (Delia Barclay), VIII, 3002 (Mary Overton), IX, 3765 (Emma Taylor).

able, and reproduction was encouraged. Women often had their first child while in their late teens and then had another every two years until they were in their forties. Even with the very high infant mortality of that age, many women had four or five living children by the time they reached the age of thirty, and some had spectacularly large families. For example, in 1859, a forty-five-year-old Brazos County woman named China had children aged twenty-eight, twenty-four, twenty-two, twenty, eighteen, sixteen, fourteen, twelve, ten, eight, seven, six, four, and an infant. Of course, white families also tended to be large during this era.[11]

Slave families, regardless of how they were created or their size, played a vital role in providing the mental and emotional strength necessary to endure bondage. Family ties gave slaves love, individual identity, and a sense of personal worth—all from relationships with people like themselves, not from their masters or from others of a clearly superior status. "If you love me like I love you," a Harrison County slave woman wrote her husband in 1862 while he served his master in the Confederate army, "no knife can cut our love into [sic]." Judge John Scott wrote to Ashbel Smith about what happened as he prepared to ride his circuit in 1839 and take a hired slave with him as a body servant. "I agreed with Dr. Anderson for his man Thornton," he wrote, "but the rascal runaway, & will not go with me, alleging that he wishes to sleep with his dear wife, etc." One of Smith's own slaves also objected to leaving home even briefly. "Albert got home, safely, on Monday night," M. S. Tunnell informed Smith. "He takes the separation from his family to heart considerably. He said he would rather be set up and shot, then the trouble would be soon over."[12] Clearly the relationships between these men and women were vital parts of their everyday lives.

11. Estate of John Millican, Brazos County Probate Records (Probate Minutes, Book E). Inventories of slave property in county probate records frequently reported sixteen- to eighteen-year-old women as the mothers of children. The families of white Texans averaged 5.5 persons in 1860. See, United States Bureau of the Census, *Statistics of the United States (Including Mortality, Property, etc.) in 1860; Compiled from the Original Returns and Being the Final Exhibit of the Eighth Census* (Washington, D.C., 1866), 349.

12. Fannie to "My Dear Husband," December 28, 1862, in Person Family Papers; John Scott to Ashbel Smith, September 28, 1839, and M. S. Tunnell to Ashbel Smith, January 7, 1859, both in Smith Papers.

The importance and strength of the slave family across the antebellum South is documented best in Gutman, *Black Family in Slavery and Freedom*, but see also Richard H. Steckel, "Slave Marriage and the Family," *Journal of Family History*, V (1980), 406–21, and Herman R. Lantz, "Family and Kin as Revealed in the Narratives of Ex-Slaves," *Social Science Quarterly*, LX (1980), 667–75.

Slave husbands and wives apparently wanted to divide responsibilities as much as possible along the lines that were traditional in mid-nineteenth-century families. Men, for example, hunted and fished when they could in order to provide additional food. Women kept their homes and took care of the children.[13]

Slave children received love, support, and discipline from their parents. Delia Barclay, for example, remembered how weekend visits from her father who lived on a nearby plantation were a special part of her life. On one occasion, she became so excited at his arrival that she ran across the porch, caught her toe in a crack between the planks, and nearly pulled it off. Martha Spence Bruton told her WPA interviewer that after her mother died her father had to be "mammy and pappy." On Sunday morning, she said, "He'd get out of bed and make a big fire and say 'Jiminy cripes! you children stay in bed and I'll make the biscuits.'" Mollie Dawson described the way children who misbehaved got a good spanking. All most parents had to do, she said, "was to look out the corner of the eye at the kids and they got good right now." Mandy Morrow recalled what happened when she decided to sneak off to the barn and try smoking a pipe. Her mother missed her because things were too quiet and found her in the barn. "She pulled me out of there. Now, white man, there am plenty of fire put on my rear and I see lots of smoke." Finally, the experience of Hannah Mullins at the time of emancipation showed the meaning of her family. She had been living at her master's house as a playmate for his children, but at freedom "my pappy comes after me and we'uns all live together in the cabin instead of me living in the master's house with the kids."[14]

Families were one focal point for survival for many slaves, and yet, paradoxically, families also could bring almost unbearable pain. Husbands generally could not protect their wives from whippings or from sexual abuse by white men. Wives at times saw their husbands beaten and humiliated by overseers and masters. Children had to see their parents unable to protect each other or themselves. Jacob Branch, for example, remembered how awful it was to see his mother whipped. "Many's the time I edges up," he said, "and tries to take some of them licks off my mama." The greatest pain from family relationships, how-

13. *Am. Slave, Supp.*, Ser. 2, VI, 2404 (Sue Lockridge), VII, 2602–2603, 2607 (Louise Mathews).

14. *Ibid.*, II, 156–57 (Delia Barclay), IV, 1125–26 (Mollie Dawson), VII, 2775–76 (Mandy Morrow), VII, 6 (Hannah Mullins); *ibid.*, Ser. 1, IV, Pt. 1, p. 175 (Martha Spence Bruton).

ever, came from the fact that they were always subject to disruption by the actions of slaveowners.[15]

Some owners showed notable concern that the family ties of their bondsmen not be disrupted. These masters not only kept husbands, wives, and children together while they lived, they also wrote wills directing that family ties be respected in the settling of their estates. John J. Webster of Harrison County, for example, wrote: "It is my further will that my Negroes be so distributed as to allot the families by families in the partition, that members of the same family may remain together." Dr. E. Stevens of Brazoria County directed his executors to sell all his property for cash but added the proviso that "the slaves shall be sold in families." Richard Carter of Brazos County left all his slaves to his wife. At her death, one large family (a man, his wife, and their eight children) plus four "orphan" Negroes would become the property of his daughter. The other slaves were to be sold, provided that another large family of eight "shall all be sold together to a purchaser, so that they may not be seperated." Samuel McGowen of Polk County bequeathed all his sixty-four slaves in family units, adding a special instruction that two of the families "shall choose for themselves whichever of my children they may like to live with (the one chosen paying the other a fair consideration)." These masters, and the many others who gave similar directions concerning at least some of their bondsmen, obviously appreciated the strength and importance of the slave family.[16]

Estate administrators and the guardians of minors with slave property also expressed concern at times for the preservation of families. One guardian in Colorado County asked the probate court's approval for hiring to herself the seven slaves belonging to her wards because "it would be painful to separate Negroes united by ties of blood." Rebecca Hagerty proposed to buy part of a Cass County plantation as a place to work the slaves under her care as guardian of Anna Hawkins. This was best, she told the court, because the bondsmen "consist of famillies, say, men, women, and children all of which are unsuitable to hire out." Other guardians and administrators went ahead and hired out slaves but kept families together in the process. For example, the administrator of

15. *Ibid.*, Ser. 2, II, 410 (Jacob Branch).

16. Estate of John B. Webster, Harrison County Probate Records (Estate Records, Book E); Estate of Dr. E. Stevens, Brazoria County Probate Records (Wills, etc., Book D); Estate of Richard Carter, Brazos County Probate Records (Probate Minutes, Book E); Estate of Samuel McGowen, Polk County Probate Records (Wills) and (Probate Record, Books C and D).

William A. Nail's Colorado County estate sought and obtained the court's permission to hire out a family together for 1856. David G. Mills, as administrator of Sterling McNeel's huge Brazoria County plantation, hired out six families in 1857. Several large families belonging to William Routt's estate in Washington County were hired out for 1858, although the administrator reported that John, his wife, and their five children were "not hired no one wanting them." [17]

While some owners and estate managers made notable efforts to keep slave families together, others went only so far as was not terribly inconvenient. The will of Dr. John L. Graves is a good example. His wish was that "in making a division the Negroes shall be so divided as to avoid as far as practicable consistently with a just apportionment the separation of the persons constituting a family." Amelia Swanson of Harrison County directed that her slaves' families be kept together as much as possible. The administrator of Susan A. S. Gardner's estate in Colorado County petitioned to hire out two families of slaves for 1857. He kept one family together but hired three members of the second to one hirer and two to another. [18]

Thus, many Texas slaves belonged to masters or came under the control of estate managers who made at least some effort to preserve families; many others, however, were the property of owners who showed absolutely no concern for family ties. In some cases, relationships among husbands, wives, and children were disrupted by the move to Texas from older southern states. For example, Ben Chambers of Jasper County remembered how the move to Texas from Alabama had disrupted his family. He and his mother belonged to Lazarus Goolsby who migrated, while his father's master remained behind. Chambers never saw his father again. John Bates told a similar story: "My mother belonged to Harry Hogan and my father belonged to Mock Bateman . . . I don't know much

17. Estate of John T. and Martha A. Earp (minors), Colorado County Probate Records (Probate Records, Book C); Estate of Anna Hawkins (minor), Cass County Probate Records (Final Record Probate Court, Book 2); Estate of William A. Nail, Colorado County Probate Records (Probate Records, Book E); Estate of Sterling McNeel, Brazoria County Probate Records (Wills, etc., Book B); Estate of William Routt, Washington County Probate Records (Final Record, Book G).
18. Estate of Dr. John L. Graves, Washington County Probate Records (Final Record, Book F); Estate of Amelia Swanson, Harrison County Probate Records (Estate Record, Book I-J); Estate of Susan A. S. Gardner, Colorado County Probate Records (Probate Records, Book D).

about him [father] because we moved to Limestone County Texas while I was small leaving my pappy in Arkansas. I never saw him no more." Eli Davison's owner decided in 1858 to leave his own wife in Dunbar, Virginia (now West Virginia), take a few slaves, including young Eli, and begin anew in Texas. Davison was permanently separated from his mother and father. Some young slaves were not even fortunate enough to come to Texas with one of their parents or their original owner. Instead, they were bought elsewhere and brought to the Lone Star state by a new master. Sarah Perkins and her brother, for example, traveled from Tennessee after being sold to Charlie Jones. The boy died en route and was buried beside the road; Sarah was so sickly that she was given away in San Antonio. Ashbel Smith bought three slaves, aged ten, twelve, and seventeen, in 1838 in New Orleans and shipped them to Galveston. Smith's bill of sale and shipping manifest provide no evidence, of course, on the family relations of these young bondsmen, but it is obvious that they were purchased and brought to Texas without their fathers or mothers.[19]

Slave families that survived migration or were formed in Texas also were subject to disruption at any time. Contemporary observers, newspaper advertisements, and former slaves all provide evidence that masters could and did sell bondsmen without regard to age or family ties. Nicholas Doran P. Maillard described an auction during 1840 in Fort Bend County in which a family of four was sold to three different purchasers—the father to one, the wife and an infant to another, and a boy to a third. The Clarksville *Northern Standard* carried an advertisement in 1857 offering a thirteen-year-old girl for sale or barter for a boy or cattle. Lizzie Atkins remembered having two brothers and a sister sold from her family when she was six or seven years old. James Brown described slave families being broken up on the auction block, and Josie Brown saw "children too little to walk split from their mammys and sold right on the block in Woodville."[20]

Perhaps the ultimate example of selling a young slave occurred in Aus-

19. *Am. Slave, Supp.*, Ser. 2, III, 670–71 (Ben Chambers), II, 213 (John Bates), X, 1096–97 (Eli Davison) (the experiences of Jacob Branch [*ibid.*, II, 405] and Reeves Tucker, [*ibid.*, X, 3891] were similar), VIII, 3071–73 (Sarah Perkins); Bill of Sale, April 14, 1838, and Cargo Manifest, April 16, 1838, both in Smith Papers.

20. Maillard, *History of the Republic of Texas*, 265; Clarksville *Northern Standard*, December 26, 1857; *Am. Slave, Supp.*, Ser. 2, II, 93 (Lizzie Atkins), III, 477 (James Brown), III, 483 (Josie Brown).

tin County during May, 1859, when James Strawther, who was in severe financial difficulty, sold a six-week-old female for $75. Strawther warranted the infant a slave for life, but did "not warrant her soundness in any manner." The purchaser was Strawther's sister, who soon became the administrator of his estate and a partial heir of his property, so perhaps the infant was never separated from her mother. Nevertheless, the transaction reveals that there was no limit on the age at which slaves could be, and were, sold.[21]

Slave children sometimes were given away as well as sold. Sarah G. Burleson of Hays County, for example, gave her daughter-in-law, Louisa, "a certain negro boy named Phillip of copper complexion and about six years of age." The boy's mother had already been given to one of Burleson's sons (not Louisa's husband). Minerva Bratcher at age six was part of the "dowry" accompanying one of her master's daughters who married in the mid-1850s. The 1862 will of David Barton of Burnet County directed that a girl named Caroline be given to the yet-unborn child being carried by his wife.[22]

Slave families were broken up by migration, sales, and gifts. However, the death of a master created an even greater likelihood of disruption. In many cases, immediately after an owner died, his farm or plantation came under the management of an administrator who then hired out the bondsmen belonging to the estate and in the process often broke up slave families, sometimes year after year. For example, William Steen's De Witt County estate included four nuclear families when it was inventoried in January, 1847. The estate's administrator immediately hired out its slaves for the remainder of that year and in the process disrupted all four families. In Rusk County, six slaves belonging to one estate, including a forty-year-old man, a thirty-year-old woman, and her three children aged fourteen, twelve, and six, were each hired to different renters each year from 1859 to 1862. The boy was separated from his mother and served four different masters before he reached the age of ten.[23]

21. Bill of Sale, May 17, 1859, in Austin County, County Clerk's Miscellaneous Records (Records, 1849–65).
22. Deed, in Sarah G. Burleson Collection, Sul Ross State University Library, Alpine, Tex.; *Am. Slave, Supp.*, Ser. 2, II, 420–21 (Minerva Bratcher); Estate of David Barton, Burnet County Probate Records (Probate Records, Book B).
23. Estate of William Steen, De Witt County Probate Records (Final Record Deceased Persons, Book A); Estate of William B. Holloway, Rusk County Probate Records (Probate Record, Book F).

Hiring out constituted a temporary disruption, but final estate settlements, some of which took place soon after a slaveholder's death and others not until after years of administration, often resulted in the permanent breakup of slave families. Although some slaveowners in their wills sought to protect families, many others made no such provision or even directed the separation of husbands, wives, and children. William C. Sparks of Bell County, for example, left his ten slaves to his six children "share and share alike." Robert O. Reeves of Grayson County and Thomas H. Snow of Polk County also wrote wills that left slave families at the mercy of an equitable division of their estates. Lewis M. H. Washington of Travis County left one slave couple to his wife, but his will also directed that a woman named Charlotte be sold and that each of his four stepchildren be given one of Charlotte's five children. The fifth child went to Washington's wife. Ephraim D. Moore's will bequeathed one slave to each of his seven children. Any slaves born before the will took effect, Moore wrote, will be "kept by them that may have their mother." In similar fashion, John Robbins divided six slaves among his five heirs. The youngest bondsman involved was only four. Isaac Vandorn of Matagorda County wanted his wife to keep all his slaves together during her lifetime. At her death, however, each of his three children was to pick one slave, and the others were to be divided equally.[24] Clearly, these wills permitted or necessitated the disruption of families.

In cases where slaveowners died intestate, settlements partitioning estates according to state laws on the subject often broke up slave families. William Steen's estate again provides a good example. When this estate was partitioned into eight "lots" of approximately equal value in April, 1848, all four families were disrupted in some way. For example, Armystead, a thirty-four-year-old blacksmith, saw his wife Aggey and three children combined with another man to create Lot #3, while he was placed in Lot #6 with a fifteen-year-old girl. Peter W. Gautier, Sr., of Brazoria County had fifteen slaves who comprised six families when his estate was inventoried and partitioned in 1848. In the partition, four of

24. Estate of William C. Sparks, Bell County Probate Records (Will Record); Estate of Robert O. Reeves, Grayson County Probate Papers; Estate of Thomas S. Snow, Polk County Probate Records (Wills, 1840–96); Will of L. M. H. Washington, March 29, 1847, in Lewis Mills Hobbs Washington Family Papers, Barker Texas History Center, University of Texas, Austin; Estates of Ephraim D. Moore and John Robbins, Red River County Probate Records (Will Record, Book B); Estate of Isaac Vandorn, Matagorda County Probate Records (Transcribed Will Record).

the families were kept intact but two were disrupted. Sancho and Lucy, who were both thirty-three, had their nine-year-old son placed with another family. The Polk County estate of Nicholas M. Callahan had such extensive debts that seven slaves including a twenty-two-year old woman and her four children aged six, four, two, and one, were sold in 1849. The same man bought Letty and her youngest child, but the other three children went to three different purchasers. Probate records provide case after case of this sort, but the point is obvious—estate settlements constituted a major threat to slave families in Texas.[25]

The breakup of a slave family was heart-rending. When eight-year-old Charlie Sandles was traded to a new master, he cried for a week. Tempe Elgin's master moved from Arkansas to Texas, taking her mother and sister, and leaving behind her father who belonged to a different master. The man ran away and followed them for sixty miles, urging his wife to run away and live with him. She, however, would not leave her children, so he gave up. His family never saw him again. Albert Henderson, drawing an analogy from his rural background, said that slaves when sold from each other "bawled" like cattle that had lost their calves. James Brown remembered seeing "them cry like they at the funeral when they am parted, they has to drag them away."[26]

Many slaves demonstrated a willingness to sacrifice virtually everything else in their lives in order to preserve their families. Millie Ann Smith described how she was brought to Texas with her mother and two sisters. Her father, who belonged to a different master, ran away, followed his wife and children to Texas, and begged their owner into buying him so that he could be with his family. Wash Ingram of Panola County told a similar story. His family lived in Virginia, he said, and his father ran away but remained in the neighborhood. Then his mother died, and he and the other children were sold to Jim Ingram from Texas. His father followed the children all the way to Louisiana before catching up with

25. Estate of William Steen, De Witt County Probate Records (Final Record Deceased Persons, Book A); Estate of Peter Gautier, Sr., Brazoria County Probate Records (Wills, etc., Book A); Estate of Nicholas Callahan, Polk County Probate Records (Probate Records, 1847–49). For other examples of estate settlements that separated family members, see Estate of Britain Odom, De Witt County Probate Records (Final Record Deceased Persons, Book A); Estate of Reuben D. Wood, San Augustine County Probate Records (Book of Wills, 1856–96); Estate of Samuel Craft, Travis County Probate Papers; and Estate of Thomas A. Edwards, Cass County Probate Records (Final Record Probate Court, Book 4).

26. *Am. Slave, Supp.*, Ser. 2, IX, 3445 (Charlie Sandles), IV, 1293 (Tempe Elgin), V, 1698 (Albert Henderson), III, 477 (James Brown).

them and becoming Ingram's slave also in order to be with his family. Walter Rimm told his WPA interviewer a story that, he said, "makes the impression on me all my life." At a slave auction on his master's place, a man from "outside" put a fifteen-year-old girl on the block. Suddenly, there was a scream from an older woman who had features very similar to the girl: "Ise will cut my throat is my daughter am sold." The owner talked to the woman, failed to calm her, and took the girl off the auction block. Her threat had preserved a family relationship, at least for the time.[27]

When slave families were disrupted, fathers, mothers, and children did the best they could to stay in contact and visit each other. The Christmas holidays were an especially likely time for families to be reunited, although many were able to get together more often. Charlie Sandles, for example, visited his parents from Saturday night until sundown on Sunday. Mollie Dawson's father lived on a neighboring plantation, and at times she left her home to visit him at his. One of Preston R. Rose's slaves went to California with him during the early 1850s, and somehow managed to obtain freedom and stay in the new El Dorado. In May, 1851, he wrote Rose, saying "I cannot come home this season, but would like much to have my family with me, if any arrangement could be made. Please let me know how much money it will be necessary for me to send you for their freedom." W. Steinert, a German visitor to Texas in 1849, traveled from New Braunfels to Austin by a stagecoach that included a slave woman and child among its passengers. To his surprise, when the stage reached Austin a Negro woman ran up and almost literally pulled the child from the coach, crying, "My baby, my little baby." Steinert then found that "the very happy woman was the mother of the child. The christian whites had torn mother and daughter apart by a sale. On the other hand they were humane enough to permit the visit."[28]

Some efforts to renew family ties after long periods of disruption were truly heroic. Mary Armstrong's mother was sold from her home in Missouri to Texas before the Civil War. Upon being manumitted in 1863, Armstrong decided to go to Texas in search of her mother. She was al-

27. *Ibid.*, IX, 3651 (Millie Ann Smith), V, 1852–55 (Wash Ingram), VIII, 3309–10 (Walter Rimm).

28. Maddox, "Slavery in Texas," 75–77; *Am. Slave, Supp.*, Ser. 2, IX, 3445 (Charlie Sandles), II, 156–57 (Delia Barclay), IV, 1120 (Mollie Dawson); Robert F. Rose per S. S. Snyder, his friend, to Preston Rose, May 30, 1852, in Rose Papers; Jordan (ed. and trans.), "Steinert's View of Texas in 1849," 409–410.

most returned to slavery in Austin, saving herself only with her manumission papers, before finally locating her mother in Wharton County after the war. Louisa Picquet was born in South Carolina, the child of a mulatto slave named Elizabeth Ramsey and her master. Eventually a man from Texas bought the mother, and Louisa was sold to a man in New Orleans and became his concubine. Upon his death, she was manumitted and given enough money to move to Cincinnati, where she married a mulatto named Henry Picquet. Louisa then continued a search for her mother that had begun almost as soon as they were separated. Finally, a friend who traveled to Texas told her of a Mr. Horton who fit the description of the man who had bought her mother. This was Albert C. Horton, a former lieutenant governor and acting governor of Texas and one of the state's largest slaveholders. She began a correspondence with her mother and with Horton in 1858 or 1859, seeking to buy her mother's freedom. Horton asked $1,000; Picquet convinced him to take $900 and raised the money through severe personal economies and a public request for funds. A note in the Cincinnati *Daily Gazette* of October 15, 1860, thanked everyone who had contributed to purchasing the freedom of Elizabeth Ramsey and invited them to call at the Picquets' home to be thanked personally by mother and daughter.[29]

Following the Civil War, the Freedmen's Bureau in Texas received numerous inquiries from blacks in other states concerning family members. A letter of July 20, 1866, from Topeka, Kansas, for example, contained a request from David Barber for "information concerning his wife Sophia Howard, who with her 6 children were sent to Collin Co., Texas in 1861." Charles White of Elizabeth City, North Carolina, wrote in June, 1867, asking that the bureau "procure and return to him his wife and two children John Westley & Florence who before the war were sent to Victoria, Tex." These men were attempting to restore families that had been disrupted for more than five years.[30]

No more eloquent testimony to the vital importance of the slave family can be imagined than the determination of the bondsmen themselves to

29. *Am. Slave, Supp.*, Ser. 2, II, 69–73 (Mary Armstrong); Bert James Loewenberg and Ruth Bogin (eds.), *Black Women in Nineteenth-Century American Life: Their Words, Their Thoughts, Their Feelings* (University Park, Penn., 1976), 54–69.

30. David Barber to General J. B. Kiddoo, July 20, 1866, Charles White to Kiddoo, June 24, 1867, both in Register of Letters Received, Records of the Assistant Commissioner for the State of Texas, United States Bureau of Refugees, Freedmen, and Abandoned Lands, 1865–69, RG 105, National Archives, Washington, D.C.

form and preserve bonds between husbands/fathers, wives/mothers, and children. A few may have sought to escape the heartbreak of family disruptions by avoiding such ties. William Byrd told of slaves who tried not to let children know who their parents were, and Lu Lee said women sometimes forced themselves to miscarry by taking calomel and turpentine. But this was not typical. "Nobody can tell me now," wrote Steinert after witnessing the joyous reunion of a mother and her child in Austin, "that the Negroes do not have fatherly and motherly love in their hearts." The bonds of love and support between the men, women, and children who created slave families, in spite of the fact that a majority of those families probably faced disruption at some time, provided much of the emotional strength necessary to endure servitude.[31]

Religion appears to have been second only to the family in helping slaves survive the psychological assault of bondage. Its role, however, depended on how spiritual instruction was given and how slaves heard and received the various articles of faith and religious precepts. Religion could be highly supportive of slavery when it taught that men had to obey their temporal masters in the same manner that they served their spiritual ruler. Bondsmen were instructed to be loyal, virtuous, and industrious, with the idea that, as one traveler put it, "a good christian is not a bad servant." On the other hand, Christianity could be subversive of slavery when it taught that all men, black and white, stood on an equal footing before God and were equally capable of attaining eternal salvation. Most Texans, while they certainly did not mean to undermine their Peculiar Institution, did not deny this most fundamental Christian assumption. At least, then, religion offered many slaves the promise, as Mary Gaffney put it, of an eternity "where they would not be any more slaves." At best, there was the hope for deliverance as the Bible told of people delivered from bondage and sin. Many years later, Ellen Ford remembered how her family had prayed for freedom and insisted that "emancipation wouldn't have come if it hadn't been for the prayers of my mother and grandmother."[32]

Slaveholders probably had fewer reasons to encourage or even permit

---

31. *Am. Slave, Supp.*, Ser. 2, III, 573 (William Byrd), VI, 2299 (Lu Lee); Jordan (ed. and trans.), "Steinert's View of Texas in 1849," 410.

32. Smith, *Account of a Journey Through Northeastern Texas*, 82–84; *Am. Slave, Supp.*, Ser. 2, V, 1447 (Mary Gaffney), IV, 1357 (Ellen Ford).

religious instruction and worship among their bondsmen than they had for allowing slave families. Religion was not generally as vital to the slaves' emotional well-being, and it involved nothing of such practical value as procreation. Under these circumstances, some masters did their best to prohibit all religious activities. They did not allow their bondsmen to attend church or even to worship on their own. According to Sarah Ashley, who belonged to Mose Davis near Coldspring, "there wasn't any meetings allowed in the quarters. The boss man even whip them when they have the prayer meeting." "Sometimes," she added, "us run off at night and go to . . . camp meetings, but I was plumb growed before I ever went to church." John Bates's Uncle Ben read the Bible and told the others on his place that some day they would be free. Their master heard and said, "Hell, no, you will never be free, you ain't got sense enough to make the living if you was free." He said the Bible had put bad ideas in people's heads and took it away from Ben. Bates remembered, however, that his uncle got another Bible and "he keeps this one hid all the time." In 1857, Ashbel Smith's overseer refused the slaves permission to attend services on Sunday, which they, as was their practice in all such disputes, protested to their master.[33]

Preventing religious activity was thus virtually impossible. Most masters, therefore, did not attempt to prohibit worship, and some actively encouraged it. Their purposes ranged from the cynical view that Christian virtues made better slaves to the sincere conviction that the souls of all, black as well as white, should be saved. Wes Brady complained that he heard only about obeying and not stealing. There was "nary a word about having a soul to save." But Albert C. Horton, a Baptist deacon and one of the largest slaveholders in Texas, took a genuine interest in the spiritual welfare of his bondsmen. He built a church, employed a minister, and personally read the Bible and prayed with his servants. Most slaveholders probably had mixed motives. As one Harrison County minister said of the slaveholders in his area, "all seem to understand, that while the Gospel qualifies their servants for immortality and eternal life, at the same time it makes them better servants here—better to their earthly masters—more obedient, industrious, trusty, and faithful."[34]

33. *Am. Slave, Supp.*, Ser. 2, II, 89 (Sarah Ashley), II, 176 (Joe Barnes, who told a similar story), II, 214–15 (John Bates); Benjamin Roper to Ashbel Smith, February 2, 1857, in Smith Papers.

34. *Am. Slave, Supp.*, Ser. 2, II, 401 (Wes Brady), II, 3 (Frank L. Adams, who remembered being required to attend church); LaNelle S. Douglas, "Religious Work Done by the Texas

Bondsmen on some places simply held local services that created as little bother as possible. Charlotte Beverly said that her master sometimes allowed one of the slaves who was "a sort a preacher" to speak to the others. However, he had to preach with a tub over his head, because if he got too "happy" and loud someone would come from the big house and end the "disturbance." [35]

It was common, however, for slaves to belong to organized churches and attend regularly scheduled services. Most Texan slaveholders who attended church belonged to one of the "standard" Protestant denominations—Methodist, Baptist, Presbyterian, Episcopal, Cumberland Presbyterian, and Disciples of Christ (Christian church)—and all these churches baptized slaves. The Methodist church, the largest denomination in antebellum Texas, claimed 1,000 blacks by the mid-1840s and reported nearly 7,500 Negro members and probationers in 1860. Complete membership statistics for the Baptist church, the second largest in the state in 1860, are not available, but clearly thousands of slaves belonged to it, too. In 1861, for example, the Colorado, Austin, Little River, and Grand Cane Baptist associations, which represented fewer than half of such associations in Texas, reported 1,087 Negro members. The other denominations were far smaller, but they, too, baptized slaves. Caleb Ives, the Episcopal minister who organized Christ Church at Matagorda in 1839, accepted "colored" members, and when Texas became a separate diocese in 1859, its first bishop, Alexander Gregg, ministered as regularly to slaves as to whites. The Cumberland Presbyterians accepted Negroes as full members of their local congregations. The Colorado Presbytery, for example, reported 256 white and 44 black communicants in 1860. The Disciples of Christ's pioneer "Old Liberty" Church in Collin County was founded by 16 whites and 5 slaves. In short, only a minority of Texas' slaves actually belonged to organized churches. But thousands had been baptized, many others doubtless attended services, and a good many more worshipped on their home places. Certainly most had access to some form of religion. [36]

Baptists Among the Negroes in Texas from 1836 to 1873" (M.A. thesis, Sam Houston State University, 1967), 41–42; Palm, "Slavery in Microcosm: Matagorda County," 85–86; Marshall *Texas Republican*, August 23, 1849.

35. *Am. Slave, Supp.*, Ser. 2, II, 285 (Charlotte Beverly).

36. Macum Phelan, *A History of Early Methodism in Texas, 1817–1866* (Dallas, 1924), 232, 499–500; Walter N. Vernon *et al.*, *The Methodist Excitement in Texas: A History* (Dallas, 1984), 76, 116; Hogan, *Texas Republic*, 197; James Milton Carroll, *A History of Texas Baptists: Compris-*

Some of the slaves attended worship services with their masters, sitting in pews especially designated for them. Far more common, however, were special meetings for black church members on Sunday afternoon or night. In some cases, the Methodists and Baptists permitted even more separate worship through the formation of all-black congregations. By 1860, for example, the Methodist church had thirty-seven "missions" to the slaves with a total membership of 2,585 bondsmen. The Colorado Baptist Association at its 1854 meeting permitted the "Colored Church on J. H. Jones' plantation, Matagorda County" to join as a separate congregation. The next year, however, the Union Baptist Association rejected a similar request by the "African Church at Anderson" on the grounds that "the establishment of independent Churches among our colored population would be inconsistent with their condition as servants, and with the interests of their masters." Separate worship services were acceptable, the association said, "but always to be aided in this work by the presence and counsel of some judicious white members." [37]

The matter of separate slave congregations raised a more fundamental question—who was to minister to the bondsmen? Obviously, the slaveholders intended that white preachers provide religious instruction, but, as slavery matured in Texas, black ministers were not uncom-

ing a Detailed Account of Their Activities, Their Progress, and Their Achievements, ed. J. B. Cranfill (Dallas, 1923), 260; Paul Wayne Stripling, "The Negro Excision from Baptist Churches in Texas (1861–1870)" (Ph.D. dissertation, Southwestern Baptist Theological Seminary, 1967), 260; Palm, "Slavery in Microcosm: Matagorda County," 90–95; Lawrence L. Brown, The Episcopal Church in Texas, 1838–1874 (Austin, 1963), 96–97; R. Douglas Brackenridge, Voice in the Wilderness: A History of the Cumberland Presbyterian Church in Texas (San Antonio, 1968), 71; Carter E. Boren, Religion on the Texas Frontier (San Antonio, 1968), 46–47; Minutes of the Colorado Presbytery of the Cumberland Presbyterian Church, 1843–1859, Barker Texas History Center, University of Texas, Austin. On the relative strength of the various denominations in antebellum Texas, see Richardson, Wallace, and Anderson, Texas: the Lone Star State, 213–14.

37. Phelan, History of Early Methodism, 372–74, 418, 429; William P. Harrison (comp. and ed.), The Gospel Among the Slaves (Nashville, 1893), 319–24; Stripling, "Negro Excision from Baptist Churches," 72–74. For examples of slaves worshipping at the same services as their masters, see Stripling, "Negro Excision from Baptist Churches," 84; Reba W. Palm, "Protestant Churches and Slavery in Matagorda County," East Texas Historical Journal, XIV (1976), 5; Boren, Religion on the Texas Frontier, 47; Am. Slave, Supp., Ser. 2, VII, 2729–35 (A. M. Moore). For the more typical experience of separate services, see Record of Proceedings of the First Baptist Church of Galveston, Texas, Rosenberg Library, Galveston; Brackenridge, Voice in the Wilderness, 77; John Lee Eighmy, "The Baptists and Slavery: An Examination of the Origins and Benefits of Segregation," Social Science Quarterly, XLIX (1968), 671; Douglas, "Religious Work Done by the Texas Baptists," 14, 34.

mon. In Washington County during the 1840s, a slave named John Mark preached so well to white and black alike that, when his owner moved, local planters bought and deeded him to three ministers in trust for the Methodist church. In 1853, the Texas Conference of the Methodist Episcopal Church, South, elected John Mark "to deacon's orders as a local preacher." The Trinity Presbytery of the Cumberland Presbyterian church in 1848 authorized a man called "Brother Henry," the property of William Roberts, to preach, to baptize other blacks, and to "administer the sacraments of the supplies" to them. Slaves in the Indian Creek community of Jasper County built the Dixie Baptist Church in 1853 with the aid of Joshua Seale. One of Seale's slaves, Richard, was the church's founding minister. Bondsmen in the area reportedly "flocked into the wooden church every Sunday and dared not think of missing." Some black preachers, of course, ministered without the formal approval of any denomination. Some were recognized locally and preached on their own places and adjoining plantations, while others repeated and interpreted what they heard from white ministers. In any case, extensive evidence from church records and from the slaves themselves indicates that many and probably most had the opportunity to hear a religious message presented by a fellow slave. Indeed, black ministers were numerous enough by 1860 that the Texas Conference of the Methodist Church received a recommendation from its committee on African missions to withdraw approval from meetings "conducted by colored men" and stop "licensing or renewing the licenses of colored men to preach."[38]

What did bondsmen hear when they attended worship services? White ministers, as noted above, generally told the slaves to be loyal, honest, and industrious in order to attain ultimate salvation. Blacks who led worship services often had their words carefully monitored by slaveowners or other white supervisors. Nancy Jackson and Simpson Camp-

38. Hogan, *Texas Republic*, 197; Harrison (comp. and ed.), *Gospel Among the Slaves*, 355–59. Harrison also tells of a black minister in Austin named Nace Duval who had a "large class of colored Methodists." Jonnie Lockhart Wallis and L. L. Hill (eds.), *Sixty Years on the Brazos: The Life and Letters of Dr. John Washington Lockhart, 1824–1900* (New York, 1966), 54, says that John Mark attained freedom. Brackenridge, *Voice in the Wilderness*, 77–78; Douglas, "Religious Work Done by the Texas Baptists," 22–23; Webb, Carroll, and Branda (eds.), *Handbook of Texas*, III, 866–67. For examples of slaves who heard black ministers, see *Am. Slave, Supp.*, Ser. 2, V, 1524 (Andy Goodman), V, 1817 (Lizzie Hughes), II, 342 (Betty Bormer), II, 356 (Isabella Boyd), III, 708 (Jeptha Choice), II, 13 (Will Adams). There were many others. Marshall *Texas Republican*, February 11, 1860 (quotation); on this subject, also see Vernon *et al.*, *Methodist Excitement in Texas*, 111–12.

bell, for example, both remembered how their ministers were instructed to preach obedience to earthly masters. Josie Brown said that the slaves on her place had to hold their church meeting "in the yard, so the white folks could see the kind of religion expounded." Those who preached "wrong" views were likely to have short careers. Sarah Ford told about a preacher named "Uncle Lew" who said that the Lord had created all men equal. "Uncle Jake," the black driver, told the master, and "Uncle Lew" found himself a field hand again the next day. And yet, in spite of all efforts to insure that slaves heard only the "right" religious message, those who worshipped were well aware of the other implications of a belief in God and Jesus. Even without an "Uncle Lew" to tell them, they understood that all men stood equally before their creator. This meant, at the very least, the promise of salvation for all, and, at best, it was a promise of redemption. Religious faith helped many thousands of slaves to endure.[39]

In Texas, as elsewhere across the South, slaves' music contributed significantly to their adjustment to servitude. Music was an acceptable form of expression that served the needs of blacks in a variety of ways. Slaves sang to set a pace for their work and to express their emotions. As Vinnie Brunson told a WPA interviewer, "the Negro used to sing to nearly everything he did. It was the way he expressed his feelings and it made him relieved, if he was happy, it made him happy, if he was sad, it made him feel better, and so he naturally sings his feelings." Slaves also used music as a deceptive form of communication. Richard Carruthers of Bastrop County remembered how, as a youth with the job of managing livestock, he watched for the overseer, Tom Hill, and used a song to warn his fellow bondsmen in the cotton field. When Carruthers sang "Hold up, hold up, American spirit," the field hands knew that they were about to receive a visit from "Devil Hill." In a similar vein, when one of Rosina Hoard's owner's sons tried to teach some of the slaves the ABCs, lookouts stood ready to give a musical warning if the master approached. Above all, slave music contained protests against bondage and expressions of the dream of freedom. One song protested:

39. *Am. Slave, Supp.*, Ser. 2, III, 535 (Wesley Burrell), III, 630 (Richard Carruthers), V, 1911–12 (Nancy Jackson), III, 614–15 (Simpson Campbell), III, 483 (Josie Brown), IV, 1364 (Sarah Ford), IV, 1033–34 (Parilee Daniels). Webber, *Deep Like the Rivers*, 80–90, argues that, across the South, slaves distinguished between the concepts of true Christianity and the falsehoods of slaveholders' preachings and prayed for deliverance on judgment day.

Master sleeps in the feather bed,
Nigger sleeps on the floor
When we all get to Heaven,
They'll be no slaves no more!

"We hummed our religious songs in the field while we was working," Millie Ann Smith of Rusk County said. "It was our way of praying for freedom, but the white folks didn't know it." Slave music was thus a means of expression, communication, and protest. Bondsmen often said a great deal more through song than their masters knew or cared to recognize, and in the process they exercised one more means of withstanding the psychological pressure of slavery.[40]

Many Texas slaves had some opportunity for education in reading and writing because the Lone Star state had no laws intended to prevent slave literacy. Some owners deliberately sought to prevent any education of slaves because it would lead to running away and other expressions of discontent. Even in some of these cases, however, members of the white family, usually children, ignored the objections of the master and mistress and tried to teach young slaves to read. Susan Merritt, for example, remembered being hit with a whip when her mistress caught her being taught to read by one of the family's daughters. Many owners, however, had no objections if their slaves were taught, and others sought deliberately to give a minimal education and take advantage of it. Andrew Goodman's master, for example, urged his bondsmen to learn all they could, and Robert Prout attended a Sunday morning "school" taught by his owner. W. L. Sloan of Harrison County educated some of his slaves to the point that they could keep records on cotton picking and other plantation work. Others had similar opportunities, although not all cared to learn. Liza Jones, for example, said that she cried to go out and play when one of her master's daughters tried to teach her to read and write. Such reluctance may have been nothing more than the expression of a child's desire to play rather than work, but it may also have been an indication that formal education was relatively unimportant to slaves. It seems that literacy did not confer any special status, unless combined with preaching, and had no particular mental or emotional benefits. No doubt infor-

---

40. *Am. Slave, Supp.*, Ser. 2, III, 517 (Vinnie Brunson), III, 631 (Richard Carruthers), V, 1732 (Rosina Hoard), IX, 3653 (Millie Ann Smith); Maddox, "Slavery in Texas," 78; Cal M. Logue, "Transcending Coercion: The Communicative Strategies of Black Slaves on Antebellum Plantations," *Quarterly Journal of Speech*, LXVII (1981), 31–46.

mal education—the knowledge of what it meant to be a slave and how to get along in the system—was more important than formal learning. This type of education, however, was provided by families and other slaves in the quarters and cannot be documented.[41]

Texas slaves, as they endured bondage, generally gained mental and emotional strength from their families, religion, and music. Still, however, they had to adjust their attitudes and day-to-day behavior to the pressures of bondage. How Texas blacks behaved as they faced the widespread harshness and essential hopelessness of slavery constitutes another vital aspect of the psychological conditions of servitude.

41. *Am. Slave, Supp.*, Ser. 2, VII, 2643–44 (Susan Merritt), III, 535 (Wesley Burrell), IX, 3653 (Millie Ann Smith), V, 1524 (Andy Goodman), VIII, 3197 (Robert Prout), III, 614 (Simpson Campbell), VIII, 3003 (Mary Overton), IV, 1428–29 (Rosanna Frazier), VI, 2120–21 (Liza Jones).

NINE

· · · · · · · · · ·

Behavioral Patterns and the Desire for Freedom

''THE BEST WE COULD''

The behavior patterns of Texas slaves varied greatly from individual to individual, but most bondsmen fell into one of three general categories. Some apparently surrendered to their circumstances and became faithful servants who identified with their masters. In total contrast, others were rebels who seized every opportunity to resist servitude. Between these two extremes there were the slaves who, as one put it, did "the best we could," neither surrendering nor rebelling but seeking to endure on the best terms possible consistent with their own dignity and self-respect.[1]

It is impossible to say how many bondsmen surrendered psychologically to slavery. The records of slaveholders are replete with references to "faithful servants" who served loyally all their lives. Such slaves often were greatly mourned at their deaths or given special consideration in wills written by their masters. James Stephens of McLennan County, for example, provided that Dolly, "a faithful slave and nurse for me and my family for many years," be given to a friend with the stipulation that she not be "considered bound to service or labor for anyone." Martha B. Hardin's will directed that Bet, in light of her loyal service, be exempted from the property partition and allowed to live with whichever of the Hardin children she wished. "I will," wrote Catlett James Atkins of Grayson County, "that my old and faithful servant Jim be at liberty to do as

---

1. *Am. Slave, Supp.*, Ser. 2, IV, 1132 (Mollie Dawson).

177

he pleases either to live with his Miss Jane [Atkin's wife] or return to the
Creek nation and live with his wife." Testimony of this sort concerning
faithful slaves has a serious limitation, however. It provides evidence that
is probably valid concerning the outward behavior of "loyal servants" in
the presence of their masters, but it does not necessarily prove that those
bondsmen had surrendered and "loved" or identified with their owners.[2]

Slaves themselves offer some testimony concerning "loyal servants,"
but there are difficulties with it, too. Hagar Lewis remembered that, as
children, she and her sister wanted to "turn white." This is compelling
evidence of the psychological impact of a system involving white masters
and black slaves, but it tells little about the attitudes or actions of adults.
Felix Haywood described a discussion with his father about why Texas
slaves had not done more to help the North win the Civil War. They had
concluded, he said, that "we couldn't help [but] stick to our masters. We
could no more shoot them than we could fly." It was, of course, a long
way from being unable to kill one's owner to surrendering completely to
slavery. Sarah Ford told about a black driver called "Uncle Jake" who
served his owner so faithfully in working and disciplining the other
bondsmen that none of them would have anything to do with him after
freedom. Ford's father relented enough to allow "Uncle Jake" to live in
their corn crib until he died. Of course, a man like "Uncle Jake" may not
have been a "loyal servant" so much as he was simply an opportunist
who abused his power in an effort to ingratiate himself with his master.[3]

In short, some slaves apparently surrendered psychologically to their
situation as bondsmen and lost any sense of personal identity or self-
worth. Their cases cannot be documented with any degree of certainty,
however, because it is impossible to distinguish between those who in-
ternalized the behavior patterns of the loyal servant and those who engaged in conscious accommodation for the purpose of getting along with
masters. Black folklore has many stories of slaves who consciously played
at being faithful and loyal while outwitting their masters. One story, for
example, involves a "faithful old slave" named John who stole onions
from his master. When told to catch the thief, John trapped a skunk. If

2. Estate of James Stephens, McLennan County Probate Records (Probate Records, Book
B); Estate of Martha B. Hardin, Polk County Probate Records (Wills, 1840–96); Estate of
Catlett James Atkins, Grayson County Probate Records (Probate Records, Book F).

3. *Am. Slave, Supp.*, Ser. 2, VI, 2334 (Hagar Lewis), V, 1694 (Felix Haywood), IV, 1363–69
(Sarah Ford).

his master doubted that the real culprit has been caught, John said, he could smell the skunk's breath.[4]

Far more slaves rebelled against bondage than surrendered or acted as if they had given in to it. In some cases, those who rebelled did so primarily in the ferocity of their hatred for slaveowners. Wes Brady, for example, told his WPA interviewer: "If there is a Hell, old Master sure went there for the way he used the innocent Negroes." William Moore said of his master: "I guess he is in Hell. Seems like that is where he belongs." Millie Manuel was more general. "I wouldn't trust a white man no more than a rattler," she said. "The Good Shepherd," she continued, "will give the best white man a heaven that is hotter than the worst Negro's Hell." Brady, Moore, and Manuel did not "rebel" in the usual sense of the word, but they certainly were not loyal servants.[5]

Other slaves expressed rebellion by day-to-day troublemaking and resistance. Elvira, a mulatto belonging to a Jackson County estate in the late 1830s, gave so much trouble by "her irregularity of conduct and general misbehavior" that the administrator asked permission to hire her out in 1840. Kate, who belonged to a Washington County estate, was "so vicious and unmanageable that when hired out no person to whom she was hired would keep her." A man named Anderson was equally impossible to control. The administrator of that estate solved the problem by selling Kate and Anderson. Four slaves were sold from Zachariah Abney's Harrison County estate because they could not "be controlled by any person but their owner without rigid severity," and their example had a "very bad effect upon the other negroes." N. B. Hawkins of east Texas headed for California in 1851 with his family and some slaves but ran out of money at El Paso when his wife became ill. He tried unsuccessfully to earn some money getting out lumber for a fort being built

4. Elkins, *Slavery*, contended that the institution, as it was practiced in the United States, turned the majority of black males into "Sambos" who behaved as loyal servants. He was answered effectively in Eugene D. Genovese, "Rebelliousness and Docility in the Negro Slave: A Critique of Elkins' Thesis," *Civil War History*, XIII (1967), 293–314; Kenneth M. Stampp, "Rebels and Sambos: The Search for the Negro Personality in Slavery," *Journal of Southern History*, XXXVII (1971), 367–92; and Blassingame, *The Slave Community*. Boles, *Black Southerners*, 167, 179–80, concludes that slave "Sambos" existed but were a small minority of the total. The story of John is found in John Q. Anderson, "Old John and the Master," *Southern Folklore Quarterly*, XXV (1961), 195–97. John Mason Brewer, *Dog Ghosts and Other Texas Negro Folk Tales* (Austin, 1958), is a major collection of folklore from Texas blacks.

5. *Am. Slave, Supp.*, Ser. 2, II, 403 (Wes Brady), VII, 2766 (William Moore), VII, 2568 (Millie Manuel).

there. His failure, he said, was due primarily to the slaves, who "would not work" and "killed about forty yoke of oxen for me during the winter." "I was afraid to chastize them," he added, "as we were right on the line where they could cross over into Mexico and be free."[6]

Slaves frequently went beyond being "unmanageable" and rebelled against bondage by running away. Precise statistics on the number of runaways cannot be calculated, but clearly there were thousands. Bondsmen began to escape to Mexico as soon as Texas became an independent republic. William B. DeWees, writing from Columbus in Colorado County on August 29, 1837, described how several of his neighbor's slaves had run for the Rio Grande. Efforts to capture them were thwarted when Indians attacked the pursuers at the Guadalupe River. Thirty fugitive slaves, including two who had once belonged to Sam Houston, were reported living at Matamoros in 1844. By 1851 Texans estimated the number of runaways across the border at three thousand. Frederick Law Olmsted described fugitives "constantly arriving" at Piedras Negras on the Rio Grande in 1854, and the next year "Rip" Ford, the famed Texas Ranger, claimed that four thousand runaways lived in northern Mexico. The land across the Rio Grande, said the San Antonio *Ledger* in 1852, "has long been regarded by the Texas slave as his El Dorado for accumulation, his utopia for political rights, and his Paradise for happiness." The editor claimed that slavery in the United States was more desirable than poverty and peonage in Mexico, but rebellious Texas slaves, if they heard this argument, paid no attention. As late as December, 1864, the guardian of one Travis County estate reported difficulties with a slave who had become "refractory" and "attempted to run off to Mexico."[7]

6. Estate of Mary Fleger, Jackson County Probate Records (Final Estates, Book A); Estate of Elisha D. Little, Washington County Probate Records (Final Record, Book G); Estate of Zachariah Abney, Harrison County Probate Papers; N. B. Hawkins to Rebecca Hagerty, March 6, 1852, in Rebecca McIntosh Hawkins Hagerty Papers, Barker Texas History Center, University of Texas, Austin.

The prevalence of day-to-day resistance among slaves across the South is documented in Stampp, *Peculiar Institution*, 97–109; Raymond A. Bauer and Alice H. Bauer, "Day to Day Resistance to Slavery," *Journal of Negro History*, XXVII (1942), 388–419.

7. Smithwick, *Evolution of a State*, 37, told of slaves escaping to Mexico before 1836 and contended that only ignorance of Spanish kept more from leaving. William B. DeWees, *Letters from an Early Settler of Texas* (Louisville, 1852), 211; Clarksville *Northern Standard*, May 22, 1844; Schwartz, "Runaway Negroes," 39–40; Tyler, "Slave Owners and Runaway Slaves," 22, 36; Olmsted, *Journey Through Texas*, 200, 324; Austin *Texas State Gazette*, February 16, 1850; San Antonio *Ledger*, quoted in Clarksville *Northern Standard*, December 25, 1852; Estate of Joseph Jester, Travis County Probate Records (Probate Records, Book C). Another interesting

Runaways did not necessarily seek the relatively secure freedom of Mexico. Some headed east, or at least their masters thought that they had, in an effort to return to their homes before removal to Texas. For example, a man who belonged to John Sevier of Colorado County was captured in Sabine County in 1840 as he headed for his original home in Tuscumbia, Alabama. In a similar fashion, two men from Bowie County ran toward Missouri in 1843, and one from Clarksville made for Hempstead County, Arkansas, in 1850. At times, Texas slaves also ran for protection to some of the less fierce tribes in the Indian territory to the north. One Titus County master, for example, advertised a $75.00 reward for a twenty-eight-year-old man thought to be heading for the Cherokee or Choctaw nation. In some cases, runaways were attempting to rejoin family members. An advertisement placed by C. M. Adams of Harrison County concerning a man named Anthony included the information that "he is supposed to be making his way to Nacogdoches County, where he has a wife a few miles west of the Alloyoa, at Mrs. Curl's, between San Augustine and Nacogdoches." When James F. Johnson of Travis County hired out Esther and her child to Ashbel Smith in Houston in 1839, the woman's husband Jesse ran away to join his family. Johnson captured Jesse by telling him that he would be sold to someone in the Houston area, but when they headed back toward Travis County Jesse gave him "the slip and put back directly for Houston." Finally, some slaves expressed discontent or anger by leaving simply to live in the woods for as long as they could. Julia Blanks described these bondsmen to a WPA interviewer who asked about runaways: "No Mam, I don't know if they run off to the North, but some of them runned off and stayed in the swamps, and they was mean."[8]

Runaways were primarily young males who escaped singly or in pairs, but there were instances involving men and women, females alone, and

case of slave runaways occurred in Bexar County during the early 1850s. A man named Arcienega gave one Riddle three slaves as security for a debt, but by the time the debt was paid the bondsmen had run for Mexico. *Arcienega* v. *Riddle,* 15 Tex. 330 (1855).

8. San Augustine *Journal and Advertiser,* November 9, 1840; Clarksville *Northern Standard,* July 27, 1843, April 29, 1848; Austin *Texas State Gazette,* June 1, 1850; Marshall *Texas Republican,* November 29, 1849; James F. Johnson to Ashbel Smith, June 27, August 27, 1839, both in Smith Papers; *Am. Slave,* Ser. 1, IV, Pt. 1, pp. 267–68 (Adeline Cunningham), IV, Pt. 1, p. 261 (Green Cumby), IV, Pt. 2, pp. 44–45 (Sarah Ford), V, Pt. 1, p. 135 (William Moore), IV, Pt. 1, pp. 97–98 (Julia Blanks). Lack, "Urban Slavery in the Southwest," 236–37, points out that town bondsmen often ran away to avoid being sent to the country.

even children. The Marshall *Texas Republican* of December 2, 1854, carried a typical runaway advertisement. In it, J. M. Taylor offered a "liberal reward" for Jim, a thirty-five-year-old blacksmith who stood six feet two inches tall, was "quite black," had a pleasant countenance, and walked with his toes turned out "more than is usual for negros." Sam and Betty, a husband and wife both in their early twenties, ran away together on horseback from their Robertson County owner in 1860. They had grown up in the Choctaw Nation, and she was part Indian. A reward of one hundred dollars was offered for their capture. In 1857 J. G. Gibson placed a notice in the Clarksville *Northern Standard* concerning a tall, copper-colored, twenty-three-year-old woman named Julia. She had said, according to Gibson, that "she intended to go to Clarksville and harbor, until she could get some man to take her off." The Houston *Weekly Telegraph* of January 8, 1845, carried an advertisement for a "little negro girl," eight or nine years old, with a "light black complexion," who had run away. Her owner offered a twenty-dollar reward for her return. Occasionally there was an attempt at what is termed a mass escape. Seven men, apparently led by one described as "a Methodist Preacher," ran away together from a Washington County plantation in 1842, and a most unusual group consisting of two men, a pregnant woman, and five preteenage children left Smith County in 1850. They were thought to be heading for the Wichita Mountains of the Indian Territory. In December, 1844, twenty-five mounted and armed slaves left Bastrop for Mexico. Seventeen of the runaways were captured at the Guadalupe River by the sheriff of Gonzales County on January 3, 1845, but seven or eight apparently made good their escape.[9]

The spirit of rebellion was so strong in some slaves that they were habitual runaways. One Brazos County estate administrator, for example, asked the probate court's permission to sell a "negro boy Jack," who was so "in the habit of running away" that he would be of no value unless "kept confined in chains." Jack was sold, presumably to a buyer familiar with the principle of "caveat emptor." Albert, a very intelligent slave who belonged to Ashbel Smith, habitually ran away. In 1843, for example, while Smith was serving as the Republic of Texas' minister to France, his overseer informed him that "Albert has run away 2 or 3 times

9. Marshall *Texas Republican*, December 2, 1854; Dallas *Herald*, December 19, 1860; Clarksville *Northern Standard*, December 26, 1857; Houston *Weekly Telegraph*, January 8, 15, 22, 1845; San Augustine *Red-Lander*, May 26, 1842; Austin *Texas State Gazette*, December 21, 1850.

but has been brought back again." William P. Ballinger of Galveston hired his slave Dave to Aaron Coffee in 1862, but the bondsman ran away twice within a year before Ballinger relented and let him stay at a place he owned in Houston. Dave was then content for about two years before running away again late in 1864.[10]

Runaways, although they often were armed, generally did not use violence against their pursuers. One exception involved a group who were surprised near Victoria by the sheriff of Gonzales County in 1837. They killed the sheriff, took his possessions, and went on to Mexico. Five years later, one of the runaways told the story to a Texan prisoner in Mexico, and the account proved so accurate that the sheriff's remains were located and buried.[11]

Running away generally was nonviolent, but individual acts of violence occurred with enough frequency to constitute yet another significant way slaves rebelled. In 1841, for example, two slaves in Nacogdoches attempted unsuccessfully to poison a family with jimsonweed seeds. That same year, a woman and her daughter killed their Sabine County master and then escaped from the county jail. Margaret, the twenty-one-year-old slave mistress to Solomon Barrow of Liberty, killed her master with arsenic in 1858. The Galveston Weekly News reported an obvious motive—Barrow's will manumitted Margaret at his death and left her five hundred dollars to move to a free state. A slave woman in Bonham strangled the six-year-old son of her master because the boy had said something to his mother that caused the woman's own son to be whipped. In 1851 a slave who had been hired out in Burleson County stopped at the home of William Baker to ask directions about the way back to his master's place in Travis County. Baker and a neighbor decided that the slave was a runaway and tied him up. After the neighbor left, the slave freed himself and fatally stabbed Baker and his wife. Joseph Dougherty's slave, Lucy, who was constantly in trouble with her master and mistress, killed Mrs. Dougherty with a stick of wood and hid her body in a cistern. In Clarksville, John Wilkins misjudged the anger of his slave Washington and paid with his life. He was making leg irons to put on the bondsman following a runaway attempt and trusted the recent captive to wield the

10. Estate of Barrett T. Millican, Brazos County Probate Records (Record of Estates, Book A); H. F. Gillett to Ashbel Smith, January 10, 1843, in Smith Papers; Paul D. Lack, "Dave," in Barr and Calvert (eds.), Black Leaders, 6–11; Fornell, Galveston Era, 121–25.
11. Tyler, "Slave Owners and Runaway Slaves," 7–8.

hammer. Washington crushed his master's skull, ran into nearby woods, and threatened his pursuers before being captured. Some of these violent acts and the many similar ones reported in Texas' newspapers were premeditated; others were committed in moments of panic or rage. In any case, those who resorted to violence did not surrender loyally to the slave system.[12]

The ultimate expression of slave rebellion, of course, was organized violence or insurrection aimed at freeing large numbers of Negroes and perhaps killing large numbers of whites. Insurrection, however, was not common in Texas. Indeed, the whole period to 1865 was marked by only one attempted uprising and one or two plots that were wildly exaggerated by nervous slaveholders eager to blame "free soilers" and "abolitionists" for causing trouble. The one incident that amounted to an attempt at insurrection came during October, 1835. B. J. White informed Stephen F. Austin on the seventeenth that "the negroes on Brazos made an attempt to rise." The plotters, White said, had planned to reverse roles with their masters and ship cotton grown by white labor to New Orleans. This "attempt to rise" amounted to little because one hundred slaves were arrested, many were whipped, and a few were executed. The next notable threat of insurrection came during the late summer of 1856, when a large number of Colorado County slaves, maybe as many as four hundred, plotted to rise up simultaneously, kill all the whites in the surrounding area, and fight their way to Mexico. They were heavily armed with knives, firearms, and ammunition and communicated with the ominous passwords, "Leave not a shadow behind." A slave gave away the plot, however, before it came to fruition. Two or three slaves were hanged and one or two others whipped to death. Revelation of this Colorado County plot touched off a wave of fear, and other supposed plots were discovered at Halletsville and in Rusk, Harrison, and Red River counties. Although an Ohio abolitionist named Davidson received one hundred lashes for his role in the supposed plot at Halletsville, these abortive "uprisings" were more imaginary than real. Soon, newspaper editors, even as they called for vigilance, urged avoidance of undue excitement.[13]

12. McDonald (ed.), *Hurrah for Texas!*, 51, 53–54; Malone, *Women on the Texas Frontier*, 33; Galveston *Weekly News*, January 19, 1858 (case of Solomon Barrow), January 5, 12, 19, 26, 1858 (Daugherty case); Clarksville *Northern Standard*, June 30, 1860 (Bonham murder case), August 13, 27, 1853 (Wilkins case); Austin *Texas State Gazette*, July 12, 19, August 2, 1851.

13. B. J. White to Austin, October 17, 1835, in Barker (ed.), *Austin Papers*, III, 190; Harvey

During the summer of 1860 north and northeast Texas experienced a rash of disastrous fires and many frightening stories of water-source poisonings. The result was the "Texas Troubles," as whites panicked with fear that their slaves, inspired and led by abolitionists, were about to rise against them. Perhaps as many as twenty-five whites and fifty Negroes were executed, yet it is entirely possible that there was not even a plot, let alone an actual uprising. The "Texas Troubles" will be discussed in greater detail in chapter 11; the point here is that there probably was no insurrection in 1860. If there was, the supposed involvement of white abolitionists made it something other than purely a slave uprising.[14]

Thus, few slave insurrections occurred in Texas. An uprising, however, while it was the ultimate form of rebellion, was not the only expression of resistance. Thousands of bondsmen rebelled against their circumstances in less dramatic but highly significant ways—by being recalcitrant and "unmanageable," by running away, and by individual acts of violence.

Many thousands of Texas slaves, probably the majority, neither surrendered to slavery nor rebelled against it. They did not "love" or identify with their masters, or "sell out" their fellow slaves or their own self-respect. They were not cowards or mindless victims who were simply too weak to rebel. Instead, the majority had few illusions about their masters. Josephine Howard expressed a typically clear-eyed view to her WPA interviewer during the 1930s. "I reckon old [Master] Tim," she said, "wasn't no worse than other white folks that owned slaves." Will Adams remembered his grandmother's reply when he commented on how well his master's family had treated them. "Why shouldn't they," she said, "that was their money." Moreover, a slave did not have to be weak or a

Wish, "American Slave Insurrections Before 1861," *Journal of Negro History*, XXII (1937), 307–309; Wendell G. Addington, "Slave Insurrections in Texas," *Journal of Negro History*, XXXV (1950), 414–19; Clarksville *Northern Standard*, September 27, November 1, 1856, January 17, 1857; Austin *Texas State Gazette*, September 13, November 15, 1856; Marshall *Texas Republican*, October 25, November 22, 1856; Austin *Southern Intelligencer*, November 19, 1856.

14. William W. White, "The Texas Slave Insurrection in 1860," *Southwestern Historical Quarterly*, LII (1949), 259–85, contends that there actually was a slave uprising in 1860. Addington, "Slave Insurrections," 419, concludes that there was "wild exaggeration" by the press. One of the most detailed examinations of the "Texas Troubles"—Donald E. Reynolds, *Editors Make War: Southern Newspapers in the Secession Crisis* (Nashville, 1966), 97–111—doubts that there was a plot of any sort, let alone a slave uprising. Two other studies dealing at least in part with this subject—Junkins, "Slave Plots, Insurrections, and Acts of Violence"; and Margaret J. A. Telford, "Slave Resistance in Texas" (M.A. thesis, Southern Methodist University, 1975)—add very little to existing secondary work.

coward to be impressed with the power of slaveholders, slave patrols, slave catchers, and the law-enforcement authorities of Texas. Those who expressed hatred openly or were too unmanageable faced punishment. Runaways sometimes lost their lives to pursuers; if captured, they were whipped, jailed, branded, hobbled with chains, or punished in even more gruesome fashion.[15] Individuals who committed acts of violence almost invariably paid with their lives, in some cases at the hands of mobs rather than through criminal prosecutions. Any action resembling insurrection meant certain death. On one Grayson County plantation in 1850, for example, a slave refused to obey the overseer and hit him with a hoe handle. Later, after the offender had gone back to work, the overseer attempted to punish him, only to be faced with further resistance backed by two other bondsmen. The owner then called in William Bourland and Dr. Elliott from Gainesville, who, with the overseer, summoned the three slaves and demanded that they submit to punishment. Armed with knives and clubs, the slaves refused, whereupon Bourland shot and killed two of the three. The Sherman *Patriot* reported the incident as the suppression of a planned general revolt intended to kill all whites on the plantation. Given reactions of this sort, it is remarkable that so many slaves rebelled in some fashion and not surprising that most adjusted their behavior in the fashion described so well by Mollie Dawson: "It hurt us sometimes to be treated the way some of us was treated, but we couldn't help ourselves and had to do the best we could which nearly all of us done."[16]

Slaves who neither surrendered nor rebelled but did the best they could deliberately acted, whenever possible without inviting retribution, in ways calculated to improve their circumstances. They were, for example, adept at turning privileges into "rights." "Last Saturday afternoon the negroes claimed half the day for themselves—alleging that you had given

15. *Am. Slave, Supp.*, Ser. 2, V, 1808 (Josephine Howard), II, 10 (Will Adams), V, 1579 (James Green), V, 1525 (Andy Goodman). Green and Goodman remembered running to train the dogs used to trail runaways. Adeline Cunningham told of a runaway having his eyes put out as punishment. Her story is in *Am. Slave*, Ser. 1, IV, Pt. 1, pp. 267–68. For examples of individuals being paid for hunting and catching runaways, see Estate of Samuel Craft, Travis County Probate Papers; Estate of Minor Heirs of George W. Tilly, Wharton County Probate Records (Probate Minutes, Book B). For an example of a runaway slave being killed by his pursuers, see Alfred Howell to "My Dear Brother," February 6, 1854, in Howell Letters.

16. Sherman *Patriot*, quoted in Austin *Texas State Gazette*, July 14, 1858; *Am. Slave, Supp.*, Ser. 2, IV, 1132 (Mollie Dawson).

it to them—so I did not consider it proper to make them work," John Bauer, one of Ashbel Smith's overseers, wrote his employer in 1841. "They also claim two hours in the middle of the day,—on the same grounds—which I consider just."[17]

Such bondsmen were also likely to be adamant in refusing to accept unjustified punishment. Jacob Branch told a story about a slave named Charley who worked hard and gave no trouble and was therefore never whipped by his master. His mistress, however, felt that every slave deserved a whipping from time to time and planned to administer one on an occasion when her husband was away. Charley, who was chopping corn, protested that he had done nothing wrong, but she came down the row toward him anyway. According to Branch, Charley, without raising his voice, began to wave his hoe in the air and said, "Missy, I ain't advise you come any step closer." Faced with this kind of determination from a man who was simply being forced to defend himself, the mistress backed away. Ferdinand Roemer told a similar story involving a blacksmith at the Nassau plantation during the 1840s. An inexperienced overseer threatened to whip the man (who was worth two thousand dollars) as if he were an ordinary field hand. The slave ran away and returned only after being promised that he would not be punished.[18]

Another incident involving a slave who refused unjustified punishment ended more tragically. In the spring of 1852, John, who belonged to Felix W. Robertson, had the responsibility of driving an ox wagon loaded with cotton from Washington County to Houston. His wagon bogged down in the muddy bottom just east of the Brazos River. In an effort to get out, he took down part of a fence that paralleled the road on the property of Jared E. Kirby. Failing to pull the wagon free before darkness came, John left the fence down and camped in the edge of the field. Shortly after dawn, Kirby's overseer, H. B. Hedgepeth, rode up and became enraged at what the slave had done. According to witnesses, Hedgepeth said, "I'll whip you, God damn you." John went to the other side of his oxen, and the overseer reiterated his threat, saying, "Pull off your coat, I mean what I say, sir." John replied, "I spects you does sir," but when Hedgepeth spurred his horse around the oxen, the Negro ran out of the field. Hedgepeth ordered two of Kirby's slaves who were present to catch John, but he warned them not to touch him. John then began

17. John Bauer to Ashbel Smith, June 13, 1841, in Smith Papers.
18. *Am. Slave, Supp.*, Ser. 2, II, 408–409 (Jacob Branch); Roemer, *Texas*, 163–64.

running along the road toward the river, while Hedgepeth yelled after him, "You can run, God damn you, but I'll whip you or kill you before you get home, you damned son of a bitch." The overseer sent one of his slaves to get his gun and dog. Meanwhile, a white witness went up to John and urged him to return on the grounds that if whipped at all he would not be whipped much. John refused. Thirty minutes later Kirby rode up. Hedgepeth took his gun and went off in the direction taken earlier by John. One witness reported hearing a gunshot, others said they heard nothing. In any case, John was never seen again dead or alive. He may have drowned or been murdered or escaped. Robertson successfully sued Hedgepeth and Kirby for damages arising from the loss of his slave, who was valued at more than twelve hundred dollars. This case is revealing of slavery in many ways, but the point here is that John, although having no intent to rebel, had too much self-respect to accept even a light whipping that was not justified.[19]

Bondsmen who normally were not rebels might also refuse to accept drastic changes in their lives. The case of an Austin County slave named Tomb provides a good example. Charles Fordtran sold Tomb to John Adriance, but the bondsman soon fought off an overseer and two other blacks who were going to whip him and, armed with a knife and two pistols, said he would fight to the death rather than be taken. He went back to Fordtran's place, "made," in the latter's words, "all the acknowledgements which his former conduct required," and "went to work like a fine fellow." Tomb was allowed to believe that he had been bought back until arrangements were made for his capture. "His confidence in me," Fordtran wrote, "and my guilt of having betrayed him caused me a feeling of remorse which I never before experienced." He urged Adriance not to treat Tomb "too severely" and expressed the hope that the slave would "make you as good a hand as he has here."[20]

Regardless of how they behaved, most slaves lived daily with the desire for freedom as a vital part of their mental and emotional makeup. Jeff Hamilton, Sam Houston's slave, said that he was not always thinking "like so many other slaves I knew, of some plan to escape or how I might manage to buy my freedom some day." But Mary Gaffney insisted that all the slaves thought about was "not being a slave because slavery time

19. *Hedgepeth* v. *Robertson*, 18 Tex. 858 (1857).
20. Charles Fordtran to John and Cornelius Adriance, May 14, May 26, 1846, both in Adriance Papers.

was hell." Even Jerry Moore, who belonged to such a benign owner, Mrs. Isaac Van Zandt, that other whites referred to her slaves as "Van Zandt's free Negroes," remembered the universal desire for deliverance. "All the Van Zandt negroes wanted to be free," he told his WPA interviewer. Martin Jackson made the same point. "Even with my good treatment," he said, "I spent most of my time planning and thinking of running away." For that matter, many slaveowners, regardless of what they said, knew that their human property wanted freedom. They gave this away in a very obvious way. Whenever a slave earned his master's gratitude to the point that the latter wished to make the greatest gift possible to the bondsman, manumission was the likely result. If Negroes were so well off as slaves, how was freedom such a wonderful gift? Blacks were not happy and content as bondsmen. They wanted freedom, and everyone knew it.[21]

In conclusion, the great majority of slaves found the psychological strength to survive bondage. Few were loyal servants who sang to express their happiness as they cheerfully went about their duties. This notion of slavery times is extravagantly romantic. On the other hand, most bondsmen did not live every day in sullen rage and leap at every opportunity to express their rebellion. Thousands did rebel in a variety of ways, but even more, in the words of Mollie Dawson, did "the best we could." This was not in any respect a tribute to the benevolence of slavery, but it was a testimonial to the human spirit of the enslaved blacks. Aided by their families, their religion, their music, and the ability to adjust their behavior to exceedingly difficult circumstances, they found the mental and emotional strength to endure.

21. Hamilton, *My Master*, 125; *Am. Slave, Supp.*, Ser. 2, V, 1447 (Mary Gaffney), V, 1904–1905 (Martin Jackson); *Am. Slave*, Ser. 1, V, Pt. 3, p. 122 (Jerry Moore).

TEN

· · · · · · · · · ·

Texas Slaveholders

''WORKING NEGROES TO AN ADVANTAGE''

"I can tell you," Martin Jackson said to a WPA interviewer, "that the life of the average slave was far from rosy. They were dealt out plenty of cruel suffering. But," he continued, "slavery, I believe, had a more degrading influence upon slave owners than it had upon the slaves." Jackson was not saying that slavery was "harder" on masters than on bondsmen, as has sometimes been claimed, but his statement contained a kernel of truth voiced by more than one observer of the Peculiar Institution. Much, for example, of Thomas Jefferson's aversion to slavery arose from what he termed its "unhappy influence on the manners of our people." It made men both tyrannical and lazy, he thought. Slaveholders did not pay the price for slavery that was exacted from the slaves, but, in spite of what the masters said, the institution in many ways constituted a curse to them, too.[1]

Slaveholders were always a minority among the free population of antebellum Texas. At the census of 1850, 30 percent of the state's heads of households owned bondsmen. That proportion declined to 27 percent by 1860.[2] The implications of these statistics for society in general are considered in the following chapter; the point here is to understand the slaveholders themselves. Although decreasing as a proportion of all Tex-

---

1. *Am. Slave, Supp.*, Ser. 2, V, 1904–1905 (Martin Jackson); Thomas Jefferson, *Notes on the State of Virginia* (New York, 1964), 155.
2. Campbell and Lowe, *Wealth and Power*, 27–28.

ans, they increased very rapidly in absolute numbers during the last two antebellum decades.

The number of slaveholders rose from 2,203 in 1840 to 7,747 in 1850 and 21,878 by 1860, an increase of nearly 900 percent in twenty years. In some cases, more than one slaveholder lived in the same household, but generally only the head of the household owned bondsmen or was reported as the owner. Typically, a household in antebellum Texas had five to six residents. Thus, at least 42,000 men, women, and children in 1850 and 120,000 in 1860 had a direct interest in the ownership and management of slaves.[3]

As would be expected, slaveholding households were headed primarily by natives of the older southern states (89 percent in 1850 and 90 percent in 1860), but immigrants from the free states were nearly as well represented among slaveholders (7 percent in 1850 and 6 percent in 1860) as they were in the total population (10 percent in 1850 and 8 percent in 1860). Only the foreign born, who constituted approximately 14 percent of Texas' household heads in 1850 and 1860, were notably underrepresented among slaveholders (only 4 percent in 1850 and 3 percent in 1860). Slaveholders generally were a little older, averaging forty-one years of age in 1850 and forty-three in 1860, than the typical head of household in Texas, who was on the average thirty-eight in 1850 and thirty-nine in 1860.[4]

Most slaveholders were male, but female owners were not uncommon. An act of January, 1840, by the Republic of Texas defined land and slaves belonging to females at the time of marriage or received later as gifts or bequests as the "separate property of the wife." A wife's slaves and their increase were to remain her separate possessions throughout the marriage, provided that "the husband shall have the sole management of such . . . slaves." The Constitution of 1845 provided that all property belonging to a woman before marriage or acquired thereafter

3. The source for the number of slaveholders in 1840 is Gifford E. White (comp.), *The 1840 Census of the Republic of Texas* (Austin, 1966), which is in reality a compilation of the county tax rolls. Six of the republic's thirty-two counties are missing, so 2,203 is an understatement of the number of slaveholders in Texas at that time. The number of slaveholders in 1850 is from DeBow (ed.), *Statistical View of the United States*, 95; the total for 1860 is from U.S. Bureau of the Census, *Agriculture of the United States in 1860*, 242.

4. These statistics and comparisons are drawn from the samples of five thousand households from the censuses of 1850 and 1860 described in Campbell and Lowe, *Wealth and Power*, 13–31.

"by gift, devise or descent, shall be her separate property." Females also had an equal right to the common property owned jointly with their spouses. Under these circumstances, women could maintain separate ownership of slaves throughout their married lives and, if they outlived their husbands, also share in the common property created during their marriage. The case of Mary Avery from Cherokee County provides a good example of Texas laws for female slaveholders. She owned a slave when she married James Avery in Georgia, but under the laws of that state all property went into her husband's name. Under the pressure of financial difficulties, he sold her slave, but then, when his circumstances improved following a move to Louisiana, he replaced the bondsman and gave Mary the bill of sale. The Averys then moved to Texas, where James died. The administrator of his estate, Richard Avery, claimed that Mary's slave belonged with the others owned as common property, but she insisted that it was hers alone. The dispute reached the Texas supreme court, which ruled in 1854 that Mary Avery was correct in asserting her separate property rights to the slave.[5]

Slaveholding gave some women positions of economic power far greater than those enjoyed by most men in antebellum Texas. In 1851, Emily M. Perry, Stephen F. Austin's sister, willed 34 slaves, which she owned as separate property, to her husband James F. Perry. Elizabeth G. Compton and Elizabeth J. Worrall, both of whom were widowed during the 1850s, left plantation-sized estates including 33 and 42 slaves respectively at the end of the decade. An 1859 inventory of the estate belonging to Thomas J. and Melinda Coffee showed that the latter owned 87 slaves valued at $64,915, while her husband held 48 bondsmen worth $37,300. Sarah Mims of Brazoria County, who was widowed before 1850, headed a household until 1861 and left 116 slaves to be partitioned among her seven heirs. Rebecca McIntosh Hawkins Hagerty of Marion County, a shrewd businesswoman who knew how to manage both people and property, survived two husbands and reported the ownership or control of 102 slaves in 1860.[6]

5. Gammel (comp.), *Laws of Texas*, II, 177–78, 1293. *Avery and Another* v. *Avery*, 12 Tex. 54 (1854). Another case involving separate property in slaves is found in the will of William R. Butler, which directed that all his property be sold to pay debts, except one female who was his wife's "own property inherited by heirship." Estate of William R. Butler, Polk County Probate Records (Wills, 1840–96).

6. Estate of Emily M. Perry, Brazoria County Probate Records (Wills, etc., Book B); Estates of Mrs. E. G. Compton, Mrs. E. J. Worrall, Thomas J. and Melinda G. Coffee, and Sarah Mims, Brazoria County Probate Records (Wills, etc., Book C); Judith N. McArthur, "Myth,

Table 14. Distribution of Slaveowners According to Size of Holdings,
1840, 1850, and 1860

Size of Slaveholding	1–4	5–9	10–19	20–49	50–99	100+
1840						
Number of owners	1,395	481	227	89	10	1
Percentage of owners	63.3	21.8	10.3	4.0	.5	.1
1850						
Number of owners	4,575	1,585	1,121	374	82	10
Percentage of owners	59.1	20.5	14.5	4.8	1.0	.1
1860						
Number of owners	11,342	4,950	3,423	1,827	282	54
Percentage of owners	51.8	22.6	15.6	8.4	1.3	.2

Slaveholdings on the scale of those just cited, owned by either men or women, were far from typical in antebellum Texas (see table 14). In spite of a trend toward larger holdings, as the number of owners reporting twenty or more bondsmen rose from 5 percent of the total in 1840 to 6 percent in 1850 and 10 percent in 1860, the majority of all owners during this period had fewer than five slaves. In fact, nearly one quarter owned only a single bondsman.[7]

Although the typical master had only a few slaves, the degree of concentration was so great that the minority of large holders owned most of the state's bondsmen (see table 15). In both 1850 and 1860, the approximately one quarter of slaveowners who held ten or more bondsmen had more than 60 percent of the total. By 1860, nearly half of all slaves belonged to large planters owning twenty or more bondsmen who constituted a little more than 10 percent of the slaveholding class. On a percentile basis, the top 20 percent of slaveholders ranked according to the size of their holdings owned 96 percent of all slaves.[8]

In spite of this high degree of concentration, only a relative handful of Texans owned 100 or more slaves and could be considered members of a

---

Reality, and Anomaly: The Complex World of Rebecca Hagerty," *East Texas Historical Journal,* XXIV (1986), 18–32.

7. White (comp.), *1840 Census of Republic of Texas, passim;* DeBow (comp.), *Statistical View of the United States,* 95; U.S. Bureau of the Census, *Agriculture of the United States in 1860,* 240–42.

8. These statistics are based on the census samples drawn by Campbell and Lowe as indicated above in note 4.

Table 15. Distribution of Slaves According to Size of Slaveholding, 1850 and 1860

Size of Slaveholding	1–4	5–9	10–19	20–49	50–99	100+
1850						
Percentage of slaveholders	54.5	24.0	14.1	6.4	.9	.1
Percentage of slaves	15.8	22.4	26.3	25.3	8.0	2.2
1860						
Percentage of slaveholders	47.6	23.7	17.5	9.3	1.5	.4
Percentage of slaves	11.5	17.1	25.8	29.6	10.6	5.4

planter elite. Property arrangements were often so complex in the case of very wealthy individuals that it is impossible to say with certainty just how many slaveholders had 100 bondsmen or more. However, approximately sixty Texans fell into this category. These individuals could be found scattered across the state, but most were concentrated in the counties along the lower Brazos and Colorado rivers. Brazoria County alone had ten, including David G. Mills, who with his brother Robert had the largest slaveholding in Texas. They reported 344 bondsmen in the census of 1860 and paid taxes on 430 in 1864, the last year that slaves were assessed before freedom.[9]

The planter elite, although in no way rivals of the greatest slaveholders in the older southern states, enjoyed fabulous wealth by Texas standards. Thomas and Melinda Coffee had an estate worth $212,848 in 1859, and Sarah Mims's property was assessed at $226,033 in 1861. By comparison, the average head of household statewide had $6,393 in total wealth at the census of 1860. John C. Clark of Wharton County built his slaveholding from 36 bondsmen in 1850 to 116 by 1860, when he reported total wealth of $236,860. At Clark's death in 1862, he had two plantations, one with 56 slaves and the other with 81. The acreage (8,739 acres in the two plantations) and slaves alone were appraised at $232,736, but the estate also had nearly $5,000 worth of livestock and more than $10,000 in cotton on hand.[10]

9. Ralph A. Wooster, "Notes on Texas' Largest Slaveholders, 1860," *Southwestern Historical Quarterly*, LXV (1961), 72–79. For a listing of Texas' largest slaveholders in 1860, see Appendix 4. For information on the Millses, see Eighth Census, 1860, Schedule 2 (Slave Inhabitants), and Brazoria County Tax Rolls, 1864. A few counties assessed slaves for tax purposes in 1865, but most did not.

10. Estates of Thomas J. and Melinda G. Coffee and Sarah Mims, Brazoria County Probate Records (Wills, etc., Book C); Estate of John C. Clark, Wharton County Probate Papers; Seventh Census, 1850, Schedule 2 (Slave Inhabitants); Eighth Census, 1860, Schedule 1 (Free

Texas slaveholders had no tradition of absentee ownership, not even among the planter elite. A few, such as Beverly Holcomb of Marshall, lived in town rather than on their plantations. Robert and D. G. Mills spent most of their time managing their commission merchant business in Galveston. Ashbel Smith, for one reason or another, was rarely at his home. Typically, however, slaveholders lived on their own farms and plantations, managing them directly or through overseers. John C. Clark, for example, had two overseers, one for each of his plantations.[11]

Articulate slaveowners, from planters to those who held only a single bondsman, generally preferred to see themselves as benevolent paternalists. Their slaves, they said, were like members of their families. In some cases, references to "family Negroes" meant only those who were household servants, but many masters insisted that all their bondsmen were "family." "My slaves to me," wrote Thomas M. League of Galveston, "are part of my Family, and I would as soon think of selling one of my own Children as one of them." "That some are badly treated there is no doubt," he continued, "but in the main they are an hundred fold better off than the Free blacks in the North." "You will call me a single man without a family," Otis M. Wheeler wrote his parents and sister in Massachusetts, but if you had "my crowd to feed," you would have a better understanding of my circumstances. "My family consists in the first place of my *noble self* 1 clerk 1 collector 1 overseer & 18 negroes 22 all told, a single man with two families." "Tell the Black folks howde [*sic*]," Thomas B. Huling wrote his wife in 1860, "and say to them I want to hear a good account of them when I come home."[12]

Some slaveholders attempted to deal with their bondsmen according to this paternalistic ethos. As the slaves themselves testified, some mas-

Inhabitants), and Schedule 2 (Slave Inhabitants). The average wealthholding in Texas in 1860 is calculated from the Campbell-Lowe sample.

11. Curlee, "Texas Slave Plantations," 85; Silverthorne, *Ashbel Smith, passim*; Webb, Carroll, and Branda (eds.), *Handbook of Texas*, II, 200; Eighth Census, 1860, Schedule 1 (Free Inhabitants).

12. Amelia Barr claimed that large slaveholders were noted for "indulgence" to their slaves and for "the footing the slaves held of being of the family." Philip Graham (ed.), "Texas Memoirs of Amelia E. Barr," *Southwestern Historical Quarterly*, LXIX (1966), 487. For references to house servants as "family slaves," see Roemer, *Texas*, 62; Estate of Mary Slade, Polk County Probate Papers; Estate of James C. English, a Minor, and Martha Waggoner, Fayette County Probate Records (Probate Records, Book E). Thomas M. League to Thomas J. League, August 21, 1850, in Thomas M. League Papers, Rosenberg Library, Galveston, Tex.; Otis M. Wheeler to "Beloved Parents and Sister," July 9, 1844, in Turner Papers; Thomas B. Huling to his wife, January 16, 1860, in Huling Papers.

ters never used the whip, encouraged and protected family relationships, and even sought to extend kindness to bondsmen on neighboring
farms and plantations. Laura Cornish's owner provides the ultimate example, being called "Papa" rather than "Master." Samuel L. Flournoy of
Tyler, according to the Quitman *Texas Free Press*, occasionally indulged
his slaves with visits to "public shows." The paper praised his "patriarchal spirit." Mrs. Isaac Van Zandt provided money to send her Negro
children to the circus. When J. W. Walton offered to sell six bondsmen to
Ashbel Smith in 1847 because, he said, they should have a "good master," slaveholders and slaves alike across Texas would have understood
his meaning.[13]

Not uncommonly, slaveholders placed complete trust in particular
bondsmen and created conditions of considerable closeness with them.
Thomas Blackshear's diary entry for July 13, 1861, read: "My good negro
man Edmund died. He was an honest, truthful, and industrious man
and a faithful servant and I shall miss his services and influence a great
deal." As has been explained, slaves became drivers, were entrusted
with jobs and errands that took them far from home, and were given the
responsibility for the health and safety of their master's children. White
and black grew up playing together. Trusted slaves carried firearms on
their masters' property and hunted for themselves and with their owners. "Our hunter affectionately called 'Uncle Sam' has shot two rabbits,"
Lucadia N. Pease wrote her husband in 1859. In a letter to his brother,
Alfred Howell described an adventure with a group of Hunt County
slaves in 1854. While 'possum hunting at night, they felt themselves men-
aced by a pack of prairie wolves. Howell told the "boys" with him to pick
a tree and be ready to "climb & fight." A Lamar County hunt, on which
a firepan was being used to shine the eyes of deer at night, ended in
misfortune when a slave was ordered to fire at a pair of eyes in the dark
and killed a mare belonging to a third party.[14]

13. Austin *Texas State Gazette*, November 8, 1856; *Am. Slave*, Ser. 1, V, Pt. 3, p. 122 (Laura
Cornish); J. W. Walton to Ashbel Smith, September 12, 1847, in Smith Papers.
14. Diary for 1861, in Blackshear Papers; Lucadia N. Pease to E. M. Pease, April 5, 1859,
in Pease-Graham-Niles Family Papers. It was common enough for slaves to carry firearms
that some masters got into legal trouble for permitting their bondsmen to do so off their home
places. See *Carter* v. *The State*, 20 Tex. 339 (1857) and *Greer* v. *The State*, 22 Tex. 588 (1858).
S. M. Swenson to John Adriance, September, 1844, in Adriance Papers, describes a slave
whose master had given him the responsibility of looking for a new owner. Alfred Howell to
"My Dear Brother," May 24, 1854, in Howell Letters; *Guffey* v. *Moseley*, 21 Tex. 408 (1858).

Examples of familiarity and trust are found also in masters' wills, which frequently contained special provisions concerning the treatment of favorite, usually old, servants. Isaac Guest of Red River County provided in 1861 "that my old Negro woman who has been a faithful servant shall not work any more and that she have Cynthia to take care of her." "As to my old cookwoman Violet," wrote George Thomas of Harrison County, "I don't want any of them [his heirs] to have her, but she is to remain on the place and under the control and management of my son William and in her old age he is to take care of her." In 1849 John P. Thompson from the same county described "an old favorite Negro man by the name of Barrow whom I desire to maintain on the place with his mistress and to perform easy labor, but I do not wish him to be regarded as the property of anyone." Benjamin Thomas of Austin County dictated a will on March 27, 1837, that freed Tom, Rachel, and their five children and gave them all the property he owned in Texas. Special provisions in wills, of course, are not necessarily carried out. After Thomas' death, the administrator of his estate petitioned the county court to disallow the will on the grounds that it contained provisions "contrary to law and which render it impossible . . . to be established under the law." Ten years after the will was first dictated, Tom, Rachel, and their thirteen children and grandchildren still belonged to the estate and were being hired out annually. Many of the other slaves who were the subject of special provisions in their masters' wills may have been just as unfortunate; nevertheless, the slaveholders who left these documents clearly recognized some of their bondsmen as a great deal more than anonymous pieces of property.[15]

Slaveholders and their apologists eventually created a romantic legend concerning the trust and kindness that masters extended to their bondsmen. Like most legends, it had some basis in fact. As has just been demonstrated, "good masters" who liked to express what one called "that interest and sympathy which naturally finds its origin in the relation of master and slave" did exist. Some of their slaves undoubtedly benefited

15. Estate of Isaac Guest, Red River County Probate Records (Will Record, Book B); Estate of George Thomas, Harrison County Probate Records (Estate Record, Book I-J); Estate of John P. Thompson, Harrison County Probate Records (Estate Record, Book B); Estate of Benjamin Thomas, Austin County Probate Records (Succession Record, Books B, C, and D). Stearlin Arnwine, a slave who lived near Jacksonville, said that a promise of freedom was violated in his case. *Am. Slave, Supp.*, Ser. 2, I, 80–81.

from such sentiments, too. For most slaveowners, however, trust, kindness, and feelings of closeness were far less fundamental to the master-slave relationship than were management and discipline. Their slaves were, as one observer put it, "careless and troublesome" and required constant attention that emphasized anything but trust and kindness.[16]

Testimony concerning the "troublesome" nature of slave property is available from a great variety of sources. Frederick Law Olmsted provided numerous examples. Of course slaves are careless about their work, he wrote, "their time isn't any value to themselves." Olmsted's abolitionism led him to see only the worst in slavery, but other, more moderate, northerners were equally critical of Negro workers. Rutherford B. Hayes, while visiting his college classmate Guy M. Bryan at the Peach Point plantation in 1849, wrote his mother: "A good 'manager' here has quite as much 'vexation of spirit' as ever you have who are changing 'girls' once a fortnight." "It may be I am mistaken," he concluded, "but I don't think Job was ever 'tried' by a gang of genuine 'Sambos'!" John P. Osterhout told his mother in Pennsylvania in 1853 that she would not want a slave woman as a worker even if the latter would labor for nothing and support herself.[17]

Southerners and slaveholders often expressed similar complaints and criticisms. In June, 1852, for example, Benjamin E. Roper, Ashbel Smith's overseer at Evergreen plantation, became utterly frustrated with the bondsmen under his "control" there. He wrote Smith: "I was born the owner of slaves and have been so during my whole life. I have always lived amongst slaves and have never been for thirty days in my life beyond the dominion of slavery, yet I have never in my life seen a set of negroes that are more unmanageable than yours. My life is a continued scene of vexation and ill humour and if I could do so with propriety I would not remain on your place an hour." Lizzie Neblett found her slaves

16. For examples of the romantic legend of master-slave relations, see John H. McLean, *Reminiscences of Reverend John H. McLean* (Dallas, 1918), 131–34; Louise Wigfall Wright, *A Southern Girl in '61* (New York, 1905), 16; Petition of L. Hudspeth concerning Susan Hudspeth, a freedwoman, December 2, 1865, Lavaca County Probate Records (Record of Estates, Book A); Amelia M. Murray, *Letters from the United States, Cuba, and Canada* (New York, 1856), 202.

17. Olmsted, *Journey Through Texas*, 56–58, 144, 148–49; Charles Richard Williams (ed.), *Diary and Letters of Rutherford Birchard Hayes, Nineteenth President of the United States* (5 vols.; Columbus, Oh., 1922–26), I, 255; John P. Osterhout to "Dear Mother," March 12, 1856, in Osterhout Papers.

anything but helpful when her husband was away in the Confederate army. "I am awful tired of them," she wrote. "Ten thousand times I have wished you had listened to me—sold them all but what we wanted to wait on us, years ago. I don't say much about them, but they are a great trouble to me—a perfect vexation." Even business advertisers recognized slaves' reputation for carelessness. The Singer Sewing Machine Company informed prospective Texas purchasers in 1860 that its product had a three-year warranty "even in the charge of negroes."[18]

Slaveholders, being unable to admit that any of these problems arose from their system of involuntary servitude, claimed that Negroes, with perhaps a few exceptions, were inherently lazy, careless, and dishonest. Masters generally made an effort to find slaves of "good" character and conduct for household servants and positions of responsibility, but beyond that, the tendency was to lump all bondsmen together and emphasize management techniques. Charles William Tait, for example, explained to his father at some length his problems with two slaves named Nicey and Frank. The former could no longer be kept "about the house," and the latter, although "doing better lately," had a "character for honesty [that] is not very good." By contrast, Tait's "Plantation Rules" contained extensive advice, not for dealing with slaves as individuals, but for managing uniformly troublesome pieces of property. "Never punish a negro when in a passion," he wrote. "No one is capable of properly regulating the punishment for an offense when angry." He also advised letting slaves know exactly why they were being punished and taking care not to show any pleasure in the punishment.[19]

Tait's "Plantation Rules" were written only for overseers employed on his place, but formal advice on slave management was readily available for any Texas master who was interested. For example, Thomas Affleck, who began his career as a planter in Mississippi before moving to Texas

18. Benjamin E. Roper to Ashbel Smith, June 23, 1852, in Smith Papers; Lizzie S. Neblett to Will Neblett, February 12, 1864, in Lizzie Scott Neblett Papers, Barker Texas History Center, University of Texas, Austin; Marshall *Texas Republican*, April 7, 1860. Ann Raney Thomas Coleman told of how she could not get a six-year-old girl to mind her and angered her husband, who said that she (his wife) threatened too much without action. See Reminiscences of Ann R. T. Coleman, in Coleman Papers. Robert Barr, Amelia Barr's husband, thought slavery morally wrong, but she was convinced that his feelings would be altered if he had to deal with the "thieving, lying, and laziness" of their kitchen help. Thomas W. Cutrer, *The English Texans* (San Antonio, 1985), 83–84.

19. Wright, *Southern Girl in '61*, 18; Charles W. Tait to James A. Tait, October 16, 1853, in Tait Papers; "Plantation Rules," in *ibid*.

in 1858, published a variety of plantation record and account books that contained extensive advice on the subject. His material on the duties of overseers in turn appeared in popular publications such as *De Bow's Review*. Affleck's advice was predictable, but apparently readers found it useful. He told masters and overseers to be consistent (keep your word and treat all alike), gentle but firm (stocks were more effective than whipping), and whenever possible to use incentives rather than punishments. But, above all, Affleck cautioned constant attentiveness to both labor and leisure time. "The only way to keep a negro honest," he wrote, "is not to trust him."[20]

Individual slaveholders, of course, had their own ideas about what the British observer William Bollaert called the "great secret" of how to manage bondsmen. Many of them, while no doubt agreeing with Affleck on the black's untrustworthiness, placed much greater faith in punishment. After Elise K. Willrich and her husband settled near LaGrange during the 1840s, they tried owning slaves but soon sold them. "It is said," she wrote her father, "that Germans don't know how to handle negroes—are too good to them. . . . The black people, we are told, are often in need of whipping." Churchill Jones of Falls County criticized his overseer, George H. Daffan, in 1853, saying, "I am afraid you have got the negroes to like you and not fear you. . . . They must know when you speak they have to obey, and to do this you have to stand square up to them and show yourself master. You cannot coax a negro to do his duty. You have to force him." Ashbel Smith's Evergreen plantation slaves continued to be the despair of everyone who tried to manage them, leading W. S. Smith to write their owner in 1854: "I wish you could get some pushing thorough going man up there to take charge here. . . . You must have a nockdown [*sic*] man to do any good[.] negroes cannot stand good treatment[.] nothing short of rigid discipline will do them." Lewis in particular, Smith said, "will not do without whipping."[21]

In short, emphasis on benevolent paternalism among Texas slaveholders was more than matched by concern for discipline through punishment. Benevolence may have permitted affection, but authority was vital.

20. Webb, Carroll, and Branda (eds.), *Handbook of Texas*, I, 11; "The Duties of an Overseer," *DeBow's Review*, XVIII (1855), 339–45.

21. W. Eugene Hollon and Ruth Lapham Butler (eds.), *William Bollaert's Texas* (Norman, Okla., 1956), 293; Elise K. Willrich to Georg Ludwig Luckuck, April 18, 1848, in Ragsdale (ed.), *Golden Free Land*, 54–55; Churchill Jones to George H. Daffan, July 25, 1853, in Jones Papers; W. S. Smith to Ashbel Smith, July 7, 1854, in Smith Papers.

Churchill Jones made this point to his overseer. Having your slaves like you is not enough, he wrote, for "if they only like you and not fear you they will soon hate you and get tired of you. That is the nature of Negroes, but to make them fear you and like you both you can do anything you want with them." In the same vein, Ferdinand Roemer wrote, "it requires a combination of great determination and a certain amount of indulgence in order to strike a happy medium [in managing slaves] and one must have an intimate knowledge of the disposition of the negro."[22]

The power to make slaves stand in fear hardly had an ennobling effect on slaveholders. Instead, it tended to create ill-tempered tyrants. "The haughty and imperious part of a man develops rapidly on one of these lonely sugar plantations, where the owner rarely meets with any except his slaves and minions," Rutherford B. Hayes wrote after visiting Sterling McNeel's plantation. Olmsted observed an eight-year-old beating and cursing a puppy and commented that "his tone was an evident imitation of his father's mode of dealing with his slaves." John H. McLean, himself a slaveholder, reminisced that the "owner was liable to become an autocrat, being in full control of the slave, and having him responding to his every beck and call." McLean also thought that slavery inclined masters to "idleness and needless self-indulgence," a view that was supported by observers such as Frances L. Trask, W. Steinert, and Mrs. Matilda Houstoun.[23]

Although the practice was publicly frowned on as the worst form of self-indulgence, some slaveowners used their power as a basis for sexual relations with their slaves. Wiley W. Pridgen of Harrison County committed adultery with at least five of his slave women between 1845 and 1850 before his wife Mary sued for divorce. She won custody of their children and half the slaves (twenty-nine), but Pridgen kept the others and moved to De Witt County, where he probably continued the conduct that had led to the divorce. When Pink and Williford Cartwright married in 1834, he owned a slave named Jane and her daughter Mary. Over the years, Jane bore four more children and Mary had two. Then in 1848 Williford Cartwright divorced her husband, charging in part that he had

22. Jones to Daffan, July 25, 1853, in Jones Papers; Roemer, *Texas*, 164.

23. Williams (ed.), *Diary and Letters of Hayes*, I, 254; Olmsted, *Journey Through Texas*, 55; McLean, *Reminiscences*, 130; Hogan, *Texas Republic*, 109 (quoting Frances L. Trask); Sibley, *Travelers in Texas*, 140; Jordan (ed. and trans.), "Steinert's View of Texas in 1849," 61.

abandoned her bed and board and "lived in improper intimacy with the negress Jane." Adeline Marshall of Brazoria County said that her master kept a black woman at his house and fathered lots of "no nation" children. In Matagorda County, a man named Fitzgerald gave Caroline Hillard a young slave girl, his "reputed natural daughter," to be reared until she was old enough to support herself and then set free. William Bracken of Jackson County wrote a will recognizing three mulatto children who were to share equally in the property of his estate. John C. Clark of Wharton County, one of Texas' largest planters, lived with a slave woman named Sobrina from the early 1830s until his death in 1862 and left three children who eventually claimed to be his legitimate heirs. Norris Wright Cuney, one of Texas' most prominent black Republicans after Reconstruction, was the son of Philip Cuney, a white planter who lived near Hempstead. Rebecca Hagerty accused Spire Hagerty of giving a woman, with whom he had had "adulterous intercourse," and two children to his sister after she (Rebecca) began divorce proceedings. This action, she said, illegally denied her a share of those three slaves as community property.[24]

There were some not-so-subtle differences in the way whites handled the relationships involved in these sexual liaisons. Pridgen went from woman to woman, whereas Cartwright eventually left his wife to live with Jane. Fitzgerald and Bracken made special provisions for their mulatto children, and Cuney sent his son to school in Pittsburgh. By contrast, Clark never gave any indication that Sobrina's offspring were his. When Clark's three children sued for shares of his estate in 1871, black witnesses testified that Sobrina habitually had shared his bed and table and exercised the authority of a mistress of the house, while white witnesses denied that he had ever treated Sobrina or her children "with any perceptible consideration." All agreed that Clark was a singularly unsocial man who concentrated only on accumulating property, yet the white community apparently was reluctant to admit that he could have had a close relationship with a black woman. On the other hand, although the two cases are not perfectly comparable, Justice Abner S. Lipscomb of the Texas supreme court readily agreed that Spire Hagerty could and should

24. Harrison County District Court Civil Case Papers, Case #1697; *Cartwright* v. *Cartwright*, 18 Tex. 626 (1858); *Am. Slave, Supp.*, Ser. 2, V, 2578 (Adeline Marshall); *Hilliard* v. *Frantz*, 21 Tex. 192 (1858); *Hunt* v. *White*, 24 Tex. 643 (1859); *Honey* v. *Clark*, 37 Tex. 686 (1872–73); Lawrence D. Rice, *The Negro in Texas, 1874–1900* (Baton Rouge, 1971), 36–37; *Hagerty* v. *Harwell*, 16 Tex. 663 (1856).

have been motivated by concern for his alleged slave mistress and children. "We do not wish to be understood as giving our judicial sanction to adultery," he wrote, "but if the sin has been committed," the "principal party" in it should not neglect "the partner in his guilt and her unoffending offspring." Hagerty naturally "should trust the mother and her children in such cases to the kindness of his own sister," Justice Lipscomb continued, "rather than leave them to the injured and infuriated wife, who would possibly, yea probably, inflict severity, cruelty and hardship on them when the offender was beyond the reach of her angry passions." In general, although sexual liaisons stemmed essentially from the master's power, some were simply exploitative while others involved varying degrees of affection and support.[25]

A few slaveholders demonstrated problems of conscience where their slave mistresses and mulatto children were concerned, but was it possible that some had feelings of guilt where the entire Peculiar Institution was concerned? Frederick Law Olmsted thought that he at times sensed an underlying uneasiness about the morality of slavery. "There seems to be the consciousness of a wrong relation and a determination to face conscience down and continue it," he wrote. In contrast, however, he found "many cultivated, agreeable and talented persons" in Austin who appeared absolutely convinced that slavery was a "beneficial" institution, justified by the benefits it brought to slave and master alike. Evidence to corroborate the view of slavery Olmsted found in Austin is plentiful and direct; that to support his sense of an underlying uneasiness over the moral issue is indirect and circumstantial. Slaveholders frequently expressed their belief in the institution, and their spokesmen developed a wide-ranging proslavery argument praising it from every possible angle. Negative comments about slavery, when they did appear in private correspondence, generally criticized it on practical rather than moral grounds. Expressions of moral concern revealed little urgency. Benjamin Lundy, for example, found that William Stafford, a former Quaker turned sugar planter, "thinks slavery a bad thing." Stafford, however, saw no harm in holding slaves until all agreed to free them and colonize them elsewhere.[26]

25. Rice, *Negro in Texas*, 36; *Honey* v. *Clark*, 37 Tex. 686 (1872–73); *Hagerty* v. *Harwell*, 16 Tex. 663 (1856).

26. Olmsted, *Journey Through Texas*, 52, 59. For a good example of a slaveholder's letter critical of slavery on practical grounds, see James Morgan to Mrs. Jane Storms, January 26, 1844, in Morgan Papers. Lundy, *Life, Travels, and Opinions of Lundy*, 38.

Texas slaveholders thus gave virtually no direct testimony to indicate the presence of a moral dilemma created by the Peculiar Institution. Few, if any, it seems, lived day-to-day with a strong feeling that slavery, which they called good, was actually an evil, a moral wrong. On the other hand, most slaveholders did not have the sort of godlike certainty in the righteousness of their institution that would allow them to withstand constant criticism without becoming sensitive and defensive. To some extent, the proslavery argument arose from slaveowners' need to convince themselves as well as nonslaveholding southerners that the ownership of human property was right and just. Critics outside the South could hardly be persuaded, so proslavery propaganda must have been directed to a less distant audience. Other indications of sensitivity and defensiveness are found in private expressions by individual slaveowners. Otis Marshall Wheeler, for example, a native of Massachusetts who became a Polk County planter, wrote his sister in 1857: "Tell your children to write to me [even] if they do say that I am a Negro whipper in Texas I am only Uncle Marshall yet." Two years later, Wheeler told his sister about the burning of a church in their hometown (Lincoln, Massachusetts). "If it had been done in this semibarbarian slaveholding country," he wrote, "it need not be wondered at but in New England oh—." Ashbel Smith confided to his journal in 1849 that European criticism of slavery arose from a desire to destroy a productive labor system in America. At times, slaveholder sensitivity appeared even in attempts at humor. Will Neblett named a half-Newfoundland, half-bloodhound puppy "Stowe," after the author of *Uncle Tom's Cabin*.[27]

Texas newspapers also demonstrated sensitivity and defensiveness by leaping at any opportunity to publicize cases of slaveholder benevolence or justice. In 1851, for example, a lawyer from Memphis arrived in Clarksville and claimed freedom for a slave girl belonging to Mary Moran on the grounds that the girl's mother back in Tennessee was free. Mrs. Moran let the girl go without a legal battle. Charles DeMorse, the Massachusetts-born editor of the Clarksville *Northern Standard*, held up this as an example of southern justice in the face of unfair attacks from abolitionist fanatics.[28]

Finally, slaveholders, through voluntary acts of manumission, be-

27. Otis M. Wheeler to "Dear Sister," July 29, 1857, December 16, 1859, both in Turner Papers; Ashbel Smith's Journal, February 21, 1849, in Smith Papers; Lizzie S. Neblett to Babe Scott, January 27, 1861, in Neblett Papers.
28. Clarksville *Northern Standard*, February 22, 1851.

trayed their lack of complete confidence in slavery's righteousness, or at least in a necessary corollary—that the inherently inferior blacks could survive only as slaves and were happy and content as such. Masters said slavery was a blessing for their bondsmen, and then, when they wished to give the greatest gift possible to a slave, they granted freedom. Manumission usually occurred through wills and came as a reward for loyal service over many years. William Vince of Austin's Colony directed in 1834 that his slave Sally, due to her "faithful services" and "obedient and submissive conduct," be freed at his death. Vince did not die until after the revolution, when manumission had become more difficult in that emancipated slaves had to be sent outside the republic, unless their masters received permission for them to live in Texas. Allen Vince, who served as administrator of his brother's estate, did not free Sally until 1839, when a jury ruled that the bequest was valid and a judge ordered her liberated. James Routh and Sinclair D. Gervais also successfully emancipated bondsmen by will during the era of the republic. Gervais' slave Peggy, freed in 1838 "on account of her faithful behavior," lived in the town of Matagorda for many years and left a will of her own in 1855. Some masters, rather than providing eventual freedom through provisions in a will, sought congressional approval for immediate acts of emancipation. In January, 1840, congress gave its approval for Thomas F. McKinney's slave Cary and Wiley Martin's man Peter to be manumitted and remain in Texas as free men. The legislature was so reluctant, however, to permit freed blacks to live in Texas that it rejected thirteen other petitions for manumission.[29]

Following statehood in 1845, legislators virtually never gave formal permission to newly emancipated blacks to live in Texas.[30] Acts of manumission continued, however, apparently in many cases with the belief that in a state as large and loosely governed as Texas free blacks who gave no trouble would simply be left alone in a gray zone between slavery and freedom. The Texas supreme court recognized this possibility after the Civil War when it ruled that Betsy Webster, who was freed in 1856 and

29. Act of Manumission by William Vince, September 22, 1834, in Dr. William E. Howard Collection, San Jacinto Historical Museum, San Jacinto State Park, San Jacinto, Tex.; Muir, "Free Negro in Harris County," 225–29; Newsome, "Antislavery Sentiment in Texas," 42–45; Estates of Sinclair D. Gervais and Peggy Gervais, Matagorda County Probate Records (Transcribed Will Record); Schoen, "Free Negro in Republic of Texas," 112–13.

30. For exceptions to this generalization, see Gammel (comp.), Laws of Texas, III, 1042 (Mary Madison of Galveston County and Thomas Cevallos of Bexar County).

given all her master's estate, could not have been free or held the property left to her without leaving Texas. But until she moved (which she
had not), the property could be held in trust for her, and she was free to
leave when she chose. Put another way, there was no time limit on when
manumitted slaves had to leave Texas. In the meantime, they would not
be owned or worked by anyone, nor would they be free citizens with the
right to hold property.[31]

Most manumissions after 1845 made no clear provision for removal
from the state and therefore placed the freedmen in this ambiguous position. William T. Weathersby, for example, freed three slaves, leaving
them "under the charge of my sister Lucinda Sherrod, to be settled near
her . . . and if the State of Texas, or any of my relations should object . . .
I give my sister full power to send them to a free State, or to Liberia, as
she and the negroes may agree." George J. Hunt of Cass County directed
that Jack be hired out for six years to earn enough to be set free "with the
choice of staying in this County and having fifty acres of land out of my
tract of any of the unimproved part or be carried to Ohio or some other
free state at my expense, and there set free." According to the 1857 will
of Gideon W. Adams, his one slave, a ten-year-old girl, was to stay with
his wife and upon her death "be as free as the laws of Texas will allow
her to be" or, if then living in another state, "to have all the liberty and
privileges of a free person." Other wills providing for manumission were
even less specific about where the slaves would live but seemed to as-
sume that there could be some sort of freedom for their bondsmen in
Texas. Samuel Allen of Travis County, for example, simply directed that
John and Lucy, as soon as they had earned enough by hiring out to pay
his debts, be "set at liberty," be "entirely free," and "have their freedom
as perfectly as though they had never been slaves." (Incidentally, each of
Allen's heirs received ten cents from his estate.)[32]

Texas slaveholders freed only a handful of the state's bondsmen; nevertheless, proslavery advocates, recognizing that voluntary manumis-

31. *Webster* v. *Heard*, 32 Tex. 685 (1870).
32. *Purvis* v. *Sherrod*, 12 Tex. 140 (1854); Will of George J. Hunt, Cass County District
Court Minutes (Book 3-A); Estate of Gideon W. Adams, Brazoria County Probate Records
(Wills, etc., Book B); Estate of Samuel Allen, Travis County Probate Records (Probate Records, Book A). For other examples of manumission by will, see Estate of D. H. Yeiser,
Brazoria County Probate Records (Wills, etc., Book B); Estate of David Funderburke, Harrison County Probate Papers; Estate of Letitia Simpson, San Augustine County Probate Records (Book of Wills, 1856–96).

sions undermined the Peculiar Institution, angrily attacked the practice. The Austin *Southern Intelligencer* commented in January, 1859: "Of all the enemies of the institution of slavery, those misadvised owners who, by their last wills manumit their slaves, are the worst. Negro slavery, as it exists in America, is either morally right or morally wrong in itself. If right in itself, the change of masters does not make it wrong." Moreover, the editor said, manumission is a disservice to slaves, who are inherently unsuited for freedom, and to society as a whole. In 1857, Louis T. Wigfall, an ultrasouthern politician who favored defending slavery at all costs, introduced a bill in the state senate to prohibit emancipation by will. His proposal did not become law, but when the Texas constitution was revised after the state joined the Confederacy in 1861 manumission was absolutely prohibited by fundamental law. Article VIII, Section 2, read as follows: "No citizen, or other person residing in this State, shall have power by deed or will, to take effect in State, or out of it, in any manner, whatsoever, directly or indirectly, to emancipate his slave or slaves."[33]

In general, Texas slaveholders, although their circumstances were far superior to those of the slaves, also paid a price for the Peculiar Institution. It tended, as Jefferson had observed many years earlier in Virginia, to make them both tyrannical and dependent while creating constant tension in their lives. Masters complained regularly about the difficulty of managing slaves and emphasized the need for strict discipline. Owners talked a great deal about their benevolent paternalism, but at the same time they instructed overseers and each other in how to punish effectively and maintain authority. Slavery did not create a crushing burden of guilt in the lives of most slaveholders, but it certainly made them prey to an unsettling sensitivity triggered by the criticism heaped upon them from outside the South. Moreover, in defending their institution as morally correct, they added a corollary argument, that Negroes were happy and content as slaves, which many knew from personal experience to be untrue. Texas slaveholders generally did not lead lives of great ease and contentment. However, they benefited enough, economically, socially, and politically, from the ownership of bondsmen to attain complete domination of antebellum Texas' society—a position they maintained at

33. U.S. Bureau of the Census, *Statistics of the United States (Including Mortality, Property, etc.) in 1860,* 337, shows that Texans manumitted only five slaves during the 1850 census year and thirty-seven in 1860. Austin *Southern Intelligencer,* January 5, 1859; *Journal of the Senate of Texas* (Austin, 1859), 269, 284, 320, 337, 339; Gammel (comp.), *Laws of Texas,* V, 22–23.

least through the Civil War. Human property, however troublesome it may have been and whatever qualms of conscience it may have caused, was something they would fight to keep.[34]

34. Lack, "Urban Slavery in the Southwest," 274–75, shows that tension among slaveholders was common even in the cities where there were relatively few bondsmen. Historians have engaged during recent years in a debate over whether planters shared the paternalistic ethos of a precapitalist society or were simply capitalistic businessmen who invested in human property. Genovese, *Roll, Jordan, Roll,* is the strongest statement of the precapitalist, paternalistic interpretation, whereas James Oakes, *The Ruling Race: A History of American Slaveholders* (New York, 1982), presents the opposing point of view. Planter paternalism existed in Texas, although it often had a practical basis in such capitalistic concerns as good management and profit.

ELEVEN

· · · · · · · · · ·

A Slaveholding Society

"THOSE WHO ARE NOT FOR US, MUST BE AGAINST US"

Antebellum Texas, although less than one-third of its families owned so much as a single slave, had all the characteristics of an advanced slaveholding society. Slaveholders dominated the state's economy, controlled its politics, and occupied the top rung on the social ladder. Their spokesmen articulated a wide-ranging proslavery argument, and discussion of public issues and Texas' future took place only within a proslavery consensus. In short, the Peculiar Institution influenced and shaped virtually every aspect of life in the Lone Star state. Yet Texas' slaveholding society regularly exhibited a siege mentality, fearing attacks by enemies from within and without. In 1860–61, these fears, coupled with the controlling influence of slaveholders, led the state to secession and Civil War.

The economic dominance of slaveholders is best documented by statistical information from United States census returns. In 1850, slaveholding households, which constituted 30 percent of the total in Texas, owned 72 percent of the state's real property. Ten years later, although slaveholding families had declined to 27 percent of the total, they still controlled 73 percent of all wealth (real and personal property combined). In 1850, slaveholding farmers, who headed 33 percent of agricultural units worked by their owners, owned 68 percent of the total improved acreage and 61 percent of the livestock (by value), and produced 65 percent of all the corn grown in Texas. By 1860, when the percentage of slaveholding farmers had decreased slightly to 32 percent, they owned 71 percent of all improved acreage and 60 percent of the livestock, and produced 72 percent of all corn. Cotton production, which was even more important as an indication of slaveholders' economic domination, was virtually a monopoly for slaveholders. The approximately one-third of all farmers who owned bondsmen grew 89 percent of the state's cotton in 1850 and 91 percent in 1860. Nonslaveholders, although a sizable majority among Texas farmers, did not participate in the cash-crop agricultural economy in any significant way.[1]

Slaveholder control of Texas politics may be shown through a profile of those who were political leaders during the years from statehood to disunion. In 1850, when slaveholders headed 30 percent of Texas' households, 58 percent of all federal, state, and local officeholders owned bondsmen. Ten years later on the eve of disunion, the 27 percent of all household heads who owned slaves provided 68 percent of the officeholders. It has been argued that such control of public office does not constitute "domination" in the sense of passing laws or implementing policies that nonslaveholders opposed. This assumes, however, that somehow a serious conflict of interest existed between those who owned slaves and those who did not. No such conflict existed across Texas. After all, nonslaveholders helped elect the slaveholders to office. Thus, slaveholders did not control politics in the sense of having to overcome opposition from nonslaveholders; yet they did hold office in greatly disproportionate numbers and, it may be assumed, made political decisions in the interests of their special form of property.[2]

The position of slaveholders toward the top of the social ladder depended simply on their wealth. Slaveholders generally owned more property than did nonholders; and the greater their wealth, the closer they stood to the top of Texas society. This meant that the planter class occupied the very top rung. They had achieved success in developing the agricultural economy and producing cash crops that brought in surplus income. By Texas standards, planters had large, well-constructed homes, enjoyed great material comforts, and often entertained lavishly. Their children had advantages that only money could buy, such as, for ex-

1. Campbell and Lowe, *Wealth and Power*, 34–37, 69–81.

2. *Ibid.*, 107–19, details the creation of a profile of federal, state, and local officeholders in antebellum Texas. Wright, *The Political Economy of the Cotton South*, 39–41. For the argument that planters were chosen democratically as leaders of the Old South (an argument that extends to Texas), see Fletcher M. Green, "Democracy in the Old South," *Journal of Southern History*, XII (1946), 23; Frank Lawrence Owsley, *Plain Folk of the Old South* (Baton Rouge, 1949), 130.

ample, the opportunity to attend good private schools and colleges outside Texas. In short, critics of slaveholding society might think it wrong,
as did Ferdinand Roemer, that the "labor of the free man is not respected," but none denied that the free man "takes a subordinate position when compared to the slave-holding planter."[3]

Given slavery's vital importance to those who dominated antebellum
Texas economically, politically, and socially and the increasingly radical
antislavery attack coming from outside the South, it is hardly surprising
that the state's politicians, newspapers, and churches vehemently defended the institution. The proslavery argument did not have to be created anew in Texas; it was already well developed in older southern
states. Texans took up most of the themes utilized by Old South apologists and directed them to the circumstances of their frontier state.[4]

A key part of the proslavery defense, one inherited from Stephen F.
Austin and Texas' first settlers, was the argument from necessity. Charles
DeMorse of the Clarksville *Northern Standard* summarized this point of
view succinctly in 1859. "We care nothing for . . . Slavery as an abstraction—but we desire the practicality; the increase of our productions; the
increase of the comforts and wealth of the population; and if slavery, or
slave labor, or Negro apprentice labor ministers to this, why that is what
we want." "The State of Texas," read a resolution introduced by John H.
Brown in the state House of Representatives in 1857, "in her vast unsettled territory, demands only labor to place her in the front rank of
civilized States." Slaves would meet that need. Only slave labor, said the
Texas Almanac for 1858, can produce the staples such as cotton; to stop
that production would bring ruin to the civilized world.[5]

Arguments emphasizing slavery's practical necessity tended, as De-
Morse's editorial indicated, toward neutrality on the moral issues raised
by the institution. They leaned heavily toward the "necessary evil" position taken by many apologists before the 1830s when proslavery advocates began to defend slavery more aggressively as a positive good. Most

3. Roemer, *Texas*, 31. For evidence on the lives of planters, see Curlee, "Texas Slave
Plantations," 69–89; Campbell, *Southern Community in Crisis*, 34–36, 111–12.
4. William Sumner Jenkins, *Pro-Slavery Thought in the Old South* (Chapel Hill, 1935); Drew
Gilpin Faust (ed.), *The Ideology of Slavery: Proslavery Thought in the Antebellum South, 1830–1860*
(Baton Rouge, 1981).
5. Clarksville *Northern Standard*, February 19, 1859; *A Report and Treatise on Slavery and the
Slavery Agitation* (Austin, 1857), 6; *The Texas Almanac for 1858: With Statistics, Historical and
Biographical Sketches, Etc., Relating to Texas* (Galveston, 1857), 132–33.

spokesmen in late antebellum Texas, therefore, while continuing to use the older argument, went a great deal further and insisted that slavery was morally correct and a blessing to everyone concerned. For proof they blended religious and racist beliefs with what they regarded as irrefutable logic.

Negroes, the argument began, were from the time of Noah and the Deluge a distinct classification of the human race, cursed to live as servants to other men. From that time forward, slavery's defenders claimed as they placed racist blocks on their biblical foundation, blacks had proven themselves inferior to all other races. Jane Cazneau described how a Texas woman made this point to an English visitor at Indianola. "A negro nation," she said, "has never attained eminence since the birth of history . . . no pure negro ever made an important invention, neither has mankind ever found among them a great teacher, whether as prophet, legislator, or poet." Since, the argument continued, Negroes constituted an inherently inferior race meant to be servants, it followed that slavery was their divinely ordained or "natural" state. Then, as a capstone to the defense, came the claim that slavery was actually a blessing to Negroes because it christianized and civilized them. As the Dallas *Herald* summed up this religious-racist argument in 1861: "The southern states are *par excellence* the guardians of the grandest interests of the world. They have for centuries fostered the institution of slavery which has resulted in the christianizing of that portion of the African race and in making them useful members of society, in restraining them in the only position that is congenial to their natures and for which they are fitted intellectually and morally." Under the "wise, humane, necessary and glorious institution" of slavery, an article in the *Texas Almanac for 1858* claimed, the inferior African has become "contented, cheerful, obedient, and a long-lived laborer." His condition is far superior to that experienced in his "wild native haunts." In fact, more Africans would benefit from the "Heaven-ordained and Heaven-approved system of Christian slavery in this country."[6]

At times the argument based on practical necessity and the more aggressive claim that slavery constituted a positive good were supplemented by assertions that Texas bondsmen enjoyed better material conditions than did the working poor elsewhere and by pre-Darwinian

---

6. Cazneau, *Eagle Pass*, 19; Dallas *Herald*, January 2, 1861; *Texas Almanac for 1858*, 132–33. For a similar argument, see Galveston *Weekly News*, October 14, 1856.

"survival of the fittest" theories. The Marshall *Texas Republican* informed its readers in 1849 that some types of "red or pale-colored ants" made slaves of black ants. Perhaps, the editor concluded, slavery was a "natural institution." "I have no more doubt," District Judge C. A. Frazier told an Upshur County grand jury in 1860, "of the right of a civilized and Christian nation to capture the African wherever he may be found, and subject him to labor, enlightenment, and religion, than I have of one of our people to capture a wild horse on the prairies of the West, and domesticate and reduce him to labor."[7]

The great majority of white Texans agreed with the proslavery argument, or at least acquiesced in its conclusions. Newspapers across the state gave virtually unanimous support to the institution. A few were willing to consider the moral issues involved, but most simply defended it with vehemence. Those who were less certain generally concluded, as did the San Antonio *Herald* in 1855, that "it is one of the institutions of the South so closely connected with her interests, that it is impracticable to eradicate it. This being the case, we consider it impolitic to even discuss it as and [sic] abstract question." Many found it "impolitic" to be even that lukewarm on the subject. Stung by a charge in 1860 that slavery had less than enthusiastic support in north Texas and, by implication, in his newspaper, Charles DeMorse, the Massachusetts-born editor of the *Northern Standard*, replied: "It does not matter what part of the Union a man comes from, or with what notions he was indoctrinated when he left home. Let him live in a slaveholding community for a few months, and he will be ready enough to acquire negro property whenever opportunity is favorable; and he will be oppressed with no qualms of conscience in so doing." It is utterly slanderous, he said, to say that the people of north Texas do not support slavery wholeheartedly.[8]

Political life in antebellum Texas existed entirely within a proslavery consensus. The Democratic party consistently defended southern rights and insisted that antislavery activists threatened the peace of the Union and the happiness of the slaves. By 1860 the party, declaring that the United States government "was founded for the benefit of the white

7. Columbia *Telegraph and Texas Register*, January 3, 1837; Marshall *Texas Republican*, May 26, 1849, December 8, 1860.

8. Marilyn McAdams Sibley, *Lone Stars and State Gazettes: Texas Newspapers Before the Civil War* (College Station, 1983), 197–98; Wesley Norton, "Religious Newspapers in Antebellum Texas," *Southwestern Historical Quarterly*, LXXIX (1975), 164–65; San Antonio *Herald*, May 22, 1855; Clarksville *Northern Standard*, February 4, 1860.

race," resolved that in the event a Republican won the presidency it would be "the duty of the people of the State of Texas to hold themselves in readiness to cooperate with our sister States of the South in convention to take into consideration such measures as may be necessary for our protection, or to secure out of the confederacy that protection of their rights which they can no longer hope for in it." The Whig, Know-Nothing, and Constitutional Union parties, which one after the other offered a relatively weak opposition to the Democrats during the antebellum years, generally took less ultrasouthern positions on sectional issues. However, they were by no means opposed to slavery. The Know-Nothings, for example, were inclined to be unionists, but in their opposition to immigration from abroad, they took delight in claiming that foreigners, especially those who settled in west Texas, opposed slavery. This charge had very little truth, but it served to establish the Know-Nothings' proslavery credentials. Neither pro-Union men who supported Sam Houston in 1859–60 nor the Constitutional Union party in that fateful election year had any intention of destroying slavery. They simply believed that their institutions had a better chance of survival within the Union than without. The Constitution of the United States protects slavery, the San Antonio *Herald* told its readers in 1860. It is "utterly impossible" for a "Black Republican president, to destroy directly the institution of slavery." Differences between the Democrats and the Opposition, as the other parties were known, were significant, but they did not extend outside the proslavery consensus.[9]

One issue involving slavery divided even the Democrats. A minority of the party's ultrasoutherners proposed in 1857 to have the African slave trade reopened. They reasoned that an influx of African bondsmen would speed the growth of Texas, increase productivity, and broaden slaveownership—all without any significant lowering of the value of human property. Indeed, the whole South would benefit from eliminating restrictions on the African trade that had stood since 1808, in that blacks would no longer be drained from the border states, and the region's representation in Congress would increase as well. This proposal received support from several influential Democratic newspapers, including the Austin *Texas State Gazette* and the Houston *Tri-Weekly Telegraph*. Other

9. Ernest William Winkler (ed.), *Platforms of Political Parties in Texas* (Austin, 1916), 83; San Antonio *Herald*, September 4, 1855, January 2, 23, 1856, January 11, 1860; Randolph B. Campbell, "Political Conflict Within the Southern Consensus: Harrison County, Texas, 1850–1880," *Civil War History*, XXVI (1980), 218–39.

strongly Democratic papers, such as the Marshall *Texas Republican* and Matagorda *Gazette*, opposed reopening the African trade. Agitation of the subject was not wise or practical, they said, since the idea was not especially popular even in the older southern states, and a great influx of slaves would reduce the values of bondsmen while driving up the costs of land, food, and clothing. This issue was decided in November, 1857, when Representative John Henry Brown of Galveston introduced resolutions in the Texas legislature calling for removing federal restrictions on the African trade. The Committee on Slaves and Slavery, pointing to the controversial nature of the proposal, recommended that no action be taken. First, however, the committee's report affirmed the justice and humanity of American slavery and agreed that the importation of additional Africans would be a blessing to those so enslaved. The majority may have disagreed with such an extreme proslavery policy, but they were careful to indicate that their stance in no way constituted opposition to slavery itself.[10]

A few articulate Germans expressed antislavery views, but, in fact, the proslavery consensus encompassed Texas' largest non-Anglo immigrant population as well. The most significant antislavery activity among Germans centered at Sisterdale, a settlement in Kendall County, after it became home to a number of immigrants fleeing political repression following the revolutions of 1848 in Europe. These "48ers," led by Eduard Degener and August Siemering, called a "political convention" at San Antonio in May, 1854, in connection with the annual *Saengerfest* and adopted a platform calling for reform in many areas of American life. One plank read: "Slavery is an evil, the abolition of which is a requirement of democratic principles; but as it only affects single States, we desire; That the Federal government abstain from all interference in the questions of slavery; but that when a single State resolves upon the abolition of the evil, such state may claim the assistance of the General Government for the purpose of carrying out such resolve." When this platform appeared in Adolph Douai's San Antonio *Zeitung* and the San Antonio *Western*

10. W. J. Carnathan, "The Attempt to Re-Open the African Slave Trade in Texas, 1857–1858," *Proceedings of the Sixth Annual Convention of the Southwestern Political and Social Science Association* (1925), 134–44; Austin *Texas State Gazette*, March 1, 1856, June 5, 12, July 17, 1858; Marshall *Texas Republican*, February 4, 1859; Matagorda *Gazette*, May 7, 1859; Curlee, "Texas Slave Plantations," 40–42; *Report and Treatise on Slavery*. Ronald T. Takaki, *A Pro-Slavery Crusade: The Agitation to Reopen the African Slave Trade* (New York, 1971), 180–85, places the issue in Texas in a regional context.

Texan, some Germans were immediately critical, but Anglo-Americans, especially those involved in the incipient Know-Nothing movement, were outraged. Douai then added to the controversy by taking a position even more critical of slavery.[11]

In reality, Texans had little basis for concern over German opposition to the Peculiar Institution. The slavery clause was, as one historian put it, "fairly harmless." After all, it clearly indicated that the institution should be dealt with state-by-state and not by the federal government—a position every proslavery advocate endorsed. Moreover, conservatives at the convention had wanted an even weaker statement on slavery, and Germans were the first to criticize the platform when it appeared in Douai's paper. A letter writer in the New Braunfels *Zeitung* protested any statement that made Germans appear as abolitionists and insisted that in the South they had an identity of interests with slaveholders. Ferdinand Lindheimer, editor of the New Braunfels paper, also protested the slavery clause, as did meetings of Germans in his town, Houston, Lockhart, and Comal Town. German readers and advertisers withdrew their patronage from Douai's San Antonio *Zeitung*. The embattled editor held on for a few months with financial assistance from Frederick Law Olmsted, who greatly admired the Sisterdale Germans after his visit to that area earlier in 1854. Soon, however, Douai sold his paper and moved to New York. His own people, in the majority, wanted no part of antislavery. There are a "few mad-caps and wild theorists" among them, said the Austin *Texas State Gazette* in 1856, but the majority are true southerners.[12]

To some extent, of course, the German reaction to the 1854 political convention arose not from support for slavery but instead from a fear of being called abolitionists. In this sense, some were forced into the proslavery consensus. Considerable evidence, however, points to the conclusion that many, and perhaps most, had no moral objections to the institution and remained nonslaveholders from purely practical consid-

11. August Siemering, "Die Lateinische Ansiedlung in Texas," trans. C. W. Geue, *Texana*, V (1967), 126–31; Rudolph L. Biesele, "The Texas State Convention of Germans in 1854," *Southwestern Historical Quarterly*, XXXIII (1930), 247–52, 255, 260–61; Translation of the Resolutions Passed at the Political Convention of Germans in Texas Held in San Antonio, May 15, 1854, in Oscar Haas Papers, Barker Texas History Center, University of Texas, Austin; Walter L. Buenger, *Secession and the Union in Texas* (Austin, 1984), 92.

12. Biesele, "Texas State Convention of Germans," 247, 255–61; Buenger, *Secession and the Union in Texas*, 92; Laura W. Roper, "Frederick Law Olmsted and the Western Texas Free-Soil Movement," *American Historical Review*, LVI (1950), 59; Austin *Texas State Gazette*, May 10, 1856.

erations. With their small-scale farms and limited capital resources, they simply could not afford slaves. Ferdinand Lindheimer said exactly that in 1859. Those who had the money bought bondsmen. The Mainz Society's Nassau Farm in Fayette County, for example, had slaves. Prince Carl of Solms-Braunfels inspected the plantation in 1844 and recommended selling it rather than continue involvement with such a stigma upon human society, but another German visitor, five years later, described the use of slave labor on Nassau Farm. Prospering German town dwellers, including Ferdinand Flake, editor of the influential Galveston *Die Union*, also acquired slaves, and Anglo-Americans, especially the Democrats fighting the antiforeign Know-Nothings, praised their commitment. The Austin *Southern Intelligencer*, for example, described the purchase of a slave man in 1857 by a "hard working German who thus showed a greater devotion to the institutions of the South than many of the intense Americans who denounce the whole German population as abolitionists." [13]

In short, *De Bow's Review* may not have been absolutely correct when it reported in 1858 "that the foreign born population [of Texas] have never shown any disposition to change the policy of the state in regard to slavery." The Germans, however, were hardly the enemies of slavery that Olmsted and a few historians have made them. Instead, as Jacob de Cordova told an English audience in 1858, Germans conducted themselves with "prudence" where slavery was concerned. Lindheimer's New Braunfels *Zeitung* agreed, saying in 1859: "The majority of the Germans are not against the institution of slave labor and will support the institution in every political struggle." This may have been less than an enthusiastic endorsement of the "slavery as a positive good" doctrine, but it clearly indicated that Germans posed no threat to the Peculiar Institution in Texas. [14]

Mexican Texans or Tejanos were less numerous than Germans in the Lone Star state by 1850, but their concentration south of San Antonio gave them considerable influence in that area. Olmsted claimed that Tejanos regarded slavery "with abhorrence," and Anglo-Texans felt that

13. Walter L. Buenger, "Secession and the Texas German Community: Editor Lindheimer vs. Editor Flake," *Southwestern Historical Quarterly*, LXXXII (1979), 383–84; Jordan (ed. and trans.), "Steinert's View of Texas in 1849," 292; Solms-Braunfels, *Texas*, 20–21; Terry G. Jordan, *German Seed in Texas Soil: Immigrant Farmers in Nineteenth-Century Texas* (Austin, 1966), 106–11; Austin *Southern Intelligencer*, April 1, 1857.

14. "Slavery in Texas," *DeBow's Review*, XXV (1858), 597; Matagorda *Gazette*, November 27, 1858 (quoting Jacob de Cordova); Buenger, *Secession and the Union in Texas*, 84.

their lack of racial prejudice indicated opposition to the institution. Tejanos did at times help slaves escape, and Mexico provided a home for runaways and showed no disposition to return them north of the Rio Grande. There is little evidence, however, that Tejanos posed a real threat to slavery in Texas. As a none-too-popular minority themselves, they had enough problems of their own without creating additional ones by challenging the proslavery consensus.[15]

Although slavery had no significant opposition anywhere within the state, Texans exhibited the extreme fear and intolerance that often characterizes a society under siege. New or different ideas received a more than skeptical reception. The Washington *Sentinel*, for example, condemned Victor Considerant's utopian socialist community at La Reunion in north Texas because it is "altogether different from our system." "Besides," the editor said, "it is an abolition system." Every rumor of an uprising or plot was accompanied by charges that nonslave agitators were involved. In part this resulted from the slaveholders' conceit that their loyal servants would never rebel unless stirred up by outsiders, but it also revealed a constant concern for internal subversion. The threats to such "abolitionists" indicated the intensity of society's fears. During the 1856 insurrection scare in Colorado County, for example, the Lockhart *Watchman* suggested a touch of hemp without benefit of a trial as proper justice for plotters, while the editor of the *Texas State Gazette* said that he "would have no more qualms of conscience in hanging the white faced but black-hearted fiend" who encouraged insurrection "than in hanging a dog."[16]

Texans' intolerant fear of internal enemies led at times to vigilantelike reprisals against Mexicans who were accused, not of fomenting rebellion, but of causing unrest and enticing bondsmen to run away. The most serious outbreak of this sort began during September, 1854, in Seguin. Local citizens, upset by the presence of transient "peons," met and passed resolutions declaring that no Mexican of the peon class could enter or live in Guadalupe County. Shortly thereafter, Austin residents took similar action against transient Mexican laborers. A citizens' meeting on

15. Olmsted, *Journey Through Texas*, 87; Arnoldo DeLeon, *The Tejano Community, 1836–1900* (Albuquerque, N.M., 1982), 15, 28; Buenger, *Secession and the Union in Texas*, 85–88.
16. William J. and Margaret F. Hammond, *La Reunion: A French Settlement in Dallas* (Dallas, 1958), 76–77; Austin *Texas State Gazette*, November 15, 22, 1856; Lockhart *Watchman*, quoted in Galveston *Weekly News*, September 30, 1856.

October 7, saying that such people made slaves "discontented and insubordinate," ordered all transients to leave within ten days or be forcibly expelled. A vigilance committee was appointed to enforce this command. By the end of October, 1854, the only Mexicans in Austin were those vouched for by "respectable citizens." While Austin dealt with its "problem," representatives from eight counties (Travis, Gonzales, De Witt, Lavaca, Hays, Caldwell, Guadalupe, and Fayette) met at Gonzales to discuss the threat posed by Mexicans to slavery. This meeting called for stronger security measures and urged Texas' federal representatives to appeal to Mexico to have its citizens leave slave property alone. Colorado and Matagorda counties drove out their Mexican populations in 1856. Such vigilante-style action then calmed down. Only a tense and defensive society would have resorted to it in the first place.[17]

Antebellum Texans thus struck hard at real or, more often, imaginary insurrectionaries and troublemakers; they were only slightly more tolerant of groups or individuals who dared to speak or write critically of slavery. "You have to be especially careful in talking about slavery," the German traveler Steinert wrote in 1849. "If you do not restrain yourself from commenting on this subject too freely, you can easily get into unpleasant quarrels." George Fellows wrote from Galveston in 1844 that a minister "can preach the truth plainly without fear if he does not touch slavery. As a private or public subject that must not be touched in any form." Steinert and Fellows disliked slavery, but defenders of the institution also felt that it was not a topic for critical discussion. Otis M. Wheeler of Coldspring inquired in March, 1860, about a friend named Sumner Bemis back in Massachusetts. Bemis, he thought, would prosper in Texas, "provided first that his notions are right upon the slave question," for "if he is an abolitionist any other country would suit him better than this." "I speak thus plainly," Wheeler wrote, "because I would not like for him to come here & be disappointed, an abolitionist would find no congenial spirit here not even a negro." The intolerant attitude described by Steinert, Fellows, and Wheeler was summarized concisely by the Galveston *Weekly News* in 1857: "Those who are not for us, must be against us. There can be no middle ground. Those who denounce slavery

17. Austin *Texas State Gazette*, September 9, October 14, 28, November 11, 1854; Brazoria *Texas Planter*, September 20, 1854; Paul D. Lack, "Slavery and Vigilantism in Austin, Texas, 1840–1860," *Southwestern Historical Quarterly*, LXXXV (1981), 4–11, 18–20; Tyler, "Slave Owners and Runaway Slaves," 37.

as an evil, in any sense, are the enemies of the South, whatever may be their pretended conservatism."[18]

The experience of Northern Methodists in Texas provides a good example of how the state's institutions, even its churches, were denied any middle ground on the slavery issue. After the Methodist church split along North-South lines in 1844–46, ministers of the Methodist Episcopal church, or Northern Methodist church as southerners called it, continued to preach in north Texas. They did not attack slavery, but their refusal to affiliate with the Methodist Episcopal Church, South, was enough to make them suspect. Alfred Howell wrote his brother from Greenville in May, 1854: "I understand preaching is going on in town tonight, by a *missionary* from the Methodist church *North*, an abolitionist, he keeps dark however on the last subject." There had been talk of silencing him, Howell noted, but it was concluded to see what he would say. Before long, north Texans became less tolerant. In March, 1859, the Arkansas Conference of the Northern Methodist Church, to which the ministers in Texas belonged, convened at Timber Creek near Bonham in Fannin County. Local citizens, already sensitive to the Northern Methodists' "abolitionism," were enraged when a visiting minister made remarks critical of slavery. Immediately, a mass meeting in Bonham adopted resolutions describing the church as a "secret foe [which] lurks in our midst" and demanding that its conference be terminated and all its preaching stopped. Our motto, one resolution said, is "peaceably if we can, forcibly if we must." A large committee—Northern Methodists called it a "mob"—then interrupted the conference's services to read the resolutions to those present. Although the conference was allowed to complete its work—only two more hours were needed—and several Northern Methodists continued to preach in Texas, John Marshall of the Austin *Texas State Gazette* applauded the resolutions but wondered if the action had been strong enough. "We would rather see a hundred such dogs bleed than one victim of a slave insurrection," he wrote.[19]

18. Jordan (ed. and trans.), "Steinert's View of Texas in 1849," 62; George Fellows to "Brother Sawyer," October, 1844, in F. E. McCoy Papers, Rosenberg Library, Galveston. Smith, *Account of a Journey Through Northeastern Texas*, 85, voiced views very similar to those of Steinert. Otis M. Wheeler to "Dear Mother," March 10, 1860, in Turner Papers; Galveston *Weekly News*, March 3, 1857.

19. Phelan, *History of Early Methodism*, 224, 236–37, 440–52; Wesley Norton, "The Methodist Episcopal Church and the Civil Disturbances in North Texas in 1859 and 1860," *Southwestern Historical Quarterly*, LXVIII (1965), 318–22; Alfred Howell to "My Dear Brother," May 1, 1854, in Howell Letters; Austin *Texas State Gazette*, April 16, 1859.

Given this attitude toward a church and its leaders, it is hardly surprising that individuals who in any way challenged the dictum "give unqualified support to slavery or be an enemy of the South" usually found themselves in serious trouble regardless of their position in society. The case of Stephen Pearl Andrews, a Massachusetts-born lawyer who came to Texas in 1839, provides a good example from the republic period. Andrews knew slavery firsthand, having lived and studied law in Louisiana, and he considered it an evil, demoralizing form of human oppression. During the early 1840s, he developed a plan that would take advantage of slavery's relative economic weakness at that time and the republic's serious financial problems in order to rid Texas of the institution. Andrews argued that Britain could be convinced to pour money into Texas as loans to the government and through purchases of land. This would enable Texas to abolish slavery with compensation for slaveholders and thereby encourage an influx of free settlers. Texas would be stronger financially and, with the protection of the British flag, could be forever independent and prosperous. His plan was meant both to take advantage of Texas' weaknesses at that time and to appeal to the self-interest of Texans. Andrews presented his ideas in general terms at a public meeting in Houston on March 16, 1843. Receiving a favorable reaction, he went immediately to Galveston with the intention of stating his abolitionist ideas more precisely. He had the apparent support of several well-to-do Texans, including Thomas League, James Love, John S. Syndnor, Andrew Janeway Yates, and Gail Borden, Jr. On the way, he met Captain Charles Elliot, the British chargé d'affaires to the Republic of Texas, who heard the plan with favor and agreed that abolition would improve Texas' position with Britain. Andrews received a friendly hearing from some of Galveston's leaders, but once his ideas became public knowledge, an armed crowd escorted him to a waiting boat and warned him "never to return to Galveston to agitate this subject."[20]

Elliot convinced Andrews that the problem had been the failure to propose direct compensation for slaveholders. The latter traveled to the second World Anti-Slavery Convention in London during June, 1843, and met with Lord Aberdeen, the British foreign secretary. Andrews received a very favorable reception, although Ashbel Smith, the Texas

20. Charles Shively, "An Option for Freedom in Texas, 1840–1844," *Journal of Negro History*, L (1965), 77–89; Madeleine B. Stern, "Stephen Pearl Andrews, Abolitionist, and the Annexation of Texas," *Southwestern Historical Quarterly*, LXVII (1964), 492–503.

chargé d'affaires in London, made it clear that he utterly disagreed with any proposals for abolishing slavery in the republic. Andrews did not receive approval for any specific plan. He returned to Texas in September, and another mob immediately drove him away. This time he left Texas permanently. Stephen Pearl Andrews had sought to find an option for freedom, but the majority of Texans, regardless of their problems in the early 1840s, opposed abolition. Their reply to Andrews' scheme for British cooperation in creating a nonslave republic was, as the *Telegraph and Texas Register* put it: "We are poor indeed, but poor as we are, all the wealth of England cannot buy us."[21]

In the mid-1850s, Lorenzo Sherwood, another Galveston lawyer, found himself in circumstances similar to those faced by Andrews. Sherwood, a native of New York who had established a very successful practice after moving to Galveston in 1846, advocated a State Plan for economic development in which banking and railroad building would be semipublic enterprises. He was bitterly opposed by advocates of the Corporate Plan, a laissez-faire approach under which state-chartered private corporations did largely as they pleased. In retrospect, Sherwood's plan appears to have had no chance of acceptance, but he presented it effectively and in 1855 won a seat in the state legislature, which provided a forum for expression of his ideas. Sherwood had a weakness, however; he did not support slavery. He had said publicly that the institution, while it might be necessary until the twentieth century, could not be maintained permanently in a democracy. Then, on November 16, 1855, in a speech to the Committee of the Whole of the legislature, he was incautious enough to make similar remarks. John Henry Brown, the rabidly proslavery spokesman from Galveston, issued a public letter claiming that Sherwood had called slavery "a moral evil, a fleeting and temporary institution destined to gradually give way to some other institution." Resolutions of censure were introduced in the house, but some felt that verbal condemnation was hardly enough. The Dallas *Herald* commented: "A man, a Texan, a southerner who could get up in the legislature of a southern State, of the most southern State, and deliberately outrage the feelings of the whole people without distinction of party, on a question so directly affecting their most vital interests, by uttering senti-

21. Shively, "Option for Freedom in Texas," 89–96; Stern, "Stephen Pearl Andrews," 504–23; Houston *Telegraph and Texas Register*, March 29, 1843, quoted in Newsome, "Antislavery Sentiment in Texas," 53.

ments that strike at the foundation of their social and political rights, possesses a heart too callous to be reached by votes of censure." Eighty or ninety pairs of boots should have kicked him out of the state capitol, the *Herald* said.[22]

Sherwood attempted to defend himself by claiming that his views had been distorted, but his enemies kept the initiative and, in June, 1856, a public meeting at Galveston called for his resignation from the legislature. Former supporters, such as Willard Richardson of the Galveston *News*, found it necessary to explain that they did not subscribe to his supposed antislavery views. Sherwood planned a public address in Galveston on July 7 to reply to his critics, but a citizens' meeting denied him the right to speak about slavery. William P. Ballinger, as secretary for the meeting, informed Sherwood that should he or any of his supporters (if he had any) try to discuss the Peculiar Institution the citizens of Galveston "will make this evening the occasion for the definite and final settlement of that issue, both as to you and to them." Sherwood surrendered to this threat, resigned from the state legislature, and gave up the fight for the State Plan. His ruin was politically inspired; nevertheless, it demonstrated the invincibility of the proslavery consensus.[23]

Public criticism of slavery or slaveholders by men of far less note than Andrews or Sherwood also brought threatening responses. When the Quitman *Texas Free Press* of March 25, 1857, carried a letter by John E. Lemon asking for an open discussion of slavery, Robert E. Loughery of the Marshall *Texas Republican* contended that anyone making such a proposition was an abolitionist who "should be driven out of the country." The Galveston *Weekly News* did not reprint Lemon's letter but kept a copy as "justification of those avengers of decency and honor, who are first to administer a dose of tar and feathers or a decoction of hemp to their miserable author." Within a few months the *Texas Free Press* ceased publication, and John E. Lemon was identified as the owner. During the summer of 1859, two Northern Methodist ministers, Solomon McKinney and William Blount, made themselves so "obnoxious" to the people of Dallas that they were "summarily expelled from the county." Charles Pryor of the Dallas *Herald* claimed that the two had petitioned the legislatures of Iowa and Wisconsin to obtain redress for them from the

22. Fornell, *Galveston Era*, 165–74; Dallas *Herald*, December 8, 1855.
23. Fornell, *Galveston Era*, 174–79.

state of Texas. If the two return, Pryor wrote, they will indeed be "re-dressed."[24]

The case of E. C. Palmer in 1859 shows that even private correspon-dence could cause trouble. Palmer, a resident of Marshall, wrote a letter to George Humphreys of Gainesville in November, 1858, which, al-though angrily antisouthern, said nothing directly about slavery. Nearly a year later, while Palmer was in Gainesville on business, the letter came to light. (Humphreys had been convicted of gambling with a Negro and moved to California, leaving the letter behind where it was found and made public.) Gainesville's citizens called a meeting and gave Palmer six hours to leave town. He went home to Marshall, only to be followed by Hercules Whaley of Gainesville carrying the incriminating letter. Palmer, protesting that he had been loyal to the South during his fourteen years of residence in the region, published a defense in the *Texas Republican* claiming that the letter was a forgery concocted by his business enemies. A meeting in Marshall decided, however, that the letter was authentic, and he was forced to flee. "No man," Loughery concluded, "imbued with anti-slavery sentiments, ought to be permitted to stay in a slave state."[25]

Beset for years by fear and intolerance, Texas' slave society finally gave in to near-total panic during the summer of 1860, just as the nation ap-proached the national elections. The "Texas Troubles," as the scare be-came known, began with the outbreak of ruinous fires in Dallas, Denton, and Pilot Point on July 8. Within the week, three other north Texas towns, Ladonia, Honey Grove, and Milford, also reported fires. The weather was extremely hot at the time—the Marshall *Texas Republican* commented on July 7 that heat rather than a "want of patriotism" had meant an un-usually quiet independence day—and the fires probably resulted from the spontaneous ignition of a new type of phosphorous match. Later, witnesses testified to seeing similar matches burst into flame on store shelves. Within a few days of the Dallas conflagration, however, a local farmer who had lost a barn to fire forced one of his slaves to confess to arson. Other interrogations followed, and suddenly Texans believed themselves threatened by a massive abolitionist-inspired "plot" aiming to

24. Marshall *Texas Republican*, April 25, 1857; Sibley, *Lone Stars and State Gazettes*, 276–77; Galveston *Weekly News*, April 14, 1857; Dallas *Herald*, August 17, 31, 1859, March 14 (quota-tion), May 11, 1860; Norton, "Methodist Episcopal Church and Civil Disturbances," 329.

25. Marshall *Texas Republican*, November 12, 19 (quotation), 26, December 3, 17, 1859; Dallas *Herald*, October 26, 1859; Frank H. Smyrl, "Unionism, Abolitionism, and Vigilantism in Texas, 1856–1865" (M.A. thesis, University of Texas, 1961), 39–44.

devastate at least all the state's northern counties. The ensuing "Texas Troubles," which in all likelihood had no basis in reality, spread fear across the entire South.[26]

Charles R. Pryor, the ultrasouthern editor of the Dallas *Herald*, did more than any other individual to spread the panic. The fire had destroyed his own press, so he publicized the "plot" by writing to other editors around the state, including John Marshall of the Austin *Texas State Gazette*, L. C. DeLisle of the Bonham *Era*, and E. H. Cushing of the Houston *Telegraph*. All three of these editors favored the Southern Democratic candidate for president, John C. Breckinridge, a fact that Pryor no doubt counted on to insure a favorable reception for his letters. His first letter, to Marshall, claimed that the "plot" was the work of McKinney and Blount, the ministers driven from Dallas a year before. Fires were to reduce the area to helplessness, and then white abolitionists would direct a servile insurrection coinciding with the state election in August. "I write in haste," Pryor said, "we sleep upon our arms and the whole country is most deeply agitated." The letters to DeLisle and Cushing added details, including the charge that the black conspirators intended to spare young white women to employ in gratifying their sexual desires. "They had even gone so far," he wrote, "as to designate their choise [*sic*], and certain ladies had already been selected as the victims of these misguided monsters."[27]

The rumors that encouraged panic and the feelings of fear and outrage that it engendered are clear in a letter written by Benjamin Bowman of Birdville in Tarrant County on July 24. Bowman was only semiliterate, but he had little difficulty in describing the situation to his brother.

Joseph, there is a great excitement in this country on the account of Negro rebellion[.] abolition Emissarys ar going through this country instigating Negros to Burne the towns and kill there Masters[.] There has all ready been some 12 or fourteen towns burnt[.] Dallasville is burnt intirely up and many others towns that i could name[.] the people of Dallasvill have sustained over a half Million of losses[.] They caught one of the ablitionst last Weake and hung him up to a limb without jug or jury tho they had proof sufficient to justify there course[.] it is Dangros for a Stranger to travel through this Country at

26. Clarksville *Northern Standard*, July 14, 1860; Marshall *Texas Republican*, July 7, 1860; Reynolds, *Editors Make War*, 97–98, 108–10.

27. Reynolds, *Editors Make War*, 100–101; Austin *Texas State Gazette*, July 28, 1860.

this time in Dallis County they ar Whipping about thirty Negros pr Day[.] the Negros ar Confessing all about the plot they say that the Abolisionists have promised them there freedom if they would burne all the towns Down in the State[.] allso they was to breake out on the Sixth Day of August when the men was all gon to the Election than kill all the Wimmin and Children that they could[.] all the likly young ladies they Was to save for Wives for themselves[.] those Secret Emmisaries promised them that they would be her with an army from Kanses about the time the Negros was to breake out[.] this they have proof of from hundreds of Negroes, What will be the result of the strife God only knows[.][28]

Reprisals against the supposed abolitionist plotters and their black allies began immediately in north Texas. A Dallas vigilance committee arrested and examined one hundred slaves, and three were executed on July 24. The man accused of actually burning the town died with a chew of tobacco in his cheek and said nothing to the end. In Fort Worth, a man accused of "tampering with slaves for several months" was hanged. Citizens there believed, in the words of one, that "it is better for us to hang ninety-nine innocent (suspicious) men than to let one guilty one pass." In the meantime, panic and the rumor that a general insurrection was planned for election day on August 6 quickly spread into east Texas. Tyler and Jefferson both reported attempts at arson in July; the town of Henderson burned on August 5. Executions spread into Anderson, Cherokee, Upshur, Ellis, and Rusk counties. Within a month or so, the alarm extended over the entire state. From Tyler County in southeastern Texas, W. L. Mann wrote that the uprising planned for August 6 was discovered only the day before. Four Negroes were whipped "very severely," and one died as a result. In Austin, news of the fires in north Texas and the burning of a mill caused, in the words of one resident there, "much apprehension of an outbreak of the negroes" and "a feeling of uneasiness among the people." Even in Matagorda County on the Gulf Coast, where no fires or disturbances had occurred, citizens were fully aroused. "Should anyone be detected in an attempt to destroy this place," the local paper said on August 22, "he need not expect a trial."[29]

28. Benjamin Bowman to "Dear Brother Joseph," July 24, 1860, in Bowman Family Papers, East Tennessee State University Library, Johnson City.

29. Austin *Texas State Gazette*, August 4, July 28, 1860; Reynolds, *Editors Make War*, 103–104 (quotation); W. L. Mann to Thomas B. Huling, August 24, 1860, in Huling Papers;

The panic gradually subsided in late August and September. No more fires were reported, and some editors pointed out how exaggerated the claims had been in the first place. Even the ultra-southerner Robert W. Loughery commented that there was "already more excitement in this community than we like to see exhibited," and the Galveston *Civilian and Gazette* commented sarcastically on how "rumor has burned almost every town in Texas this season." Unionists such as Governor Sam Houston and A. B. Norton, editor of the Austin *Southern Intelligencer*, began to charge that the insurrection plot had been fabricated to win votes for the Southern Democratic candidate for president. "There was a little excitement got up by the newspapers before the election for political effect," Mrs. E. M. Pease wrote her sister on September 20, "but the stories of fires and murders are all exaggerated."[30]

Even as the "Texas Troubles" subsided, however, they claimed one additional victim in a case that was more sensational than any of those before it. Anthony Bewley, a Northern Methodist minister active in north Texas from 1855 until the summer of 1860, left the area in July, apparently from the realization that he made an inviting target to fearful defenders of slavery. Shortly thereafter, several residents of Tarrant County found, according to their sworn statements, a letter written on July 3 by one W. H. Bailey to the "Rev. W. Buley." It discussed in detail a plot for incendiarism and slave insurrection to be executed by a secret organization known as the "Mystic-Red." Their purpose was to ruin Texas' slaveholders so that Republicans could control the state and join Abraham Lincoln in blocking the spread of slavery. Citizens' meetings in Fort Worth and Sherman concluded that the "Rev. W. Buley" was Anthony Bewley and offered a thousand-dollar reward for his capture and return. Accordingly, a group of bounty hunters pursued the minister to Missouri and brought him back to Fort Worth where he was hanged on September 13 without benefit of a trial. Claims were made that Bewley admitted being the recipient of the Bailey letter, saying that he had lost it while getting oats to feed his horse as he left Texas. In fact, however, he protested innocence

D. C. Freeman, Jr., to Mollie Freeman, July 13, 1860, in Plummer Family Papers, Garrett Collection, University of Texas at Arlington; Matagorda *Gazette*, August 22, 1860. Lack, "Urban Slavery in the Southwest," 283–88, shows that the fear had impact in Austin and even in Galveston.

30. Marshall *Texas Republic*, August 11, 1860; Reynolds, *Editors Make War*, 108, 111–21; Austin *Texas State Gazette*, September 1, 15, 1860; Lucadia N. Pease to "Sister," September 10, 1860, in Pease-Graham-Niles Family Papers.

to the end and almost certainly was guilty of nothing more than disapproving of slavery in principle. A few Texas newspapers questioned the authenticity of the Bailey letter, but the *Texas Christian Advocate*, which was published by Southern Methodists, claimed that Bewley had fallen "a victim to his lawlessness." And the Weatherford *White Man* took vicious delight in his fate, writing, "This distinguished parson, one of Sam Houston's 'vicegerents of God,' met with a sad accident at Fort Worth not long ago. By some means he got on the Abraham Lincoln-Sam Houston platform, and somehow, or somehow else, got a string entangled around his neck, and just as he stepped on the Squatter Sovereignty plank of the platform, some of the screws gave way, and down came the 'vicegerent' and broke his pious neck."[31]

Extremism in society meant extremism in politics. Even as Texas emerged from the abolitionist-insurrection panic at the end of the summer of 1860, the state's voters prepared to demonstrate overwhelming support for the Lower South's presidential candidate, John C. Breckinridge. Nominated by Southern Democrats who walked out of their party's convention rather than accept Illinois' Stephen A. Douglas as a candidate, Breckinridge represented ultra positions on nearly all questions related to slavery. The only real alternative in Texas, where voting for Douglas, the northern Democratic candidate, was almost as unthinkable as supporting the Republican candidate Abraham Lincoln, was John Bell of the Constitutional Union party. Bell, a Tennesseean, represented a conservative alternative for southern voters who wished to preserve slavery within the Union. His supporters became increasingly alarmed as the Southern Democrats persistently threatened secession if Lincoln and the "Black Republicans" won the election. Texans in 1860 were on the verge of allowing their anger at abolitionist attacks on slavery, their fears of servile insurrection, and their intolerance for any seeming dissent to still, as Sam Houston put it, "the voice of reason."[32]

In November, 1860, Breckinridge defeated Bell by a vote of 47,548 to

31. Phelan, *History of Early Methodism*, 452–58; Sibley, *Lone Stars and State Gazettes*, 288; Norton, "Methodist Episcopal Church and Civil Disturbances," 321–22, 332–36; Austin *Texas State Gazette*, August 25, September 29 (quoting the Weatherford *White Man*), October 13, 1860; Charles Elliott, *A History of the Methodist Episcopal Church in the South-West from 1844 to 1864*, ed. Leroy M. Vernon (Cincinnati, 1868), 189 (quoting the *Texas Christian Advocate*).

32. Buenger, *Secession and the Union in Texas*, is the most comprehensive study of the election of 1860 and the background to secession. For a good summary of the election of 1860, see Richardson, Wallace, and Anderson, *Texas: The Lone Star State*, 220–22.

15,463 in Texas, but Lincoln carried the free states and won the presidency. Secessionists immediately began to press for disunion. Even Governor Sam Houston could not restrain the extremists or block the convention they called for January 28, 1861, in Austin. The convention adopted an ordinance of secession on February 1 and submitted it to the voters in a referendum on February 23. Texans approved secession 46,129 to 14,697, with only a few counties rejecting the ordinance, and the state then joined the Confederate States of America in March, 1861.[33]

The decision for secession in Texas, although it came swiftly and with a momentum that apparently could not be stopped, was not a simple matter. Yet the fundamental reason for disunion is absolutely clear—it was Negro slavery. The institution provided, in the words of one historian, the "destabilizing force" in Texas society, and it "linked Texas with the Lower South," to the other states that began disunion and created the Confederacy. Determination to defend slavery motivated secession, and the secession convention itself said so very directly in its "Declaration of the Causes which Impel the State of Texas to Secede from the Federal Union." Texas, the declaration said, had joined the Union while "holding, maintaining and protecting the institution known as negro slavery—the servitude of the African to the white race within her limits; a relation that had existed from her first settlement of her wilderness by the white race, and which her people intended should continue to exist in all future time." The controlling majority in the federal government, however, had sought to exclude slavery from the territories and denied it proper protection of the law. Moreover, the declaration continued, a "great sectional party" had been formed in the North based upon hostility to the southern states and "their benificent and patriarchal system of African slavery, proclaiming the debasing doctrine of the equality of all men, irrespective of race or color, a doctrine at war with nature, in opposition to the experience of mankind, and in violation of the plainest revelations of the Divine law." In its fanatical attack on slavery, this "abolition organization" had committed many offenses against the South, including sending "hired emissaries among us to burn our towns." Accordingly, the declaration concluded, we must state "our own views," which are as follows:

33. Buenger, *Secession and the Union in Texas*, 119–77; Richardson, Wallace, and Anderson, *Texas: The Lone Star State*, 222–27. Buenger (p. 174) gives the vote on secession as 46,153 to 14,747; Richardson (p. 226), as 46,129 to 14,697.

We hold as undeniable truths that the governments of the various States, and of the Confederacy itself, were established exclusively by the white race, for themselves and their posterity; that the African race had no agency in their establishment; that they were rightfully held and regarded as an inferior and dependent race, and in that condition only could their existence in this country be rendered beneficial or tolerable.

That in this free government *all white men are and of right ought to be entitled to equal civil and political rights*; that the servitude of the African race, as existing in these States, is mutually beneficial to both bond and free, and is abundantly authorized and justified by the experience of mankind, and the revealed will of the Almighty Creator, as recognized by all Christian nations; while the destruction of the existing relations between the two races, as advocated by our sectional enemies, would bring inevitable calamities upon both and desolation upon the fifteen slaveholding states.

In defense of these truths, Texas dissolved its political connections with the United States.[34]

The extremists who had come to dominate Texas during the 1850s cheered secession and discounted the risk involved in undertaking a revolution to protect slavery. Unionists were more pessimistic. "Although the South has been driven to this measure by the Black Republicans of the north disregarding the Constitution of the U. S. in respect to Slavery," Lucadia N. Pease wrote her sister, "yet it will be a most grievous thing particularly for Texas." Sam Houston, who used every bit of his great prestige and even sacrificed his career in an unsuccessful effort to prevent secession and keep Texas out of the Confederacy, offered an even more specific prophecy. "Our people are going to war to perpetuate slavery," he told John H. Reagan, "and the first gun fired in the war will be the knell of slavery."[35]

34. Buenger, *Secession and the Union in Texas*, 7, 21; Terry G. Jordan, "The Imprint of the Upper and Lower South on Mid-Nineteenth Century Texas," *Annals of the Association of American Geographers*, LVII (1967), 688, reaches similar conclusions on the importance of slavery. Winkler (ed.), *Platforms of Political Parties in Texas*, 89–92.

35. Lucadia N. Pease to "Sister," February 11, 1861, in Pease-Graham-Niles Family Papers; John H. Reagan, "A Conversation with Governor Houston," *Quarterly of the Texas State Historical Association*, III (1900), 280.

TWELVE

. . . .

The Civil War and "Juneteenth," 1861–1865

"FREE, FREE MY LORD"

At the outbreak of the Civil War in April, 1861, Texas had nearly two hundred thousand slaves. For the next four years, as the fate of those bondsmen was settled on battlefields across the South, the Peculiar Institution remained less disturbed in Texas than in any other Confederate state. The primary reason was simple—Texas escaped any significant invasion by Federal troops, and thus the great majority of the state's slaves were not uprooted by advancing armies or given an opportunity to flee to nearby Union forces. This does not mean, however, that the war years passed without notable disruptions in the lives of slaves and masters alike before it ended with a climactic event for both—"Juneteenth."[1]

Texas faced no serious threat of a land-based invasion during the early years of the war. Its eastern boundary was protected by Louisiana. To the north lay the Indian Territory, which remained part of the Union, but William C. Young of Cooke County, in command of a force of Texans,

---

1. The 1860 U.S. census enumerated a slave population of 182,566, whereas county tax rolls for the same year showed the assessment of 160,467 bondsmen across the state. The number of slaves counted for tax purposes was 13.8 percent less than that recorded by census enumerators. In 1861, the tax roll total rose to 169,166. If this figure is increased by 13.8 percent, the total is 192,511. Thus, it is likely that Texas' slave population was approaching 200,000 at the outbreak of the Civil War. U.S. Bureau of the Census, *Population of the United States in 1860*, 484–86; County Tax Rolls, 1860 and 1861.

In contrast to the situation in Texas, slavery began to crumble in Louisiana and Georgia with the beginning of the Civil War. See Ripley, *Slaves and Freedmen in Civil War Louisiana*; Mohr, *On the Threshold of Freedom*.

crossed the Red River in May, 1861, and took Forts Arbuckle, Cobb, and Washita. This action removed any threat of Federal invasion from that direction. In the west, Confederate forces under General Henry H. Sibley failed in an attempt to conquer New Mexico in 1861–62; nevertheless, the great expanses of harsh and only semi-explored west Texas terrain gave adequate protection in that region. Indians were much more of a threat than Federal forces on the western frontier, rolling back the frontier of white settlement, especially in the northwest, during the war years when adequate forces were unavailable to protect settlers. This circumstance may have interfered slightly with the spread of slavery, but Indians hardly provided bondsmen the hope for escape that Federal armies offered.[2]

Although reasonably well protected from invasion on the east, north, and west, Texas had no such security along its more than four hundred miles of coastline stretching from Sabine Pass to the Rio Grande. Once the Federal blockade was extended to this area in July, 1861, Union forces found many inviting targets situated on the bays and rivers along the Gulf. In September, 1862, Federal blockaders forced the Confederates to abandon control of Sabine Pass, the outlet for the Sabine and Neches rivers, and followed that success with an attack on Galveston, Texas' most important port. The harbor and city fell to Union forces in early October, virtually without opposition. Later that month, United States warships, working further to the west, took control of the waters of Matagorda Bay and around Corpus Christi. These successes, however, proved temporary. Federal ships, beset by disease and frustrated by a lack of garrison troops to take advantage of their control of coastal waters, abandoned Matagorda Bay in December. Then, on January 1, 1863, Confederate troops under Major General John B. Magruder, the new commander of the Department of Texas, recaptured Galveston. Within the month, Union ships controlling Sabine Pass were driven away, too. In September, 1863, Major General Nathaniel P. Banks and Rear Admiral David G. Farragut planned a major offensive against Texas to begin with an attack at Sabine Pass. Their plans were thwarted, however, when Lieutenant Dick Dowling and a small garrison turned back the initial landing force with heavy losses. Galveston and Sabine Pass remained in Confed-

2. James Burchell Crow, "Confederate Military Operations in Texas, 1861–1865" (M.A. thesis, North Texas State College, 1957), 1–17; Richardson, Wallace, and Anderson, *Texas: The Lone Star State*, 227–29.

erate hands and open to blockade runners until the war ended. Later in 1863, Banks turned his attention to the western Gulf Coast, taking Brownsville and Rio Grande City and all key points eastward to the Matagorda Peninsula, including Indianola and Port Lavaca, but these successes posed only a limited threat to the settled interior of Texas. In the spring of 1864, wishing to disrupt the Trans-Mississippi Department, based in part at Marshall, Texas, and hit the fertile east Texas farm country, Banks planned a major campaign up the Red River past Shreveport. But he was turned back at the Battle of Mansfield (Louisiana) in April, and Texas escaped the most serious invasion threat mounted by Union forces during the war.[3]

Federal troops thus had no opportunity to create more than minor disruptions of slavery in Texas. Galveston had a sizable slave population (1,240 on the 1862 tax rolls), but masters there had ample time to evacuate their bondsmen before the Union attack. Thomas Jefferson League, for example, instructed his wife as early as June, 1862, to be ready to take their slaves and leave if the island fell. Their house could be left to its fate, he said. When Federal forces took over, their commander, Commodore William B. Renshaw, declaring that he was no abolitionist, asked all citizens to take their slaves to the mainland and issued an order stating that Negroes were not to come to him for asylum. Once Galveston was reoccupied, a good many owners and their slaves returned. The Sabine Pass area and the coastal regions west of Corpus Christi had very few slaves to be disturbed by the presence of Federal ships in their vicinities. Matagorda County, which borders Matagorda Bay, did have extensive slaveholdings, and some planters living close to the coast may have felt it necessary to abandon their places as early as the fall of 1862. The administrator of the H. J. Powell estate, for example, informed the Matagorda County Probate Court that due to evacuating the plantation during the war the Negroes under his charge were an expense to the estate rather than a benefit. Such cases were uncommon, however.[4]

3. Charles C. Cumberland, "The Confederate Loss and Recapture of Galveston, 1862–1863," *Southwestern Historical Quarterly*, LI (1947), 111–15, 123–30; Alwyn Barr, "Texas Coastal Defense, 1861–1865," *Southwestern Historical Quarterly*, LXV (1961), 13–19, 23–27; Crow, "Confederate Military Operations," 76–86. The best account of the Red River Campaign is Ludwell H. Johnson, *Red River Campaign: Politics and Cotton in the Civil War* (Baltimore, 1958).

4. Lack, "Urban Slavery in the Southwest," 303; Mary Elizabeth Massey, *Refugee Life in the Confederacy* (Baton Rouge, 1964), 6; Thomas J. League to his wife, June 2, 1862, in League

Since there was little actual fighting in Texas, the use of slave labor to build fortifications and supply other manpower needs of the Confederacy constituted the most serious disruption faced by bondsmen and their masters during the conflict. Calls on slaveowners to permit the use of their Negroes in building coastal defenses began during the first year of the war. On November 15, 1861, Brigadier General Paul O. Hebert, commander of all Confederate forces in Texas, ordered Isaac H. Dennis to go into the interior of the state and induce citizens to loan their slaves for the purpose of erecting fortifications. Voluntarism did not generally provide sufficient labor, however, and the lack of coastal defenses contributed to Federal successes along the Gulf Coast in 1862. By early 1863, some Texans were demanding that Confederate authorities authorize impressment to force slaveholders to bear their share of the war's burdens. Governor Francis R. Lubbock mentioned this problem to a special session of the state legislature in February, 1863, suggesting the passage of a law that would require masters to make their bondsmen available. "A small percentage of the slave population would suffice," Lubbock said. The state legislature did not act, but on March 26, 1863, the Confederate Congress did, passing a law authorizing military commanders to impress private property, including slaves, for public service. Bondsmen were to be held a maximum of sixty days and be paid for at a rate of fifteen dollars per month.[5]

During the spring of 1863, General Magruder, having recaptured Gal-

---

Papers; Galveston County Tax Rolls, 1862 and 1864 (which show 957 slaves); Dallas *Herald*, November 1, 1862. U.S. Bureau of the Census, *Population of the United States in 1860*, 484–85, reported only 701 slaves in Jefferson and Orange counties (near Sabine Pass), and only 223 in Nueces and Cameron, which stretched from Corpus Christi to Brownsville. Estate of H. J. Powell, Matagorda County Probate Records (Inventory Record, Book A-2).

5. Robert N. Scott (comp.), *The War of the Rebellion: A Compilation of the Official Records of the Union and Confederate Armies* (Washington, D.C., 1880–1901), Ser. I, Vol. 4, p. 140 (hereinafter this collection will be cited as *O.R.*, with appropriate series, volume, part, and page numbers). Bill Winsor, *Texas in the Confederacy: Military Installations, Economy and People* (Hillsboro, Tex., 1978), 5, provides one exception to these generalizations. Five hundred slaves helped build Fort Esperanza on Matagorda Island in late 1862. Harrison A. Trexler, "The Opposition of Planters to Employment of Slaves as Laborers by the Confederacy," *Mississippi Valley Historical Review*, XXVII (1940), 213; Robert L. Kerby, *Kirby Smith's Confederacy: The Trans-Mississippi South, 1863–1865* (New York, 1972), 56–57; Marshall *Texas Republican*, October 18, 1862; *Message of Governor F. R. Lubbock to the Extra Session of the Ninth Legislature* (Austin, 1863), 14; Bernard H. Nelson, "Confederate Slave Impressment Legislation, 1861–1865," *Journal of Negro History*, XXXI (1946), 400–401; Clement Eaton, *A History of the Southern Confederacy* (New York, 1961), 238–39.

veston in January, employed slave labor in fortifying approaches to the city. Perhaps as many as three thousand bondsmen worked on this project. Magruder also obtained the services of five hundred slaves in constructing a line of fortifications in the Sabine Pass area. Technically, this labor was provided voluntarily, but a great deal of pressure was exerted in persuading slaveowners to part with their bondsmen. The British traveler Lieutenant Colonel Arthur Fremantle spoke in May, 1863, of troops being used "to impress" slaves "for the government works at Galveston, the planters having been backward in coming forward with their darkies." Magruder, in spite of the success of his pressure tactics, felt that there had been a less than equitable sharing of the burden among slaveowners. As he planned further fortifications in June, 1863, he informed Governor Lubbock that actual impressment might well be a necessity. "I am fully aware," he wrote,

> that citizens who have been the most patriotic have heretofore borne a greater portion of the burden of furnishing slave labor than properly belonged to them. There are many reasons for this. The most selfish keep their slaves at home, and of those who furnish them, the most importunate for their return will sometimes succeed in recovering their slaves, in consequence of the change of officers and agents necessarily incident to military life. At least 1,500 slaves are necessary at this moment to work on the fortifications on the coast. I earnestly desire to be spared the painful necessity of using the power which the law of impressment gives me, and am confident that I will not have to apply it in the majority of cases; nevertheless, I will execute it with firmness when necessary, and will give credit to the patriotic for the sacrifices they have made, whilst the public interest will be protected by calling more largely upon those who have been dilatory or who have omitted entirely to contribute their quota to the public defense. A mere inspection of the map should satisfy any holder of slave property that these defenses are absolutely necessary to its security.[6]

Lubbock immediately promised full support to Magruder, expressing confidence that the general would "exercise a rigid surveillance over the

6. Trexler, "Opposition of Planters," 215; Kerby, *Kirby Smith's Confederacy*, 56–57; Lack, "Urban Slavery in the Southwest," 301; Winsor, *Texas in the Confederacy*, 3; Lord (ed.), *Fremantle Diary*, 60; O.R., Ser. I, Vol. 26, Pt. 2, p. 35.

bureau to which you entrust this duty of the impressment of slave labor" so that "the injustice heretofore operating upon a patriotic few will be speedily removed, and the burden extended, by an equitable apportionment, over the entire body of slaveholders." Before the month ended, Magruder received permission from Lieutenant General Edmund Kirby Smith, commander of the Trans-Mississippi Department, to use the power of impressment. But Kirby Smith's order indicated great concern over the sensitivity of the issue. Speaking primarily of obtaining bondsmen to serve as teamsters, he reminded Magruder that the property in question "is the last the owners are disposed to part with." Therefore it would be best to exhaust every effort to hire slaves first and then to impress "with great precaution, so as to wound the sensibilities of the people as little as possible." The order also "suggested" that Magruder wait to use this power until after the gubernatorial election in early August, so as not to provide any "additional exciting cause" to upset voters. Agreeing not to resort to impressment until after the election, Magruder established a Labor Bureau on July 1 and put it to work trying to hire slaves.[7]

Impressment began in early August, 1863. One early case arose from the need for teamsters to drive cotton wagons from the Clarksville area to the Rio Grande. Several planters in Red River and Bowie counties offered Negro drivers in return for exemptions from military duty. The Labor Bureau refused, however, and impressed the necessary teamsters. By the late summer, with General Kirby Smith's continuing support, slaves were being impressed for any purpose necessary to the Confederacy's military effort. In the Sabine Pass area, for example, bondsmen were used to improve railroad transportation and to erect additional fortifications after Dowling's successful defense. At Tyler in November, impressed slaves built a stockade to enclose the Federal prisoners of war being held at Camp Ford. Magruder's Labor Bureau not only impressed the property of Texas slaveholders; it also took bondsmen from Louisiana planters who "refugeed" to Texas to escape Federal forces. The refugee masters protested, and General Kirby Smith agreed that they not be disturbed until settled in Texas. But General Magruder argued that such preferential treatment would confuse his efforts and force him to discharge all the bondsmen already impressed. "The business of the negro bureau works well for the first time," he wrote, "and I do hope the lieutenant-general

7. O.R., Ser. I, Vol. 26, Pt. 2, pp. 36, 85–86 (quotation), 102.

[Kirby Smith] will not permit the representations of interested parties (planters from Louisiana or elsewhere) to interfere with it."[8]

Early in December, 1863, as Federal forces took control of the coast from Brownsville to Matagorda Bay and threatened to move inland, General Magruder issued a sweeping order that amounted to an impressment of all the able-bodied male slaves, except one per owner, in Texas. The planters of Brazoria, Fort Bend, and Wharton counties were to send all their able-bodied slaves except one to work on defenses for the San Bernard River and Caney Creek. Other slaveowners, depending on their geographical locations, were to send their male bondsmen either to Houston, Gonzales, Austin, or San Antonio. It is difficult to imagine the resulting confusion if every master had obeyed this order with alacrity. Magruder had been accused of becoming overly excited at the Seven Days' Battle in Virginia before he was transferred to Texas in 1862. Perhaps this characteristic emerged again in his impressment order. In any case, the call for slaves did not last long once it came to the attention of General Kirby Smith. On January 7, 1864, he informed Magruder that the circular, "unlimited in its duration, sweeping in its provisions, and drawing upon so large a proportion of the slave population and over such an extent of country, for the defense of points so distant from each other, seems to be injudicious." Moreover, Kirby Smith said, Magruder's circular violated several parts of General Order Number 138, issued by the Confederate government in October, 1863, as an interpretation of the impressment law passed in March. For example, only males aged seventeen to fifty could be impressed, and those for a period of only sixty days. He instructed Magruder to modify his call for slaves to conform to General Order Number 138 and to relax it even more "if it can be safely done." Kirby Smith also revoked the call as it affected eight northeastern counties that had already been called on for laborers to build fortifications on the upper Red River.[9]

Regardless of Kirby Smith's directive, Magruder continued to think in

8. *Ibid.*, Ser. I, Vol. 26, Pt. 2, pp. 154–55, 209–10, 268–69; Ser. I, Vol. 22, Pt. 2, pp. 994–95; Winsor, *Texas in the Confederacy*, 3; Randal B. Gilbert, "'The People of Tyler Are Relieved of Their Fears'; The Building of the Camp Ford Stockade," *Chronicles of Smith County, Texas*, XXIV (1985), 2.

9. *O.R.*, Ser. I, Vol. 34, Pt. 2, pp. 832, 838–39 (quotation on 838), Ser. IV, Vol. 2, pp. 897–898. In late November, just before issuing his sweeping impressment circular, Magruder ordered one thousand slaves to Austin to build fortifications there. *Ibid.*, Ser. I, Vol. 26, Pt. 2, pp. 444–46. The comment on Magruder's becoming "overly excited" is in Webb, Carroll, and Branda (eds.), *Handbook of Texas*, II, 131.

terms of large-scale impressment. In January, 1864, he hinted that sixty thousand bondsmen would be needed to fortify the Gulf Coast. Fearing an attack in April at the mouths of the Caney and San Bernard rivers, he issued impressment orders for one-fourth of all the male slaves aged seventeen to fifty in four coastal counties. As late as November, 1864—well after the defeat of Banks's Red River Campaign—he suggested that Confederate authorities impress slaves from northern Texas to work in Arkansas. Texas, he said, was filled with refugeed bondsmen, while Arkansas was virtually denuded of slave labor. In the meantime, on February 17, 1864, the Confederate Congress had authorized the employment of twenty thousand slaves at the same wages as privates and enrolled one-fifth of all Negro males aged eighteen to forty-five. Although this act was not so encompassing as some of Magruder's impressment orders, it doubtless lent support to his actions. Early in 1865, the last congress of the Confederacy authorized military commanders to hire or impress as many slaves as necessary. By then, however, the war was drawing to a close.[10]

Texas slaveholders generally were reluctant to have their bondsmen serve the Confederacy. The primary reason was simple—such work endangered a valuable piece of property. Impressed slaves often did heavy, dangerous work under unhealthy conditions. They depended on the government for food and housing, and supervision came from military officers or engineers. Owners feared too that their slaves, away from home in the company of large numbers of other male bondsmen, would be more likely to run away. Payments from the Confederacy, which reached thirty dollars per month during 1864, did not seem adequate compensation for the loss of labor and the potential loss of a valuable slave. Some slaveowners, as General Magruder's correspondence indicated, responded patriotically to the Confederacy's need for labor, but others, from the beginning, parted with their bondsmen very grudgingly. Lizzie Neblett, for example, explained to her husband in May, 1863, that she had made excuses to avoid sending one of their slaves to Galveston. "I fear that I have not acted for the best," she wrote, "but I did not want to send any if I could help it, but if they come again Joe will have to go, & be put under any overseer they please, etc., but I can't help it." By

10. *O.R.*, Ser. I, Vol. 34, Pt. 3, pp. 784–85, Ser. I, Vol. 41, Pt. 4, pp. 1029–30, Ser. I, Vol. 41, Pt. 2, p. 1014; Kerby, *Kirby Smith's Confederacy*, 254–56; Nelson, "Impressment Legislation," 401–402; Eaton, *History of Southern Confederacy*, 238–39.

1864, opposition to impressment became so strong that some masters advised disregarding Magruder's orders or promised to obey only "at the point of a bayonet." Others encouraged their slaves to hide from impressment officers and to run away and come home as soon as possible if they were taken.[11]

Texas slaves who were impressed had no choice in the matter, of course, but it seems likely that for once they agreed with their masters. Most had no desire to leave their homes and families and engage in work that probably posed an even greater threat of injury and disease than did their normal plantation labor. Impressment thus disturbed thousands of slaves and their owners alike and disrupted slavery in Texas far more than did military action from 1861 to 1865.

As the conflict entered its third year, the specter of defeat posed an even greater threat to slavery in Texas than did invasion or impressment. After Gettysburg and Vicksburg in mid-1863, whether southerners admitted it or not, Federal victory was only a matter of time. To what extent did this circumstance cause Texas slaveholders to lose confidence in slavery before the war came to an end?

Major newspapers continued to support the institution adamantly in 1863–65. When, for example, Confederate leaders, including President Jefferson Davis, began in 1864 to discuss using slaves as soldiers and rewarding them with freedom, the Galveston *Weekly News* apologized for even having to mention the subject: "We think it is a matter of regret that any suggestion should ever have been made in high official quarters, that any emergency can arise to compel the South to an abandonment of the foundation principle upon which the institution of slavery rests; that is, the principle that slavery is the best possible condition for the slave himself, and the only one he can occupy consistent with the welfare of the white man." *The Patriot*, published at LaGrange, agreed and pronounced the suggestion of black military service as "fatal and disastrous." In February, 1865, a public meeting at Goliad resolved "that the discussion of the question, whether it is expedient or politic to abolish southern slavery, is premature, unwise and unnecessary, and impresses the Northern

11. Lack, "Urban Slavery in the Southwest," 306; Bell I. Wiley, *Southern Negroes, 1861–1865* (New York, 1938), 124–25; Lizzie Neblett to Will H. Neblett, January 3, 1864, May 24, 1863, both in Neblett Papers; Receipt for the services of a slave, December 31, 1864, in W. L. Sloan Papers, Barker Texas History Center, University of Texas, Austin.

mind with the belief that we feel unable to sustain the institution." Slavery, these citizens said, is "not to be wrested from us by any power on earth." Robert W. Loughery of the Marshall *Texas Republican* expressed the hope as late as June 16, 1865, that the Thirteenth Amendment would not be ratified quickly. Negroes, he wrote, because of their "naturally idle and migratory" character, cannot take care of themselves outside slavery.[12]

Public expressions are one thing; however, private sentiments may be another. Did individual actions belie these statements of support to the bitter end? Some Texans became pessimistic in 1863–64, fearing that invasion and defeat would destroy their Peculiar Institution. "If the yankees invade & overrun Texas," Lizzie Neblett wrote her husband in January, 1864, "my negroes will be lost, and then, all will depend upon my exertions; and how shall I meet the emergency?" Abram Sheppard of Matagorda County wrote an elaborately detailed will in September, 1863, disposing of some ninety slaves and a plantation he owned jointly with his sister. He concluded, however, with the following: "In case the casualties or the results of the present war should greatly diminish my estate by losses of slaves or other property, . . . I hereby revoke all the bequests . . . and devise the whole of my estate of every kind to my said sister." By early 1864, Theophilus Perry, a soldier from Harrison County, had lost all confidence in slave property. He urged his wife to sell or trade their slaves for land. "I do not wish to be considered as believing that we will be subjugated," he wrote on January 18, 1864, "but whatever our fortune may be I think that our money will be worthless in all likelihood, and that our Negro property will be rendered very insecure and precarious." Slightly more than a year later, in March, 1865, Frank Moss, writing from near Crockett in Houston County, told his sister: "I believe that the Negro question has dide [*sic*] out. All hands wiling to give them up."[13]

Undoubtedly other Texans shared the pessimism of Neblett, Shep-

12. Robert F. Durden, *The Gray and the Black: The Confederate Debate on Emancipation* (Baton Rouge, 1972), 119, 198; La Grange *Patriot*, December 24, 1864; Marshall *Texas Republican*, June 16, 1865.

13. Lizzie Neblett to Will H. Neblett, January 3, 1864, in Neblett Papers; Estate of Abram Sheppard, Matagorda County Probate Records (Transcribed Will Record); Theophilus Perry to Harriet P. Perry, January 18, 1864, in Person Family Papers; Frank Moss to Mrs. A. E. Rentfrow, March 26, 1865, in A. Henry Moss Papers, Barker Texas History Center, University of Texas, Austin; Kerby, *Kirby Smith's Confederacy*, 257.

pard, Perry, and Moss, but many did not. Slaveowners continued throughout the war to write wills distributing their slave property as though they expected the institution to last indefinitely. The will of James B. Wooten provides an ultimate example of such apparent optimism. Writing on August 20, 1865, two months after "Juneteenth," he said, "Should Negroes remain as property to their owners I wish all my Negroes equally divided between my wife and three children previously mentioned." Slaves also continued to be treated as property in probate proceedings begun during the war's last stages. In February, 1865, for example, Caleb Barron's Smith County estate, which included thirty-seven slaves, was inventoried, appraised, and divided. As late as May 29, the slaves belonging to an estate in Burnet County were included in an inventory. Perhaps such cases reveal very little about attitudes toward slavery's future, in that so long as the institution had not been finally abolished slaves had to be considered as property. Nevertheless, the treatment of bondsmen in wills and estate settlements in 1863–65, without any indication that slavery was doomed, suggests some degree of confidence or hope for its future.[14]

Optimism concerning the Peculiar Institution was especially obvious in the continuing demand for slave labor during the last years of the war. In spite of an extremely unsettled monetary system, a brisk business in the hiring and the buying and selling of slaves continued until the end. Many estate managers hired out bondsmen in their charge for the year beginning in January, 1865. As late as March 17, two slaves from the Brazoria County estate of Sidney Phillips were hired out for the remainder of that year. Advertisements by potential slave purchasers appeared in the early months of 1865, and on April 25, less than two months before "Juneteenth," a man was sold at auction on Congress Street in Austin. Hire contracts, of course, represented only temporary commitments and therefore a limited risk to the hirer, but individuals who purchased slaves during the last years of the war made themselves vulnerable to significant financial losses.[15]

14. Estate of James B. Wooten, Red River County Probate Records (Will Record, Book B); Estate of Caleb Barron, Smith County Probate Papers; Estate of Joseph H. Eubank, Burnet County Probate Records (Probate Record, Book B).

15. Estate of Sidney Phillips, Brazoria County Probate Records (Wills, etc., Book D). Examples of hiring out slaves for 1865 are found in the following: Estate of Joseph M. Brown, De Witt County Probate Records (Final Record, Book C); Estate of John Burrows, Brazos County Probate Records (Probate Record, Book E); Estate of Alvan Frisby, Smith

These late-war transactions involving slaves may reflect to some extent chaotic monetary conditions and declining values rather than confidence in the institution's future. Depreciation of Confederate currency led to wildly inflated prices. On September 22, 1863, for example, six young Travis County bondsmen sold for an average of $3,857 each in Confederate money, and in 1864, adult male slaves in Houston sold for approximately $4,500 in the same currency.[16] Such prices mean very little, however, in light of the depreciated paper in use then. In fact, spending such money for slaves in 1864 probably represented trading two items of equally questionable future value. Values assigned to bondsmen in estate appraisals, which generally were stated in prewar terms, may be a better indicator of slaves' prices as the war drew to a close. These values held steady at approximately $700 from 1861 through 1864 (averages—regardless of age, sex, or condition—of $738 in 1861, $702 in 1862, $664 in 1863, and $691 in 1864) and then dropped sharply to $462 in 1865. Hire rates for that year appear to have declined also.[17] Such declining values probably encouraged business in slaves during the war's last year, but these prices still represented significant sums. Texans were willing, too, to exchange other forms of property for slaves. During 1864, David Black and Barney Sherry, both of Red River County, each traded land for bondsmen. The LaGrange *Patriot* of February 18, 1865, carried an advertisement offering to trade a flock of sheep for a Negro. Almost unbelievably, some individuals even paid for slaves with hard money, in spite of its relative scarcity in Civil War Texas. Evan Lovett of Gonzales, for example, paid $300 in specie for a twenty-year-old male on March 17, 1864, and John N. Brooks of San Augustine County executed a note on July 5, 1865, promising to pay $400 in gold for a man named Miles. Thus Texans were willing to exchange property and money of considerable value for

---

County Probate Papers; *Williams* v. *Arnis*, 30 Tex. 37 (1867). La Grange *Patriot*, February 18, 1865; Estate of Nancy J. Pugh, Travis County Probate Records (Probate Record, Book C).

16. Estate of L. L. Leonard, Travis County Probate Records (Probate Record, Book C); Winsor, *Texas in the Confederacy*, 51. Nathan Anderson of Hunt County paid $1,700 in Confederate money for a thirty-year-old in May, 1864. See bill of sale, in Slavery and Abolition Papers, Barker Texas History Center, University of Texas, Austin.

17. These values are based on appraisals found in probate records. The numbers of slaves involved were 634 in 1861, 274 in 1862, 178 in 1863, 331 in 1864, and 90 in 1865. The suggestion that hire rates fell is supported by the estate of John Burrows, which is cited above (note 15). Eight slaves who had hired out for $765 in 1864 brought only $601 in January, 1865. The single slave belonging to Joseph Miller of Brazoria County hired for $215 in 1864 and $105 in 1865. Estate of Joseph Miller, Brazoria County Probate Records (Wills, etc., Book D).

slaves even in the last year of the war. The Confederacy's waning military fortunes did not destroy all confidence in the Peculiar Institution until the very end.[18]

It is surprising that hire rates and prices did not show a greater decrease during the war, in light of the large number of slaves brought to Texas for safekeeping as Federal forces overran other Confederate states. "Refugeeing" became common in late 1862, reached a peak in 1863, and continued through much of 1864. Louisiana provided most of the planters who brought or sent their slaves to Texas, but many came from Arkansas and Missouri as well. Some refugeed bondsmen even came from as far away as Mississippi and Tennessee. At the beginning of 1863, the LaGrange *True Issue* described wagon trains of Louisiana refugees entering Texas. In May, Colonel Fremantle, as he traveled from Rusk through Marshall and on into Louisiana, observed numerous planters moving everything they owned to Texas. "The road today was alive with Negroes," he wrote on May 10, "who are being 'run' into Texas out of Banks's way. We have met hundreds of them." This human tide continued into the fall. The Marshall *Texas Republican* commented in October on refugees who were "pouring in" in such numbers that the roads were "lined with them" and all available housing filled to capacity. Banks's Red River Campaign and related actions in Arkansas during the spring of 1864 contributed further to the flood of refugees.[19]

There is no way to determine the precise number of slaves refugeed to Texas. General Magruder said in November, 1864, that he had been told that 150,000 were from Arkansas and Missouri alone. This was doubtless an exaggeration, but contemporary observers had good reason to overestimate. They saw the roads busy with refugees, and at times a single master brought more than 100 bondsmen. In December, 1863, for example, W. W. Heartsill, a soldier with the Confederate army in southern

18. *Algier* v. *Black*, 32 Tex. 168 (1869); *Castleman* v. *Sherry*, 42 Tex. 59 (1875); La Grange *Patriot*, February 18, 1865; Bill of Sale, March 17, 1864, in E. E. Townsend Collection, Sul Ross State University Library, Alpine, Tex.; *Garrett* v. *Brooks*, 41 Tex. 479 (1874); John S. Harrison's will, written on November 11, 1864, authorized his heirs to trade his property for Negroes. Estate of John S. Harrison, Bell County Probate Records (Will Record).

19. Massey, *Refugee Life*, 90–93; Lord (ed.), *Fremantle Diary*, 63–68; *O.R.*, Ser. I, Vol. 41, Pt. 4, p. 1030; *Am. Slave, Supp.*, Ser. 2, II, 133–35 (Smith Austin); Wiley, *Southern Negroes*, 5; Marshall *Texas Republican*, quoted in Massey, *Refugee Life*, 92–93; Kerby, *Kirby Smith's Confederacy*, 255.

Arkansas, described refugees "bound for Texas; with hundreds and I might truthfully say thousands of slaves." Amanda Stone's overseer took 130 slaves from the Brokenburn plantation in northeastern Louisiana to Lamar County during the summer of 1863. Smith Austin remembered traveling to Texas with 100 fellow bondsmen during the war's early stages. John P. McIntosh from Franklin Parish, Louisiana, although not owning quite so many slaves, provides another well-documented case of large-scale refugeeing. When he died in Grimes County on May 11, 1864, McIntosh left 74 slaves and thousands of acres of Franklin Parish land to his heirs. Ten of the slaves, however, had no value because they were "within the Federal lines in hands of Yankees."[20]

Tax rolls provide two additional pieces of evidence, albeit of an indirect nature, on the extent of refugeeing. First, by 1864, many counties assessed taxes on at least a few very large slaveholders who had arrived since 1862, owned no land, and would disappear from the rolls by 1866. Almost certainly these masters were refugees. In Falls County, for example, fourteen individuals who fit the description given above paid taxes on 50 or more slaves in 1864. Mrs. J. M. Jordan, the largest of these holders, had 221 bondsmen. Second, the total number of slaves rendered for taxation in Texas, which had increased by 16.5 percent from 1860 (160,467) to 1862 (186,884), rose 28.5 percent from 1862 to 1864 (240,098). The state had approximately 32,000 more bondsmen in 1864 than it would have had if the rate of increase had maintained the 1860–62 pace. Given the likelihood that refugee masters were not eager to pay taxes to their temporary host, it is probable that the number was far larger than is indicated on the tax rolls.[21]

Most of the refugee masters and their slaves located in the eastern third of Texas. Coastal areas were too exposed, so most lived along the Trinity and Brazos rivers and in the northeastern counties along the Red River. Falls County, for example, the "home" of so many slaveholding refugees, is on the middle Brazos just southeast of Waco. In some cases, when refugee families found life in the Texas interior too crude for their taste, they stayed in the more exposed towns and left their slaves in

20. *O.R.*, Ser. I, Vol. 41, Pt. 4, p. 1030; Bell I. Wiley (ed.), *One Thousand Four Hundred and Ninety-One Days in the Confederate Army: A Journal Kept by W. W. Heartsill* (Jackson, Tenn., 1953), 186; John Q. Anderson (ed.), *Brokenburn: The Journal of Kate Stone, 1861–1868* (Baton Rouge, 1955), xvi; *Am. Slave, Supp.*, Ser. 2, II, 133–35 (Smith Austin); Estate of John P. McIntosh, Grimes County Probate Records (Probate Minutes, Book N).

21. County Tax Rolls (for all Texas counties), 1860, 1862, 1864.

the care of overseers. Amanda Stone's daughter Kate commented that the area around Lamar County where their slaves were taken was "the dark corner of the Confederacy." The Stone family lived in Tyler; their overseer remained in the more rural interior.[22]

Refugee masters generally intended only a brief stay in Texas and therefore did not purchase land. Some appear to have rented farms or plantations to employ their bondsmen, and others hired them out. Smith Austin, for example, remembered being hired to Rance Davis once he was settled in Ellis County. Kate Stone's diary entry for September 19, 1863, recorded a similar use of the Brokenburn slaves in Lamar County: "We have had a succession of callers lately. The unadulterated natives are all eager to hire Negroes. There is a furor for them. All the old ladies in the county are falling sick just to get their 'old man' to hire a servant. Who can blame them after their years of seeking a little rest?"[23]

While some Texans rushed to take advantage of the extra labor arriving in their state, others watched the flood of refugees with concern. Governor Lubbock's message to the legislature in November, 1863, sought to allay their fears. No reason existed, he said, to fear a "scarcity of provisions" or "other dangers," because the state had plenty of food and enough work to "keep these negroes beneficially and constantly employed." Properly policed and employed, Lubbock said, refugeed slaves would be a source of strength rather than a problem. He did not recommend any specific action, apparently feeling that existing laws regulating slaves and slavery were sufficient. Most Texans apparently agreed, although in at least one case local government took action to see that a group of idle refugees had no opportunity to cause trouble. The Hunt County Commissioners Court in January, 1864, issued an order to "P. G. Wartall Negro o[w]ner or known as agent for Wartall . . . either set your negroes to work or take them from our County or the Court will proceed to hire them at public out cry." In general, in spite of some expressions of concern, the refugees caused no serious disruption of slavery in Texas.[24]

22. Massey, *Refugee Life*, 92–93, 123–24; Anderson (ed.), *Brokenburn*, xvi, 226, 237.

23. Massey, *Refugee Life*, 92; *Am. Slave, Supp.*, Ser. 2, II, 133–35 (Smith Austin), X, 4104 (Mattie Williams, who also remembered hired-out refugee slaves); Anderson (ed.), *Brokenburn*, 242. Massey (p. 170) points out that refugees often lacked farm equipment for their slaves to use.

24. *Message of Governor F. R. Lubbock to the Tenth Legislature* (Austin, 1863), 12–13; Hunt County Commissioners' Court Minutes (Book A-2).

For the bondsmen themselves, refugeeing often constituted a serious upheaval. It may have lightened their work load, at least temporarily, but it subjected them to the danger of the trip to Texas and the problems of adjusting to an unknown country. Smith Austin said that no chains were needed when he and his fellow slaves went from Tennessee to Texas. "Us was too scared in the strange country and strange folks to run away from the ones us knowed was going to look after us. Us just marched behind the wagons like soldiers." One Louisiana refugee informed his wife that, although the slaves "were often very short of food and had many hardships to endure" on their way to Texas, not once did they "falter or cease" to be careful and considerate of their master. Refugeeing, like all movements of slaves, disrupted some families, too. After the war, the Freedmen's Bureau attempted to reunite fathers, mothers, and their children who had been separated in this way. Food was not always plentiful, and hiring out did not necessarily insure good care. In short, slavery in Texas survived refugeeing with few difficulties, but the slaves who wound up there for the last years of the war often carried additional burdens of servitude.[25]

Refugeed slaves surely were aware of the war between North and South, but some Texas bondsmen, particularly those who lived in sparsely populated frontier conditions, lived through the 1861–65 period with little or no knowledge of the war. Individuals living in Hill, Bell, Bosque, Bexar, and Wilson counties, for example, all testified that they knew nothing of the conflict. Most slaves, however, were aware of the fighting and had an idea of what was at stake. They saw young men leaving for the army, and they heard stories of what the Yankees would do. No doubt the influx of refugees caught their attention as well and brought additional information about the meaning of the war. Some slaveholders attempted to keep their bondsmen ignorant, but, as always, there were ways to learn things and pass them on. J. W. King of Washington County described how men slipped up to the master's house and listened at open windows for news of the war and then returned to whisper it to others. Churches were sources of information, too. Baptist ministers, for example, were

25. *Am. Slave, Supp.*, Ser. 2, II, 134 (Smith Austin), II, 84 (Stearlin Arnwine); Frances Fearn (ed.), *Diary of a Refugee* (New York, 1910), 30; J. M. Steele to General J. B. Kiddoo, July 20, 1866, Captain H. Skinner to Kiddoo, August 24, 1866, both in Register of Letters Received, Records of Assistant Commissioner for Texas, Bureau of Refugees, Freedmen, and Abandoned Lands.

advised by the state convention in 1863 to tell slaves that Federal prom-
ises were just empty political slogans and that masters no longer had to
protect bondsmen who fled to the enemy. This message could not be
delivered, however, without telling the blacks a good deal more than was
intended.[26]

Slaves knew that a Union victory probably meant freedom. William M.
Adams remembered a white minister who told the bondsmen how difficult freedom would be and asked all those who wished to pray for a
Confederate victory to raise their hands. "We all raised our hands because we was scared not to," Adams said, "but we sure didn't want the
South to win." As the war went on, some felt that their hopes were base-
less. J. W. King told of discouraged slaves saying, "If we is to be freed it's
a long time getting here." There were more, however, like the old men
described by Abram Sells, sitting around the fire late at night, smoking
their pipes and "whispering right low and quiet like" about what they
were going to do and where they were going to go when Mr. Lincoln set
them free. Slaves also were delighted when their young masters showed
reluctance to fight for the Confederacy. With obvious amusement, Harrison Beckett of San Augustine County related a story about how his
owner's son had joined the army in Arkansas and then run all the way
home when the first cannon fired. Little Rock is a long way off, Beckett
told his interviewer, but that is what the other slaves say happened.[27]

Slaves in Texas generally knew what the war meant, but they did relatively little to hinder the Confederate military effort or contribute to
Union victory. Bondsmen who were not removed from coastal areas or
impressed to build fortifications continued to produce food and fiber on
Texas farms and plantations throughout the years to 1865. Indeed, many
may have been given greater responsiblities than ever before. Masters so
frequently put bondsmen in charge of farms or properties detached from
their home places that the state legislature in 1862 made this action a

26. *Am. Slave, Supp.*, Ser. 2, VIII, 3004 (Mary Overton), III, 728 (Amos Clark), II, 289
(Della M. Bibles), V, 1689 (Felix M. Haywood), V, 1596 (William Green), VI, 2213–14 (J. W.
King); Douglas, "Religious Work Done by the Texas Baptists," 53.

27. *Am. Slave*, Ser. 1, IV, Pt. 1, p. 11 (William M. Adams); *ibid.*, *Supp.*, Ser. 2, VI, 2214
(J. W. King), IX, 3484 (Abram Sells), II, 227–28 (Harrison Beckett), II, 176 (Joe Barnes, who
told a story similar to Beckett's). Some slaves had a different perspective because soldiers
from slaveholding families often took personal servants with them when they joined the
Confederate army. For examples, see Campbell, *Southern Community in Crisis*, 227, 233–34,
236–37; *Batchelor-Turner Letters, 1861–1864, Written by Two of Terry's Rangers*, ed. H. J. H.
Rugeley (Austin, 1961), 8, 37–40.

criminal offense.[28] No notable rebellions took place during the war years. Running away, although still common, especially among those who got close to Mexico while serving as teamsters, did not increase dramatically. Of the 98,594 black Union soldiers recruited in the Confederate states, only 47 came from the more than 36,000 slave men of military age in Texas.[29] Texas slaveowners preferred to see this behavior as a matter, as John J. Linn put it, of "commendable loyalty to their masters." In fact, however, the slaves' "loyalty" during the war was, as always with the majority, largely a matter of their circumstances. Bondsmen elsewhere flocked to the Union army when their states were invaded; Federal troops never penetrated the Texas interior. Many masters left for the war, but other men and the managers of plantation-size slave forces remained at home. Security measures such as the slave patrol system were strengthened, too. The act of May, 1846, was amended in January, 1862, to require each patrol to go out at least once a week (rather than once a month) and more often if necessary to maintain proper control.[30]

If the physical restraints were not enough to keep Texas bondsmen from hindering the Confederacy, a variety of other considerations came into play as well. The complex psychological relationship between slave and master deterred action by some. These bondsmen, although not "loyal" to the point of wishing to remain in servitude, did not want any harm to come to their owners. As Felix Haywood put it, "we could no more shoot them than we could fly." Liza Jones, who belonged to Charles Bryant of Liberty, remembered an incident that occurred at the end of the war, which demonstrated the sort of sentiment described by Haywood. When Federal troops came to the Bryant place, her master ran for his gun. But her father, who was the driver, took the gun away and locked his owner in the smokehouse until the troops left. Other slaves' "loyalty" may have risen from certain types of calculation rather than sentiment.

28. Gammel (comp.), *Laws of Texas*, V, 484. William E. B. Du Bois, *Black Reconstruction: An Essay Toward a History of the Part Which Black Folk Played in the Attempt to Reconstruct Democracy in America, 1860–1880* (Philadelphia, 1935), suggested that slaves worked less effectively during the war and thereby hindered the Confederate cause. There is no evidence, however, of reduced labor productivity in Texas during the war.

29. Lizzie Neblett to Will H. Neblett, January 3, 1864, in Neblett Papers; Ira Berlin *et al.* (eds.), *The Black Military Experience* (New York, 1983), 12, 15, vol. II of Berlin *et al.* (eds.), *Freedom: A Documentary History of Emancipation, 1861–1867*. Masters were reluctant to allow Confederate authorities to use their slaves as teamsters in moving cotton to Matamoros for fear of losing runaways across the Rio Grande. *O.R.*, Ser. I, Vol. 26, Pt. 2, pp. 103, 105–106.

30. Linn, *Reminiscences of Fifty Years in Texas*, 357; Engelking, "Slavery in Texas," 104; Eaton, *History of Southern Confederacy*, 89–91; Gammel (comp.), *Laws of Texas*, II, 1498, V, 498.

Martin Jackson, for example, said that his father had advised him not to run or help the Yankees because he would have to live among white southerners after freedom came.[31]

The long-awaited day of jubilee came for Texas slaves on June 19, 1865, when Major General Gordon Granger arrived at Galveston and issued his General Order Number 3:

> The people of Texas are informed that, in accordance with a proclamation from the Executive of the United States, all slaves are free. This involves an absolute equality of personal rights and rights of property between former masters and slaves, and the connection heretofore existing between them becomes that between employer and hired labor. The freedmen are advised to remain quietly at their present homes and work for wages. They are informed that they will not be allowed to collect at military posts and that they will not be supported in idleness either there or elsewhere.

It took time, of course, for Granger's order to become known across the state. Some masters called their slaves together and read the proclamation of freedom, but others were slow to obey it. Josie Brown of Woodville, for example, said that slaves on her place worked a "whole year" before an official made "the white folks turn us loose." Isabella Boyd remembered, "When we all gits free, they's the long time letting us know." Former slaves from other plantations finally convinced them that forced labor had ended. Steve Robertson's mother found out about freedom only by the "grapevine," and even then she and her children had to run away in order to gain it\ Given Texas' territorial expanse, the relatively poor communication system, and the bitter hatred many owners had for Yankees, the experiences of Brown, Boyd, and Robertson were not uncommon. Still, the great majority of the state's bondsmen obtained their freedom before the end of 1865.[32]

Most slaves greeted the end of bondage with the overwhelming joy that accompanies receiving the answer to a lifelong prayer. As Felix Haywood remembered it, "Everyone was singing. We was all walking on golden clouds. Hallelujah!" According to Lu Lee, a fellow slave on her place called out "Free, free my Lord. Oh! free, free, my Lord. Free, free,

31. *Am. Slave, Supp.*, Ser. 2, V, 1694 (Felix Haywood), VI, 2115–16 (Liza Jones), V, 1905 (Martin Jackson).

32. *O.R.*, Ser. I, Vol. 48, Pt. 4, p. 929; *Am. Slave, Supp.*, Ser. 2, III, 483–84 (Josie Brown), II, 358 (Isabella Boyd), VIII, 3331–34 (Steve Robertson).

free oh my Lord." In many cases, however, such expressions of joy were not permitted by whites. A celebration at Huntsville ended when a sword-wielding man on horseback cut a Negro woman nearly in half on the street. According to Dave Byrd, the "patter rollers" whipped one hundred celebrants in Crockett. When John Mosley's master told him of freedom, the slave jumped into the air to express his delight, whereupon the master pulled a pistol and fired several shots between his legs. No more, he said, or I will shoot you between the eyes.[33]

Slaves soon found their joy constrained by the realization that, as one put it, "freedom could make folks proud but it didn't make them rich." James Boyd remembered his master interrupting their celebration to say, "How you going to eat and get clothes and such?" That "sure scared" them, Boyd said. Although some masters angrily ordered all Negroes off their places, the great majority asked their bondsmen to stay on and work for wages. Most slaves stayed, at least immediately after freedom, if for no other reason than that they had nowhere else to go. Will Adams of Harrison County said that "lots" of the slaves did not even want to be free "because they knowed nothing and had nowhere to go." A sizable minority (perhaps one-quarter), however, left their former masters immediately. Some did so as the most direct way of asserting their freedom—at least they had control of their own bodies and could come and go as they pleased. They left, in some cases, even if they had no particular place to go. "They just went," said Henry Baker. Others left to escape hated masters. When Andy Anderson's owner announced freedom and asked his slaves to stay on and work for wages, Anderson muttered, "Like Hell, I will." The master heard and demanded to know what was said. Anderson replied, "Nothing, nothing master," but the next morning he ran for the plantation of a former owner who had been kind to him.[34]

Only a minority of slaves received any special assistance from their former masters in laying a foundation for their lives as free men. There were a few owners, like Mrs. Isaac Van Zandt of Harrison County, who helped with the acquisition of land. There were others like Mose Davis

33. *Am. Slave, Supp.*, Ser. 2, V, 1691 (Felix Haywood), VI, 2302–2303 (Lu Lee), VII, 2453–54 (Andy McAdams), III, 569 (Dave Byrd), VII, 2805 (John Mosely).

34. *Ibid.*, V, 1694 (Felix Haywood), II, 367–68 (James Boyd), IV, 1105 (Eli Davison), II, 14 (Will Adams), II, 147 (Henry Baker), II, 53–54 (Andy Anderson). The statement that most slaves did not leave their masters immediately is based on the sample of 181 Texas slave narratives discussed above in chapter 3, note 4. Of these bondsmen, 51 percent remained with their owners for at least one year after emancipation.

who, according to Sarah Ashley, gave cotton and corn to his former slaves. Colonel M. T. Johnson of Tarrant County gave land and livestock and offered to help freedmen who got into any sort of trouble. The majority of slaves, however, received nothing more than the opportunity to work—not "a hoecake or a slice of bacon," as Minerva Bendy put it.[35]

A little more than two months after "Juneteenth," Lucadia N. Pease, whose former-governor husband had owned eight slaves in 1864, commented on the conclusion of the war in letters to two of her sisters. In one, she rejoiced at the "blessing of peace" but lamented "the trials and troubles the result of the war has brought upon the freedmen and women, who had no part in bringing on the war, but upon whom the evils of it will fall most heavily." Her other letter contained a more explicit definition of these "evils." Speaking of freedom for the slaves, she wrote, "I do not think of it as any loss to us, only to them, as their condition will be much worse than before, as they are uneducated, improvident and unfitted to take care of themselves." A few freedmen might have agreed with Mrs. Pease that their condition had in some ways worsened, but virtually none of Texas' approximately 250,000 former slaves would have voluntarily elected a return to bondage. As free men, they had the opportunity to move about and seek work on their own terms, hold property as a legal right, and create families and worship without fear of interference by a master. Freedom was far better than slavery. On the other hand, emancipation would mean for most only unremitting labor, poverty, and limited educational opportunities combined with, as Mrs. Pease's attitude indicated, a total denial of equality.[36] Slavery's bitter legacy had only begun to unfold.

35. *Ibid.*, Ser. 1, V, Pt. 3, p. 122 (Jerry Moore); *ibid.*, *Supp.*, Ser. 2, II, 90 (Sarah Ashley), 252 (Minerva Bendy). Only 6 percent of the sample of 181 slave narratives mentioned material help from masters.

36. Lucadia N. Pease to Maria N. Moor, August 30, 1865, Lucadia N. Pease to "Sister," August 30, 1865, both in Pease-Graham-Niles Family Papers. Tax rolls for Texas counties showed a total of 240,098 slaves at the beginning of 1864, the last time bondsmen were counted for any official purpose. Given the tendency to underreport for tax purposes and the fact that slavery continued for nearly eighteen months after January, 1864, placing the slave population at 250,000 on "Juneteenth" is probably a conservative estimate.

Conclusions

Negro slavery became important in Texas with the arrival of Anglo-American colonists during the 1820s. Most of these settlers came from the Old South and believed that Texas' fertile lands could best be populated and brought into cultivation with the aid of an institution that they knew well. Mexican governments, both federal and state, resisted the development of slavery in Texas and probably retarded its growth during the colonial period. Official opposition was limited and vacillating, however, in the face of insistence by Anglo settlers, led by Stephen F. Austin, that slavery was an economic necessity in Texas. Mexican leaders made concessions that allowed the institution to gain a significant, albeit not completely secure, foothold in the province by 1835.

Slavery constituted one underlying factor in the general clash of Anglo-American and Hispanic cultural traditions that culminated in the Texas Revolution during 1835–36. Had Mexico won the war, slavery almost certainly would have been abolished. As it was, the conflict seriously disturbed slavery in Texas and allowed some bondsmen to escape. Sam Houston's army won the Battle of San Jacinto, however, and Texans succeeded in establishing their new republic with a constitution that guaranteed slavery. The revolution did not begin primarily as a movement to protect the Peculiar Institution, but certainly one major result was, in the words of Justice Abner S. Lipscomb of the Texas Supreme Court, the removal of "all doubt and uneasiness among the citizens of Texas in regard to the tenure by which they held dominion over their slaves."[1]

Slavery expanded rapidly, both numerically and geographically, through the republic and statehood periods from 1836 to 1861. As bondsmen poured into Texas, arriving primarily with immigrant owners, their total population increased from approximately five thousand in 1836 to more than thirty thousand in 1846, when the republic became a state. By

1. *Guess* v. *Lubbock*, 5 Tex. 535 (1851).

1861, when Texas seceded and joined the Confederacy, the slave population, which had grown more rapidly than the free, was approaching two hundred thousand. Bondsmen lived in largest numbers along Texas' major rivers—the Red in the northeast, the Sabine and Trinity in the east, and the Brazos and Colorado in the south-central region down to the Gulf Coast. By 1860, however, blacks constituted at least 25 percent of the population in all settled portions of the state, except the north-central area centering on Dallas and the southwestern plains extending from the San Antonio River to the Rio Grande.

Perhaps slavery faced, as Charles Ramsdell argued, a barrier to expansion once it reached the semiarid plains of western Texas and the areas within easy reach of the Mexican border, but those limits were not reached by 1861. Slavery was still growing everywhere in the state, and the blackland prairie/Grand Prairie region of north-central Texas offered a vast expanse of suitable acreage relatively untouched by slaveholders and their bondsmen. To open that area, only transportation was needed, and the railroad would have provided that. Texas constituted a virtual empire for slavery, and on the eve of secession Texans talked with buoyant optimism of the millions of bondsmen who would build the state's future.

Slavery existed in antebellum Texas primarily as an economic institution. Those who purchased bondsmen to supply labor on farms and plantations generally found their investments profitable. Slaves produced larger and larger cotton crops, reproduced themselves, and appreciated in value through the late antebellum years. They also produced enough corn and other food crops to provide self-sufficiency in the state's agricultural economy. Finally, slavery was very flexible and highly functional, as witnessed, for example, by the hire system, so that it was economically advantageous in ways that did not appear on a profit-and-loss balance sheet. The institution may have contributed to Texas' relative backwardness in commercialization and industrialization, but there were no important demands that it be ended in order to promote diversification. Slavery flourished in Texas throughout the late antebellum period and was never in danger of failing from its own economic weakness.

Between 1836 and 1861, Texas legislators and judges developed a slave code for the Lone Star state based largely on practices elsewhere in the Old South. The law assured slaveowners of their right to own, buy, and sell bondsmen while protecting their property against criminal interference by others. It regulated the conduct of slaves and prescribed rules for the capture and return of runaways. The legal status accorded free blacks made it clear that, no matter how few, they were an unwelcome minority who would frequently be equated with slaves. Lawmakers and judges recognized that slaves were human and therefore a very special form of property. The weight of the law, however, usually rested with protection of the masters' property rights rather than concern for the slaves' humanity.

Most Texas slaves lived on farms and plantations and worked long hours clearing land, cultivating crops, and taking care of innumerable chores. Many had Saturday afternoons free from labor, but only Sundays, July 4, and Christmas week were regarded virtually without exception as days off. A minority of bondsmen, perhaps 10 to 20 percent of the total, worked as skilled craftsmen or house servants or lived in Texas' towns and few fledgling cities. Compared to agricultural workers, these slaves were less exposed to the elements and performed labor that was less burdensome physically. Some, especially the house servants, may have had longer hours, but few, it seems, wanted to change places with field workers. Slaves frequently were given positions of considerable responsibility as, for example, "drivers" and teamsters. Some had the opportunity, although the practice was illegal for most of the antebellum period, to hire their own time and seek profitable employment for themselves. Many earned at least a little money of their own, especially by working small patches of cotton and food crops.

The state of Texas had constitutional and statutory provisions concerning the material conditions of slaves' lives and the physical treatment accorded them by their masters. In all but the most extreme cases, however, these matters were left, in the words of Justice James H. Bell of the Texas Supreme Court, "to the master's judgment, discretion, and humanity."[2] Texas bondsmen generally had food adequate to provide the energy for work and the nutrition, by the standards of that era, for health. Their housing was usually uncomfortable at best and inadequate for winter weather. Clothing and shoes were made of cheap, rough materials, and slaves found them a source of considerable discomfort. When bondsmen suffered, as they often did, from diseases and accidents, masters generally provided doctors' care. Slaves were, after all, a valuable form of property. Unfortunately, medical science in mid-nineteenth-century Texas could not deal effectively with many of the diseases and injuries that

2. *Callihan* v. *Johnson*, 22 Tex. 597 (1858).

afflicted slaves. Masters, in exercising their right to obedience and submission from their bondsmen, inflicted a variety of punishments, particularly whippings. Any whipping was a fearsome prospect, and all slaves lived with the knowledge that it could happen to them, largely at the whim of their master. At times, punishments became cruel treatment and even murder, but Texas courts were extremely reluctant to interfere with the master-slave relationship. Regardless of the law, slaves' material conditions and physical treatment depended largely upon their individual masters.

Texas slaves endured the psychological pressures of bondage with the aid of strength that came from their families, their religion, and their music. The great majority of bondsmen experienced family ties, and in spite of constant threats and numerous disruptions, depended on those relationships for identity, support, and a sense of worth. Families appear to have been the focal point for survival. Thousands of Texas slaves drew strength too from religion. They listened to white ministers emphasize the virtues of loyal and honest servants, but they heard the underlying message, often brought to them by black preachers, of salvation for all and perhaps even deliverance. Music provided psychological strength also because it served as a means of expression, communication, and protest.

Behavior patterns among Texas slaves varied widely. At one extreme was the loyal servant who apparently loved and identified with his master; at the other was the rebel who resisted bondage at every opportunity, especially by running away. Most common, however, were the bondsmen who, in the words of one woman, did "the best we could."[3] Neither loyal servants nor rebels, they recognized the limitations of their situation and sought to endure on the best terms possible. Such slaves expected certain types of treatment and became rebellious if they did not receive it. Regardless of their behavioral adjustments, the vast majority of blacks wanted freedom, and everyone knew it. In short, the enslaved blacks were simply human. They employed their intelligence and their moral and spiritual resources to survive in and attempt to influence the world in which they found themselves. Some were capable and strong; others were incapable and weak. In any case, the enslaved blacks were not an inherently inferior part of the human race, and slavery was no school for civilization.

3. *Am. Slave, Supp.*, Ser. 2, IV, 1132 (Mollie Dawson).

A minority of Texans owned slaves, and only a handful achieved elite status as planters. Slaveholders generally found the institution to be a source of tension in their lives. Slaves proved so difficult to manage that owners, while they enjoyed picturing themselves as benevolent paternalists, spent a good deal more time discussing means of punishing effectively. Masters did not labor, it seems, under a great burden of guilt, but constant criticism from outside the South also created tension. Texas slaveholders thus found the institution troublesome and unsettling, but, at the same time, it benefited them to the extent that they would attempt a revolution to keep it.

Slaveholders dominated economic, political, and social life in antebellum Texas. They produced 90 percent of the state's cotton, dominated officeholding at all levels of government, and by virtue of their wealth occupied the top rungs of the social ladder. Not surprisingly under these circumstances, most articulate Texans such as newspaper editors and ministers defended slavery with every imaginable argument, and the vast majority of the state's people either supported or quietly acquiesced in the institution. A few German immigrants found it unworthy of a democratic, liberal nation, but most had no serious objections.

In spite of the proslavery consensus that had no significant opposition anywhere in the state, antebellum Texans often demonstrated the fear and intolerance typical of a society under siege. They struck hard at anyone suspected of preaching abolitionism or fomenting insurrection and were only slightly less tolerant of individuals or groups who did not support the system enthusiastically. As the Galveston *Weekly News* expressed it, "Those who are not for us, must be against us."[4] The potential for terror inherent in this attitude was realized most fully during the summer of 1860, when a series of disastrous fires in north-central counties led to a widespread panic called the "Texas Troubles." Vigilante action to deal with the supposed abolitionist-inspired insurrection plot signaled by the fires claimed an undetermined number of victims, white as well as black. Within a year, "the voice of reason," as Governor Sam Houston termed it, was stilled entirely as Texas seceded and joined the Confederate States of America. The decision for secession involved a variety of considerations for Texans depending on their backgrounds and their circumstances in the Lone Star state, but the fundamental reason for having to decide at all was absolutely clear—it was Negro slavery.

4. Galveston *Weekly News*, March 3, 1857.

During the Civil War, slavery remained less disturbed in Texas than in other areas of the Confederacy because Federal troops did not invade the state's interior. The most significant disruptions resulted from the impressment of bondsmen to serve Confederate authorities in building fortifications and, to a lesser extent, from the arrival of thousands of "refugeed" slaves fleeing Federal invaders in other states. Most slaves were aware of the war and its implications for their future freedom. They hoped for a Union victory but were in no position to contribute to it or to hinder the Confederate military effort. When the day of jubilee, June 19, 1865, finally came with the arrival of General Gordon Granger at Galveston and the reading of the Emancipation Proclamation, most Texas slaves celebrated their freedom as the answer to a lifelong prayer.

Slavery in Texas did not differ in any fundamental way from the institution as it existed elsewhere in the United States. Claims that somehow Negro bondage was "milder" or "worse" in the Lone Star state are morally pointless and historically inaccurate.[5] Material conditions and physical treatment had nothing to do with making slavery right or wrong. Even if it could be demonstrated convincingly, for example, that Texas slaves had a better diet, worked fewer hours in a milder climate, and were whipped less often than bondsmen elsewhere, the moral nature of a system that held humans as property would remain the same. It was still wrong.

On a day-to-day basis, of course, material conditions and physical treatment were of great importance to Texas slaves themselves. Studies of the institution in other states, however, provide no basis for claiming that it was generally "milder" or "worse" in the Lone Star state. Bondsmen in older southern states were subject to essentially the same laws and, except in very special areas, lived under relatively similar circumstances in terms of work, material conditions, discipline and punishment,

5. An article entitled "Texas" in *DeBow's Review*, X (1851), 637, asserted that bondsmen in Texas were "invested with more liberty, and are less liable to abuse, than the slaves of the southern states generally." For a similar claim that slavery was "milder" in Texas, see Curlee, "Texas Slave Plantations," 146–47. Existing studies of slavery in Texas do not claim that the institution was "worse" in the Lone Star state than elsewhere, but it is entirely possible to make such a charge. Sydnor, *Slavery in Mississippi*, viii, notes that, since Mississippi was a frontier state that imported slaves and devoted itself almost entirely to cotton planting, the lives of its slaves should have been "harder and more laborious" than those of bondsmen in the upper South. Texas might be regarded in the same light. Incidentally, Sydnor concluded (p. 253) that "except for the omnipresent danger of being sold . . . being a slave was not for the average Negro a dreadful lot." Thus it would seem that he rejected his own hypothesis about the harshness of bondage in a state such as Mississippi.

formation and preservation of families, religion, and so on.[6] This should be expected. After all, the immigrants who brought slavery to Texas learned its ways in the Old South. They were not likely to change significantly once they reached a new home unless the area was dramatically different from any previously experienced. Granted that Texas constituted a frontier region during the antebellum period, those portions of the state having large numbers of slaves by the 1840s and 1850s were not so different in terms of climate and topography or so wild and unsettled as to change common patterns of labor and management. Slavery in Texas was simply American Negro slavery; nothing about the Lone Star state led or forced slaveholders there to accord their bondsmen appreciably different treatment than the variations common from master to master across the South.[7]

Far from being unimportant, slavery played a vital role in shaping antebellum Texas and determining its future. The state could not have grown as it did without the labor of its slave population. Secession and participation in the tragedy of civil war resulted primarily from the desire to preserve an institution that was flourishing and had seemingly unlim-

6. These state studies, all cited in note 9 of the Introduction, include Ballagh, *Slavery in Virginia*; Bassett, *Slavery in the State of North Carolina*; Brackett, *Negro in Maryland*; Coleman, *Slavery Times in Kentucky*; Fields, *Slavery and Freedom on the Middle Ground*; Flanders, *Slavery in Georgia*; Mooney, *Slavery in Tennessee*; Sellers, *Slavery in Alabama*; Smith, *Slavery and Plantation Growth in Antebellum Florida*; Sydnor, *Slavery in Mississippi*; J. G. Taylor, *Negro Slavery in Louisiana*; O. W. Taylor, *Negro Slavery in Arkansas*; R. H. Taylor, *Slaveholding in North Carolina*; Trexler, *Slavery in Missouri*. Several of these studies made strong claims about how mild slavery was in their particular states. Bassett, *Slavery in the State of North Carolina*, 89, for example, concluded that his evidence showed "that slavery in North Carolina was not so harsh as elsewhere." Coleman, *Slavery Times in Kentucky*, vii, found that observers in that state "saw slavery . . . in its mildest form, better than in any other slave state, with the possible exception of Maryland or Virginia." Mooney, *Slavery in Tennessee*, 86, suggested that "perhaps" slave life in that state was not so hard as in the true plantation states.

7. Genovese, *Roll, Jordan, Roll*, 7–9, tends to reject the idea that slavery can be said to have been "better" in one place than another. Fields, *Slavery and Freedom on the Middle Ground*, 23, refuses to accept the often-made claim that slavery was "milder" in Maryland and says that the safest generalization is that in matters of material care and physical treatment slaveholders in that state exhibited the same range of concern and benevolence as their fellows in the Lower South.

Even comparative studies of slavery in Latin American countries such as Brazil and Cuba have tended to conclude that Negro bondage was, in the words of David Brion Davis, "a single phenomenon whose variations were less significant than underlying patterns of unity." Little effort is now devoted to proving that slavery was "better" or "worse" in one place than another. Peter Kolchin, "Comparing American History," *Reviews in American History*, X (1982), 69–74.

ited potential in 1861. Once defeat destroyed slavery and emancipated approximately 250,000 blacks, most white Texans for generation after generation regarded them and their descendants as more of a problem than an asset. The Peculiar Institution continued to exact a huge price from Texans well after "Juneteenth"—but that is another story.

APPENDIX 1

The Federal Writers' Project Slave Narratives As A Historical Source

In *This Stubborn Soil*, the autobiographical story of his north Texas childhood, William Owens recounted a visit to the Lamar County home of two aged ex-slaves. Imbued with the view, common among whites in the early twentieth century, that slavery had been an essentially benign institution, Owens decided to talk to his hosts about what it was like to be a slave. Thinking to himself: "They got everything furnished when they needed it, and were taken care of when they got old," he said, "You'd a been better off staying slaves." "Don't say that," the old man replied. "You don't know what you saying. Somebody else done said it and you believed 'em. . . . Don't let them tell you nothing about slavery, . . . You don't know nothing about being a slave until you been one."[1]

The old man was correct. Only those who experienced slavery could tell how it felt to be owned. Only they knew the physical sufferings of bondage and the psychological impact of being constantly reminded that blacks were inferior to whites. Thus the testimony of ex-slaves is essential to any attempt, as in chapters 6 through 9 of this study, to look inside the institution and see what it was like to be a slave.

There are two major sources of ex-slaves' testimony concerning the Peculiar Institution—autobiographies by blacks who experienced bondage and narratives resulting from interviews with aged former bondsmen conducted by Federal Writers' Project employees between 1936 and 1938. Most of the ex-slave autobiographers wrote and published their stories during the nineteenth century. The interview narratives remained in manuscript form in the Library of Congress and other depositories until 1972, when Greenwood Press began publication of the entire collection under the editorship of George P. Rawick. Entitled *The American Slave: A Composite Autobiography*, this collection eventually grew to a total of forty-one volumes. Series 1 consists of volumes 1–7, the first of which is Rawick's own important interpretation of slave life, *From Sundown to Sunup, The Making of a Black Community*. Series 2 of *The American Slave* comprises volumes 8–19. These nine-

1. William A. Owens, *This Stubborn Soil* (New York, 1966), 138–39.

teen volumes were followed in 1977 by a twelve-volume *Supplement, Series 1* and in 1979 by a ten-volume *Supplement, Series 2*.

Virtually none of the thousands of slaves in Texas published autobiographies. This is unfortunate, especially since individuals who prepared the stories of their lives were likely to be outstandingly perceptive and articulate.[2] There are, however, literally hundreds of narratives resulting from interviews conducted with ex-slaves in Texas during 1936–38. Volumes 4 and 5 of *The American Slave, Series 1* (1972), and volumes 2 through 10 of the *Supplement, Series 2* (1979) contain more than 600 such narratives. Some of the interviews were with ex-bondsmen who had come to Texas after emancipation, but the two volumes of series 1 alone had the narratives of 181 individuals who actually experienced bondage in the Lone Star state. Their interviews constituted a sample for a quantitative analysis of matters such as the quality of food, housing, and clothing, the frequency of whippings, and the frequency of family disruptions.[3]

Obviously, an investigation of the slave's view of bondage in Texas must utilize material from the narratives collection. There simply are no comparable sources. Many historians, however, have questioned the reliability of the slave narratives, and with good reason. First, the interviews were conducted during the late 1930s when all the ex-slaves were at least in their seventies, and two-thirds were eighty or older. In general, they had known slavery only as children, and their memories were burdened with the many decades since. Second, whites conducted most of the interviews. Given the racial atmosphere of the 1930s, this circumstance had to have an impact on what was said and left unsaid. Should blacks have been expected to give white interviewers straightforward answers to questions about treatment by their owners, whether they were better off as slaves, and so on? Finally, interviews were sometimes revised and edited before they were typed. Many narratives were thus filtered through white consciousness rather than presented verbatim.[4]

In spite of these problems, this study used the slave narratives extensively in describing the lives of slaves in Texas. The primary reason, as noted above, is simple. They are the only source available, and refusing to use them would in effect constitute a refusal to address one vitally important aspect of the Peculiar Institution in the Lone Star state. Moreover, as C. Vann Woodward pointed in a review of *The American Slave*, the narratives are just as reliable as many other historical sources. Newspapers, diaries, travelers' accounts, and politicians'

---

2. Two of the best recent articles on the testimony of ex-slaves found no autobiographies by Texas slaves. See John Blassingame, "Using the Testimony of Ex-Slaves: Approaches and Problems," *Journal of Southern History*, XLI (1975), 480; David Thomas Bailey, "A Divided Prism: Two Sources of Black Testimony on Slavery," *Journal of Southern History*, XLVI (1980), 387. Hamilton, *My Master*, contains a great deal of personal information and is the only ex-slave autobiographical account located and used in this study.

3. Some of the narratives in the *Supplement*, Ser. 2 were simply longer versions of interviews that had appeared in Ser. 1, but most were originals not previously published.

4. For discussions of the weaknesses of the narratives, see Blassingame, "Using the Testimony of Ex-Slaves," 81–87; Bailey, "A Divided Prism," 402–404.

speeches, for example, often contain contradictions, evasions, distortions, and even outright lies. Use of the narratives, Woodward wrote, requires "caution and discrimination," but "the necessary precautions . . . are no more elaborate or burdensome than those required by many other types of sources."[5] The slave narratives are an essential and acceptably reliable source on the slave's view of bondage in Texas.

5. C. Vann Woodward, "History from Slave Sources," *American Historical Review*, LXXVIX (1974), 475, 480. For other articles that evaluate the slave narratives in an essentially positive fashion, see Norman R. Yetman, "The Background of the Slave Narrative Collection," *American Quarterly*, XIX (1967), 534–53; Thomas F. Soapes, "The Federal Writers' Project Slave Interviews: Useful Data or Misleading Source?" *Oral History Review* (1977), 33–38. For a detailed statistical and literary analysis of the narratives, see Paul D. Escott, *Slavery Remembered: A Record of Twentieth-Century Slave Narratives* (Chapel Hill, 1979).

APPENDIX 2

Slave Populations of Texas Counties in Selected Years, 1837–1864
(Compiled from County Tax Rolls)

County	1837	1840	1845	1846	1850	1855	1860	1864
Anderson (1846)[1]	—	—	—	237	506	1,917	3,154	5,429
Angelina (1846)	—	—	—	142	167	291	497	826
Atascosa (1856)	—	—	—	—	—	—	84	102
Austin (1837)	n/a	447	1,093	1,162	1,356	2,353	3,199	4,702
Bandera (1856)	—	—	—	—	—	—	6	14
Bastrop (1837)	111	299	408	491	743	1,748	2,417	3,068
Bee (1858)	—	—	—	—	—	—	70	90
Bell (1850)	—	—	—	—	50	466	918	1,429
Bexar (1837)	3	20	25	n/a	248	979	993	1,193
Blanco (1858)	—	—	—	—	—	—	64	52
Bosque (1854)	—	—	—	—	—	34	252	810
Bowie (1841)	—	—	1,765	1,013	1,114	1,866	2,474	4,138
Brazoria (1837)	892	1,665[2]	2,094	2,520	3,161	4,292	4,782	5,125
Brazos (1843)	—	—	153	101	132	427	735	2,013
Brown (1857)	—	—	—	—	—	—	n/a	29
Burleson (1846)	—	—	—	332	428	1,047	1,932	2,905
Burnet (1854)	—	—	—	—	—	150	220	278
Caldwell (1848)	—	—	—	—	237	1,171	1,490	1,743
Calhoun (1846)	—	—	—	26	180	310	333	175
Cameron (1846)	—	—	—	0	20	15	1	n/a
Cass (1846)	—	—	—	722	1,467	3,518	3,515	5,189
Chambers (1858)	—	—	—	—	—	—	430	474
Cherokee (1846)	—	—	—	270	1,180	2,286	2,706	4,992
Clay (1857)	—	—	—	—	—	—	n/a	0
Collin (1846)	—	—	—	68	100	432	933	1,593
Colorado (1837)	170	416	872	527	644	1,580	3,198	4,086
Comal (1846)	—	—	—	68	56	126	141	206
Comanche (1856)	—	—	—	—	—	—	88	48
Cooke (1848)	—	—	—	—	0	123	340	493
Coryell (1854)	—	—	—	—	—	139	281	419
Dallas (1846)	—	—	—	62	168	481	923	2,482
Denton (1846)	—	—	—	2	9	74	256	588
De Witt (1846)	—	—	—	44	443	963	1,362	1,552
Ellis (1850)	—	—	—	—	69	517	1,008	2,086
El Paso (1850)	—	—	—	—	—	0	8	n/a
Erath (1856)	—	—	—	—	—	—	107	308

Slave Populations of Texas Counties in Selected Years, 1837–1864 (cont.)
(Compiled from County Tax Rolls)

County	1837	1840	1845	1846	1850	1855	1860	1864
Falls (1850)	—	—	—	—	33	851	1,569	4,230
Fannin (1838)	—	92	353	333	437	1,019	1,464	2,339
Fayette (1838)	—	206	590	526	820	2,072	3,190	4,501
Fort Bend (1838)	—	572	1,172	1,005	1,023	1,746	3,532	4,253
Freestone (1851)	—	—	—	—	—	2,167	2,997	5,613
Galveston (1839)	—	156	558	497	456	761	1,407	957
Gillespie (1848)	—	—	—	—	0	63	30	41
Goliad (1837)	n/a	n/a	n/a	41	193	416	634	707
Gonzales (1837)	n/a	56	323	193	493	2,136	2,702	3,545
Grayson (1846)	—	—	—	109	142	602	1,194	2,205
Grimes (1846)	—	—	—	1,169	1,471	3,124	4,850	7,005
Guadalupe (1846)	—	—	—	92	291	1,637	1,622	1,887
Hamilton (1858)	—	—	—	—	—	—	22	103
Hardin (1858)	—	—	—	—	—	—	194	331
Harris (1837)	236	393	542	773	814	1,084	1,565	n/a
Harrison (1839)	—	n/a	2,795	2,625	4,839	7,013	8,101	8,681
Hays (1843)	—	—	n/a	n/a	103	517	740	868
Henderson (1846)	—	—	—	57	3	411	1,021	1,861
Hidalgo (1852)	—	—	—	—	—	0	n/a	n/a
Hill (1853)	—	—	—	—	—	254	594	1,226
Hopkins (1846)	—	—	—	71	150	352	918	2,101
Houston (1837)	n/a	308	718	535	545	1,595	2,446	4,310
Hunt (1846)	—	—	—	5	41	198	517	1,238
Jack (1857)	—	—	—	—	—	—	37	41
Jackson (1837)	96	120	265	301	288	717	1,015	1,169
Jasper (1837)	131	275	412	200	435	991	1,466	1,816
Jefferson (1837)	103	176	168	122	243	216	287	348
Johnson (1854)	—	—	—	—	—	120	416	994
Karnes (1854)	—	—	—	—	—	212	334	266
Kaufman (1848)	—	—	—	—	49	329	506	1,345
Kendall (1862)	—	—	—	—	—	—	—	89
Kerr (1856)	—	—	—	—	—	—	45	38
Lamar (1841)	—	—	596	565	973	1,296	2,424	4,230
Lampasas (1856)	—	—	—	—	—	—	146	224
Lavaca (1846)	—	—	—	110	379	1,004	1,654	2,713
Leon (1846)	—	—	—	344	531	1,455	2,225	3,456
Liberty (1837)	n/a	532	1,199	780	749	922	904	1,798
Limestone (1846)	—	—	—	364	488	680	844	1,475
Live Oak (1856)	—	—	—	—	—.	—	43	41
Llano (1856)	—	—	—	—	—	—	68	74
McLennan (1850)	—	—	—	—	49	1,048	2,105	3,807
Madison (1854)	—	—	—	—	—	429	648	902
Marion (1860)	—	—	—	—	—	—	1,742	2,445
Mason (1858)	—	—	—	—	—	—	15	15
Matagorda (1837)	n/a	n/a	1,067	648	1,153	1,529	1,875	2,369
Medina (1848)	—	—	—	—	10	25	84	79
Milam (1837)	n/a	n/a	391	134	173	713	1,136	2,147

Slave Populations of Texas Counties in Selected Years, 1837–1864 (cont.)
(Compiled from County Tax Rolls)

County	1837	1840	1845	1846	1850	1855	1860	1864
Montague (1858)	—	—	—	—	—	—	n/a	82
Montgomery (1837)	n/a	854	1,969	555	689	1,448	2,416	3,356
Nacogdoches (1837)	385	940	1,466	1,138	1,336	1,702	2,238	3,104
Navarro (1846)	—	—	—	96	205	1,135	1,724	3,913
Newton (1846)	—	—	—	n/a	332	602	900	1,185
Nueces (1846)	—	—	—	12	42	89	150	n/a
Orange (1852)	—	—	—	—	—	185	298	329
Palo Pinto (1857)	—	—	—	—	—	—	115	82
Panola (1846)	—	—	—	574	957	1,990	2,540	3,110
Parker (1855)	—	—	—	—	—	—	324	390
Polk (1846)	—	—	—	414	722	1,427	3,639	5,481
Presidio (1857)	—	—	—	—	—	—	n/a	n/a
Red River (1837)	n/a	1,789	1,204	1,042	1,232	1,807	2,513	4,655
Refugio (1837)	n/a	n/a	n/a	n/a	22	148	202	193
Robertson (1838)	—	292	587	238	263	1,239	1,955	4,392
Rusk (1843)	—	—	519	344	1,633	3,620	5,398	7,864
Sabine (1837)	114	534	667	667	719	800	1,112	1,294
San Augustine (1837)	520	991	1,363	1,436	1,492	1,382	1,490	1,674
San Patricio (1837)	n/a	n/a	n/a	1	2	21	47	77
San Saba (1856)	—	—	—	—	—	—	81	90
Shelby (1837)	186	367	734	615	791	775	1,423	1,913
Smith (1846)	—	—	—	n/a	517	2,414	3,995	7,212
Starr (1848)	—	—	—	—	2	0	0	n/a
Stephens (1858)[3]	—	—	—	—	—	—	n/a	33
Tarrant (1850)	—	—	—	—	32	280	730	1,772
Titus (1846)	—	—	—	243	448	1,208	2,040	3,580
Travis (1840)	—	288	n/a	287	594	2,068	2,104	3,019
Trinity (1850)	—	—	—	—	44	260	666	1,227
Tyler (1846)	—	—	—	n/a	420	752	1,097	1,526
Upshur (1846)	—	—	—	87	479	1,784	3,611	5,871
Uvalde (1856)	—	—	—	—	—	—	33	49
Van Zandt (1848)	—	—	—	—	5	125	291	1,461
Victoria (1837)	n/a	73	164	368	488	850	1,533	1,478
Walker (1846)	—	—	—	720	1,129	2,758	3,766	5,275
Washington (1837)	583	709[2]	1,323	1,581	2,218	4,399	6,616	8,663
Webb (1848)	—	—	—	—	n/a	n/a	n/a	n/a
Wharton (1846)	—	—	—	701	1,156	1,798	2,633	3,445
Williamson (1848)	—	—	—	—	127	757	844	1,074
Wilson (1860)	—	—	—	—	n/a	n/a	310	433
Wise (1856)	—	—	—	—	—	—	95	161
Wood (1850)	—	—	—	—	17	354	923	2,084
Young (1856)	—	—	—	—	—	—	78	31

[1] Dates in parentheses indicate year of county formation.

[2] Rolls incomplete.

[3] Stephens County was created originally in 1858 as Buchanan County and renamed for Alexander Hamilton Stephens in 1861.

Totals for the number of slaves in each county in 1837, 1846, and 1864 had to be determined from the original tax rolls completed by county tax assessor/collectors. In most cases, assessors totaled slaves and other key forms of taxable property at the end of each year's rolls. These totals were accepted as correct, so it was relatively easy to collect the necessary data.

County-by-county totals for the other years given in the table above—1840, 1845, 1850, 1855, and 1860—were available in printed sources. When the printed sources did not have the total for a particular county, the original rolls were consulted to see that the information was indeed not available. If the returns were found in the original, they were included in the table. A list of these printed sources follows:

1840. Gifford White (comp.), *The 1840 Census of the Republic of Texas* (Austin, 1966). This is a reproduction of tax rolls rather than a true census.

1845. "Report of the Secretary of the Treasury," in *Appendix to the Journals of the Senate of the First Legislature of the State of Texas* (Clarksville, Tex., 1848).

1850. *Biennial Report of the Comptroller, for the Years, 1850 and 1851* (Austin, 1851).

1855. *Report of the Comptroller of the State of Texas . . . for the Two Years Terminating October 31, 1855* (Austin, 1856).

1860. *Biennial Report of the Comptroller of Texas . . . 1860–1861* (Austin, 1861).

APPENDIX 3

County Records as a Source
Of Information on Slavery in Texas

Primary research materials on slavery in Texas are relatively abundant. Traditional sources such as manuscript collections, travelers' accounts, and newspapers contain essential narrative information. United States census returns and tax rolls provide the quantitative data necessary for a statistical view of the institution's growth and profitability. These materials are so familiar to most readers that bibliographical entries offer a sufficient explanation of their use. County government records, however, constitute another, albeit generally less familiar, source of primary material utilized in this study. Documents housed in county courthouses are used infrequently if at all by most historians, and yet they have great potential for contributing to the narrative and quantitative history of slavery as well as many other aspects of antebellum social and economic life. Thus, this appendix offers a brief description of the most useful of these records and a list of those utilized in studying slavery in Texas.

Probate records may be the single most important local source on slavery and society in antebellum Texas. Preserved in the county clerks' offices, these records, which were created by the estates of deceased persons going through probate, consist of Probate Case Papers, Probate Minutes, and the Final Record (often called the Estate Record or, somewhat confusingly, the Probate Record). Case Papers consist of the original documents filed on each estate as it went through probate. They are generally preserved in legal-case jackets and offer the advantage of having all the documentation pertaining to a particular estate collected in one place. Probate Minutes indicate when the various aspects of the case came before the court and what actions were taken. They have little detail and are therefore much less valuable than the Case Papers. The Final Record consists of bound volumes containing copies of all the major original documents filed in the case. These volumes offer the advantage of high-quality paper and generally legible handwriting, although not all of the documents pertaining to a particular estate are necessarily recorded on consecutive pages. Most counties have name indexes to all three types of records.

Texans being the law-abiding individuals that they are, no two counties have kept their probate records in exactly the same way over the years. Nevertheless, every county created before 1865, excepting those that have suffered courthouse fires, has either Case Papers or the Final Record or both, containing a number of extremely useful documents concerning slavery and society. First, there are wills written by the deceased. These can be very revealing of attitudes toward slaves and the treatment accorded them. (Some counties have special books for the recording of wills only.) Second, there are inventories and appraisals of each estate's property made by three disinterested members of the community. These constitute the best source available for data on the value of slaves according to age, sex, and condition. Third, there are the annual reports of guardians and administrators on the management and condition of estates under their control. These are unmatched for information concerning the hiring of slaves in rural agricultural areas. Finally, there are the final accounts of estate settlements, which are very informative on the subject of the preservation and disruption of slave families.

District Court Records constitute a second major set of local government documents that are highly revealing of a slaveholding society's concerns. Antebellum Texas district courts heard all felony criminal cases, all civil cases where the claims involved amounted to one hundred dollars or more, and all divorce actions. The records generated by these courts included Case Papers and Minute Books. Case Papers contain the original documentation provided by both parties, the lawyers, and the witnesses in each legal action. They touch on slavery and slaveholding society in actions ranging from divorce cases in which adultery with slaves was charged to criminal prosecutions brought by the state for cruelty to bondsmen. The slave-hire system also generated a great deal of district court litigation and, therefore, original records related to this practice. District Court Minutes are generally just records of cases decided and actions taken without any explanatory detail. At times, however, clerks included highly revealing material in these records also.

Local records offer a special advantage to students of an emotionally charged subject such as slavery in that the documents were not created with the intention of saying anything about the Peculiar Institution as such. Traditional sources such as newspapers, travelers' accounts, and even to some extent letters and diaries tended to be very self-conscious and either highly critical or extremely defensive in commenting on slavery. They often told more about the author than about the institution. Probate records and court papers, however, were legal documents created with the purpose of managing property concerns and settling disputes. They had no reason to misrepresent the nature of slavery. Perhaps the most reliable and revealing historical sources on any controversial subject are those not consciously created as statements on that particular subject. County government records have that quality.

Finally, there is the matter of availability. County records pertaining to slavery may be found in every part of Texas where the institution existed. Research is not limited by whether or not an area had a town large enough to publish a newspaper or by the vagaries of the preservation of manuscript collections. Moreover, the only chronological limit is the founding date of the county. Local records have availability too in the sense that many have been filmed by the Mormons as part of their genealogical work and may be obtained through Texas' regional archives system.

The following is a list of the county records consulted, either in the original or on microfilm, for material utilized in this study of slavery in Texas. The list includes the county, the county seat, the office having custody of the records used, and the records themselves.

Anderson County. Palestine. County Clerk: Probate Minutes, Books D, E, and G.

Austin County. Bellville. County Clerk: Succession Record, Books A, B, C, and D; Book entitled "Records, 1849–1865."

Bell County. Belton. County Clerk: Inventory and Appraisal Record, Book 1; Will Record; Commissioners' Court Minutes.

Brazoria County. Angleton. County Clerk: Record entitled "Wills, etc.," Books A, B, C, and D.

Brazos County. Bryan. County Clerk: Record of Estates, Book A; Probate Minutes, Book E.

Burleson County. Caldwell. County Clerk: Probate Minutes, Books 1 and 2; Probate Record, Book 4.

Burnet County. Burnet. County Clerk: Probate Record, Books A and B.

Caldwell County. Lockhart. County Clerk: Probate Record, Books A, B, C, and D.

Cass County. Linden. County Clerk: Final Record of the Probate Court, Books 1, 2, 3, 4, and 5. District Clerk: District Court Civil Minutes, Books 3A and B.

Cherokee County. Rusk. County Clerk: Probate Minutes, Books C2, D, E, and F.

Collin County. McKinney. County Clerk: Probate Case Papers; Probate Minutes, Book A1.

Colorado County. Columbus. County Clerk: Probate Record, Books B, D, E, and F.

Cooke County. Gainesville. County Clerk: Probate Records and Minutes.

De Witt County. Cuero. County Clerk: Final Record of Deceased Persons, Books A, B, and C.

Falls County. Marlin. District Clerk: District Court Minutes, Books A and B.

Fannin County. Bonham. County Clerk: Probate Minutes, Books A, C, D, and E.

Fayette County. La Grange. County Clerk: Probate Record, Books A, B, E, and F.

Fort Bend County. Richmond. County Clerk: Probate Record, Books A, A2, and B1.

Freestone County. Fairfield. County Clerk: Probate Minutes, Book for 1859–67.

Galveston County. Galveston. County Clerk: Inventory Record, Book 1; Probate Minutes, Book 2; Will Book A.

Gonzales County. Gonzales. County Clerk: Probate Case Papers.

Grayson County. Sherman. County Clerk: Probate Case Papers; Probate Record, Books AB, D, E, and F. District Clerk: District Court Civil Minutes, Books A and B.

Grimes County. Anderson. County Clerk: Probate Minutes, Books 1 and N.

Harrison County. Marshall. County Clerk: Probate Case Papers; Estate Record, Books B, D, E, F, H, I–J, and N; Commissioners' Court Minutes. District Clerk: District Court Civil Papers.

Henderson County. Athens. County Clerk: Inventory and Appraisal Record, Book B2.

Hunt County. Greenville. County Clerk: Probate Final Record, Book A; Commissioners Court Minutes. District Clerk: District Court Minutes, Book A.

Jackson County. Edna. County Clerk: Final Record of Estates, Books A, B, C, and D.

Jasper County. Jasper. County Clerk: Probate Minutes, Books B and C.

Lavaca County. Hallettsville. County Clerk: Record of Estates, Book A.

Leon County. Centerville. County Clerk: Probate Record, Books D, F, H, and I.

McLennan County. Waco. County Clerk: Probate Record, Books B, C, and D.

Matagorda County. Bay City. County Clerk: Inventory Record, Books A, A2, B, and C; Transcribed Will Record.

Montgomery County. Conroe. County Clerk: Probate Minutes, Books D5, E7, F8, G9, 10, and 11.

Nacogdoches County. Nacogdoches. County Clerk: Book of Wills; "Slave Bundle"; Record of Inventories, Book A.

Navarro County. Corsicana. County Clerk: Deed Record, Books C, H, L, and O.

Newton County. Newton. County Clerk: Probate Minutes, Books A and B.

Nueces County. Corpus Christi. County Clerk: Probate Record, Book B.

Polk County. Livingston. County Clerk: Probate Record, Books A, B, and C; Book of Wills, 1840–96; Probate Case Papers; Justice of the Peace Record Books; Commissioners' Court Minutes. District Clerk: District Court Civil Papers.

Red River County. Clarksville. County Clerk: Probate Minutes, Books C, E, F, G, and H; Will Record, Book B. District Clerk: District Court Minutes, Books E and F.

Rusk County. Henderson. County Clerk: Probate Case Papers; Probate Record, Books D, E, F, G, H, and I.

San Augustine County. San Augustine. County Clerk: Book of Wills, 1856–96; Probate Minutes, Books for 1837–44 and 1844–51.

Smith County. Tyler. County Clerk: Probate Case Papers; Probate Minutes, Books B and B1; Commissioners' Court Minutes; Justice of the Peace Case Papers. District Clerk: District Court Criminal Papers; District Court Civil Minutes, Book D.

Travis County. Austin. County Clerk: Probate Case Papers; Probate Record, Books A, B, and C; Commissioners' Court Minutes. District Clerk: District Court Civil Minutes.

Van Zandt County. Canton. County Clerk: Probate Minutes, Book AA.

Washington County. Brenham. County Clerk: Final Record, Books B, C, F, and G.

Wharton County. Wharton. County Clerk: Probate Minutes, Books A, B, and B2.

Williamson County. Georgetown. County Clerk: Probate Minutes, Books 2A and 3R.

APPENDIX 4
Texas' Largest Slaveholders in 1860

Texas' Largest Slaveholders in 1860

County	Name of slaveholder	Age	State of birth	Slaves	Real property	Personal property	Improved acreage	Corn (bushels)	Cotton (bales)	Sugar (hhds.)
Anderson	F. S. Jackson	51	Va.	119	29,000	80,000	1,200	10,000	419	0
Austin[1]	L. W. Groce	54	Ga.	129	100,000	225,000	1,200	7,000	590	0
	P. M. Cuney	52	La.	105	293,900	31,100	550	7,000	412	0
	J. E. Kirby	40	Ga.	139	285,000	175,000	2,800	10,000	700	0
	A. T. Oliver	40	Ga.	103	85,000	120,000	1,500	5,000	275	0
	T. C. Cliett	48	Ga.	100	0	115,000	850	5,000	468	0
	E. A. Glover[2]	n/a	n/a	159	n/a	n/a	1,700	12,000	937	0
Brazoria	Joel Spencer	65	S.C.	102	22,000	51,000	650	700	175	0
	David G. Mills	46	Ky.	344	364,234	250,000	2,500	25,000	0	712
	John G. McNeel	58	Ky.	176	100,150	216,400	1,550	15,000	275	300
	Abner Jackson	50	Va.	286	84,415	88,360	2,550	21,500	622	586
	Sarah Mims[3]	55	Ala.	103	73,480	96,030	700	7,000	105	65
	Levi Jordan	66	Ga.	134	69,200	130,740	600	3,000	77	193
	William H. Kennedy	22	S.C.	124	36,800	127,380	975	600	807	0
	Hamlin Bass	54	Ga.	213	163,830	97,705	1,450	8,000	0	200
	John A. Wharton	29	Tenn.	133	113,000	123,950	700	7,000	100	185
	Aaron Coffee[4]	27	Miss.	157	100,000	167,350	1,153	10,000	600	120
Brazos	Thomas D. Wilson	48	Tenn.	105	40,600	106,095	1,000	6,000	225	0
Burleson	William Davis	55	Ga.	121	157,160	200,000	900	7,000	700	0
Cass	Willis Whitaker, Sr.	61	S.C.	142	60,000	100,400	1,000	2,000	150	0
	Reece Hughes	47	Tenn.	147	100,000	130,540	2,000	10,000	511	0
Colorado	John H. Crisp	63	N.C.	146	32,000	98,200	800	6,000	260	0
	H. D. Rhodes	41	Ala.	103	61,000	105,000	585	4,000	412	0
	John Mathews	63	Va.	140	80,000	145,000	800	10,000	589	0
	William J. Harbert	37	Ala.	123	32,000	28,000	830	4,500	465	0
Falls	Churchill Jones	54	Va.	127	200,000	153,150	1,200	1,000	312	0
Fort Bend	J. D. Waters[5]	n/a	n/a	216	n/a	n/a	1,400	14,000	800	200
	C. W. Buckley	45	N.C.	108	200,000	125,000	1,000	5,000	400	0

County	Name	Age	State							
	James Simonton & Theophilus Simonton[6]	38 / 33	N.C. / N.C.	105	200,000	155,000	975	11,000	600	0
Freestone	W. J. Kyle[7] & B. F. Terry[8]	50 / 39	Tenn. / Ky.	105	68,000	105,750	1,100	8,000	300	250
	L. M. Stroud	42	Ga.	112	3,000	67,665	300	1,000	120	0
	W. M. Bonner	76	N.C.	112	6,200	104,920	150	900	98	0
Grayson	J. E. Hudson	62	S.C.	105	18,000	75,000	250	3,000	150	0
	George Stonum	74	Va.	115	50,000	107,500	100	6,000	362	0
Grimes	Thomas E. Blackshear	57	Ga.	123	45,000	105,000	900	800	400	0
Harrison	William T. Scott	49	Miss.	104	90,000	248,202	2,010	5,000	356	0
Lavaca	W. G. L. Foley	79	N.C.	124	50,000	142,000	600	2,000	291	0
Limestone	L. A. Stroud[9]	45	Ga.	100	49,600	69,200	600	6,000	188	0
Marion	Rebecca Hagerty[10]	45	Ga.	103	35,000	85,000	n/a	n/a	n/a	n/a
Matagorda	James B. Hawkins	46	N.C.	101	100,660	60,750	800	8,000	225	175
	W. G. Warren	55	N.C.	111	85,000	76,000	800	10,000	0	143
Montgomery	G. Wood	68	Ga.	105	16,964	80,750	650	10,000	333	0
	George Goldthwaite[11]	n/a	n/a	102	n/a	n/a	700	10,000	437	0
Nacogdoches	John J. Hayter	70	Va.	150	60,792	85,460	1,500	12,000	249	0
Navarro	Anderson Ingraham	61	Ga.	126	29,740	70,150	900	6,500	382	0
Polk	Byrd M. Grace	47	Ga.	114	30,000	150,000	500	2,800	150	0
	E. J. Carrington	61	Va.	103	22,600	70,000	500	2,500	200	0
Red River	James E. Hopkins &	54	Ky.		32,000	50,000				
	R. M. Hopkins[12]	51	Ky.	139	44,000	55,000	1,200	10,000	385	0
Robertson	B. F. Hammond	40	Ala.	106	20,000	194,840	500	4,000	300	0
	Reuben Anderson	66	Ga.	100	80,426	93,380	950	6,000	644	0
Rusk	John Pruitt	56	Tenn.	105	18,750	70,800	800	12,000	350	0
San Augustine	William Garrett	49	Tenn.	132	36,751	134,900	1,150	10,000	400	0
Trinity	F. B. Sublett	30	Tex.	117	80,000	90,000	120	5,000	400	0
Walker	Joshua A. Thomason	49	Ga.	128	60,180	169,650	950	10,000	603	0
Washington	Gabriel Felder	63	S.C.	130	32,250	111,700	850	9,000	470	0
	Asa Hoxey	60	Ga.	103	200,000	100,000	1,075	6,000	500	0

Texas' Largest Slaveholders in 1860

County	Name of slaveholder	Age	State of birth	Slaves	Real property	Personal property	Improved acreage	Corn (bushels)	Cotton (bales)	Sugar (hhds.)
Wharton	Albert C. Horton[13]	60	Ga.	167	200,000	119,000	1,400	12,000	600	0
	R. H. D. Sewell[14]	n/a	n/a	123	n/a	n/a	750	7,000	300	0
	M. G. Stith	46	Va.	118	0	0	1,160	6,000	520	0
	John C. Clark[15]	62	S.C.	116	132,145	104,715	500	2,500	225	0
	David G. Stevens	55	Ala.	109	240,000	242,000	1,200	10,000	500	0

[1] Austin County presents special difficulties in determining the number of slaves owned by large planters because the census enumerator placed multiple numbers of bondsmen of the same age and sex on the same line. Page 5 of the slave schedule, for example, reported 270 slaves on 80 lines.

[2] E. A. Glover does not appear in Schedule 1 for any county in Texas. He was either not a resident of Texas or not in the state when the census was taken.

[3] The Mims plantation and slaves appear in the name of Alexander Mims, the thirty-year-old son of Sarah Mims. She was the actual owner, however, and the property was in her name on the tax rolls. Brazoria County Tax Rolls, 1860.

[4] Aaron Coffee reported only 25 slaves in his own name, but he was the administrator of the estate of his parents, Thomas J. and Melinda Coffee, which had an additional 132 slaves.

[5] J. D. Waters was not present at the census of 1860, but he appeared in the 1850 census as a forty-year-old planter from South Carolina. His plantation was being managed in 1860 by thirty-eight-year-old J. P. Waters from South Carolina.

[6] James Simonton and Theophilus Simonton operated as partners.

[7] William J. Kyle also appeared in the census for Brazoria County in 1860. He had real property valued at $112,500 and personal property valued at $65,750. He and Terry had seventy-five slaves in Brazoria County and a plantation with six hundred improved acres that produced three thousand bushels of corn, fifty bales of cotton, and two hundred hogsheads of sugar. Thus, Kyle and Terry were almost large enough to appear on this list for both Brazoria and Fort Bend counties.

[8] William J. Kyle and B. F. Terry operated as partners.

[9] Stroud and his wife owned one hundred slaves. He was also the agent for an estate having seventy slaves.

[10] Hagerty's plantation was not listed on those pages of the agricultural schedule that were microfilmed. Apparently, the originals were lost. They are not with the Marion County agricultural schedule in the Texas State Archives.

[11] George Goldthwaite was a thirty-year-old lawyer from South Carolina who lived in Houston. He reported only $3,000 in real and $1,000 in personal property. Although the census listed the slaves on the Montgomery County plantation in his name, and tax rolls indicate that he paid taxes on them, he may well have been only the agent for an absentee owner.

[12] James E. Hopkins and R. M. Hopkins operated as partners.

[13] Albert C. Horton was reported on Schedule 1 as a resident of Matagorda County. His plantation and slaves were in Wharton County.

[14] R. H. D. Sewell was not listed in Schedule 1 for any county in Texas.

[15] John C. Clark had two plantations that were reported separately in the census of Wharton County.

BIBLIOGRAPHY

Primary Sources

MANUSCRIPTS

Austin Public Library, Austin, Texas
  Pease-Graham-Niles. Family Papers.

Baylor University, Waco,Texas. Texas Collection
  Trask Family Papers.

Cornell University Libraries, Ithaca, N.Y. Department of Manuscripts and University Archives
  Turner, Avery. Papers.

Dallas Historical Society Archives, Dallas, Texas
  Howard, Dr. W. E. Collection.

Duke University, Durham, N.C. Perkins Library
  Person Family Papers.

East Tennessee State University Library, Johnson City
  Bowman Family Papers.

East Texas Baptist University Library, Marshall
  Webster, John B. Plantation Journal, 1858–59.

National Archives, Washington, D.C.
  Eighth Census of the United States, 1860. Schedule 1 (Free Inhabitants), and Schedule 2 (Slave Inhabitants).
  Ninth Census of the United States, 1870. Schedule 1 (Inhabitants).
  Records of the Department of War. Record Group 105.
    Records of the Assistant Commissioner for the State of Texas, United States Bureau of Refugees, Freedmen, and Abandoned Lands, 1865–69.
  Seventh Census of the United States, 1850. Schedule 1 (Free Inhabitants) and Schedule 2 (Slave Inhabitants).

Rice University, Houston, Texas. Fondren Library
  Osterhout, John Patterson. Papers.

Rosenberg Library, Galveston, Texas
  League, Thomas M. Papers.
  McCoy, F. E. Papers.
  Morgan, James. Papers.

Record of Proceedings of the First Baptist Church of Galveston, Texas.
Williams, Samuel May. Papers.

Sam Houston Regional Library and Research Center, Liberty, Texas
Neyland, Watson A. Collection.

San Jacinto Historical Museum, San Jacinto State Park, San Jacinto, Texas
Howard, Dr. William E. Collection.

Sul Ross State University Library, Alpine, Texas
Burleson, Sarah G. Collection.
Townsend, E. E. Collection.
Travis, William Barret. Collection.

Tennessee State Library, Nashville
Howell, Alfred. Letters.

Texas State Library and Archives, Austin
Biennial Report of the Comptroller of the State of Texas for the Two Fiscal Years
Ending August 21, 1863.
Eighth Census of the United States, 1860. Schedule 4 (Productions of Agricul-
ture), Schedule 5 (Products of Industry), and Schedule 6 (Social Statistics).
Papers of the Comptroller of Public Accounts.
Records of the Comptroller of Public Accounts, Ad Valorem Tax Division,
County Real and Personal Property Tax Rolls, 1837–65.
Seventh Census of the United States, 1850. Schedule 4 (Productions of Agricul-
ture), Schedule 5 (Products of Industry), and Schedule 6 (Social Statistics).

University of Texas at Arlington Library, Arlington. Garrett Collection
Maas, Samuel. Family Papers.
Plummer Family Papers.

University of Texas, Austin. Barker Texas History Center
Adriance, John. Papers.
Billingsley, James B. and Virginia C. Papers.
Blackshear, Thomas E. Papers
Burnet, David G. Papers.
Chambers, Thomas W. Papers.
Coleman, Ann Raney Thomas. Papers.
Cumberland Presbyterian Church. Minutes of the Colorado Presbytery.
Devereux, Julien Sydney. Papers.
Duncan, Green C. Papers.
Haas, Oscar. Papers.
Hagerty, Rebecca McIntosh Hawkins. Papers.
Hill, John R. Papers.
Hornsby, Reuben. Papers.
Huling, Thomas Byers. Papers.
Jones, Churchill. Papers.
Lawrance, James W. Papers.
Moss, A. Henry. Papers.

Neblett, Lizzie, Scott. Papers.
Perry, James F. and Stephen S. Papers.
Rose, Preston R. Papers.
Slavery and Abolition Papers.
Sloan, W. L. Papers.
Smith, Ashbel. Papers.
Tait, Charles William. Papers.
Washington, Lewis Mills Hobbs. Family Papers.

NEWSPAPERS

Austin *Southern Intelligencer*, 1856–60.
Austin *Texas State Gazette*, 1849–65.
Brazoria *Texas Planter*, September 20, 1854.
Brazoria *Texas Republican*, September 26, 1835.
Clarksville *Northern Standard*, 1842–65.
Columbia *Telegraph and Texas Register*, January 3, 1837.
Dallas *Herald*, 1855–65.
Dallas *Morning News*, November 17, 1985, December 5, 1986.
Galveston *Weekly News*, 1844–60.
Houston *Telegraph and Texas Register*, 1837–53.
La Grange *Patriot*, December 24, 1864, February 18, 1865.
La Grange *True Issue*, October 29, 1859, July 5, 1860.
Marshall *Texas Republican*, 1849–65.
Matagorda *Bulletin*, October 18, 1838.
Matagorda *Gazette*, 1858–60.
[New Orleans], *DeBow's Review*, January, 1855, July, 1858.
San Antonio *Herald*, 1855–63.
San Augustine *Journal and Advertiser*, November 9, 1840.
San Augustine *Red-Lander*, September 9, 1841, May 26, 1842.
San Felipe de Austin *Telegraph and Texas Register*, October 17, 1835, March 12, 1836.
San Felipe de Austin *Texas Gazette*, January 30, April 3, 1830.

PUBLISHED DOCUMENTS

Appendix to the Journal of the House of Representatives, Fifth Legislature. Austin, 1853.
Barker, Eugene C., ed. "Minutes of the Ayuntamiento of San Felipe de Austin, 1828–1832." *Southwestern Historical Quarterly*, XXI (1918), 299–326.
Berlin, Ira *et al.*, eds. *The Black Military Experience.* New York, 1983. Vol. II of Berlin *et al.*, eds., *Freedom: A Documentary History of Emancipation, 1861–1867*
Biennial Report of the Comptroller, for the Years 1850 and 1851. Austin, 1851.
Biennial Report of the Comptroller of the State of Texas for the Years 1856 and 1857. Austin, 1858.
Biennial Report of the Comptroller of the State of Texas for the Fiscal Years 1858–59. Austin, 1859.
Biennial Report of the Comptroller of Texas . . . 1860–1861. Austin, 1861.

Dallam, James Wilmer, comp. *A Digest of the Laws of Texas*. Baltimore, 1845.

DeBow, James D. B., comp. *Statistical View of the United States . . . Being a Compendium of the Seventh Census*. Washington, D.C., 1854.

Gammel, H. P. N., comp. *The Laws of Texas, 1822–1897*. 10 volumes. Austin, 1898–1902.

Hartley, Oliver C., comp. *A Digest of the Laws of Texas*. Philadelphia, 1850.

Hogan, William R., comp. "The State Census of 1847." *Southwestern Historical Quarterly*, L (1946), 116–18.

Journals of the Senate of the State of Texas [6th-8th Legislatures]. Austin, 1856–59.

Leal, Carmela, ed. "Translations of Statistical and Census Reports of Texas, 1782–1836, and Sources Documenting the Black in Texas, 1603–1803." Microfilm publication. San Antonio, 1979.

Message of Governor F. R. Lubbock to the Extra Session of the Ninth Legislature. Austin, 1863.

Message of Governor F. R. Lubbock to the Tenth Legislature. Austin, 1863.

Oldham, Williamson S., and George W. White, comps. *A Digest of the General Statute Laws of the State of Texas*. Austin, 1859.

Osburn, Mary M., ed. "The Atascosito Census of 1826." *Texana*, I (1963), 299–321.

A Report and Treatise on Slavery and the Slavery Agitation. Austin, 1857.

Report of the Comptroller of the State of Texas . . . for the Two Years Terminating October 31, 1855. Austin, 1856.

Report of the Directors, Superintendent and Agent of the Texas Penitentiary for the Years 1856 and 1857. Austin, 1857.

"Report of the Secretary of the Treasury." *Appendix to the Journals of the Senate of the First Legislature of the State of Texas*. Clarksville, Tex., 1848.

Reports of Cases Argued and Decided in the Supreme Court of the State of Texas. 65 volumes. St. Louis, 1848–86.

Reports of the Comptroller and Treasurer for the Years 1848 and 1849. Austin, 1849.

Scott, Robert N., comp. *The War of the Rebellion: A Compilation of the Official Records of the Union and Confederate Armies*. 70 vols. in 128. Washington, D.C., 1880–1901.

Smither, Harriet, ed. *Journals of the Fourth Congress of the Republic of Texas, 1839–1840*. 3 volumes. Austin, 1929.

Statistical History of the United States from Colonial Times to the Present. Stamford, Conn., 1965.

United States Bureau of the Census. *Population of the United States in 1860: Compiled from the Original Returns of the Eighth Census*. Washington, D.C., 1864.

————. *Agriculture of the United States in 1860: Compiled from the Original Returns of the Eighth Census*. Washington, D.C., 1864.

————. *Statistics of the United States (Including Mortality, Property, etc.) in 1860: Compiled from the Original Returns and Being the Final Exhibit of the Eighth Census*. Washington, D.C., 1866.

————. *Report on the Productions of Agriculture as Returned at the Tenth Census, 1880*. Washington, D.C., 1883.

Wallace, Ernest, and David M. Vigness, eds. *Documents of Texas History*. Austin, 1963.

Weeks, William F., reporter. *Debates of the Texas Convention.* Houston, 1846.
White, Gifford E., comp. *The 1840 Census of the Republic of Texas.* Austin, 1966.
Winkler, Ernest William, ed. *Platforms of Political Parties in Texas.* Austin, 1916.

PUBLISHED LETTERS AND CORRESPONDENCE

Barker, Eugene C., ed. *The Papers of Stephen F. Austin.* 3 vols. Washington, D.C., 1924, 1928; Austin, 1926.
Batchelor-Turner Letters, 1861–1864, Written by Two of Terry's Rangers. Edited by H. J. H. Rugeley. Austin, 1961.
Binkley, William C., ed. *Official Correspondence of the Texas Revolution, 1835–1836.* 2 vols. New York, 1936.
Clopper, A. M. "The Clopper Correspondence, 1834–1838." *Quarterly of the Texas State Historical Association,* XIII (1909), 128–44.
Garrison, George P., ed. *Diplomatic Correspondence of the Republic of Texas.* 3 vols. Washington, D.C., 1908–11.
Hoxey, Asa. Letter to Robert M. Williamson from Montgomery, Alabama, on December 2, 1832. In "Notes and Fragments," *Quarterly of the Texas State Historical Association,* IX (1906), 285–86.
Jenkins, John Holmes, ed. *The Papers of the Texas Revolution, 1835–1836.* 10 vols. Austin, 1973.
Leathers, Frances Jane, ed. "Christopher Columbus Goodman: Soldier, Indian Fighter, Farmer, 1818–1861." *Southwestern Historical Quarterly,* LXIX (1966), 353–76.
Reichstein, Andreas, ed. "The Austin-Leaming Correspondence, 1828–1836." *Southwestern Historical Quarterly,* LXXXVIII (1985), 247–82.
Williams, Amelia W., and Eugene C. Barker, eds. *The Writings of Sam Houston.* 8 vols. Austin, 1938–43.
Williams, Charles Richard, ed. *Diary and Letters of Rutherford Birchard Hayes, Nineteenth President of the United States.* 5 vols. Columbus, Ohio, 1922–26.

PUBLISHED MEMOIRS, TRAVELERS' ACCOUNTS, AND CONTEMPORARY BOOKS

Almonte, Juan N. "Statistical Report on Texas, 1835." Translated by Carlos E. Castañeda. *Southwestern Historical Quarterly,* XXVIII (1925), 177–222.
Anderson, John Q., ed. *Brokenburn: The Journal of Kate Stone, 1861–1868.* Baton Rouge, 1955.
Bracht, Viktor. *Texas in 1848.* Translated by C. F. Schmidt. San Antonio, 1931.
Cazneau, Jane McManus [Cora Montgomery]. *Eagle Pass: or Life on the Border.* New York, 1852.
Covey, Cyclone, trans. and ed. *Cabeza de Vaca's Adventures in the Unknown Interior of America.* Albuquerque, N.M., 1983.
De la Peña, José Enrique. *With Santa Anna in Texas: A Personal Narrative of the Revolution.* Translated and edited by Carmen Perry. College Station, Tex., 1975.
DeWees, William B. *Letters from an Early Settler of Texas.* Louisville, 1852.
Fearn, Frances, ed. *Diary of a Refugee.* New York, 1910.

Featherstonhaugh, George W. *Excursion Through the Slave States: From Washington on the Potomac to the Frontier of Mexico, with Sketches of Popular Manners and Geological Notices.* New York, 1844.

Field, Joseph E. *Three Years in Texas: Including a View of the Texas Revolution and an Account of the Principal Battles, Together with Descriptions of the Soil, Commercial and Agricultural Advantages.* 1836; rpr. Austin, 1935.

Gaillardet, Frederic. *Sketches of Early Texas and Louisiana.* Translated and edited by James L. Shepherd, III. Austin, 1966.

[Cocke, James D. (?)]. *A Glance at the Currency and Resources Generally of the Republic of Texas, By a Citizen of the Country.* Houston, 1838.

Graham, Philip, ed. "Texas Memoirs of Amelia E. Barr." *Southwestern Historical Quarterly,* LXIX (1966), 473–98.

Gray, Allen Charles, ed. *From Virginia to Texas, 1835: Diary of Col. Wm. F. Gray Giving Details of His Journey to Texas and Return in 1835–1836 and Second Journey to Texas in 1837.* Houston, 1909.

Hamilton, Jeff. *My Master: The Inside Story of Sam Houston and His Times.* Edited by Lenoir Hunt. Dallas, 1940.

Harris, Dilue. "Reminiscences of Mrs. Dilue Harris." *Quarterly of the Texas State Historical Association,* IV (1900–1901), 85–127, 155–89.

Hollon, E. Eugene, and Ruth Lapham Butler, eds. *William Bollaert's Texas.* Norman, Okla., 1956.

Jefferson, Thomas. *Notes on the State of Virginia.* 1861; rpr. New York, 1964.

Jordan, Gilbert J., ed. and trans. "W. Steinert's View of Texas in 1849." *Southwestern Historical Quarterly,* LXXX (1976), 57–78, 177–200; (1977), 283–301, 399–416; LXXXI (1977), 45–72.

Kennedy, William. *Texas: The Rise, Progress, and Prospects of the Republic of Texas.* London, 1841.

Kuykendall, J. H., ed. "Recollections of Early Texans." *Quarterly of the Texas State Historical Association,* VI (1903), 236–53, 311–30; VII (1903), 29–64.

[Lawrence, A. B.]. *Texas in 1840: Or, The Emigrant's Guide to the New Republic, Being the Result of Observations, Inquiry, and Travel in that Beautiful Country.* New York, 1840.

Linn, John J. *Reminiscences of Fifty Years in Texas.* New York, 1883.

Loewenberg, Bert James, and Ruth Bogin, eds. *Black Women in Nineteenth-Century American Life: Their Words, Their Thoughts, Their Feelings.* University Park, Penn., 1976.

Lord, Walter, ed. *The Fremantle Diary, Being the Journal of Lieutenant Colonel Arthur James Lyon Fremantle, Coldstream Guards, on His Three Months in the Southern States.* Boston, 1954.

Lundy, Benjamin. *The Life, Travels, and Opinions of Benjamin Lundy, Including His Journeys to Texas and Mexico.* Compiled by Thomas Earle. 1847; rpr. New York, 1971.

———. *The War in Texas: A Review of Facts and Circumstances Showing that This Contest Is a Crusade . . . to Re-establish, Extend, and Perpetuate the System of Slavery and the Slave Trade.* Philadelphia, 1837.

McCormick, Andrew Phelps. *Scotch-Irish in Ireland and in America as Shown in*

Sketches of . . . Pioneer Scotch-Irish Families . . . in North Carolina, Kentucky, Missouri, and Texas. New Orleans, 1897.

McDonald, Archie P., ed. *Hurrah for Texas! The Diary of Adolphus Sterne, 1838–1851.* Waco, 1969.

McLean, John H. *Reminiscences of Reverend John H. McLean.* Dallas, 1918.

Maillard, Nicholas Doran P. *The History of the Republic of Texas: From the Discovery of the Country to the Present Time and the Causes of Her Separation from the Republic of Mexico.* London, 1842.

The Mexican Side of the Texas Revolution [1836] by the Chief Mexican Participants. Translated by Carlos E. Castañeda. Dallas, 1928.

Murray, Amelia M. *Letters from the United States, Cuba, and Canada.* New York, 1856.

Oates, Stephen B., ed. *Rip Ford's Texas.* Austin, 1963.

Olmsted, Frederick Law. *A Journey Through Texas: Or, A Saddle-Trip on the Southwestern Frontier, With a Statistical Appendix.* New York, 1857.

Parker, Amos Andrew. *Trip to the West and Texas . . . in the Autumn and Winter of 1834–5.* Concord, N.H., 1835.

Pratt, Willis W., ed. *Galveston Island, or, a Few Months Off the Coast of Texas: The Journal of Francis C. Sheridan, 1839–1840.* Austin, 1954.

Ragsdale, Crystal Sasse, ed. *The Golden Free Land: The Reminiscences and Letters of Women on an American Frontier.* Austin, 1976.

Raines, C. W., ed. *Six Decades in Texas, or Memoirs of Francis Richard Lubbock, Civil War Governor.* Austin, 1900.

Rawick, George P., ed. *The American Slave: A Composite Autobiography.* Series 1, 7 vols.; Series 2, 12 vols.; *Supplement,* Series 1, 12 vols.; *Supplement,* Series 2, 10 vols. Westport, Conn., 1972, 1977, 1979.

Reagan, John H. "A Conversation with Governor Houston." *Quarterly of the Texas State Historical Association,* III (1900), 279–82.

Roemer, Ferdinand. *Texas: With Particular Reference to German Immigration and the Physical Appearance of the Country.* Translated by Oswald Mueller. San Antonio, 1935.

Scoble, John. *Texas: Its Claims to be Recognized as an Independent Power by Great Britain; Examined in a Series of Letters.* London, 1839.

Siemering, August. "Die Latinische Ansiedlung in Texas." Translated by C. W. Geue. *Texana,* V (1967), 126–31.

Smith, Edward. *Account of a Journey Through Northeastern Texas Undertaken in 1849 for the Purposes of Emigration.* London, 1849.

Smithwick, Noah. *The Evolution of a State, or Recollections of Old Texas Days.* Compiled by Nanna Smithwick Donaldson. Austin, 1900.

Solms-Braunfels, Prince Carl of. *Texas, 1844–1845.* Houston, 1936.

The Texas Almanac for 1857: With Statistics, Historical and Biographical Sketches, Etc., Relating to Texas. Galveston, 1856.

The Texas Almanac for 1858: With Statistics, Historical and Biographical Sketches, Etc., Relating to Texas. Galveston, 1857.

The Texas Almanac for 1861: With Statistics, Historical and Biographical Sketches, Etc., Relating to Texas. Galveston, 1860.

Tyler, Ronnie C., and Lawrence R. Murphy, eds. *The Slave Narratives of Texas.* Austin, 1974.

[Anonymous.] *A Visit to Texas: Being a Journal of a Traveller Through Those Parts Most Interesting to American Settlers with Descriptions of Scenery, Habits, Etc. Etc.* 1834; rpr. Austin, 1952.

Wallis, Jonnie Lockhart, and L. L. Hill, eds. *Sixty Years on the Brazos: The Life and Letters of Dr. John Washington Lockhart, 1824–1900.* New York, 1966.

Wiley, Bell I., ed. *One Thousand Four Hundred and Ninety-One Days in the Confederate Army: A Journal Kept by W. W. Heartsill.* Jackson, Tenn., 1953.

Wright, Louise Wigfall. *A Southern Girl in '61.* New York, 1905.

Secondary Sources

BOOKS

Ballagh, James Curtis. *A History of Slavery in Virginia.* Baltimore, 1902.

Bancroft, Frederic. *Slave-Trading in the Old South.* Baltimore, 1931.

Barker, Eugene C. *The Life of Stephen F. Austin: Founder of Texas, 1793–1836.* Nashville, 1925.

———. *Mexico and Texas, 1821–1835.* Dallas, 1928.

Barr, Alwyn. *Black Texans: A History of Negroes in Texas, 1528–1971.* Austin, 1973.

Barr, Alwyn, and Robert A. Calvert, eds. *Black Leaders: Texans for Their Times.* Austin, 1981.

Bassett, John Spencer. *Slavery in the State of North Carolina.* Baltimore, 1899.

Bateman, Fred, and Thomas Weiss. *A Deplorable Scarcity: The Failure of Industrialization in the Slave Economy.* Chapel Hill, 1981.

Berlin, Ira. *Slaves Without Masters: The Free Negro in the Antebellum South.* New York, 1974.

Blassingame, John W. *The Slave Community: Plantation Life in the Antebellum South.* New York, 1972.

Boles, John B. *Black Southerners, 1619–1869.* Lexington, Ky., 1983.

Boren, Carter E. *Religion on the Texas Frontier.* San Antonio, 1968.

Brackenridge, R. Douglas. *Voice in the Wilderness: A History of the Cumberland Presbyterian Church in Texas.* San Antonio, 1968.

Brackett, Jeffrey R. *The Negro in Maryland: A Study of the Institution of Slavery.* Baltimore, 1889.

Brewer, John Mason. *Dog Ghosts and Other Texas Negro Folk Tales.* Austin, 1958.

Brown, Lawrence L. *The Episcopal Church in Texas, 1838–1874.* Austin, 1963.

Buenger, Walter L. *Secession and the Union in Texas.* Austin, 1984.

Campbell, Randolph B. *A Southern Community in Crisis: Harrison County, Texas, 1850–1880.* Austin, 1983.

Campbell, Randolph B., and Richard G. Lowe. *Wealth and Power in Antebellum Texas.* College Station, 1977.

Carroll, James Milton. *A History of Texas Baptists: Comprising a Detailed Account of Their Activities, Their Progress, and Their Achievements.* Edited by J. B. Cranfill. Dallas, 1923.

Clarke, John H., ed. *William Styron's Nat Turner: Ten Black Writers Respond*. Boston, 1968.

Clarke, Mary Whatley. *David G. Burnet*. Austin, 1969.

Coleman, J. Winston, Jr. *Slavery Times in Kentucky*. Chapel Hill, 1940.

Cutrer, Thomas W. *The English Texans*. San Antonio, 1985.

David, Paul A., et al. *Reckoning with Slavery: Critical Essays in the Quantitative History of American Negro Slavery*. New York, 1976.

DeLeon, Arnoldo. *The Tejano Community, 1836–1900*. Albuquerque, 1982.

Du Bois, William E. B. *Black Reconstruction: An Essay Toward a History of the Part Which Black Folk Played in the Attempt to Reconstruct Democracy in America, 1860–1880*. Philadelphia, 1935.

Durden, Robert F. *The Gray and the Black: The Confederate Debate on Emancipation*. Baton Rouge, 1972.

Durham, Philip, and Everett L. Jones. *The Negro Cowboys*. New York, 1965.

Eaton, Clement. *A History of the Southern Confederacy*. New York, 1961.

Elkins, Stanley M. *Slavery: A Problem in American Institutional and Intellectual Life*. Chicago, 1959.

Elliott, Charles. *A History of the Methodist Episcopal Church in the South-West from 1844 to 1864*. Revised and edited by Leroy M. Vernon. Cincinnati, 1868.

Escott, Paul D. *Slavery Remembered: A Record of Twentieth-Century Slave Narratives*. Chapel Hill, 1979.

Faust, Drew Gilpin, ed. *The Ideology of Slavery: Proslavery Thought in the Antebellum South, 1830–1860*. Baton Rouge, 1981.

Fields, Barbara Jeanne. *Slavery and Freedom on the Middle Ground: Maryland During the Nineteenth Century*. New Haven, 1985.

Flanders, Ralph Betts. *Plantation Slavery in Georgia*. Chapel Hill, 1933.

Fogel, Robert William, and Stanley L. Engerman. *Time on the Cross: The Economics of American Negro Slavery*. 2 vols. Boston, 1974.

Fornell, Earl Wesley. *The Galveston Era: The Texas Crescent on the Eve of Secession*. Austin, 1961.

Genovese, Eugene D. *Roll, Jordan, Roll: The World The Slaves Made*. New York, 1974.

Goldin, Claudia Dale. *Urban Slavery in the American South, 1820–1860: A Quantitative View*. Chicago, 1976.

Graham, Don. *Cowboys and Cadillacs: How Hollywood Looks at Texas*. Austin, 1983.

Gutman, Herbert G. *The Black Family in Slavery and Freedom, 1750–1925*. New York, 1976.

———. *Slavery and the Numbers Game: A Critique of "Time on the Cross."* Urbana, Ill. 1975.

Hammond, William J., and Margaret F. Hammond. *La Reunion: A French Settlement in Dallas*. Dallas, 1958.

Harrison, William P., comp. and ed. *The Gospel Among the Slaves*. Nashville, 1893.

Henson, Margaret Swett. *Juan Davis Bradburn: A Reappraisal of the Mexican Commander at Anahuac*. College Station, 1982.

Hogan, William R. *The Texas Republic: A Social and Economic History*. Norman, Okla., 1946.

Huston, James L. *The Panic of 1857 and the Coming of the Civil War.* Baton Rouge, 1987.

Jenkins, William Sumner. *Pro-Slavery Thought in the Old South.* Chapel Hill, 1935.

Johnson, Ludwell H. *Red River Campaign: Politics and Cotton in the Civil War.* Baltimore, 1958.

Jones, Jacqueline. *Labor of Love, Labor of Sorrow: Black Women, Work, and the Family from Slavery to the Present.* New York, 1985.

Jones, Oakah L., Jr. *Santa Anna.* New York, 1968.

Jordan, Terry G. *German Seed in Texas Soil: Immigrant Farmers in Nineteenth-Century Texas.* Austin, 1966.

————. *Trails to Texas: Southern Roots of Western Cattle Ranching.* Lincoln, Nebr., 1981.

Kerby, Robert L. *Kirby Smith's Confederacy: The Trans-Mississippi South, 1863–1865.* New York, 1972.

Kingston, Mike, ed. *The 1986–1987 Texas Almanac and State Industrial Guide.* Dallas, 1985.

Klingberg, Frank. *The Negro in Colonial South Carolina: A Study in Americanization.* Washington, D.C., 1941.

Lane, Ann J., ed. *The Debate over Slavery: Stanley Elkins and His Critics.* Urbana, Ill., 1971.

Levine, Lawrence W. *Black Culture and Black Consciousness: Afro-American Thought from Slavery to Freedom.* New York, 1977.

Lowe, Richard G., and Randolph B. Campbell. *Planters and Plain Folk: Agriculture in Antebellum Texas.* Dallas, 1987.

Lowrie, Samuel Harmon. *Culture Conflict in Texas, 1821–1835.* New York, 1932.

Malone, Ann Patton. *Women on the Texas Frontier: A Cross-Cultural Perspective.* El Paso, 1983.

Massey, Mary Elizabeth. *Refugee Life in the Confederacy.* Baton Rouge, 1964.

Mohr, Clarence L. *On the Threshold of Freedom: Masters and Slaves in Civil War Georgia.* Athens, Ga., 1986.

Mooney, Chase C. *Slavery in Tennessee.* Bloomington, 1957.

Morgan, Edmund S. *American Slavery, American Freedom: The Ordeal of Colonial Virginia.* New York, 1975.

Morton, Ohland. *Terán and Texas: A Chapter in Texas-American Relations.* Austin, 1948.

Oakes, James. *The Ruling Race: A History of American Slaveholders.* New York, 1982.

Owens, Leslie Howard. *This Species of Property: Slave Life and Culture in the Old South.* New York, 1976.

Owens, William A. *This Stubborn Soil.* New York, 1966.

Owsley, Frank Lawrence. *Plain Folk of the Old South.* Baton Rouge, 1949.

Partlow, Miriam. *Liberty, Liberty County, and the Atascosito District.* Austin, 1974.

Phelan, Macum. *A History of Early Methodism in Texas, 1817–1866.* Dallas, 1924.

Phillips, Ulrich Bonnell. *American Negro Slavery: A Survey of the Supply, Employment, and Control of Negro Labor as Determined by the Plantation Regime.* New York, 1918.

Porter, Kenneth Wiggins. *The Negro on the American Frontier.* New York, 1971.

Procter, Ben, and Archie P. McDonald, eds. *The Texas Heritage*. St. Louis, 1980.

Raboteau, Albert J. *Slave Religion: The "Invisible Institution" in the Antebellum South.* New York, 1978.

Rawick, George P. *From Sundown to Sunup: The Making of a Black Community*. Westport, Conn., 1972.

Red, William Stuart. *A History of the Presbyterian Church in Texas*. Austin, 1936.

Reynolds, Donald E. *Editors Make War: Southern Newspapers in the Secession Crisis.* Nashville, 1966.

Rice, Lawrence D. *The Negro in Texas, 1874–1900*. Baton Rouge, 1971.

Richardson, Rupert Norval. *The Comanche Barrier to South Plains Settlement: A Century and a Half of Savage Resistance to the Advancing White Frontier*. Glendale, Cal., 1933.

Richardson, Rupert Norval, Ernest Wallace, and Adrian N. Anderson. *Texas: The Lone Star State*. 4th ed. Englewood Cliffs, N.J., 1981.

Ripley, C. Peter. *Slaves and Freedmen in Civil War Louisiana*. Baton Rouge, 1976.

Schwartz, Rosalie. *Across the Rio to Freedom: United States Negroes in Mexico*. El Paso, 1975.

Sellers, James Benson. *Slavery in Alabama*. University, Ala., 1950.

Sibley, Marilyn McAdams. *Lone Stars and State Gazettes: Texas Newspapers Before the Civil War*. College Station, 1983.

———. *Travelers in Texas, 1761–1860*. Austin, 1967.

Silverthorne, Elizabeth. *Ashbel Smith of Texas: Pioneer, Patriot, Statesman, 1805– 1886*. College Station, 1982.

———. *Plantation Life in Texas*. College Station, 1986.

Smith, John David. *An Old Creed for the New South: Proslavery Ideology and Historiography, 1865–1918*. Westport, Conn., 1985.

Smith, Julia Floyd. *Slavery and Plantation Growth in Antebellum Florida, 1821–1860*. Gainesville, 1973.

Speer, Ocie. *A Treatise on the Law of Married Women in Texas*. Rochester, N.Y., 1901.

Stampp, Kenneth M. *The Peculiar Institution: Slavery in the Ante-Bellum South*. New York, 1956.

Starobin, Robert S. *Industrial Slavery in the Old South*. New York, 1970.

Styron, William. *The Confessions of Nat Turner*. New York, 1966.

Sydnor, Charles Sackett. *Slavery in Mississippi*. New York, 1933.

Takaki, Ronald T. *A Pro-Slavery Crusade: The Agitation to Reopen the African Slave Trade*. New York, 1971.

Taylor, Joe Gray. *Negro Slavery in Louisiana*. Baton Rouge, 1963.

Taylor, Orville W. *Negro Slavery in Arkansas*. Durham, 1958.

Taylor, Rosser Howard. *Slaveholding in North Carolina: An Economic View*. Chapel Hill, 1926.

Trexler, Harrison Anthony. *Slavery in Missouri, 1804–1865*. Baltimore, 1914.

Turner, Martha Anne. *The Yellow Rose of Texas: Her Saga and Her Song*. Austin, 1976.

Tushnet, Mark. *The American Law of Slavery, 1810–1860: Considerations of Humanity and Interest*. Princeton, 1981.

Van Deburg, William L. *The Slave Drivers: Black Agricultural Labor Supervisors in the Antebellum South*. Westport, Conn., 1979.

Vandiver, Frank E. *The Southwest: South or West?* College Station, 1975.
Vernon, Walter N., et al. *The Methodist Excitement in Texas: A History.* Dallas, 1984.
Wade, Richard C. *Slavery in the Cities: The South, 1820–1860.* New York, 1964.
Webb, Walter Prescott, H. Bailey Carroll, and Eldon S. Branda, eds. *The Handbook of Texas.* 3 vols. Austin, 1952, 1976.
Webber, Thomas L. *Deep Like the Rivers: Education in the Slave Quarter Community, 1831–1865.* New York, 1978.
Weber, David J. *The Mexican Frontier, 1821–1846: The American Southwest Under Mexico.* Albuquerque, 1982.
Wheeler, Kenneth W. *To Wear a City's Crown: The Beginnings of Urban Growth in Texas, 1836–1865.* Cambridge, Mass., 1968.
White, Deborah Gray. *Ar'n't I A Woman? Female Slaves in the Plantation South.* New York, 1985.
Wiley, Bell I. *Southern Negroes, 1861–1865.* New York, 1938.
Williams, Annie Lee. *A History of Wharton County, 1846–1961.* Austin, 1964.
Winfrey, Dorman H. *Julien Sidney Devereux and His Monte Verdi Plantation.* Waco, 1962.
Winsor, Bill. *Texas in the Confederacy: Military Installations, Economy and People.* Hillsboro, Tex., 1978.
Wood, Betty. *Slavery in Colonial Georgia, 1730–1775.* Athens, Ga., 1984.
Wood, Peter. *Black Majority: Negroes in Colonial South Carolina from 1670 Through the Stono Rebellion.* New York, 1974.
Woodward, C. Vann. *The Burden of Southern History.* Baton Rouge, 1960.
Wooten, Dudley G., ed. *A Comprehensive History of Texas, 1685 to 1897.* 2 vols. Dallas, 1898.
Wright, Gavin. *The Political Economy of the Cotton South: Households, Markets, and Wealth in the Nineteenth Century.* New York, 1978.

ARTICLES

Addington, Wendell G. "Slave Insurrections in Texas." *Journal of Negro History,* XXXV (1950), 408–24.
Anderson, James D. "Aunt Jemima in Dialectics: Genovese on Slave Culture." *Journal of Negro History,* XLI (1976), 99–114.
Anderson, John Q. "Old John and the Master." *Southern Folklore Quarterly,* XXV (1961), 195–97.
Anderson, Robert V., and Robert E. Gallman. "Slaves as Fixed Capital: Slave Labor and Southern Economic Development." *Journal of American History,* LXIV (1977), 24–46.
Bailey, David Thomas. "A Divided Prism: Two Sources of Black Testimony on Slavery." *Journal of Southern History,* XLVI (1980), 381–404.
Barker, Eugene C. "The African Slave Trade in Texas." *Quarterly of the Texas State Historical Association,* VI (1902), 145–58.
———. "The Influence of Slavery in the Colonization of Texas." *Southwestern Historical Quarterly,* XXVIII (1924), 1–33.
———. "Public Opinion in Texas Preceding the Revolution." *Annual Report of the*

American Historical Association for the Year 1911. Washington, D.C., 1913. pp. 219–28.

Barr, Alwyn. "Texas Coastal Defense, 1861–1865." *Southwestern Historical Quarterly,* LXV (1961), 1–31.

Bauer, Raymond A., and Alice H. Bauer. "Day to Day Resistance to Slavery." *Journal of Negro History,* XXVII (1942), 388–419.

Berleth, Rosa Groce. "Jared Ellison Groce." *Quarterly of the Texas State Historical Association,* XX (1917), 358–68.

Biesele, Rudolph L. "The Texas State Convention of Germans in 1854." *Southwestern Historical Quarterly,* XXXIII (1930), 247–61.

Blassingame, John W. "Using the Testimony of Ex-Slaves: Approaches and Problems." *Journal of Southern History,* XLI (1975), 473–92.

Brindley, Anne A. "Jane Long." *Southwestern Historical Quarterly,* LVI (1952), 211–38.

Buenger, Walter L. "Secession and the Texas German Community: Editor Lindheimer vs. Editor Flake." *Southwestern Historical Quarterly,* LXXXII (1979), 379–402.

Bugbee, Lester E. "Slavery in Early Texas." *Political Science Quarterly,* XIII (1898), 389–412, 648–88.

Campbell, Randolph B. "Political Conflict Within the Southern Consensus: Harrison County, Texas, 1850–1880." *Civil War History,* XXVI (1980), 218–39.

Carnathan, W. J. "The Attempt to Re-Open the African Slave Trade in Texas, 1857–1858." *Proceedings of the Sixth Annual Convention of the Southwestern Political and Social Science Association* (1925), 134–44.

Conrad, Alfred H., and John R. Meyer. "The Economics of Slavery in the Ante Bellum South." *Journal of Political Economy,* LXVI (1958), 95–130.

Cumberland, Charles C. "The Confederate Loss and Recapture of Galveston, 1862–1863." *Southwestern Historical Quarterly,* LI (1947), 109–30.

Curlee, Abigail. "The History of a Texas Slave Plantation, 1831–1863." *Southwestern Historical Quarterly,* XXVI (1922), 79–127.

Dugas, Vera Lee. "Texas Industry, 1860–1880." *Southwestern Historical Quarterly,* LIX (1955), 151–85.

Earle, Carville, and Ronald Hoffman. "The Foundation of the Modern Economy: Agriculture and the Costs of Labor in the United States and England, 1800–1860." *American Historical Review,* LXXXV (1980), 1055–94.

Eighmy, John Lee. "The Baptists and Slavery: An Examination of the Origins and Benefits of Segregation." *Social Science Quarterly,* XLIX (1968), 666–73.

Fleisig, Heywood. "Slavery, the Supply of Agricultural Labor, and the Industrialization of the South." *Journal of Economic History,* XXXVI (1976), 572–97.

Gallman, Robert E. "Slavery and Southern Economic Growth." *Southern Economic Journal,* XLV (1979), 1007–22.

Genovese, Eugene D. "Rebelliousness and Docility in the Negro Slave: A Critique of Elkins' Thesis." *Civil War History,* XIII (1967), 293–314.

Gilbert, Randal B. "'The People of Tyler Are Relieved of Their Fears': The Building of the Camp Ford Stockade." *Chronicles of Smith County, Texas,* XXIV (1985), 1–9.

Green, Fletcher M. "Democracy in the Old South." *Journal of Southern History*, XII (1946), 3–23.

Harper, Cecil, Jr. "Slavery Without Cotton: Hunt County, Texas, 1846–1864." *Southwestern Historical Quarterly*, LXXXVIII (1985), 387–405.

Harrigan, Stephen. "The Yellow Rose of Texas." *Texas Monthly*, XII (April, 1984), 152.

Harris, Helen Willits. "Almonte's Inspection of Texas in 1834." *Southwestern Historical Quarterly*, XLI (1938), 195–211.

Henson, Margaret S. "She's The Real Thing." *Texas Highways*, XXXIII (April, 1986), 60–61.

Howren, Alleine. "Causes and Origins of the Decree of April 6, 1830." *Southwestern Historical Quarterly*, XVI (1913), 378–422.

Jackson, Susan. "Slavery in Houston: The 1850s." *Houston Review*, II (1980), 66–82.

Jordan, Terry G. "The Imprint of the Upper and Lower South on Mid-Nineteenth Century Texas." *Annals of the Association of American Geographers*, LVII (1967), 667–90.

Kolchin, Peter. "Comparing American History." *Reviews in American History*, X (1982), 64–81.

Lack, Paul D. "Slavery and the Texas Revolution." *Southwestern Historical Quarterly*, LXXXIX (1985), 181–202.

———. "Slavery and Vigilantism in Austin, Texas, 1840–1860." *Southwestern Historical Quarterly*, LXXXV (1981), 1–20.

Lantz, Herman R. "Family and Kin as Revealed in the Narratives of Ex-Slaves." *Social Science Quarterly*, LX (1980), 667–75.

Ledbetter, Barbara A. "Black and Mexican Slaves in Young County, Texas, 1856–1865." *West Texas Historical Association Yearbook*, LVI (1980), 100–102.

Logue, Cal M. "Transcending Coercion: The Communicative Strategies of Black Slaves on Antebellum Plantations." *Quarterly Journal of Speech*, LXVII (1981), 31–46.

Lowe, Richard G., and Randolph B. Campbell. "The Slave-Breeding Hypothesis: A Demographic Comment on the 'Buying' and 'Selling' States." *Journal of Southern History*, XLII (1976), 401–12.

McArthur, Judith N. "Myth, Reality, and Anomaly: The Complex World of Rebecca Hagerty." *East Texas Historical Journal*, XXIV (1986), 18–32.

McKnight, Joseph W. "Stephen F. Austin's Legalistic Concerns." *Southwestern Historical Quarterly*, LXXXIX (1986), 239–68.

Muir, Andrew Forest. "The Free Negro in Harris County, Texas." *Southwestern Historical Quarterly*, XLVI (1943), 214–38.

———. "The Free Negro in Jefferson and Orange Counties, Texas." *Journal of Negro History*, XXXV (1950), 183–206.

Nash, A. E. Keir. "The Texas Supreme Court and the Trial Rights of Blacks, 1845–1860." *Journal of American History*, LVIII (1971), 622–42.

Nelson, Bernard H. "Confederate Slave Impressment Legislation, 1861–1865." *Journal of Negro History*, XXXI (1946), 392–410.

Norton, Wesley. "The Methodist Episcopal Church and the Civil Disturbances in

North Texas in 1859 and 1860." *Southwestern Historical Quarterly*, LXVIII (1965), 317–41.

———. "Religious Newspapers in Antebellum Texas." *Southwestern Historical Quarterly*, LXXIX (1975), 145–65.

Palm, Reba W. "Protestant Churches and Slavery in Matagorda County." *East Texas Historical Journal*, XIV (1976), 3–8.

Pohl, James W., and Stephen L. Hardin. "The Military History of the Texas Revolution: An Overview." *Southwestern Historical Quarterly*, LXXXIX (1986), 269–308.

Ramsdell, Charles W. "The Natural Limits of Slavery Expansion." *Mississippi Valley Historical Review*, XVI (1929), 151–71.

Rippy, J. Fred. "Border Troubles Along the Rio Grande." *Southwestern Historical Quarterly*, XXIII (1919), 91–111.

Roper, Laura W. "Frederick Law Olmsted and the Western Texas Free-Soil Movement." *American Historical Review*, LVI (1950), 58–64.

Schoen, Harold. "The Free Negro in the Republic of Texas." *Southwestern Historical Quarterly*, XXXIX (1936), 292–308; XL (1936), 26–34, 85–113; XL (1937), 169–99, 267–89; XLI (1937), 83–108.

Shively, Charles. "An Option for Freedom in Texas, 1840–1844." *Journal of Negro History*, L (1965), 77–96.

Soapes, Thomas F. "The Federal Writers' Project Slave Interviews: Useful Data or Misleading Source?" *Oral History Review* (1977), 33–38.

Stampp, Kenneth M. "Rebels and Sambos: The Search for the Negro Personality in Slavery." *Journal of Southern History*, XXXVII (1971), 367–92.

Steckel, Richard H. "Slave Marriage and the Family." *Journal of Family History*, V (1980), 406–21.

Stern, Madeleine B. "Stephen Pearl Andrews, Abolitionist, and the Annexation of Texas." *Southwestern Historical Quarterly*, LXVII (1964), 491–523.

Tjarks, Alicia V. "Comparative Demographic Analysis of Texas, 1777–1793." *Southwestern Historical Quarterly*, LXXVII (1974), 291–338.

Trexler, Harrison A. "The Opposition of Planters to Employment of Slaves as Laborers by the Confederacy." *Mississippi Valley Historical Review*, XXVII (1940), 211–24.

Tyler, Ronnie C. "The Callahan Expedition of 1855: Indians or Negroes?" *Southwestern Historical Quarterly*, LXX (1967), 574–85.

———. "Fugitive Slaves in Mexico." *Journal of Negro History*, LVII (1972), 1–12.

Vázquez, Josefina Zoraida. "The Texas Question in Mexican Politics, 1836–1845." *Southwestern Historical Quarterly*, LXXXIX (1986), 309–44.

Vlach, John Michael. "Afro-American Folk Crafts in Nineteenth Century Texas." *Western Folklore*, XL (1981), 149–61.

White, Laura A. "The South in the 1850s as Seen by British Consuls." *Journal of Southern History*, I (1935), 29–48.

White, Raymond E. "Cotton Ginning in Texas to 1861." *Southwestern Historical Quarterly*, LXI (1957), 255–69.

White, William W. "The Texas Slave Insurrection in 1860." *Southwestern Historical Quarterly*, LII (1949), 259–85.

Williams, Amelia. "A Critical Study of the Siege of the Alamo and of the Personnel of Its Defenders." *Southwestern Historical Quarterly*, XXXVII (1933), 79–115.

Wish, Harvey. "American Slave Insurrections Before 1861." *Journal of Negro History*, XXII (1937), 299–320.

———. "The Slave Insurrection Panic of 1856." *Journal of Southern History*, V (1939), 206–22.

Woodward, C. Vann. "History from Slave Sources." *American Historical Review*, LXXVIX (1974), 470–81.

Woolfolk, George R. "Cotton Capitalism and Slave Labor in Texas." *Southwestern Social Science Quarterly*, XXXVII (1956), 43–52.

Wooster, Ralph A. "Notes on Texas' Largest Slaveholders, 1860." *Southwestern Historical Quarterly*, LXV (1961), 72–79.

Wyatt-Brown, Bertram. Review of *The Ruling Race: A History of American Slaveholders*, by James Oakes. *Journal of Southern History*, XLVIII (1982), 559–61.

Yetman, Norman R. "The Background of the Slave Narrative Collection." *American Quarterly*, XIX (1967), 534–53.

THESES AND DISSERTATIONS

Atkinson, Lillie E. "Slavery in the Economy of Colorado County, 1822–1863." M.A. thesis, Prairie View A & M College, 1954.

Barrett, Faydell Lomma. "Slavery in the Economy of San Augustine County, Texas, 1837–1860." M.A. thesis, Prairie View A & M College, 1963.

Bornholst, Jacquelyn Wooley. "Plantation Settlement in the Brazos River Valley, 1820–1860." M.A. thesis, Texas A & M University, 1971.

Crow, John Burchell. "Confederate Military Operations in Texas, 1861–1865." M.A. thesis, North Texas State College, 1957.

Curlee, Abigail. "A Study of Texas Slave Plantations, 1822–1865." Ph.D. dissertation, University of Texas, 1932.

Douglas, LaNelle S. "Religious Work Done by the Texas Baptists Among the Negroes in Texas from 1836 to 1873." M.A. thesis, Sam Houston State University, 1967.

Engelking, Johanna Rosa. "Slavery in Texas." M.A. thesis, Baylor University, 1933.

Henson, Margaret Swett. "Development of Slave Codes in Texas, 1821–1845." M.A. thesis, University of Houston, 1969.

Junkins, Enda. "Slave Plots, Insurrections, and Acts of Violence in the State of Texas, 1828–1865." M.A. thesis, Baylor University, 1969.

Kahn, Joan M. "Slave Labor on an Ante-Bellum Texas Plantation as Revealed in the Ashbel Smith Papers." M.A. thesis, Columbia University, 1951.

Kite, Jodella D. "The War and Peace Parties of Pre-Revolutionary Texas, 1832–1835." M.A. thesis, Texas Tech University, 1986.

Lack, Paul Dean. "Urban Slavery in the Southwest." Ph.D. dissertation, Texas Tech University, 1973.

McPherson, Hallie M. "Slavery in Texas." M.A. thesis, University of Chicago, 1924.

Maddox, Joleene. "Slavery in Texas, 1836–1860." M.A. thesis, Southwest Texas State University, 1969.

Meier, Frederick L. "A Study of Slavery in Microcosm: Lamar County, Texas, 1850–1860." M.A. thesis, Fort Hays State University, 1971.

Newsome, Zoie Odom. "Antislavery Sentiment in Texas, 1821–1861." M.A. thesis, Texas Tech University, 1968.

Palm, Reba W. "Slavery in Microcosm: Matagorda County, Texas." M.S. thesis, Texas A & I University, 1971.

Prince, Diane Elizabeth. "William Goyens, Free Negro on the Texas Frontier." M.A. thesis, Stephen F. Austin State College, 1967.

Purcell, Linda M. "Slavery in the Republic of Texas." M.S. thesis, North Texas State University, 1982.

Robbins, Fred H. "The Origins and Development of the African Slave Trade into Texas, 1816–1860." M.A. thesis, University of Houston, 1972.

Robbins, Hal. "Slavery in the Economy of Matagorda County, Texas, 1839–1860." M.A. thesis, Prairie View A & M College, 1952.

Schwartz, Rosalie. "Runaway Negroes: Mexico as an Alternative for United States Blacks, 1825–1860." M.A. thesis, San Diego State University, 1974.

Smyrl, Frank H. "Unionism, Abolitionism, and Vigilantism in Texas, 1856–1865." M.A. thesis, University of Texas, 1961.

Strickland, Rex Wallace. "Anglo-American Activities in Northeastern Texas, 1803–1845." Ph.D. dissertation, University of Texas, 1937.

Stripling, Paul Wayne. "The Negro Excision from Baptist Churches in Texas (1861–1870)." Ph.D. dissertation, Southwestern Baptist Theological Seminary, 1967.

Telford, Margaret J. A. "Slave Resistance in Texas." M.A. thesis, Southern Methodist University, 1975.

Tyler, Ronnie C. "Slave Owners and Runaway Slaves in Texas." M.A. thesis, Texas Christian University, 1966.

Watson, Tom V. "A Study of Agriculture in Colonial Texas, 1821–1836." M.A. thesis, Texas Tech University, 1935.

Wortham, Sue Clark. "The Role of the Negro on the Texas Frontier, 1821–1836." M.A. thesis, Southwestern Texas State University, 1970.

Index